How to Do Everything

Microsoft® Expression® Web 2

About the Authors

Donna L. Baker is a graphic designer who has been working on the Internet since the late 1980s, when online time was paid for by the hour. She has written numerous books on web and graphic design.

Rick Leinecker has written more than 12 retail video games for the PC, written hundreds of articles, written dozens of books, and made sure it was all fun.

About the Technical Editor

Since 1995, and under the cover of darkness, **Bill Bruns** has been a technical editor, working on more than 125 books relating to operating systems, the Internet, web servers, HTML, and Office applications. In his day job, he is the webmaster for the Student Center at Southern Illinois University Carbondale (www.siucstudentcenter .org). He is also involved with several other not-for-profit organizations as a stalwart volunteer, always being asked to undertake the challenge of "webmaster." Bill holds bachelor's degrees in Telecommunications and English Literature from Indiana University and a Masters of Public Administration from New York University.

How to Do Everything

Microsoft® Expression® Web 2

Donna L. Baker
Rick Leinecker

McGraw Hill

New York Chicago San Francisco Lisbon
London Madrid Mexico City Milan New Delhi
San Juan Seoul Singapore Sydney Toronto

The McGraw-Hill Companies

Cataloging-in-Publication Data is on file with the Library of Congress

McGraw-Hill books are available at special quantity discounts to use as premiums and sales promotions, or for use in corporate training programs. To contact a special sales representative, please visit the Contact Us page at www.mhprofessional.com.

How to Do Everything: Microsoft® Expression® Web 2

1 2 3 4 5 6 7 8 9 0 DOC DOC 0 1 9

ISBN 978-0-07-154587-7
MHID 0-07-154587-5

Sponsoring Editor
Megg Morin

Editorial Supervisor
Jody McKenzie

Project Manager
Vasundhara Sawhney, International Typesetting and Composition

Acquisitions Coordinator
Carly Stapleton

Technical Editor
Bill Bruns

Copy Editor
Sally Engelfried

Proofreader
Paul Tyler

Indexer
Broccoli Information Management

Production Supervisor
Jean Bodeaux

Composition
International Typesetting and Composition

Illustration
International Typesetting and Composition

Cover Designer
Jeff Weeks

For Terry. You're so cool.

—Donna Baker

To the three greatest daughters in the world: Jane, Judy, and Beth.

—Rick Leinecker

Contents at a Glance

Contents

Acknowledgments

I want to thank the terrific gang at McGraw-Hill for the opportunity to write this book. Many thanks to Rick Leinecker for agreeing to take on this project with me, and to Margot Hutchison, our incomparable agent at Waterside, for making it all happen. My thanks to Megg Morin, who has handled this book with her usual level of skill, finesse, and humor. Thanks to Carly Stapleton, organizational diva, for keeping the project on track. And finally, thanks to Bill Bruns for his masterful tech editing.

Many thanks to my dear hubby Terry for his tireless support, supply of fresh coffee, and my brand new art studio. Of course, thanks to my girls—Erin, Deena, Daisy, and Benni—for your companionship and amusement. As always, thanks to Tom Waits, my ongoing inspiration and muse.

—Donna Baker

I want to thank Donna Baker for letting me in on this very cool project. I've enjoyed it immensely. Thanks are also extended to Margot Hutchison, Megg Morin, Carly Stapleton, and Bill Bruns.

I'd also like to thank my colleagues at Rockingham Community College for their support as I disappeared from the radar screen fairly often to work on this book.

—Rick Leinecker

Introduction

Expression Web 2 helps you build standards-based sites with as much assistance as you need. Whether you are a comfortable hand coder, strictly a great visual designer, or have never built a web page before, you're sure to find Expression Web 2 a comfortable program to use.

The program interface offers a clear display of menus and task panes that offer labels and tooltips to keep you on track. Your work centers around the Editing window, which can show different views for hand or visual coding, as well as displaying reports and other structural information.

If you are under the impression that Expression Web 2 is simply an updated version of FrontPage, think again. The program was built separately from any influence of earlier Microsoft products. Although there are visual similarities in the program interface, the program works in an entirely different way. Unlike with its limited-feature predecessor, FrontPage, your pages aren't filled with superfluous formatting tags and other background bloating.

Expression Web 2

This book is about Expression Web 2, part of the Microsoft Expression suite of graphic and web products. It's usually a difficult task to capture every nuance of a subject within the confines of a book's pages, and this book is no exception. We have covered the program from touring the interface to publishing your site, but we had to make some decisions on how much emphasis to place on a particular topic area or process. ASP.NET, for example, could have easily made up half the book, if not more. Our approach to emphasizing one tool or process over another is based on what the average user would turn to for assistance in building their own web sites.

Information About the Book

To bring important information to your attention, we've included short Notes and Tips throughout the book that offer a tidbit of information about the topic at hand or refer you to other areas in the book for further exploration.

You'll find sidebars in each chapter that come in two variations. Some are "How To" sidebars that explain an aspect of an Expression Web 2 feature or tool in depth; such as "How to Resample Images with Confidence" in Chapter 3, which describes how and why resizing and resampling are used for adjusting images in Expression Web 2.

Other sidebars offer expanded information or branching topics from the subject at hand. The "Did You Know?" sidebars aren't required for you to have an understanding of the book's material or Expression Web 2 functionality. For example, the Chapter 7 sidebar, "Did You Know You Can Make It Easier to View the Blank Layout Page?" describes how you can assign colors and borders to a set of tags used to configure a column layout for a web page. You don't need that information in order to use the column layout feature, but, as the sidebar explains, it's easier to visualize the page components.

Finally, the Spotlight section in the center of this book profiles a workflow the average business person can use to create and style their own web site. Cafe Margo is a fictitious enterprise, as is the web site. However, you'll find dozens of techniques and tricks for building a solid web site in just a few pages.

Welcome to Expression Web 2.

Files for Download

Many of the files shown as examples or projects in the book are available for download from McGraw-Hill Professional's web site:

1. Open www.mhprofessional.com in your browser.
2. Scroll down the page and click the Computing category.
3. Look for the Downloads link about halfway down the left side of the page.
4. Click the link for *How to Do Everything: Microsoft Expression Web 2* to download the files automatically.

Some files are located on http://rickleinecker.com and will be mentioned in their particular chapter.

Here's what you'll find in the download files on www.mhprofessional.com.

Spotlight Project: "Cafe Margo: You Can Almost Smell the Coffee"

Many of the example files used in the first part of the book are featured in the Spotlight project. The project contains two folders, cafeR and cafeF.

cafeR This folder contains the "raw" files, such as images, HTML, basic CSS files, and source text files, including:

- A subfolder named *images*, containing the images used in the site's pages
- *menu.css*, a style sheet used for the horizontal menus in the site
- *cafe.text*, the text used on the pages
- *cafe_margo.css*, the partially completed style sheet for the site

cafeF This folder contains the finished site, including:

- The *images* subfolder, containing the site's images
- *cafe_margo.css* and *menu.css* style sheets
- *default.html, bakery.html*, and *summer.html* web pages
- *cafe.txt*, the original text file

Chapter 8: Lay Out Pages with Templates and Layers

- *example1.dwt*, example dynamic web template file from Chapter 8

Chapter 9: Organize Content in Tables and Frames

- *TableDemoSamples.zip*, example of using tables to lay out a web application

Chapter 11: Insert Media Elements

- *1highway528.zip*, free sample flash script
- *flashiness.zip*, free sample flash script
- *HelloSilverlight.xap*, simple hello world Silverlight application
- *HelloSilverlightPrj.zip*, simple hello world Silverlight project
- *LearnSilverlightPrjCS.zip*, simple C# Silverlight project
- *LearnSilverlightPrjVB.zip*, simple VB Silverlight project

Chapter 14: Work with ASP.NET Pages

- *CalcAreaPerimeterPage.zip*, ASP.NET application to calculate area and perimeter
- *FPNWIND.zip*, sample database for example
- *LibraryGeniusPrj.zip*, sample ASP.NET project

PART I

Build a Site with Microsoft Expression Web 2

Over the past two decades, the World Wide Web has grown to become a workplace, meeting place, social environment, shopping center—you name it, you're sure to discover it somewhere online.

Designers and programmers work together to create the content you interact with on a daily basis (just as a designer and programmer worked together to write this book!). To meet the needs of designers and other nonprogrammers, WYSIWYG (What You See Is What You Get) editors revolutionized web page development in the last decade by hiding the coded innards of a page behind a visual display of the output.

Web page editing software has taken giant leaps forward from its early days; now editing software uses both design and programmatic methods for constructing web pages and sites. In this part, we'll look at Microsoft Expression Web 2 and its streamlined method for web page development and site construction, from both the design and code perspectives.

1

Take a Program Tour and Start Your Site

HOW TO...

- Find features in the Expression Web program
- View and manage task panes
- Customize program preferences
- Start a new web site from scratch or using other content
- Check out different features of a web site

Developing a web page that is visually pleasing, useful, and standards-compliant takes a lot of planning and consideration, and so does organizing and managing the pages that go into a web site. Fortunately, Expression Web 2 offers many ways to help you both in your design and organization tasks.

In this chapter, you'll see how to make your way around the Expression 2 interface and learn what goes into the construction of a new web site. You'll see a number of options to start a web site and get an overview of its structure and components.

Get Around the Expression Web Interface

Anyone who has worked with Microsoft Office 2003 products, such as Word, will find many features in the Expression 2 interface familiar. For example, the layout includes menus and toolbars arrayed at the top of the window, and a collapsible task pane at the right of the program window. Of course, there are also differences, such as another group of task panes at the left side. Figure 1-1 identifies the major components of the program window.

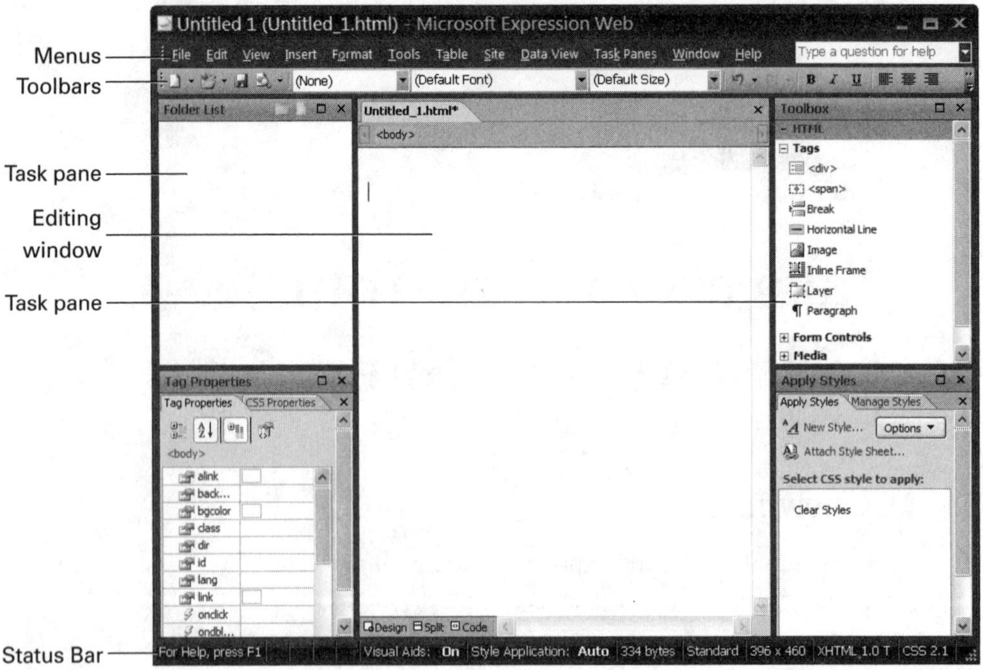

FIGURE 1-1 **The Microsoft Expression Web 2 interface contains several functional areas.**

The Ins and Outs of Task Panes

As you saw in Figure 1-1, two columns of task panes surround the Expression Web working area. Task panes make it easy for you to find tools and information quickly and are easy to configure to meet your needs as you work on your web design. You can return to the default layout at any time, simply by choosing Task Panes | Reset Workspace Layout.

If you are starting out with Expression Web, you're unlikely to leave the program's default layout and arrangement. As your skill and familiarity develops, keep an eye on how you work and adjust the interface to suit your needs better.

Here are some ways you can work with the task panes:

Maximize the Task Pane You can maximize any task pane displayed on the program window, as you see next. Click the Maximize Window icon to collapse the other task panes normally displayed on that side of the program window. You might maximize a task pane when you are working with its features, like the Folder List, and want to see the entire structure. When you're finished, click the Restore Window icon to resize the task pane's contents.

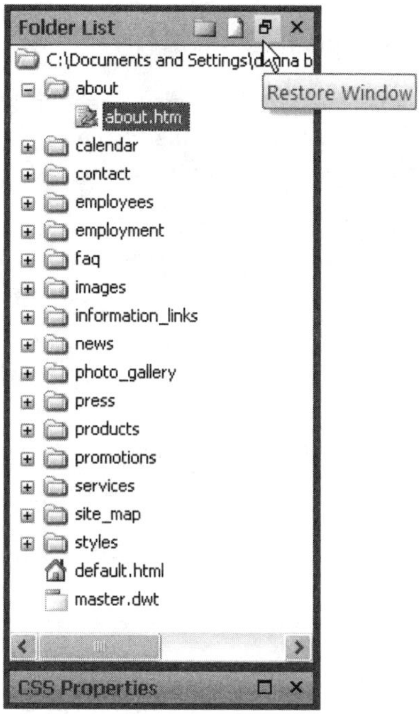

Move Task Panes Rather than have a task pane dock at one side or the other, you can float it and position it anywhere on the program window. Simply drag from the task pane's name tab away from the docking area and drop the pane where you like.

Combine and Recombine Task Panes The Expression Web 2 program layout shows task panes collected into groups by default. You can add more by dragging from another task pane group. However, the task pane area can become crowded if there are several grouped task panes. In that case, look for a pair of small arrows to the upper right of the set of tabs; click the appropriate arrow to move left or right through the panes (Figure 1-2).

Tip The name of the active task pane shows as the name of the group of task panes. For example, in Figure 1-2, the Manage Styles task pane is active and shown as the group's name.

Check Out the Default Task Panes

The default display in Expression Web contains several task pane areas, each responsible for managing web site components and features. Here's a quick rundown of what you see in the program and what it does.

How to... Show Even More Task Panes

If the left and right task pane displays aren't enough, you can also use the bottom of the Editing window by dragging the task pane to the lower middle of the program window. Of course, that doesn't leave much room for working!

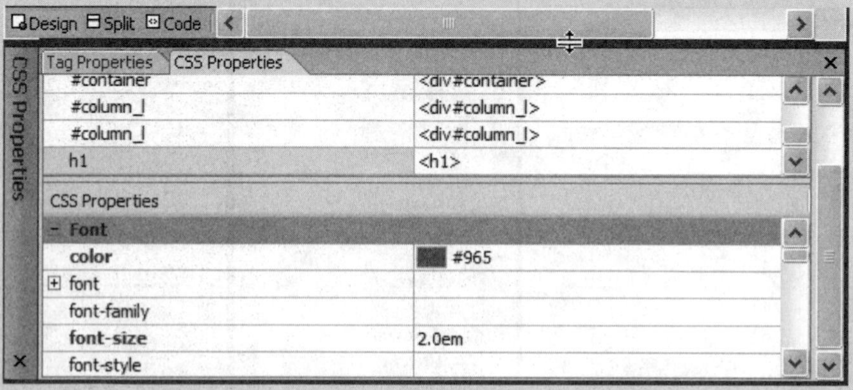

Another group of task panes shows in the program after running a program task, such as generating Accessibility or Hyperlinks reports. Resize these tabs by dragging their edge, as you see here. Click the "X" to close the group of panes, or drag them to one side of the program window for docking.

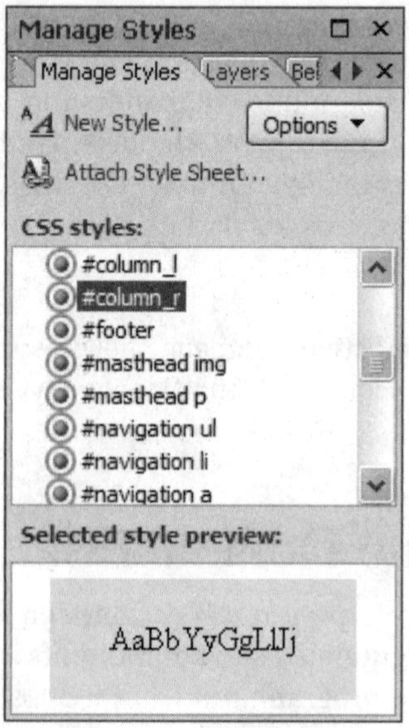

FIGURE 1-2 Navigate through several task panes.

Use the Folder List Task Pane to Stay Organized

The Folder List task pane lists all the folders and files used for a web site and serves as a file manager for working in Expression Web. You can add new folders and pages, rename existing content, or right-click to access shortcut menu commands to configure the list contents further (Figure 1-3).

Note Read more about the Folder List later in the chapter.

Configure Elements in the Properties Task Pane

There is a wealth of information available for each and every element you add to a web page—a heading, bullet list, image, blank space—the list is endless. Expression Web includes Tag Properties and CSS Properties task panes. An example of the Tag Properties for a heading is shown in Figure 1-4.

Tip Tag properties pertain to XHTML tags used for defining the content and its structure; CSS properties pertain to Cascading Style Sheet properties: visual characteristics assigned to page elements, which may or may not be XHTML tags. Read all about tags and styles in Chapters 5–7.

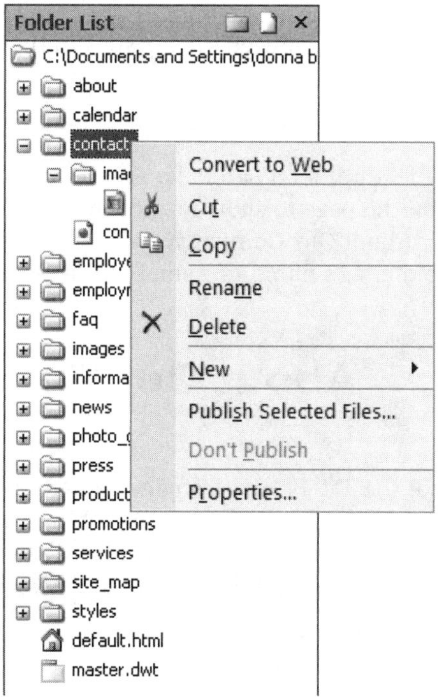

FIGURE 1-3 Manage web site files in the Folder List task pane.

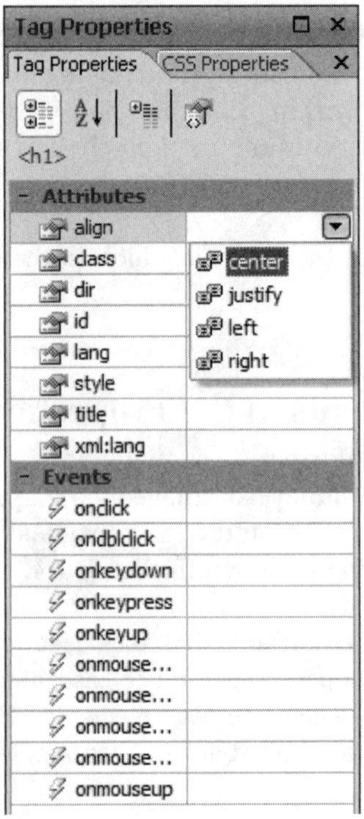

FIGURE 1-4 Specify and view characteristics in the Tag Properties pane.

Use the list of features for a particular tag to set its *attributes*, or visual characteristics. Select an object on the page to show its attributes in the Tag Properties pane. For example, the text "About Our Company" displays as a large heading size, centered on the page. You see the tag's name in a small tab above the heading as well.

Now, if you look at the Tag Properties pane shown in Figure 1-4, you'll see the list of attributes for the `<h1>` tag, or Heading 1, which is the largest heading. Click the line next to an attribute to display a drop-down arrow as you see in Figure 1-4, and pick a setting. Some attributes don't offer drop-down lists, while others open separate dialog boxes.

Note The Content tab to the left of the <h1> tab doesn't refer to a tag. It is a named item of a web template, a set of preconfigured elements used to create consistent pages. You'll learn about templates in Chapter 8.

The Toolbox Task Pane

Speaking of tags, you can find tags for everything from images to text fields in the Toolbox task pane. If you pause your mouse over a listing, you'll see a short description in a pop-up, like the one shown here.

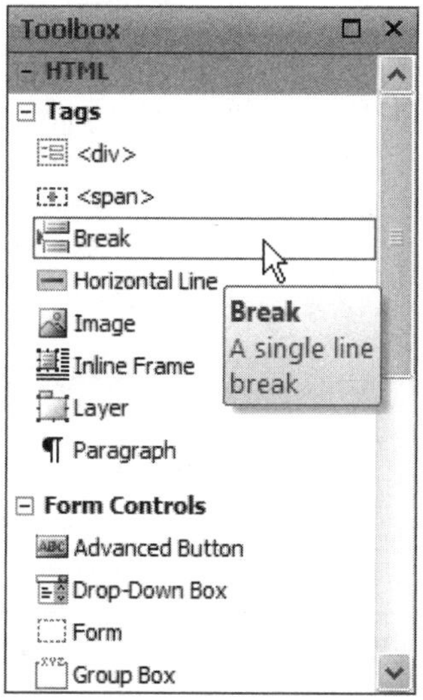

Along with tags for building page elements and forms, the Toolbox also offers tools for inserting media, such as Flash or Silverlight, as well as a collection of ASP.NET controls for adding active content like field validation and logins.

Note Read about using media in Chapter 11; check out ASP.NET pages in Chapter 14.

Handling Styles for Page Elements

The task panes at the lower right of the Expression Web program window go hand in hand. The Manage Styles pane shows the CSS styles configured for your page (Figure 1-5). On this pane, along with previewing a selected style, you can modify, rename, and apply styles.

The tabbed Apply Styles pane shows the styles differently, in that you see what styles are applicable to a particular page element. Read about using the Manage Styles and Apply Styles task panes in Chapter 5.

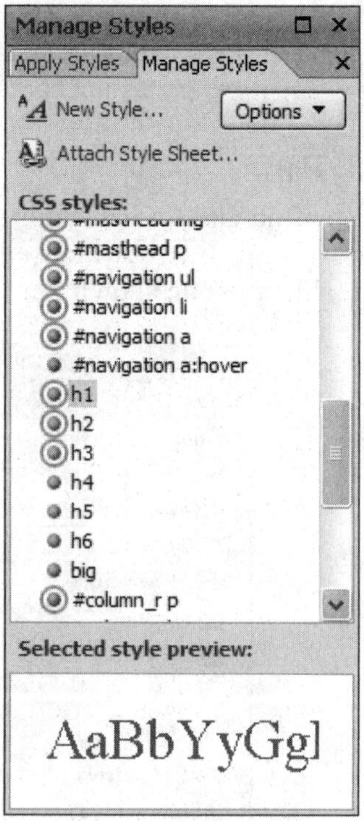

FIGURE 1-5 Select and preview styles in the pane.

The Editing Window

In Expression Web 2 you lay out and structure pages and sites in the Editing window, and you keep track of various page and site features in the Status Bar.

Note Learn more about customizing the Editing window in Chapter 2.

View the Editing Window

Modify the Editing window's layout to show different features like visual aids and nonprinting characters such as paragraph marks, as you see in Figure 1-6.

You can show different views to help pinpoint elements on the page. The Design view, shown by default (and seen in Figure 1-1), renders the page as it would be seen in a browser. The Split view, shown in Figure 1-6, shows the design and code in separate sections of the Editing window; the Code view shows the code alone.

Note In a Split view, an item selected in the Code view section of the page is also selected on the Design view side of the page, and vice versa.

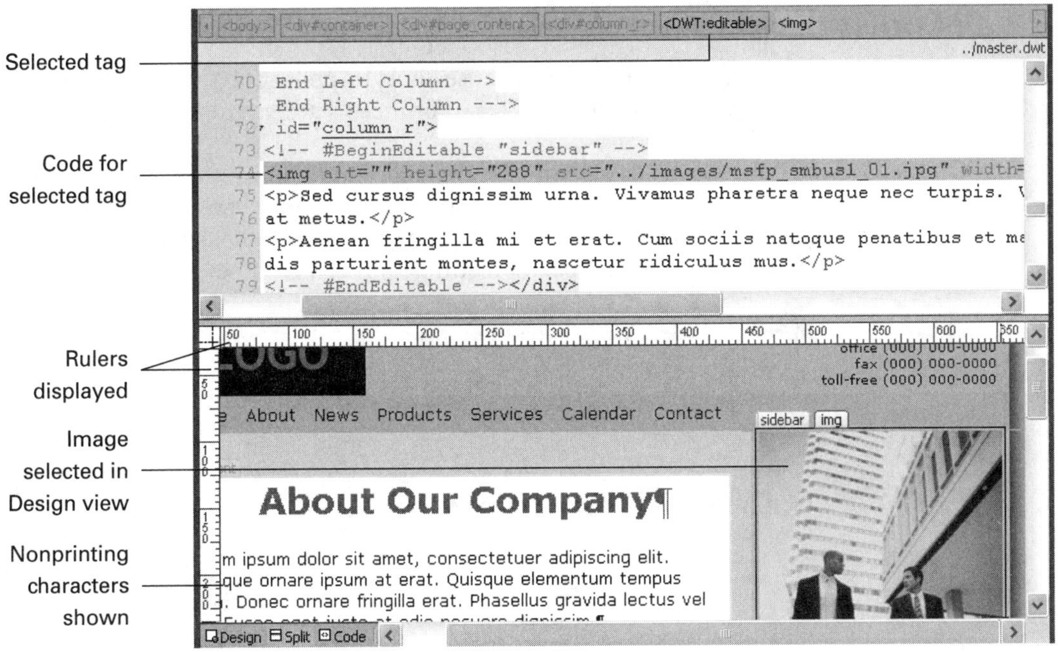

FIGURE 1-6 Display different features for easier editing.

Keep Track of Page Features

The final stop on the tour is the Status Bar, shown along the bottom of the program window. Here you'll find information about different aspects of your page, such as the web standards applied to the page, the page size, and so on.

If you see an indicator in the Status Bar that shows a white page with a red circle overlay like the one shown here, look for errors in the page's code.

Customize Preferences to Suit Your Work Style

Check through the Expression Web 2 preferences to see what sorts of features can be modified and what will work for you. You can configure preferences for the program as well as for pages.

Modify Expression Web 2 Options

To check out the program preferences, choose Tools | Application Options to open the four-tab Application Options dialog box. Look for these settings:

On the General Tab Select the Open Last Web Site Automatically When Expression Web Starts check box to save time. If you work with numerous web sites on an ongoing basis, deselect this option. Select the Show Status Bar check box to show an ongoing snapshot of your site and page's features; this is a great timesaver.

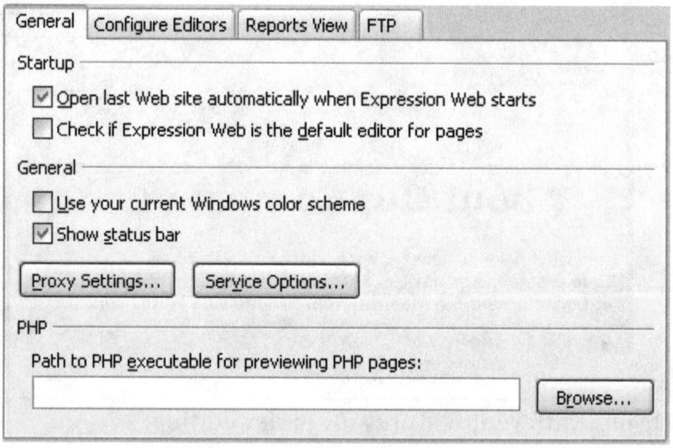

Note Also on the General tab, you can specify a path for previewing PHP pages. Read about using PHP in Chapter 13.

On the Configure Editors Tab Select and specify the program used to open files of different formats. For example, a file with a CSS extension can open in Expression Web as a CSS file or as a text file, or it can open in Notepad. Unless you are working with unusual file formats, you can leave these settings as they are.

On the Reports View Tab There are several settings you may want to adjust, based on how you like to work and your environment (Figure 1-7). Expression Web defines default time frames and terms to use in reports that might mean different things to you. For example, a file that is called *Recent* is less than 30 days old, an *Older* file is more than 72 days old, a *Slow* page takes at least 30 seconds to download, and the assumed connection speed is 56Kbps. Be sure to adjust these settings if you commonly use different frames of reference or if you know your typical visitor's connection speed. One option you might like to choose is Display Gridlines When Viewing Reports. You'll see gridlines in the figures showing reports in some examples in this book.

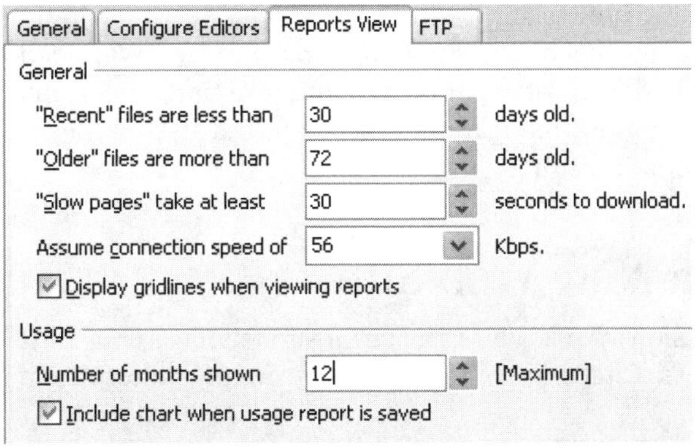

FIGURE 1-7 Specify time frames that are useful to your workflow.

Note Once your site is online, your service provider may have reporting tools that give you information about your visitors, including their connection speed. Other programs you may subscribe to, like Google Analytics, offer in-depth reporting. Use this report information to modify your page settings.

On the FTP Tab The final tab covers a list of extensions for transfer via FTP. Again, unless you are working with unusual file formats, you can leave these settings as is.

Modify Expression Web 2 Page Editing Options

The other customizable options pertain to viewing and editing web pages. Choose Tools | Page Editor Options to open the Page Editor Options dialog box, where you'll see 12 tabs of settings. Many of the settings relate to the appearance of different items on the page, such as the color for different types of code in Code view or the fonts used.

Often, Expression Web 2 shows a link to the Page Editor Options dialog box from other dialog boxes, such as the New Page dialog box, where you can make changes on the fly. You'll find references to different settings throughout the book.

Build a New Site

A web site is more than a group of web pages. Sites usually contain images, style sheets, scripts, and other content needed to maintain and run the site.

The basic decisions to make before you start include:

- Where do I want to store the site?
- What content do I want to use for the site?

Deciding how to start a web site is like deciding whether the chicken or the egg came first. You need pages to make up a site, and you need a site to hold pages. There are literally dozens of other design and functional decisions to make regarding the style, layout, flow, navigation, and so on. Discussing these items would be (and has been) a book in itself!

Start a New Web Site

In Expression Web 2, you can start a site from scratch, start with a single page, use a template as a starting point, or utilize existing content for a site.

Create a Simple Site

Expression Web 2 offers different ways to start a simple web site. Follow these steps:

1. Choose File | New | Web Site to open the New dialog box. You'll see tabs for starting a new page or a new web site, with the Web Site tab active.
2. Click General to display the options (Figure 1-8). Choices include a web site holding one page, a blank site, or importing a site into Expression Web 2. Choose One Page Web Site.
3. Click Browse at the bottom of the dialog box to open the Web Site Location dialog box; locate and select the folder where you want to store the site. To use the default location, select the My Web Sites folder Expression Web 2 creates automatically in your My Documents folder and then click Open.

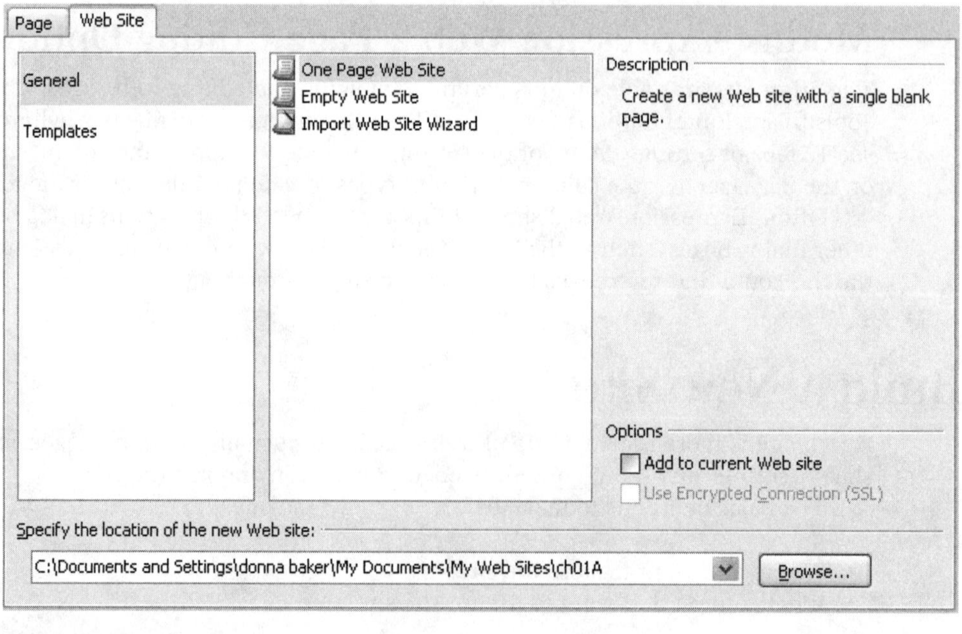

FIGURE 1-8 Configure a simple site in the dialog box.

4. You return to the New dialog box—the location you selected in the previous step shows in the dialog box. Type the name for the site at the end of the location string following the \. You only have to type the site's name, such as "ch01A" since the rest of the location and punctuation is provided, and click OK.
5. Expression Web 2 configures your site, building the single page using the default name *default* and the default `html` format.

Note Check with your Internet service provider—in some cases, the start page should be named *index.html* rather than *default.html*.

Start from a Web Site Template

Expression Web 2 offers a collection of terrific templates you can use to start your web site. Choose from three categories: organization, personal, or business site. The characteristics of each site, as well as the content included in the template, vary according to the category. For example, in an organization's site, you're not likely to need a hobbies page; in a personal site, you won't need a product page. Learn to work with existing and new templates in Chapter 8.

To use a template, follow these steps:

1. Choose File | New | Web Site to open the New dialog box, which displays the Web Site tab.
2. Click Templates to display the list of options. You'll find a number of Organization, Personal, and Small Business templates listed.
3. Click a template name to show a preview. As you look through the previews, you'll see a variety of layouts and color schemes. Pick the layout closest to your requirements. You can make adjustments as needed—see how in Chapter 8.

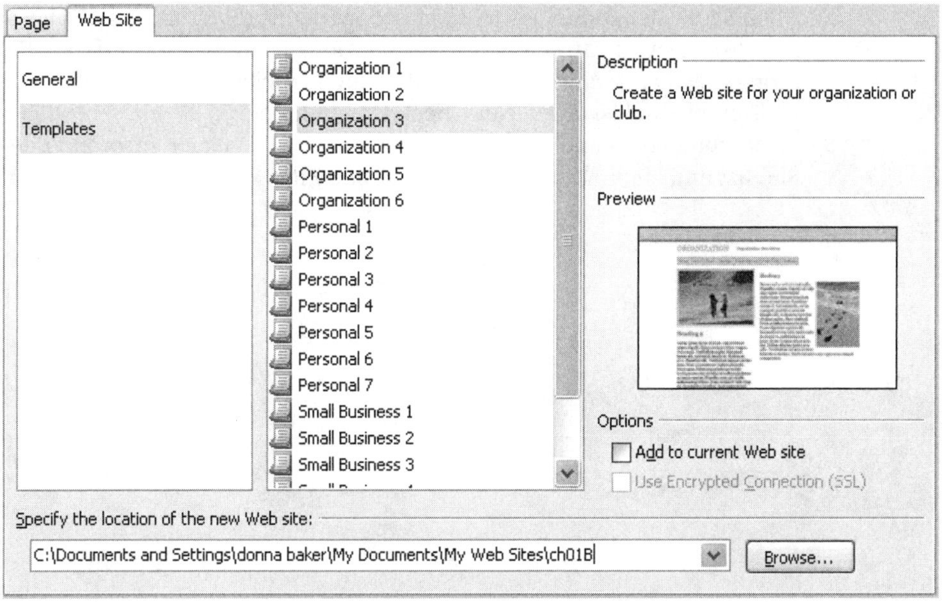

4. As in steps 3 and 4 in the previous set of steps to create a simple site, choose a location, name the file, and click OK to close the dialog box and construct the site.

Tip If you plan to store the site in the same location as the others you've worked with, all you have to do is replace the site's name at the end of the location string on the dialog box with a name for the new site. Click OK to name the site and add it to the specified storage location.

Import Content from Other Locations

It's not uncommon to bring content in from other web sites. You may have been working in another web editing program or inherited a web site from a colleague. Expression Web 2 offers several ways to incorporate content from other sources. In the case of a Personal Web Package, you have to create it first, or import it from a colleague or other source.

Use a Personal Web Package

A Personal Web Package lets you combine any or all parts of a site into a single file that you can share or incorporate into another web site. You—or another person working with Expression Web 2—have to generate the package first before using it in a different site.

Open the site in Expression Web 2 and then follow these steps to create the package:

1. Choose File | Export | Personal Web Package to open the Export Web Package dialog box.
2. Click Show Dependencies to display dependent relationships of files as you select them; you can select different options from the Dependency Checking drop-down list, including Check All Dependencies, Except Hyperlinks, Check All Dependencies, or Do Not Check Dependencies.
3. Select the folders and files for the Personal Web Package from the Files in Web Site list and click Add to copy them to the Files in Package list, as shown next.

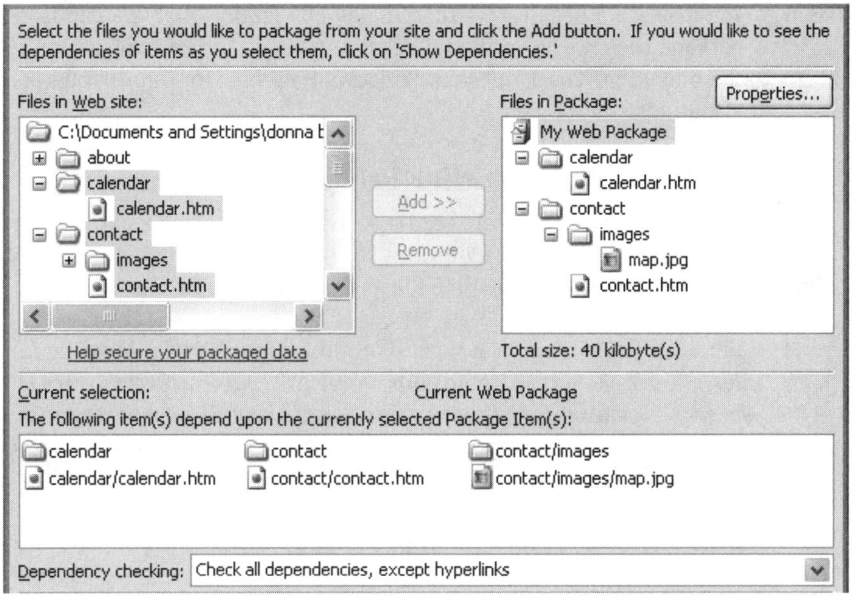

Tip You'll see a dialog box asking if you want to include the contents of a folder as you add it to your package. Click No to add just the set of empty folders. Click Yes to add the folder contents.

4. If you like, click Properties to specify information about the package, such as the Author, Company, Title, and Description.
5. Click OK to close the Export Web Package dialog box and open the File Save dialog box. Name the package and select a storage location. Click Save to close the dialog box and save the file as a Web Package using the FWP file extension.

Importing the Personal Web Package into an existing site is quick. Follow these steps:

1. Open the site to receive the content, and then choose File | Import | Personal Web Package. In the File Open dialog box, locate and select your Web Package file, and click Open to display the Import Web Package dialog box. You'll see the folders listed that you included in the Web Package, as well as those with relationships to the selected folders.
2. Deselect any folders you don't want to use, open the folders you want to import (be sure to check that the individual components like pages and images are selected), and click Import.
3. The content is processed and you'll see the folders and files added to your site.

Tip You may see a Security Warning dialog box stating that the publisher of the package couldn't be verified. Click Run to open the content or Don't Run to stop the operation. Check out your Windows Help files for information on digital signatures.

Import a Site from Another Program

Expression Web 2 offers a wizard for importing an entire web site from another program. Start a blank site, save it in Expression Web 2, and then choose File | Import | Import Site Wizard to open the dialog box. Step through the wizard:

1. On the initial pane of the wizard, choose a method for locating and selecting the files: FrontPage Server Extensions, WebDAV, FTP, File System, or HTTP (Figure 1-9). Specify a location for the site's files, and a root directory if required. Click Next.
2. The source location is processed. Specify the location for saving a local copy. You can choose any location on your computer, local network, or a web server running SharePoint Services or FrontPage Server Extensions. Click Next.
3. Expression Web 2 processes the storage location and states the process is complete; click Finish.

Note Read more about different storage and site options in Chapter 16.

FIGURE 1-9 Specify the type of site to import.

Combine Sites

Suppose you are building a new web site for your recreation center and decide you can use the old site as part of the new one. Expression Web 2 lets you add one site into another by combining the content and its hidden data.

Add More to a Web Site

Expression Web 2 lets you easily add one site into another. In the New dialog box, shown in Figure 1-8, click the Add to Current Web Site check box in the lower right to add the content into the named site.

The metadata from the imported content is added to that of the existing web site. You may prefer not to have Expression Web 2 try to maintain and update the metadata as you combine the content and would rather restore it once you have everything in place and named. To remove the metadata files, choose Site | Site Settings to open the General tab of the Site Settings dialog box. If it's active, deselect the Manage the Web Site Using Hidden Metadata Files check box shown here.

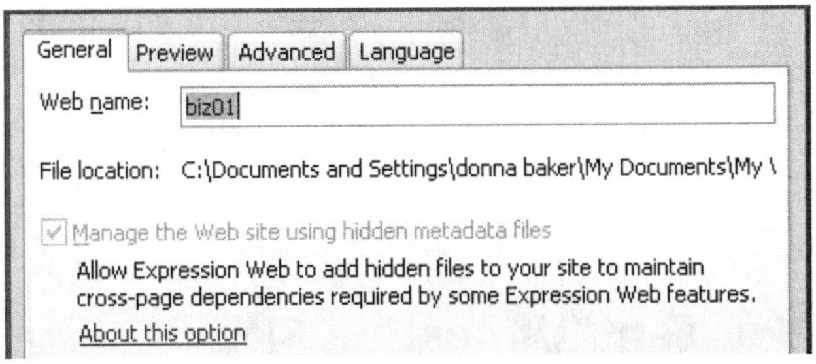

Note There's one exception: If you have saved a web site in the My Web Sites folder, you can't remove the metadata. In that case, move the site to another storage folder and try again.

Nest Web Sites

You can create a web site nested within a web site, called a *subsite*. Consider using subsites if your business offers several product lines, for example, or your personal site contains very different areas, such as your kennel club activities and your vacation plans.

Expression Web 2 can build a subsite for you, provided you have the metadata feature enabled. If you don't, the program can't recognize your subsite as a separate web site, and you may encounter errors running or using the site.

To add a subsite, right-click the folder location for your site in the Folder List, and choose New | Subsite to open the New dialog box. From here, choose one of the options to start a site. Expression Web 2 specifies the storage location as a folder named *subsite* within your site (Figure 1-10).

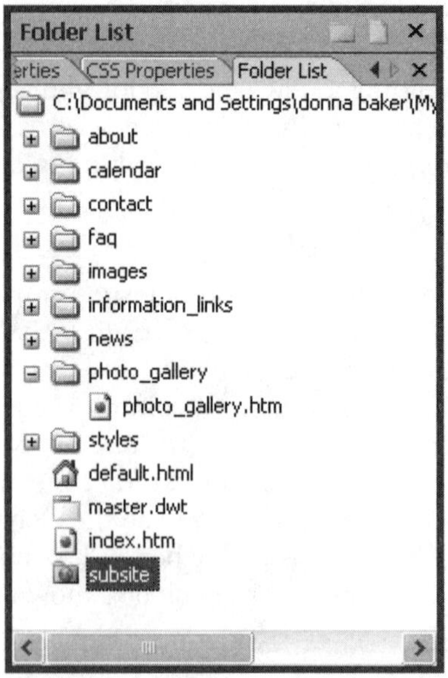

FIGURE 1-10 A new subsite added to an existing web site

Did You Know?

You Can "Unnest" a Site

Using a subsite may or may not work for you, depending on how you like to work and your sites' contents. If you like to see everything you have to work with at the same time, a subsite isn't a good idea, as it has to open in a separate program window—you can't see its files from the parent site's Folder List.

On the other hand, if you are working on a site for your community club, for example, and have four or five sites for different sports teams, separating the content into subsites may work. You are likely to have similar types and names of pages, and having each team's site open in a separate Expression Web 2 window may help keep your tasks straight.

If you make a subsite or two and decide it's not the thing for you, simply right-click the subsite's listing in the Folder List, and choose Convert to Folder. The subsite becomes a folder within your parent site, removing the nested structure for the subsite.

Converting a subsite into folders causes some changes in the pages, including:

- Themes change to match the parent site's theme.
- Access to the converted subsite is restricted to those having access to the parent site.
- External hyperlinks to the pages in the subsite are lost.

Rename the *subsite* folder if you like, or choose an alternate storage location. To prevent losing or misplacing your web site (which can easily happen!), use the same storage location. Click OK to close the dialog box.

Choose a Web Site Location

Regardless of where the content for your site comes from, you need to decide what type of site storage you want to use. Your choices include disk-based, FTP-based, or HTTP-based sites.

Disk-Based Web Site

The sites shown in the examples in this chapter are disk-based web sites. In all cases, the site is stored at a particular hard drive location. A disk-based site can be stored on your hard drive, a remote hard drive, or removable drives.

Note You can use Microsoft Expression Development Server to test disk-based sites that contain ASP.NET and PHP content. Read about ASP.NET in Chapter 14 and PHP in Chapter 13.

FTP Web Site

Usually an FTP web site is on a remote server, like the one your web host likely provides you to upload your web site to. Usually, you build your site locally, and then transfer it by FTP to your web host.

In Expression Web 2, you can work live directly on the FTP site. Choose File | Open Site, type the FTP path to your hosting server, and click Open. You choose to edit the web site live, or edit a local copy and then publish the changes. If you choose to edit live, any changes you make to your pages are visible on your web site as soon as you save the changes.

Note Read more about using FTP in Chapter 16.

HTTP Web Sites

You can use HTTP (hypertext transfer protocol), the technology used for displaying your site in a browser, if you have access to FrontPage Server Extensions on your web server. When you start a site, type the URL for the web site as the location for the new web site, as shown here.

Options
Add to current Web site
Use Encrypted Connection (SSL)
Specify the location of the new Web site:
https:\\www.howtodoeverything.ca
Browse...

Optionally, if you need more security and your server allows, click the Use Encrypted Connection (SSL) check box at the bottom of the dialog box to create a web site using SSL (secure socket layer) technology. In that case, the site uses HTTPS, a secured version of HTTP. Read more about using HTTP in Chapter 16.

Tip You don't have to type the "s" in the protocol—if you select or deselect the SSL option, the address changes automatically.

Configure Web Site Settings

Information about the structure and data in a web site is stored as metadata in folders named with a *_vti* prefix. The metadata files are stored in the same location as the rest of your web site but aren't seen in the Expression Web 2 Folders List. However, you can see the folders and their contents by opening your folders from your desktop (Figure 1-11).

The metadata provides ongoing tracking of changes in your web site, such as updating links for moved or renamed pages, although you can choose a preference to prevent saving metadata. Regardless of metadata tracking, there's no effect on your web site and its functions.

Produce Website Reports

Don't wait until you're ready to upload your site pages before checking them for accuracy.

Tip It's a lot easier to check your site at the end of every work session or every day and make corrections than it is to check through an entire multipage site the day it is supposed to go live!

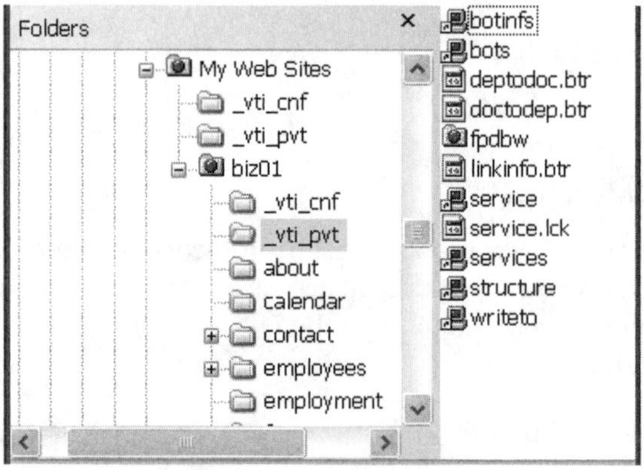

FIGURE 1-11 View the metadata files from your hard drive.

TABLE 1-1 List of Available Web Site Reports

Report Type	What It Describes
All files	The files in the web site, including their folder location, size, type, and modification dates
Pictures	The images attached to the current web site
File links	Files not linked from the site's home page, files that link from the site's home page. Read more about links in Chapter 4.
Time-based reports	Slow pages that download over an established time frame, files older than a certain date, files that haven't been modified within a specified time frame, or files that have been added recently. The time frames for these reports are set in the Report View settings, described earlier in the section "Modify Expression Web 2 Options."
Hyperlinks	Several reports display information about hyperlinks, including a list of all hyperlinks, those that are unverified (haven't been checked to see if the pages they are linked to are still there) or broken (the target files are unavailable or no longer exist), those that point to files that are not inside your set of web folders, and those that point to other files in the current web site. Read about hyperlinks in Chapter 4.
Shared content	Style sheet links in the web site, a list of files associated with a Dynamic Web Template, and those associated with a Master Page. Read about shared content in Chapters 5 and 8.

Expression Web 2 offers over a dozen site reports that you'll use at different stages of your project development. You'll read about different reports in different chapters in this book. For quick reference, Table 1-1 lists groups of available reports.

To view a report, follow these steps:

1. Click Reports at the bottom of the Web Site window, shown in Figure 1-12.
2. Click the link for the report's name to display the contents of the report in the Web Site window.
3. Once you've read through the report and made any corrections, click the link at the upper left of the report window—the link takes on the name of the active report, such as Site Summary—to open a drop-down menu. Click Site Summary to return to the view shown in Figure 1-12. If you like, you can select another report directly from the drop-down menu.

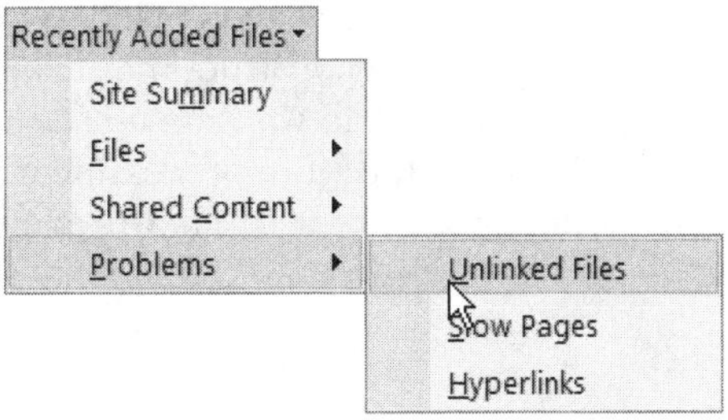

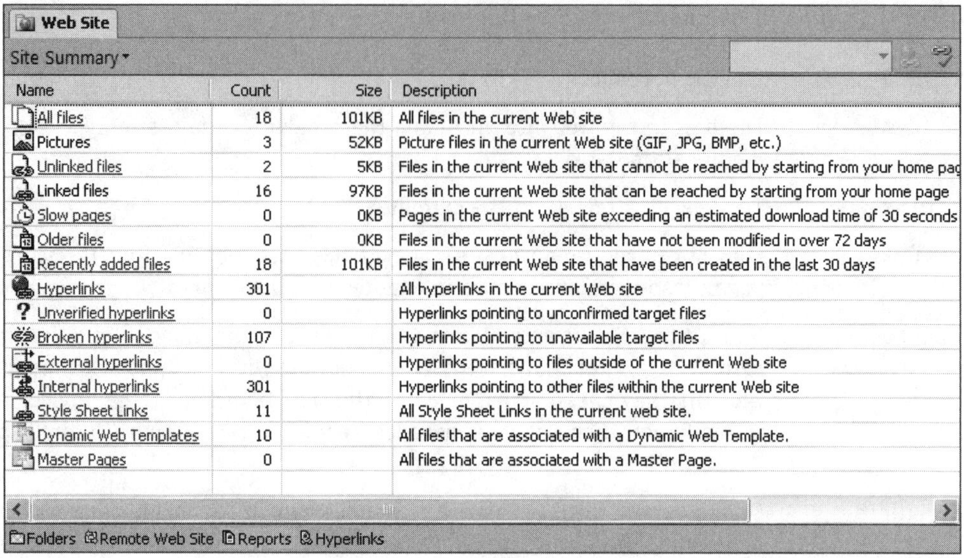

Web Site

Site Summary

Name	Count	Size	Description
All files	18	101KB	All files in the current Web site
Pictures	3	52KB	Picture files in the current Web site (GIF, JPG, BMP, etc.)
Unlinked files	2	5KB	Files in the current Web site that cannot be reached by starting from your home pag
Linked files	16	97KB	Files in the current Web site that can be reached by starting from your home page
Slow pages	0	0KB	Pages in the current Web site exceeding an estimated download time of 30 seconds
Older files	0	0KB	Files in the current Web site that have not been modified in over 72 days
Recently added files	18	101KB	Files in the current Web site that have been created in the last 30 days
Hyperlinks	301		All hyperlinks in the current Web site
Unverified hyperlinks	0		Hyperlinks pointing to unconfirmed target files
Broken hyperlinks	107		Hyperlinks pointing to unavailable target files
External hyperlinks	0		Hyperlinks pointing to files outside of the current Web site
Internal hyperlinks	301		Hyperlinks pointing to other files within the current Web site
Style Sheet Links	11		All Style Sheet Links in the current web site.
Dynamic Web Templates	10		All files that are associated with a Dynamic Web Template.
Master Pages	0		All files that are associated with a Master Page.

Folders Remote Web Site Reports Hyperlinks

FIGURE 1-12 Monitor your site's features using a number of reports.

Summary

In this chapter, you saw the features that make up the Expression Web 2 program and how to construct a web site. After an overview of the program interface, you learned how to make your way around the interface on a short tour of the major task pane groups in the program. Like most programs, Expression Web 2 offers many ways to customize the program's preferences, both for the overall program and its components.

Expression Web offers multiple ways to start a new web site. You can start with a blank page and then establish a site, or start from the basic web site and a single page. The web site approach lets you start from one of many preconfigured web templates. You can use templates for organization, personal, or business sites that have you up and running quickly.

Every web site is made up of pages—in Chapter 2, you'll learn how Expression Web 2 helps construct the structure of a web page. You'll see different visual aids you can use to work on a page, and how to define the page's structure and coding. Utilizing the word processing features in Expression Web 2, you'll also see how to add and configure text. There's even a thesaurus!

2

Build a Page and Add Text

HOW TO...

- Create a new document
- Specify page characteristics
- Use visual aids to assist design and layout
- Add and configure text
- Apply word processing features

A web page is much more than what you see in a browser window and requires a number of behind-the-scenes components. Fortunately, Expression Web 2 can manage the coding detail for you.

In this chapter, you'll learn about different page structures using Expression Web 2 to build some pages. You'll see how to use the many layout and text configuration features for quick and easy page design.

Create a New Page

The fundamental element of a web site is, of course, a page. You see words and text on the page along with images and other elements, all supported and controlled by different code and structures.

Begin the Page's Design

You can find the New Page command in several program locations. If you want a generic page, click the New Page icon on the Folder List panel or the Common toolbar. If you want to choose the type of page to start, follow these steps:

1. Choose File | New | Page from the program menu to open the New dialog box. The General page types are listed by default, and the HTML page option is selected by default (Figure 2-1).

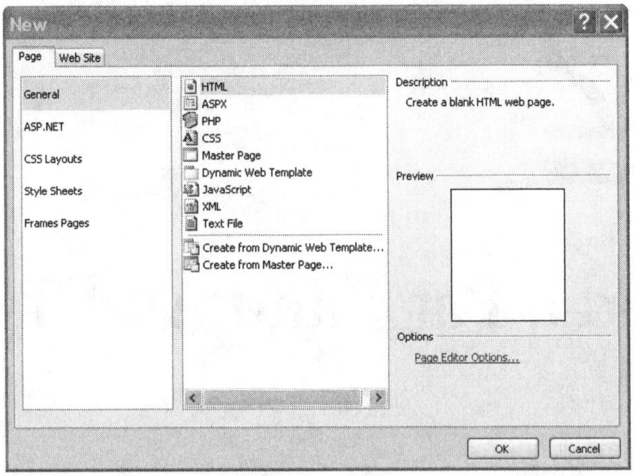

FIGURE 2-1 Specify the type of page you want to create.

Tip Click the New Page icon's drop-down arrow on the Common toolbar to open the same list of page types as the General list shown in Figure 2-1.

2. At the upper right of the dialog box, you'll see a description and preview of the file. Click the Page Editor Options link to open the Page Editor Options dialog box.
3. Click the Authoring tab to show the features available for new documents.

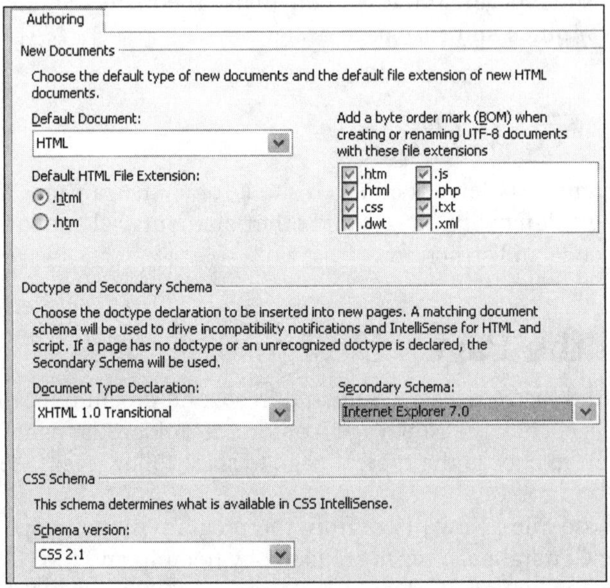

On this tab, you'll find three categories of settings to configure, including:

- **Default Document** The default document type in Expression Web 2 is HTML. You can choose from several other types such as text, ASP, or CSS from the drop-down list. Below the document type are two options for the file extension. The default is .html, although you can use .htm. There is no fundamental difference—the .htm extension was used in the early days of the Web when all file extensions were three characters in length. In this book, we use the .html extension.
- **Doctype and Secondary Schema** A *doctype* is a tag at the start of a web page's code that states what version of HTML or XHTML is used in the document. Browsers read the doctype and display the content accordingly. In this book, most pages are XHTML 1.0 Transitional, which is the Expression Web 2 default. If a page doesn't show a doctype or there is an error in how it is written, Expression Web 2 uses a secondary document type. In the Secondary Schema drop-down list, you'll find the variations of HTML and XHTML doctypes, as well as schemas (similar to a doctype) for several versions of Internet Explorer.
- **CSS Schema** Finally, choose the schema you'll use for writing and evaluating the CSS on your pages. The default is CSS 2.1. You'll learn about CSS in Part II of this book.

4. Click OK to close the Page Editor Options dialog box, which returns you to the New dialog box; click OK again to close the dialog box and create the new page.
5. Click Save on the Common toolbar, or choose File | Save to open the Save As dialog box. Choose the location where you want to save the file. Type a name for the file and specify the type of file you're saving. The default is a web page.
6. Check the page title shown on the page, if you've added one to the page before saving. If not, or if you want to change the content, click Change Title to open the small Set Page Title dialog box shown here. Type the new title and click OK.

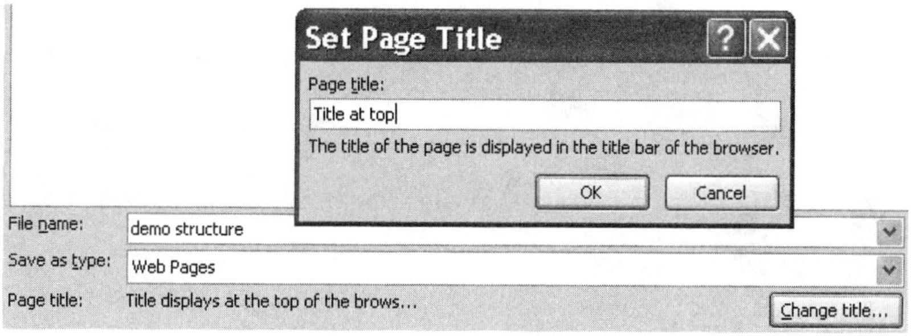

7. Click Save to save the file and close the dialog box.

Identify the Parts of the Page

A new page is shown in the Editing window. Click Split at the bottom left of the Editing window to show both the code and design layouts for the page (Figure 2-2).

There are a number of program and page features shown in Figure 2-2, including:

- The new page is named Untitled_*x*.html by default and isn't included as part of a web site until you name and save the file into a specific web site.
- The Editing window is split between the Code view and Design view, also known as the Design *surface*. You'll see the code at the top of the page, and the page as it is interpreted for a browser at the bottom of the page.
- In the Code area of the Editing window, notice that the <!DOCTYPE> declaration tag is written in Lines 1 and 2. The code is inserted automatically based on the items selected in the previous section. A doctype is written prior to any of the page tags.
- Expression Web 2 inserts a set of page tags; each tag is paired with an opening tag—the tag's name shown in braces—and a closing tag—the tag's name again shown in braces with "/" prefacing the tag's name. All tags are written in lowercase and as opening and closing pairs to comply with XHTML requirements. The default set of tags includes:

```
<html>
     <head>
          <title> A name for the page shown on the browser window </title>
     </head>
<body>
All the text, images, tables, forms, and anything else you see on the page
</body>
</html>
```

- As you see in Figure 2-2, the heading "What do We Have Here?" is selected. At the top left of the heading's text you see a tab showing *h1* again. If you check out Line 14 in the Code area of the Editing window, you'll see the <h1> tag, the text, and the closing </h1> tag.
- The top of the Editing window shows the hierarchy of tags that identify the active item, called the Quick Select bar. In Figure 2-2, notice that the tag <h1> is shown in an orange highlight.

Note You can read much more about working with tags and their attributes in Chapter 7.

How to... Save a Lot of Time

Expression Web 2 offers plenty of contextual menus. Before you start hunting through the program menu for a command, right-click the item or area you're working in and check the shortcut menu.

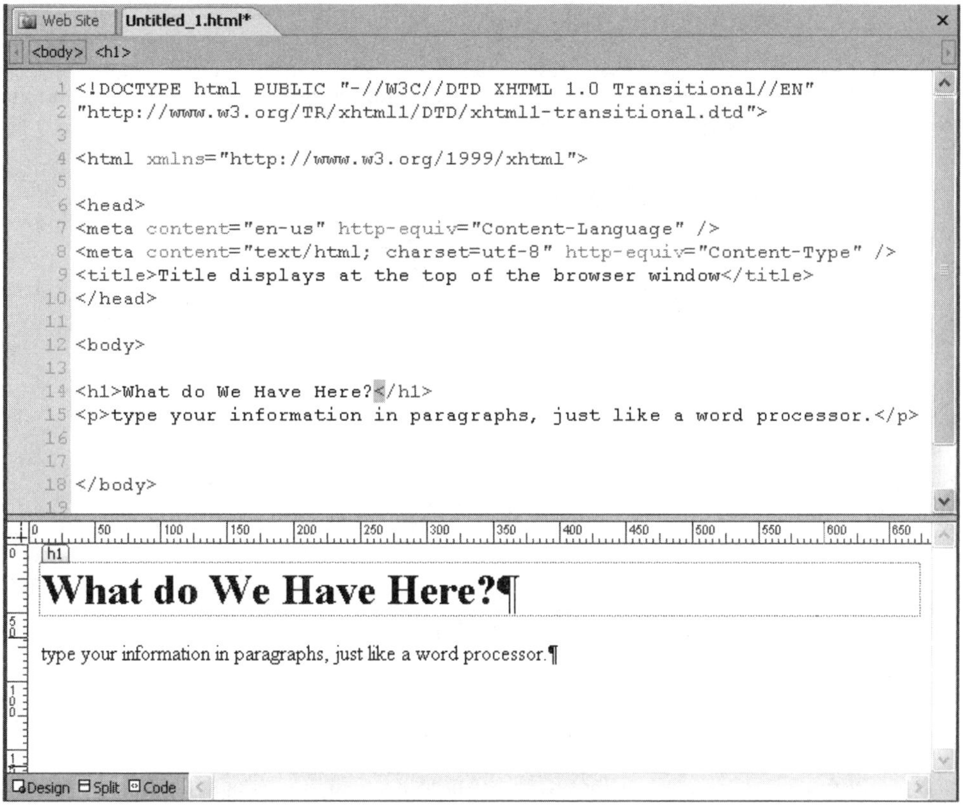

FIGURE 2-2 View the content and features of the new page in the Editing window.

Specify Page Characteristics

Once your basic page is constructed you can add more detail to the page's properties: Expression Web 2 offers a number of ways to modify the page, ranging from a page description to background colors.

Right-click the page in Design view, and choose Page Properties from the shortcut menu (or choose File | Page Properties) to open the five-tab Page Properties dialog box. Once you've chosen your settings, click OK to close the dialog box and apply the changes to the page.

Add Metatags for Indexing

On the General tab, add content to provide an overview of your page and its contents. The easier it is for a search engine to find and categorize your content, the greater the flow of traffic will be to your site.

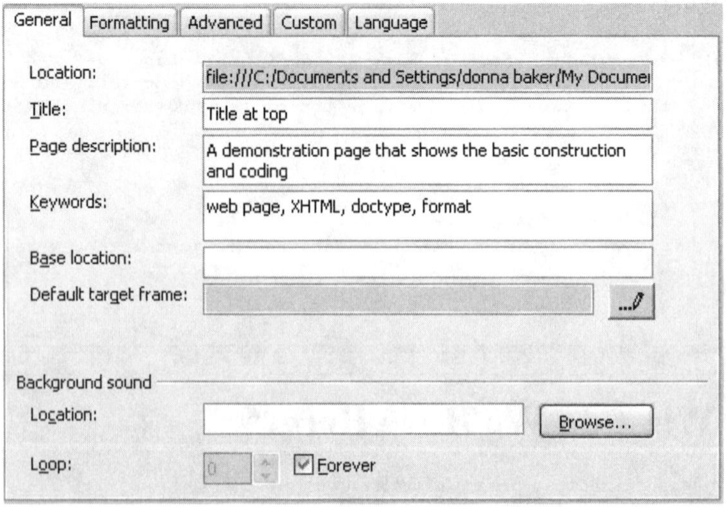

Consider these three types of information:

- The page title is shown on the title bar on most browser windows (described in the earlier section, "Begin the Page's Design").
- The page description identifies the fundamental purpose of the web page, used in a variety of ways. For example, some search engines use the description as part of the returns on a search, while other search engines use the description as a part of the site indexing process.
- Keywords are used in different ways, such as indexing by search engines and allocating targeted advertising.

Note On the General tab, you can also specify a base location, a URL identifying where the page is stored (if you are storing it in a location other than the default root location).

Once you've added the data in the dialog box, you'll see it used as part of the content in the page's <head> tag. Keywords and descriptions are listed using *metatags*, an HTML element that describes page contents, as you see in the following code snippet:

```
<head>
<title>Title at top</title>
<meta content="web page, XHTML, doctype, format" name="keywords" />
```

```
<meta content="A demonstration page that shows the basic construction
and coding" name="description" />
</head>
```

Tip The General tab also includes options for adding background music to your page. With few exceptions—such as a site for a musician or a guitar luthier—there's no good reason to include background music, as the files unnecessarily add to the download size. Besides, if your visitors are listening to their own music, they won't likely appreciate the intrusion of *"Eine kleine Nachtmusik"* or similar.

Format the Page Color and Background

Use the settings on the Formatting tab as a quick way to add a page background image or color and set colors for links, text, and the background. To use a background, select the check box; to use a *watermark* (a semi-transparent version of a background image), select both the Background Picture and Make It a Watermark check boxes. Click Browse to open a dialog box where you can locate and select the image file.

Any sort of image file can be used, as long as Expression Web 2 can read the file format. The example uses a WMF (Windows Metafile format) image exported from an Adobe Illustrator project.

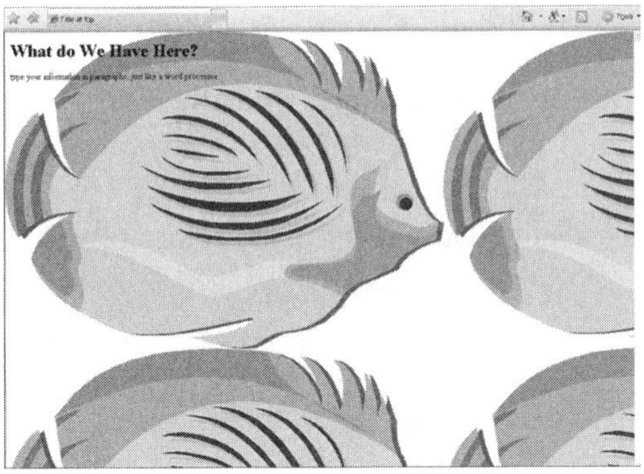

Tip The fish page shows a common issue, called *tiling*, where multiple copies of the background image are displayed due to a difference between the image size and the size of the page displayed in the browser. The workaround without using styles is to create the image at a size larger than that of the browser window. The better method is to use a style, where you can configure the placement, tiling, and other features of the background image. Read about styles in Part II.

For the colors, click the drop-down arrow for the component you want to change and choose a color from the palettes displayed (Figure 2-3). Click More Colors to open a standard color palette; click Custom Colors to open a Color Picker where you can configure colors.

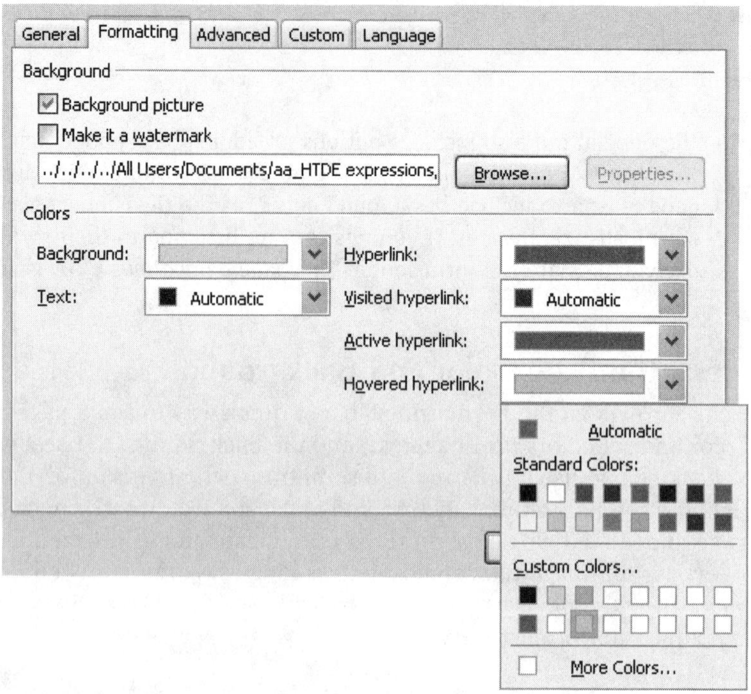

FIGURE 2-3 Specify color schemes quickly.

Note Read more about choosing and using color in Part II.

Choose Additional Page Properties

You can define other properties in the Page Properties dialog box.

Define Page Margins Click the Advanced tab to set margins for the page if you like. For the most part (and in this book), margins are defined using CSS.

Apply Custom Settings Use settings on the Custom tab to manage custom code snippets. If you add keywords or a description in the General tab, you'll see the content listed on the Custom tab.

Specify Language On the Language tab, specify the page language and HTML encoding to apply to the page. The default for HTML encoding uses Unicode (UTF-8) encoding.

Preview Pages in a Browser

Viewing the page on your computer screen using your browser is one thing—seeing how the page looks and behaves in different browsers using different screen sizes and resolutions is another.

To preview the page, press F12 to display the page in the default browser (Internet Explorer 7.0) or choose File | Preview in Browser and select an option from the list. You can choose combinations of page sizes and browsers. The available choices depend on the resolution set for the page you're viewing as well as lower resolutions.

A page has to be saved before previewing. Rather than saving manually, choose File | Preview in Browser | Edit Browser List. Select the Automatically Save Page Before Previewing check box in the Edit Browser List dialog box. While you are viewing the dialog box, check the options for window sizes and browsers you want to use for display.

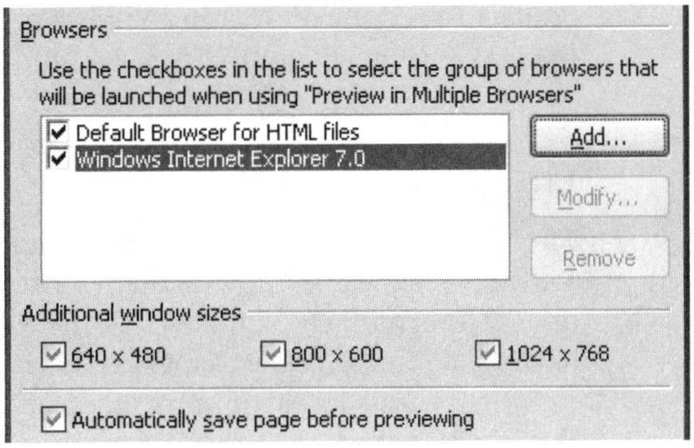

Word Processing in Expression Web 2

You use the same sorts of tools, text features, and formatting in Expression Web 2 that you are accustomed to working with in Microsoft Office programs. In addition to simply typing and formatting text directly on the page, place preconfigured text into areas on a template. Read about templates in Chapter 8.

Each item you add to a page is placed into a container defined by an HTML tag. As you add and format items, you'll see the formatted content shown in Design view, along with any customizations, specified as *styles*.

Note Configuring the text as you write the page isn't the most efficient way to construct a page. It's more efficient (and easier to control) using styles, as you'll see in Part II. Not only can you design a specific style for a specific purpose—such as a bullet list for one type of list on your site—you can also redefine the default appearance of basic tags, such as headings and paragraphs. Check how that's done in Chapter 7.

The logical way to lay out a page in Expression Web 2 uses *semantic markup*, similar to using an outline in a Word document. That is, the subject of the page should be the largest heading; the content divided into sections; and the sections further subdivided as necessary—just as in this book. Define lists by list tags, quotes by blockquote tags, and so on. Using the proper hierarchy of tags in a logical order describes your page to a search engine in a way it can understand.

Even without a style sheet attached to a web page, using a semantic markup structure is readable for you and understandable by a browser. Not only is it easier for your readers to follow along when you use an outline structure, it's also important because it makes your pages accessible to users working with assistive devices like screen readers.

Show Layout Assistants

Anyone who has worked in a word processing program such as Microsoft Word can easily insert and edit text in Expression Web 2. To help you visualize how a browser reads the page, lay out the content, and troubleshoot for layout issues, Expression Web 2 offers visual aids and formatting marks.

Display Visual Aids

The visual aids help you see empty elements or those with invisible borders. Choose View | Visual Aids | Show to open a list of options, and select/deselect those you want to use. Alternatively, double-click the Visual Aids label on the status bar at the bottom of the program window to toggle the visual aids' visibility.

Figure 2-4 shows common aids you'll see when working on a simple page. By the way, the figure shows a composite image as you can't show all the features as illustrated at once.

Several visual aids help you visualize and design a basic page layout.

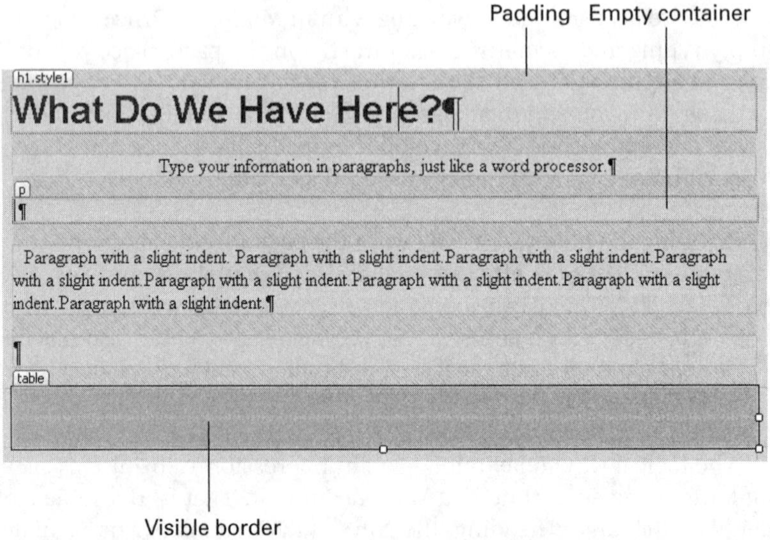

FIGURE 2-4 Use visual aids for identifying spacing and invisible features on the page.

Block Selections Clicking within the limits of a block-level element like a paragraph or heading shows a dotted rectangle around the item and displays the tag in a tab at the top of the item.

Empty Containers A common practice is to press ENTER to add empty space separating paragraphs or other content on the page. If you use the Empty Containers aid, you'll be able to see where you've added extra spaces that should be removed and replaced by styles.

Visible Borders Making borders visible lets you see where an object will be placed on the page, such as a table.

Margins and Padding Headings include padding, an amount of space to separate the heading from the text preceding and following it. Click the element's tab to display margins or padding.

Note There are numerous other visual aids used for CSS (read about them in Part II), templates (described in Chapter 8), and ASP (see Chapter 14 for details).

Reveal Formatting Marks

Some people are comfortable switching from Design to Code view and back, while others find working in Design view far simpler. If you are in the latter group, consider showing some of the Expression Web 2 formatting marks to keep track of your page's layout. To show formatting, choose View | Formatting Marks | Show. Once the marks are visible, you can toggle the different options visible or hidden by selecting them on the menu.

For example, in Figure 2-5 the paragraph marks indicate carriage returns, which lets you see if you have unnecessary blank lines. The spaces are shown, to see if there are unnecessary spaces. Finally, the tag marks are displayed, which is like a shorthand version of a Split view.

You may find the formatting marks clutter up your design as you are writing and constructing the layout. If so, simply deselect the ones you don't want to use, or turn them off altogether.

Tip Displaying visible tag marks is a terrific learning tool if you want to learn about XHTML as you learn to use Expression Web 2. As you design the content, you'll see the tags added. Over time, the tags will become very familiar and help you read and write code yourself.

Edit Text

Typing text into the Expression Web 2 Editing window is no different from typing text into a Word document. Simply click to activate the text cursor and enter your text. Similarly, selecting, deleting, copy/cut/paste, and other actions are also the same.

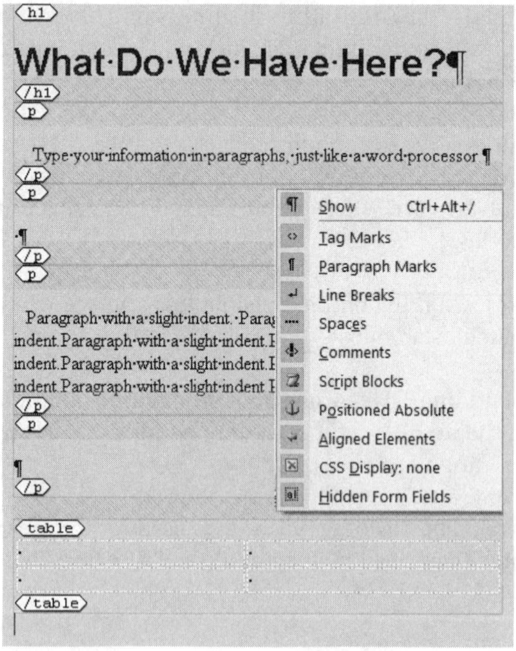

FIGURE 2-5 Show various formatting marks for assistance.

There are some differences, predominantly related to pasting text and assigning the type of line breaks to use, as you'll see later in this section.

Make Historical Corrections

To make corrections, use the Undo and Redo buttons, located on the Common toolbar. You can modify by single or multiple items:

- Click the Undo button to cancel your most recent action.
- Click the Redo button to restore the last action you revoked.
- Click the Undo button arrow to open a history list, and select the consecutive actions you want to cancel.
- Click the Redo button arrow to open a history list, and select the consecutive actions you want to reapply.

Specify Default Fonts

Expression Web 2 uses a set of default text attributes when you insert text on the page. In Design view, you can change the default proportional and fixed-width fonts.

Tip Proportional fonts are those that have variable sizes for the characters, like the text you see on this page; fixed-width fonts use constant character widths and spacing, like the text used for writing code.

To change the default fonts, follow these steps:

1. Choose Tools | Page Editor Options to open the dialog box; click the Default Fonts tab (Figure 2-6).
2. Select the language to use as the default.
3. Select default fonts to use for Design view.
4. Select the default font and its size to use for Code view.
5. Click OK to close the dialog box.

Format Text Visually

You've likely used the text formatting buttons on the toolbars in Word to apply features like bold or italics. Expression Web 2 offers numerous text enhancements accessible from the Common toolbar, shown in this abbreviated view of the toolbar.

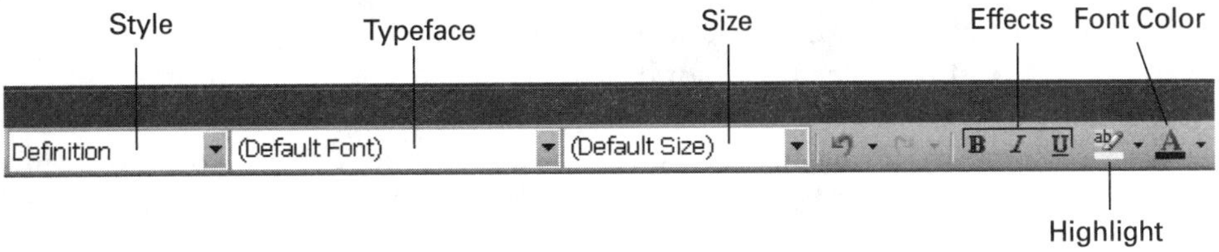

Tip The Common toolbar shows most common settings from the Standard and Formatting toolbars. To display or hide toolbars, choose View | Toolbars and make a selection from the list. Alternatively, right-click in the toolbar area at the top of the program window and choose a toolbar from the pop-up list. If you're using the Formatting toolbar rather than the Common toolbar, you can click the Increase Font Size or Decrease Font Size buttons to change the sizes incrementally.

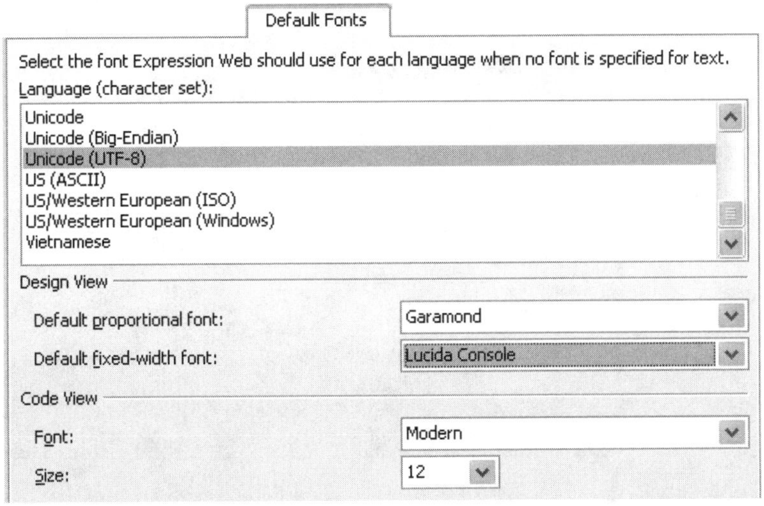

FIGURE 2-6 Specify the fonts for Design and Code views.

Configure Text Features

Rather than using the toolbar, you can use the Font dialog box to make multiple changes to selected text. Follow these steps:

1. Select the text you want to format on the page.
2. Select Format | Font to open the Font dialog box (Figure 2-7).
3. Choose features on the dialog box, including:
   - **Font** Scroll through the list and select a font family (described in the section "Define Font Families") or choose a font by name.
   - **Font style** Choose a style for the font face. All fonts are capable of simulating italic, bold, and bold italic appearances, whether or not their font information includes those features.
   - **Size** Scroll through the list and select a font size. The sizes are listed using HTML font descriptions, such as xx-small or large. Their equivalent point sizes are shown in brackets for reference.
   - **Color** Click the Color drop-down arrow and choose a color from the palette. You can choose from the set of 16 standard colors, or a default set of document colors. To specify your own color, click More Colors to open the More Colors dialog box; click Custom to open a further Color Picker for defining color numerically. Read about using and specifying color in Chapter 6.

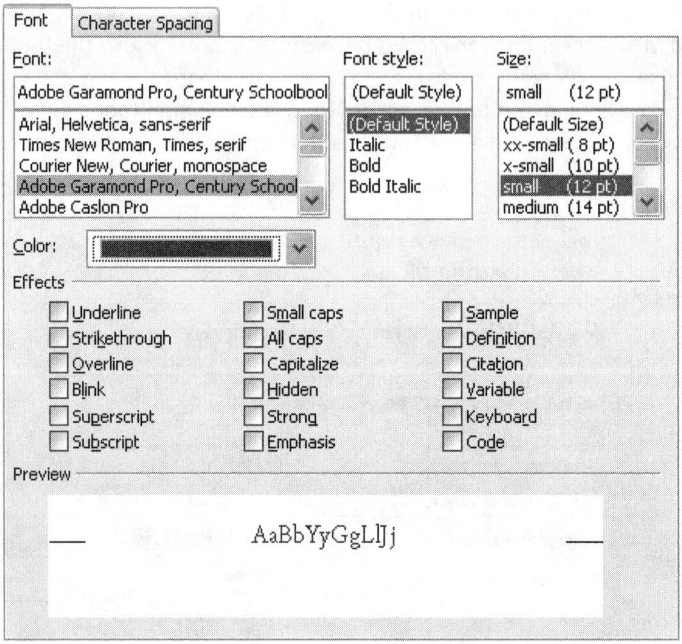

FIGURE 2-7 Define the appearance of selected text on the page.

- **Effects** Choose from many visual appearances for text.

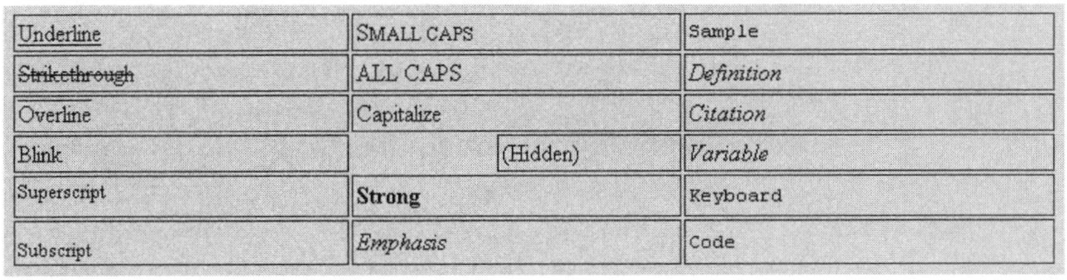

Tip Although some of the text effects look similar, such as the Emphasis and Definition choices, the names refer to different HTML tags.

4. Click Apply to set the font appearance, and click OK to close the dialog box.

Define Font Families

A *font family* is a list of usually three fonts for displaying text online. When you view a web page, the first font in the list is tested. If the viewer has the font installed on their system, it is used. If not, the second font is tested and shown if available. If neither is available, the default serif or sans serif font is shown.

To specify a font family, follow these steps:

1. Choose Tools | Page Editor Options | Font Families to open the Font Families tab.
2. Click New Font Family, then select a font in the list and click Add.
3. Add additional fonts as desired (Figure 2-8).

Note To ensure your viewers can see some text, be sure to include a default serif, sans serif, or monospace font option.

Apply Default Styles

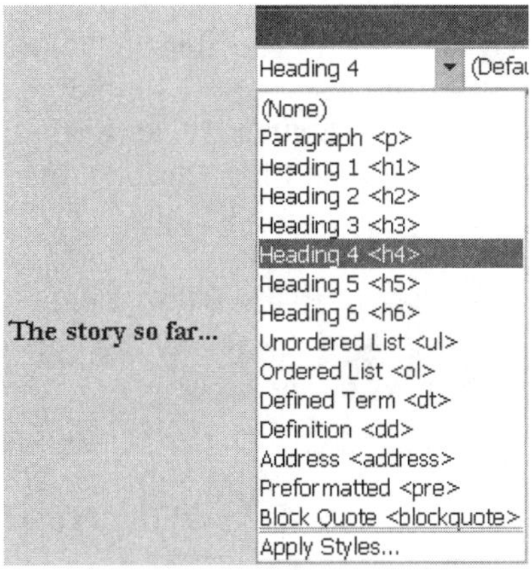

Use the built-in styles in Expression Web 2 to apply formatting to text. The styles are based on HTML tags, such as paragraphs, headings, and blockquotes.

To use a style, select the text on the page, and click the Style arrow on the Common toolbar to display the list.

The default features, such as font size and weight, indentations, and other formatting, are applied automatically. In the page's code, the selected text is contained within the corresponding tags.

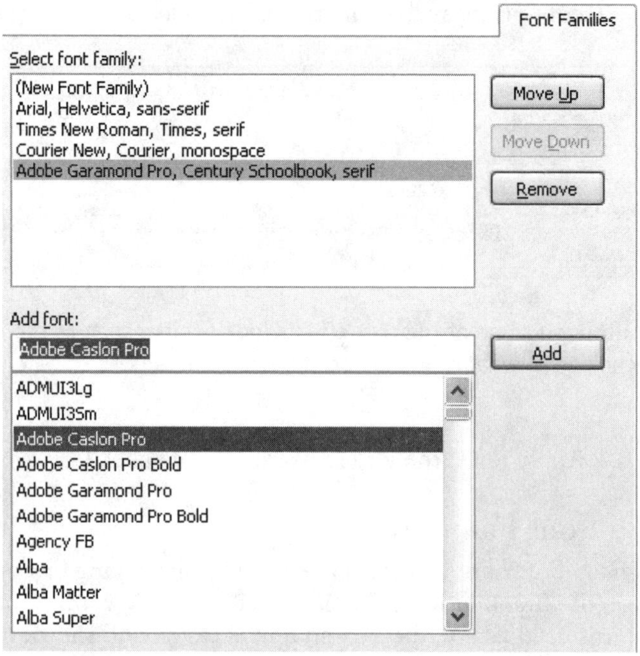

FIGURE 2-8 Use a font family to offer viewing options.

Note You can modify and define styles yourself, which are then stored in the page as a new style. Read about using styles, HTML styles, and style sheets in Part II.

Use Special HTML Characters

Often you need to add special characters such as a currency sign, © symbol, or a mathematical term. To use a symbol, click the page at the insertion location and choose Insert | Symbol to display the dialog box. Click the symbol you want to use, from either the Recently Used Symbol list or the Main Font Symbol display, and click Insert. Click Close to dismiss the dialog box, as it doesn't close automatically when you make a choice.

Tip Click the Font drop-down arrow to display a font list to choose another font; click the Subset drop-down arrow to filter the displayed font by subset, such as currency or arrows.

Paste Content into a Page

Instead of writing a page from scratch, you can insert content originating in different document formats or extensions, including Word DOC and DOCX formats, RTF,

TXT, and HTM or HTML files. Expression Web 2 offers different ways to control the appearance of the text as you paste it into your web page.

Maintain Styles

Expression Web 2 lets you copy and paste text including the formatting from the specified file. For example, you can use one option to match an imported style to your web page style; another option imports the style to use in the web page.

To paste content from a file into an existing web page and control formatting, follow these steps:

1. Open your source file and copy the text you want to reuse.
2. In Expression Web 2, click to identify the insertion location in your web page.
3. Choose Edit | Paste to place the text on the page at your insertion point.
4. Click the Paste Options button that displays close to the pasted text and choose an option:
   - **Match Destination Formatting** Choose this option to use the styles in the web page that correspond to the styles attached to the imported content. For example, text using a Heading 1 style in a Word document becomes `<h1>` tags when imported.
   - **Keep Source Formatting** To paste both the content and the style from the source document, choose this option. For example, a list bullet configured in Word maintains its appearance as a list bullet when placed into a web page, regardless of how Expression Web 2 defines the bullet.
   - **Remove Formatting** Choose this option to simply paste the content as plain text using the line breaks and spacing specified in your original page.
   - **Keep HTML Only** Use this option to import a page of HTML code for displaying as rendered code. For example, `<blockquote>` tags are interpreted to display the content contained in the tag using the style; the actual code tags aren't shown.
   - **Keep Text Only** Remove all formatting from the pasted text with this option. Text is pasted as plain text, and you choose options for line breaks and spacing.

Control Line Breaks and Spacing

If you want to preserve the text you're importing and also control the spacing and line breaks, use the Paste Text command. Regardless of your choice, all styles are removed from the text—which is terrific when you only want the content and intend to apply styles later.

To place content from a file into an existing web page, follow these steps:

1. Open your source file and copy the text you want to reuse.
2. In Expression Web 2, click to identify the insertion location in your web page.
3. Choose Edit | Paste Text to open the Paste Text dialog box.
4. Specify the breaks you want inserted in the text, using an option shown in Table 2-1.

TABLE 2-1 Specify the Appearance for Pasted Text

Option	Text Appearance
Plain text	Pastes as plain text; line breaks replaced by spaces
<pre> formatted paragraph	All line breaks of pasted text use the <pre> (preformatted) tag
Normal paragraphs and line breaks	Line breaks convert to < /br> (break) tags; paragraph breaks convert to <p> tag
Normal paragraphs without line breaks	Only paragraph breaks are modified and converted to <p> tag

Lay Out a Web Page

Most of the content in a page is made up of headings, paragraphs, and different types of breaks. Expression Web 2 offers a range of default options based on HTML tags for headings, paragraphs, and lists.

Put Together Pages with Headings and Paragraphs

Use the provided heading levels to develop a hierarchy of information in your page. To add a heading, select the text, click the Style drop-down arrow on the Common toolbar to display the list, and choose a style. The options range from Heading 1 through Heading 6 inclusive. An applied heading is identified by the corresponding HTML <h1> through <h6> tags.

Once your paragraphs are typed or pasted, you need to stylize their appearance. Expression Web 2 offers ways to configure the appearance of paragraphs. Select the paragraph you want to change, and use some simple choices on the Common toolbar, including:

- Click Increase Indent Position to shuffle the paragraph to the right; conversely, click Decrease Indent Position to shuffle the paragraph left.
- Click the Align Left, Center, or Align Right buttons to align a paragraph. Left alignment is the program default.

The appearance of paragraphs on your web page can be configured precisely in the Paragraph Properties dialog box. Select the content on the page, and then choose Format | Paragraph to open the dialog box (Figure 2-9).

In the dialog box, choose an option from the Alignment drop-down list, which includes Justified Text, as well as the options shown on the Common toolbar. Any settings you configure are shown in the Preview area at the bottom of the dialog box.

Indentation Choices Set off a paragraph by indenting it from the right or left side. To select an indentation for the entire paragraph, type a value in points in the Left

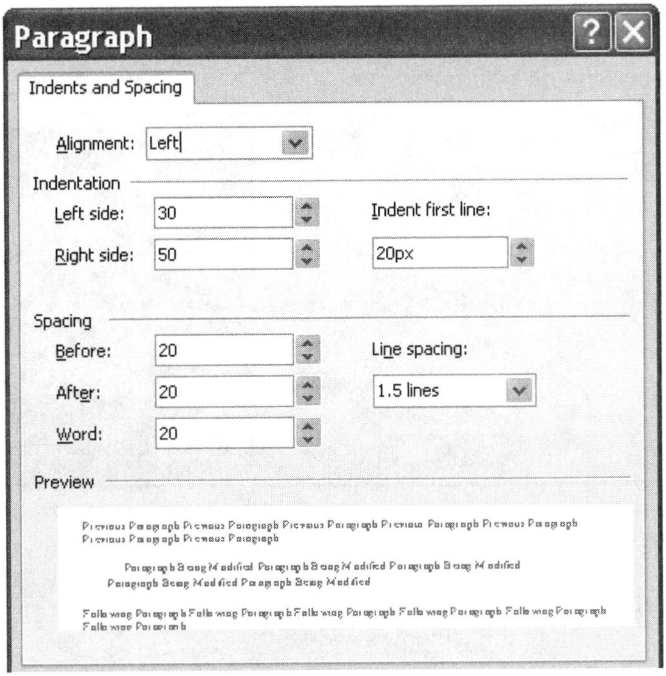

FIGURE 2-9 Choose the characteristics for a paragraph's appearance.

Side or Right Side fields. To indent just the first line of a paragraph, type a value for the Indent First Line field in pixels.

Note If you want to indent the paragraph from both sides, consider the `<blockquote>` tag rather than a `<p>` tag for the content.

Spacing Options Text on a web page is single-spaced by default. To increase the line spacing, which draws attention to the text, click the Line Spacing drop-down arrow and choose an alternative spacing, such as 1.5 or double spacing. Another way to add impact is to change the spacing between paragraphs, such as setting off the introductory paragraph. To do that, type a value in the Before, After, or Word fields, or click their arrows to add space in points.

Separate Content with Horizontal Lines

One simple device for separating content on a page is a horizontal rule, or line. To add a rule, click the page at the insertion location and choose Insert | HTML | Horizontal Line.

If you want to modify the line's appearance, double-click it on the page to open the Horizontal Line Properties dialog box. Modify the line and click OK to close the dialog box and make the changes.

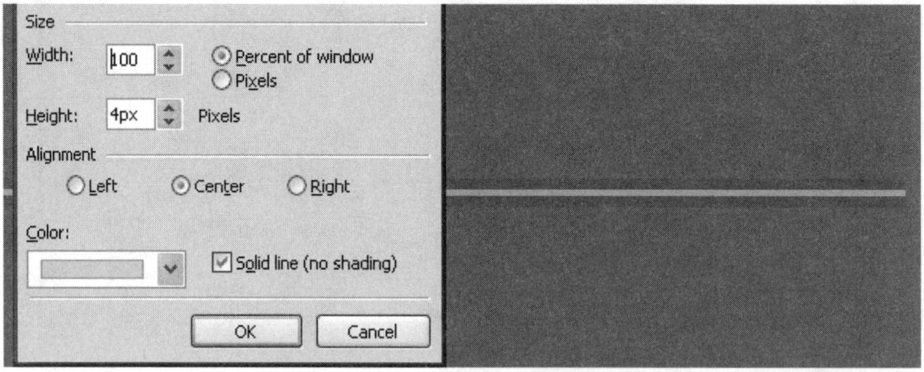

You can make these modifications:

- Specify the width as a percent of the window's width or in pixels; the default is 100 percent of the window's width.
- Set the height of the line in pixels; the default is 2 pixels.
- Define an alignment for the stroke as left, center (default), or right.
- Choose a color from the Color drop-down list and select whether to use a solid line only or use the shaded default.

Organize Text with Lists

Use Expression Web 2 to quickly generate both numbered (called *ordered*) and bulleted (called *unordered*) lists. You can customize the list with different numbering structures and different bullet appearances and even use your own images as bullets.

If you modify the structure of the list, such as adding or moving an item, Expression Web 2 automatically reorders the list for you. Regardless of the type of list you're using, press ENTER to start a new list item; press ENTER twice to end the list.

Tip To create a list, type a single item and choose the settings on the Common toolbar, or type the text, select it, and then apply a list appearance.

Configure Text as a List

To define a list, select the text to change into a list, or click the page where you want to start the list. Click the Bullets or Numbering button on the Common toolbar to apply the default list appearances.

To customize a list's appearance, select the list items on the web page, and choose Format | Bullets and Numbering to open the List Properties dialog box. Click the appropriate tab to display choices for the Picture Bullets, Plain Bullets, Numbers, or

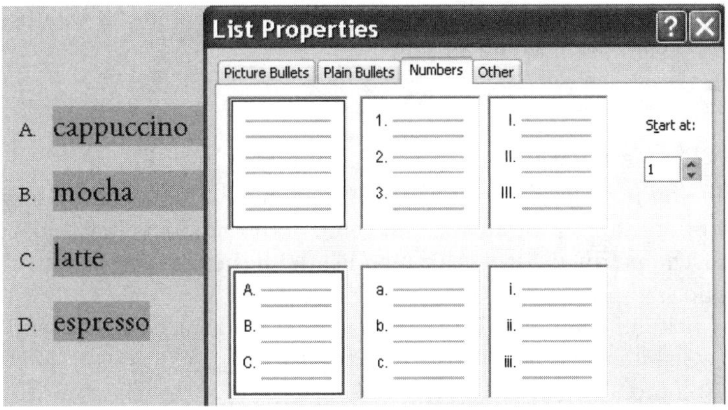

FIGURE 2-10 Specify the appearance of numbered and bulleted lists.

Other types of lists (Figure 2-10). Choose the style you want to use, and click OK to close the dialog box and apply the list style.

Use Images in a Bullet List

Customize your pages with image bullets, such as a portion of your logo used as an image element on your web pages. Expression Web 2 accepts any web image format, bitmap files, or Windows metafiles. Be sure to resize the image prior to configuring the bullets, as the program won't do it for you.

To customize a bullet list, follow these steps:

1. Select or type your list on the page, and then select the list items.
2. Choose Format | Bullets and Numbering to display the List Properties dialog box; click the Picture Bullets tab.
3. Select the Specify Picture radio button, click Browse to locate and select your image and click OK to load the image.
4. Click OK to close the dialog box and change your bullet appearance.

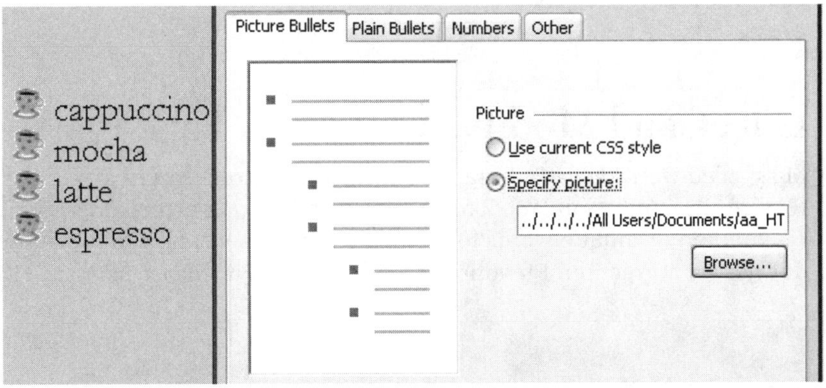

Tip Customize the location, spacing, and other features of your list further using styles. See how in Part II.

Insert a Sublist

Often you need to organize a set of items in a hierarchy. For example, your business may offer different products, and some of the products may be available in different sizes. The products form their own list, with the sizes as sublists for the pertinent products.

Click the end of the line where you want to start a sublist and press ENTER to insert a new list item. To demote the list for a sublist, press TAB, or click Increase Indent on the Common toolbar.

Tip If you want to insert another level (a sub-sublist), press TAB again, or click Increase Indent again.

Define Your Terms

In sites and pages related to technical material, it's common to see a list of terms, particularly if the layperson will be using the content. You can create a specialized type of list that shows terms and meanings called a *definition list*:

1. Click the page where you want the definition to appear.
2. On the Common toolbar, click the Style drop-down arrow and choose Defined Term. Type the name and press ENTER.
3. Type a definition for the term and press ENTER.
4. Continue adding name and definition pairs. To finish the list, press ENTER twice.

On the page, the term is indented and identified by the `<dt>` tag; the definition is defined with the <dd> tag, and the list is enclosed in a `<dl>` container, such as:

```
<dl>
<dt> name of term </dt>
<dd> definition </dd>
</dl>
```

Check and Modify Words on a Page

Misspelled words always detract from the professionalism of a site. Use the Spelling features in Expression Web 2 to check for and correct errors. To save time, add uncommon or unique words to the dictionary as necessary to prevent repeated queries for correction. Prevent overuse of certain words by using the Expression

Web 2 Thesaurus. If you need to change content, use the Find and Replace feature to locate and change content.

Check Spelling Page by Page

You can correct spelling in a page or an entire site. Choose Tools | Spelling | Spelling to run the spell checker. For each item found that isn't in the program dictionary, choose an option:

- Click Ignore to ignore one instance, or Ignore All to ignore all occurrences of a word, such as a proper name.
- Click Add to include a queried word in the dictionary.
- Select the misspelled word on the page, and retype to correct the error.

When you're finished, click OK.

Check Spelling Site-wide

Rather than correcting spelling errors page by page, incorporate a site-wide spell check into your routine prior to uploading a site or revisions. Follow these steps:

1. Select the site or pages you want to check from the Folder List.
2. Choose Tools | Spelling | Spelling, and select either the Entire Web Site option or the Selected Page(s) option.
3. Click Start. Expression Web 2 processes the first page in the site or selected list and opens the Spelling dialog box when it encounters a misspelled word. Choose Change or click Ignore to continue. The Continue with the Next Page dialog box opens when you've finished responding to errors; click OK to continue.
4. Click Back To List to return to the page list, or click Cancel to close the dialog box.

Tip If you rely heavily on the dictionary, customize how Expression Web 2 reviews your contents. Choose Tools | Spelling | Spelling Options | Custom Dictionaries, and create a custom dictionary. Start with a language and a default set of values, and then add, edit, or delete content. To use your custom dictionary, specify it as the default dictionary.

Make Corrections on the Fly

You can have Expression Web 2 show you spelling and errors as you type; some people prefer this, while others find the wavy red underlines distracting. You can also choose synonyms as you type by using the thesaurus. In all cases, look for the right-click shortcut menu options to modify the selected item, add it to the dictionary, and so on.

Check Spelling If you want to use the spell checker as you work, choose Tools | Spelling | Spelling Options and select the Check Spelling as You Type check box. Click OK to close the dialog box and apply the setting. As you type, you'll see errors on the page underlined with a wavy red line.

Everything with Google Tools offerss a special Spotlight project
o check out the Hart of Glass Studio blog, live online at Blogger.
ct follows Jody Hart, the owner of the fictius Hart of Glass St
help of a variety of Google Tools to estab
ect, you'll read how she:
es pictures in Picasa, and creates a Web Al
fictions
factious
fiction
fifties
factions
fictions'
Ignore All
Add

Make Word Substitutions Vary the words used in your sentences to minimize repetition using the thesaurus. Select the word you want to change, and choose Thesaurus from the shortcut menu. If there are suggestions, you'll see them displayed in the shortcut menu. Select the word to substitute.

Note You can also choose Tools | Thesaurus to open the menu, select a word, and replace it.

Did You Know?

You Can Use Expression Web 2 in Different Languages

Like other Microsoft programs, you can change the language that appears on the screen. Once a language is installed, you can use it as the default for a web page, web site, and a dictionary.

To mark text as another language, follow these steps:

1. Select the text to mark on the page.
2. Choose Tools | Set Language and select the language to use from the list.
3. Click OK.

Find and Replace Content on One or More Pages

Sometimes you realize you've made a consistent error throughout a page or a site, such as misspelling a name or an address. You can scan all the pages and make corrections as you come across them, or you can take the quick route to find and replace the content.

Note Find and Replace works equally well with text and code, both on a single page and site wide. Suppose you decide to define a style for a heading level. Rather than scanning each page and typing the style name for the heading, let the program do the work for you. See how to use Find and Replace for code in Chapter 7.

To make changes to one or more pages, follow these steps:

1. Select the page or pages you want to evaluate in the Folder List.
2. Choose Edit | Find to open the Find and Replace dialog box, or use the CTRL-F keystroke combination.
3. Click the tab corresponding to what you want to work with:
   - **Find** In the Find tab, type the text you want to locate in the page or pages selected. You can specify a page range and direction. In addition, choose specific features to help filter the results, such as matching the case or finding whole words only. Click Find All to identify all the items in the page or pages you selected, or click Find Next to view each search result systematically.
   - **Replace** The Replace tab is a duplicate of the Find tab, with the addition of a second field where you can type replacement text. Once you've specified the text and search options, you can have Expression Web 2 replace all instances automatically, or click Find Next to display the next instance, where you can click either Replace or Find Next to go on to the next instance (Figure 2-11).
4. Click Close when you're finished.

Find Content Using Expressions

Many times you need to find text or code, but don't know exactly how it is written. Other times, you may be looking for similar items. To simplify the search, use regular expressions following the steps in the previous section.

A *regular expression* is a string of text you use in combination with rules to define a search query. There are many regular expressions, but here are a few of the most common:

- **Single character** Use a . (period) to specify a missing character. For example, `88.2` returns anything from *8802* to *8892*.
- **Maximal** Use * (asterisk) as part of a term or string of code if you aren't sure of the content. Also, you can find similar items using a wildcard combining a period and asterisk. For example, `exp*.ion` returns *expansion*, *expulsion*, *expression*, and so on.
- **Minimal** Use # (sharp) as part of the string to show returns using a specified number of characters. For example, `44.#0` would return *4400* or *4410*, but not *44789022*; 44.##3 would return 44123, but not 4445678.

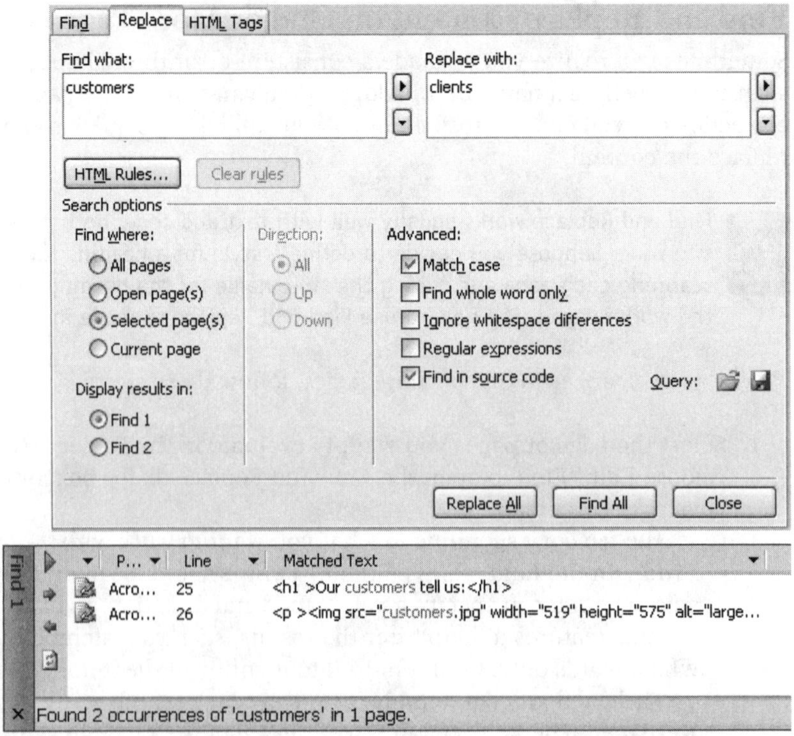

FIGURE 2-11 Specify search parameters and terms for replacement.

Note Locating and replacing text on a web site is similar to using the commands for one or more selected pages. The differences lie in how the returns are displayed. Select the web site you want to search in the Folder List, open the Find dialog box, and specify the search parameters in the Find or Replace tabs. Click Find All to show the results at the bottom of the program window in the Find pane. Double-click a page to open the page, highlighting the search term. Continue in the open and subsequent pages by clicking the Next or Back arrows in the Find pane.

How to... Save Search Results

You can save searches as a query. Perform a search using the Find and Replace dialog box, and then click the Save Query button, available on all tabs of the dialog box. In the resulting dialog box, name the file and specify its storage location. Later, click the Open button to locate and select your query file to open it again.

Summary

In this chapter, you saw how to create a new page and specify its characteristics. There are many ways you can modify text within Expression Web 2 without configuring a style sheet. The program offers similar features to a regular word processor, such as default styles and fonts, and includes multiple toolbar commands for setting heading, paragraph, and list appearances.

Features you add to the text are configurable in a variety of associated dialog boxes, such as setting spacing between paragraphs, or the type of bullet to use for a list. Expression Web 2 also offers a number of editing features, such as Redo/Undo, spell checkers, and a thesaurus.

In the next chapter, you'll see how Expression Web 2 handles images. You'll be impressed by the way most any image can be readily configured to add to your web pages.

3

Configure Images on a Page

HOW TO...

- Add images to a page
- Edit images for your site
- Import Photoshop images
- Specify image layouts
- Set off images on a page

Back in the early days of the Internet, the introduction of images was big news. Today, however, it's very difficult to imagine a web site that doesn't use images.

Online images have specific requirements, primarily related to the need to balance the image quality with the file size. In this chapter, you'll see how Expression Web 2 assists in using and managing images for your web pages.

Once an image is on the page, there are numerous ways to enhance the image and page, ranging from using a graphic as a tracing layout to working with layered images to defining page alignments and text wrapping.

Manage Graphics in Expression Web 2

Whether you're using images for illustration or as page elements like bullets, links, and page backgrounds, Expression Web 2 can help you manage your image files. By the way, Expression Web 2 refers to all image and graphic files as *pictures*.

Graphic File Formats

Images can be imported into Expression Web 2 in a variety of formats. Some are better for illustration while others are better for photographic images (Figure 3-1). The two most common image formats for online use are GIF and JPG. In the last few years, PNG (Portable Network Graphic) format has become increasingly popular.

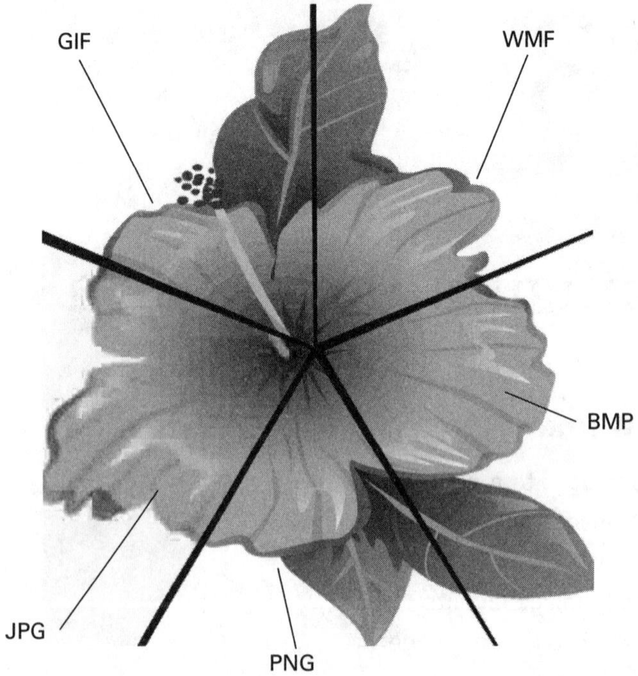

FIGURE 3-1 Use different image formats in your web page.

You can import images in any of the following formats.

GIF Format GIF (Graphic Interchange Format) files are best for illustrations and images with solid blocks of color. GIF images can use up to 256 colors, one of which can be specified as transparent to blend a foreground graphic with the page background. (The section "Specify Transparency" later in the chapter describes how to designate the transparent color.)

JPG Format JPG (Joint Photographic Experts Group) files are best used for photographs and images containing color gradients and thousands or millions of colors. The quality of a JPG image has a great effect on its appearance. A low quality image shows blocks of overlapping color. In addition, JPG is *lossy compression*, meaning that pixels are deleted from the image in order to compress its size.

BMP Format BMP (Bitmap Format) is the Microsoft Windows raster file format, that is, an image made up of an arrangement of screen dots, or pixels. If one of these images uses a low resolution (a low number of pixels per inch), you tend to find the edges of images and transitions between colors jagged.

PNG Format PNG (Portable Network Graphics) is designed to replace GIF images as the format for displaying simple images and illustrations. PNG offers *lossless* *compression*, meaning that pixels aren't deleted from the image in order to compress its size. In addition to working with simple images, PNG images can produce background transparency without jagged edges, common in GIF images due to the limited number of colors used. PNG also offers support for images with millions of colors, like JPG format, often in a smaller file size.

WMF Format WMF (Microsoft Windows Metafile) supports vector and EPS (Encapsulated PostScript) images. Illustrations created in Adobe Illustrator can be used in Expression Web 2 when exported in WMF format. In addition, Microsoft Clip Organizer images are in WMF format.

When you save files that are imported in formats other than GIF or JPG formats, Expression Web 2 converts the files when you save the page. In addition to GIF and JPG, you can also use PNG files as default formats. Choose and change settings in the Page Editor Options.

Define Graphic Defaults

Although Expression Web 2 lets you import images in formats like WMF, the images aren't saved in your web page in their native formats. Instead, the files are converted using default formats—to GIF if there are fewer than 256 colors or to JPG if there are over 256 colors.

To view and modify the default formats, follow these steps:

1. Select Tools | Page Editor Options and select the Picture tab.
2. Click File Types Settings to open the Picture File Type dialog box to view and specify settings for GIF and JPG images:
   - GIF image options are deselected by default. Choose Interlace to specify a sequential download of the image's contents. In the "old days," downloading even simple images was a lengthy process. Today, rather than waiting to see content, an interlaced GIF is shown in horizontal sections that fill in as the image content is downloaded. Choose Set Transparent Color to specify one color in the image as transparent.

Tip Rather than using the transparency settings in the options, use the Transparency feature on the Picture toolbar to let you customize the color choice. Read how in the upcoming section, "Specify Transparency."

   - JPG image options include quality and progressive passes. The default quality is 90, which provides very good image quality at a reasonable file size. Type a different value or use the arrows to the right of the field to increase or decrease the quality. Progressive Passes is inactive by default. Click the field to type a value if you want to display images in sequential passes (Figure 3-2).

Note Progressive Passes gradually display the image—specify the number of passes (usually three or four) if your web page is likely to be used by viewers with slow Internet connections. As each pass occurs, more of the detail of the image is shown.

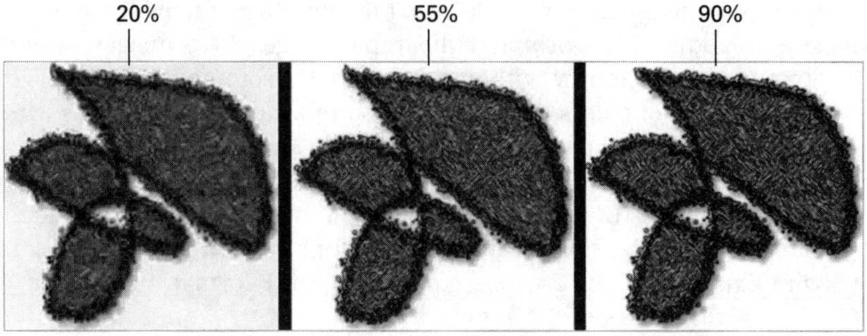

FIGURE 3-2 A progressive JPG draws over several passes.

3. Click OK to close the dialog box and return to the Picture tab.
4. Select formats for the Default File Type Conversion and Paste Settings. The default choices are GIF for images with less than 256 colors and JPG for those with over 256 colors. To change either option, click the drop-down arrow and choose from GIF, JPG, and PNG formats.
5. Click OK to close the Page Editor Options dialog box.

Specify an Image Editor

You can edit an image directly from the Expression Web 2 page, but first you have to define an image editing program in the Expression Web 2 options. You can choose different editors for different file types. For example, you might want to edit JPG images in Photoshop or Paint Shop Pro but use Fireworks to edit GIF files.

Follow these steps to select and define image editors:

1. Select Tools | Application Options to open the Application Options dialog box; click the Configure Editors tab.

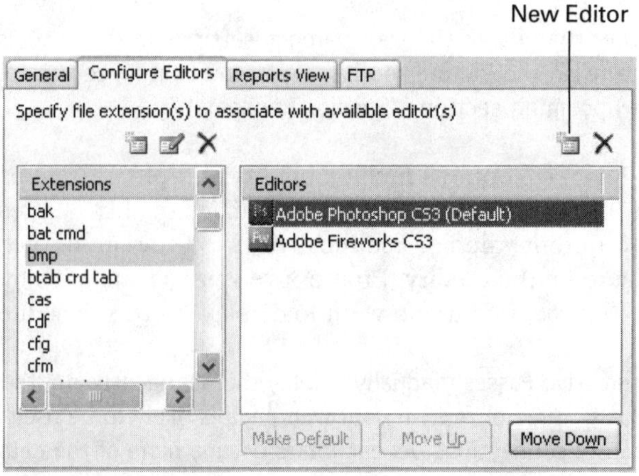

2. In the Extensions list, select the file extension you want to associate with an editing program. You'll see the default shown in the Editors list (for example, BMP files are associated with Paint by default, or by a designated program such as Photoshop as you see above).
3. Click the New Editor button, shown above the list of Editors to display the Open With dialog box. You'll see a Recommended Programs list, followed by an Other Programs list.
4. Scroll through the list and select the program you want to associate with the file format. Click OK to close the dialog box and add the program to the Editors list.

Tip If the program you want to use isn't listed, click Browse for More to open a Windows Explorer dialog box. Locate and select the program's EXE file. Click Open to close the dialog boxes and add the program to the Editors list.

5. To add another editor, repeat steps 3 and 4. To delete an existing editor, select it in the Editors list and click DELETE. Reorder the list as you like. The editor at the top of the list is automatically defined as the Default.
6. Click OK to close the dialog box.

Use the Pictures Toolbar

Expression Web 2 offers the Pictures toolbar with an array of tools and settings to use for managing and editing images on your web pages. Click an image on the page in Design or Split views to display the Pictures toolbar, or choose View | Toolbars | Pictures (Figure 3-3).

The toolbar is broken into several sections, as shown in Figure 3-3. You'll see how the different tools work throughout the chapter.

Tip Once you start working on images for your site's pages, drag the Pictures toolbar up until it docks, or joins up, with the other toolbars. It's out of the way, but easy to access.

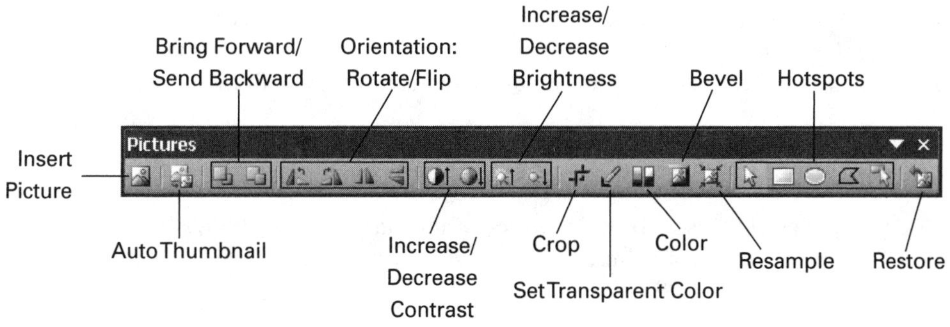

FIGURE 3-3 Use the features on the toolbar to manipulate the image.

Add Images to a Page

You have a lot of freedom when working with images in Expression Web 2. For example, you don't have to assemble all your image files in a folder before starting work. As you collect and insert your images, Expression Web 2 moves copies to your web site's folder. You can insert images directly from a scanner or camera and even use a Photoshop image.

Insert Graphics from a File

The most common way to add images and graphics to your web page is to use a file stored on your computer. Open the web page you're working with and click to define the insertion point for the image.

Add an Image

You can specify an image from any location to include in a web page. Follow these steps to insert an image:

1. Choose Insert | Picture | From File, or click the Insert Picture from File button at the far left of the Pictures toolbar to open the Picture dialog box.
2. Locate and select the file you want to add to the page and click Insert. The Picture dialog box closes, and the Accessibility Properties dialog box opens.
3. Type alternate text for the image, which will display for persons using screen reading devices and those using text-only browsers, and click OK. The dialog box closes, and your image is placed on the page.

Note For a complex image, such as a graph or chart, you can use a long description, which is often a text file or another HTML file. Click Browse to open a dialog box to locate and select the file. Read about accessibility issues in Chapter 15.

Embed Image Files

Any files you insert from locations other than your web site's root folder are processed when you save your file.

Follow these steps to embed your image(s) in your site's root folder:

1. Once the page contains the image or images, choose File | Save to save the web page complete with its images. The Save Embedded Files dialog box displays if you sourced pictures from various locations on your hard drive
2. If the graphics are not already included in the web site folder, the Save Embedded Files dialog box opens, listing the unsaved images. If you like, select an image's name to view a preview.
3. Specify any modifications you want to make to the file by clicking the appropriate button at the bottom of the dialog box (Figure 3-4):
   - **Rename** Activates the file's name text so you can type a different name.
   - **Change Folder** Opens the Change Folder dialog box, displaying the folder and file structure for your web site. If you have several locations where you intend to store image files, choose the folder and click OK.
   - **Set Action** Opens a dialog box where you can choose one of two options. Leave the default action to save the file, or click Don't Save This File, which then writes a path to the current file's location on your computer.
   - **Picture File Types** Opens the Picture File Type dialog box. The file format for the selected image is preselected. You can change to one of the other formats listed, including GIF, JPG, PNG-8, and PNG-24. Click OK to return to the Save Embedded File dialog box.
4. When you're finished, click OK to close the dialog box and process the files.

Insert Graphics from the Folder List

Adding images from your web site's folders to an open web page is a simple drag-and-drop process. Open the page on your site where you want to place the image. Then drag it from the Folder List and drop it at the insertion point on the page. You'll see the Accessibility Properties dialog box open so you can type alternate text. Type a description and click OK to close the dialog box and add the image.

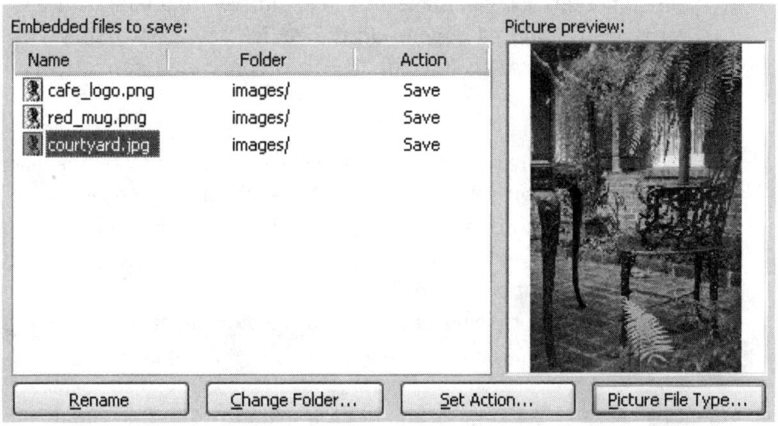

FIGURE 3-4 Specify some settings for images prior to embedding them in your web site.

Note Since the files are already within your web site's folder, you can simply save the file without any embedding requirements.

Did You Know?

You Can Download Images Directly into Your Web Page

If you have a digital still or video camera, a web camera, or a scanner connected to your computer, you can place an image directly from your device on to a web page.

The steps required depend on the device you are working with. Regardless of your image source, be sure the device is configured correctly and then follow these steps:

1. Click the location on the page where you want to insert the image.
2. Choose Insert | Picture | From Scanner or Camera to open the dialog box.
3. Click the Device drop-down arrow and choose a device from the list.
4. Specify the resolution you want. For online use, click Web Quality, which provides good resolution at a low file size.
5. Click Insert to import the image using program defaults. To use your own settings, click Custom Insert and follow the device dialog boxes to insert the image.

Note By default, images are added to the Clip Organizer.

Use a Photoshop File in Expression Web 2

Here's a really cool feature in Expression Web 2: You can generate a web-optimized image to use in Expression Web 2 from a layered Photoshop PSD file. Not only can you select the layers you want to use, but you can also open the original PSD file from the file in Expression Web 2.

Image Requirements

There are a number of properties that must be included in the Photoshop file—fortunately, the properties are those you'd commonly use in a Photoshop workflow, including:

- 8-bit color/channel
- RGB, grayscale, or indexed color (you have to convert CMYK to one of these color spaces)
- Image size no greater than 200MB
- Maximize File Compatibility Preference active (this is a default preference, and you'll see it every time you save a Photoshop file until you disable the message box)
- PSD format

Insert a Photoshop Image

You can insert the entire flattened Photoshop image, or specify layers to import following these steps:

1. Open the web page and click the page to place the insertion point where you want to insert the image.
2. Choose Insert | Picture | From Adobe Photoshop (.psd) to display the Open dialog box.
3. Locate and select the file you want to use and click Open.
4. Specify the characteristics for the image (Figure 3-5). Your options include:
    - **Select a layer option** Click All Layers to import a flattened version of the image; click Selected Layers and choose the layers to import. If the PSD file is flattened to a single layer, only the All Layers option is available as the default selection.
    - **Specify a file format** Click the Encoding drop-down arrow and choose a file format, including a quality setting for JPG import.
    - **Choose your view** Click the Optimized tab to view the image you'll import; or click the Original tab to view the original file.
5. Click Import. In the pop-up that displays, type alternative text for accessibility use, and then click OK. The dialog box closes, and your image is placed on the page.

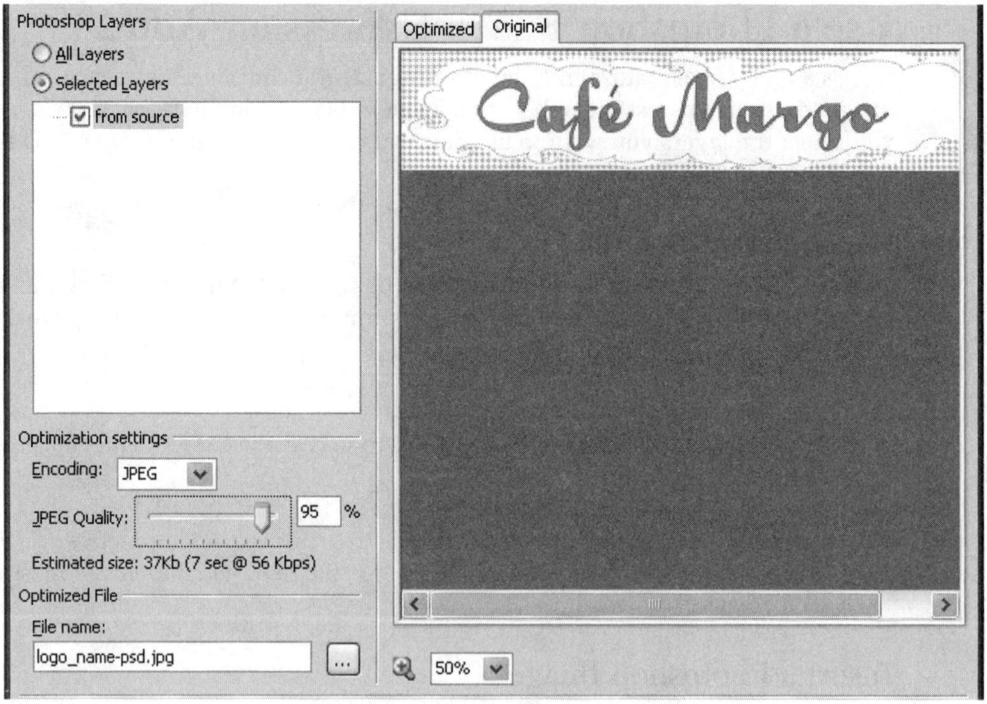

FIGURE 3-5 Specify the features for the imported Photoshop file.

Update a Photoshop Image

The PSD files you use in Expression Web 2 aren't static items. That is, there's a link between the image you see on the web page and the original file. For that reason, you can *round-trip edit* the image directly from the web page.

To start, right-click the image in Design view to display the shortcut menu, and choose Adobe Photoshop PSD | Edit Source [*path to file\filename*]. The default application opens and displays the PSD file. Make the edits as desired, save the file, and close the program.

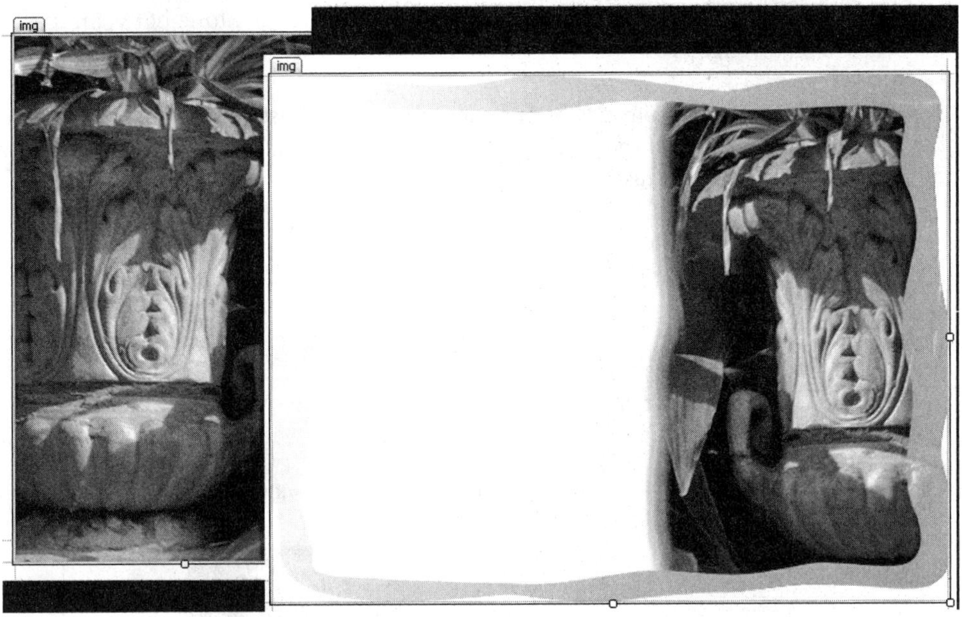

When you return to the Expression Web 2 program and your web page, right-click the image and choose Adobe Photoshop PSD | Update from Source. Specify the import settings (described in the previous section) and click Import.

Edit Image Features

Dropping or inserting images on your web page gives you a good idea of how and where your images work best. If you haven't done a lot of planning beforehand, or if you are new to the web design process, the odds are good that your images aren't going to be exactly as you'd like. Fortunately, you can use tools on the Pictures toolbar to adjust different aspects of an image's coloring and brightness. You can also make changes to the resolution and even wash out an image—great for a page or section background.

Modify Image Colors

Expression Web 2 offers a few tools that change the color characteristics of your images. Use them for correcting images or for creating effects.

Adjust Brightness and Contrast

Many of us confuse the terms *brightness* and *contrast*. They are different, although the outcome may be similar. *Brightness* refers to the overall level of light shown by each pixel in an image, while *contrast* defines the difference in tone between dark and light areas on an image.

Note Often an image needs both brightness and contrast correction. In that case, start with brightness to increase the range of pixel colors, and then finish with adjusting contrast.

To start, open the web page containing the graphic and select the image on the page. You'll see the selection frame, and the Pictures toolbar displays:

- Click More Brightness or Less Brightness to lighten or darken your image, shown in the upper row of examples.
- Click More Contrast or Less Contrast to increase or decrease the difference between light and dark areas on the image, shown in the lower row of examples.

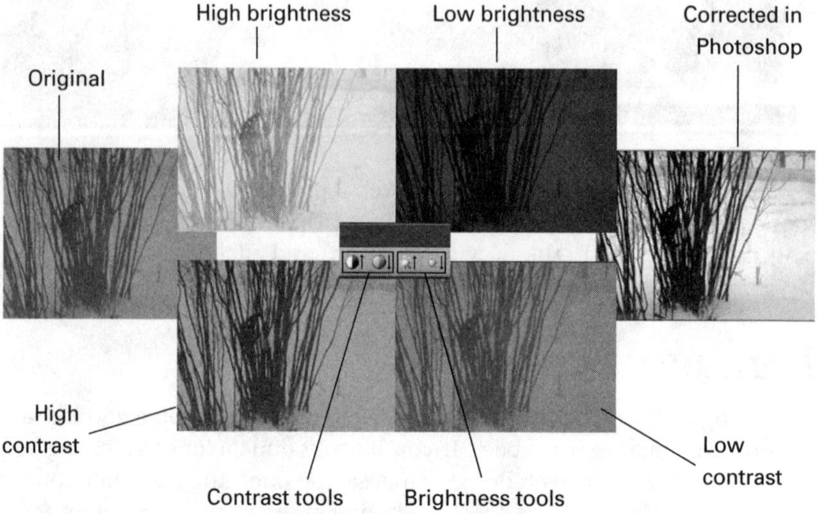

Tip As you see in the image, using the tools in Expression Web 2 helps, but the image required more correction than the Picture tools could offer.

Change Color Intensity

A common color edit that can add interest to your page is to desaturate the images. *Saturation* is the color intensity of an image. When you *desaturate* the image, you remove the intensity. Remove all the color, and you have a grayscale image.

Select the image on the page that you want to change, and click Color on the Pictures toolbar to open a list of options:

- Select Wash Out to produce a faded version of the original image.
- Select Grayscale to produce an image without color, using only shades of gray.

Specify Transparency

Setting a transparent color in an image helps integrate the images with the web page background. Open the page containing the image and select the graphic on the page. In the Pictures toolbar, click Set Transparent Color, and click the tool over the color you want to remove from the selected graphic.

If your image is in any format other than GIF, Expression Web 2 opens a message dialog box explaining the file has to be converted to GIF format first, before continuing with the color sampling. Click OK to close the message and click the image to select the color for removal; or click Cancel to stop the process. If you don't want the format changed, you can specify transparency in another program.

Although the Expression Web 2 Picture tools are great for making some quick edits to your images, they don't necessarily give you the best results. If you make changes using the Picture tools and don't like the results, open the file in your editing program (Figure 3-6).

The left image uses the Expression Web 2 Picture tool to set the transparent color, the center shows a GIF, and the right image a PNG, both imported with a predetermined transparent color. The figure is magnified to show the differences clearly.

Change Dimensions and Appearance

Often, graphic images aren't the size you want for the finished page. In Expression Web 2, you can resize the graphics using resizing or resampling.

Resizing and Resampling Graphics

Resizing duplicates pixels to increase the image size or deletes pixels to decrease the image size. *Resampling* increases image size by adding additional pixels or decreases image size by removing or shrinking pixels. Expression Web 2 resizes images automatically but leaves the decision whether or not to resample up to you. Read more about resampling in the sidebar, "Resample Images with Confidence."

Manually Resizing an Image To resize an image, select it on the page and drag a corner resize handle. Press SHIFT as you drag to preserve the proportions. As you resize, the dimensions in pixels are shown in a tooltip. Release the mouse when the

FIGURE 3-6 Transparency quality varies with program and file format used.

image is the desired size. Click the Picture Actions button that displays at the lower right edge of the image to open a list of two options shown here.

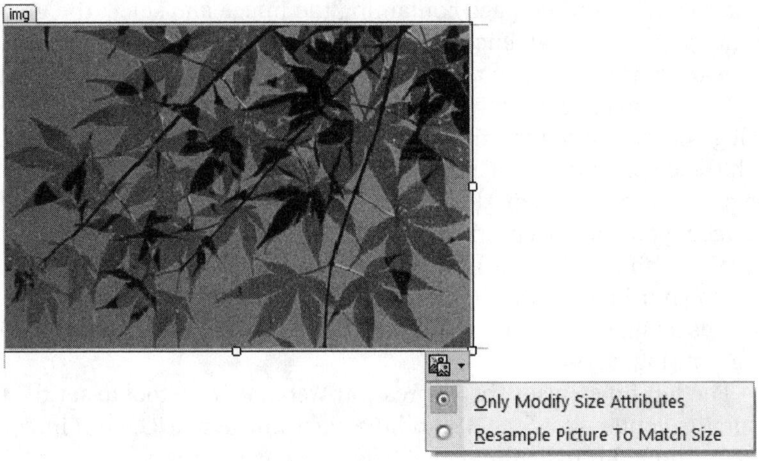

The default choice is Only Modify Size Attributes. You can also select Resample Picture to Match Size, which adds or removes pixels according to the image's resolution.

Resizing an Image Numerically Open and display the web page you want to use. Double-click the image to open the Picture Properties dialog box; click the Appearance tab. In the Size area at the bottom of the dialog box, specify the height and width in pixels or as a percent of the original. Select the Keep Aspect Ratio check box to maintain the image's proportions.

Click OK to close the dialog box and make the adjustment. Along with resizing the image on the Display view, the image's dimensions are also adjusted in the page's HTML code.

Tip You don't have to resample an image immediately. Any time the web page is open, you can resample it using the Resample command on the Pictures toolbar.

Create Thumbnails

Often you see thumbnail previews of larger images on web pages. Offering a thumbnail view is a convenient way for your site's visitors to decide if they want to download and view the larger image. Expression Web 2 can create thumbnails automatically. Right-click the image on the page and choose Auto Thumbnail, or use the shortcut keystroke CTRL + T to replace a graphic on the page with a thumbnail and a link to the original image.

How to... Resample Images with Confidence

Expression Web 2 offers tools to change image sizes dimensionally and through resampling. Suppose you have an image that is 4 inches wide, at a resolution of 100 ppi (pixels per inch). If you increase the size of the image to 6 inches wide dimensionally, the 400 original pixels stretch to fit the space, often resulting in a jagged appearance. If you resample the image, you actually add more pixels to it. So, in the example, the 6-inch wide image contains 600 pixels per inch. Resampling applies an algorithm to estimate the new pixels' color based on surrounding pixels. The simpler the image, the better the results.

Conversely, decreasing an image dimensions by resampling (downsampling) removes pixels. The resulting image looks fine online.

The results of using resizing and resampling vary, depending on the characteristics of the original image:

- Decreasing the size of a high-resolution image works well by either resizing or resampling.
- Decreasing the size of a low-resolution image works well by resizing or resampling.
- Increasing the size of a high-resolution image often works, while increasing the size of a low-resolution image usually produces jagged pixels.
- Resizing is best for images with simple edges and limited colors, like a sketch or illustration. Resampling is better used for photos or complex images.

The thumbnail's appearance is based on settings specified in the Page Editor Options dialog box. Choose Tools | Page Editor Options to open the dialog box, and click the AutoThumbnail tab (Figure 3-7).

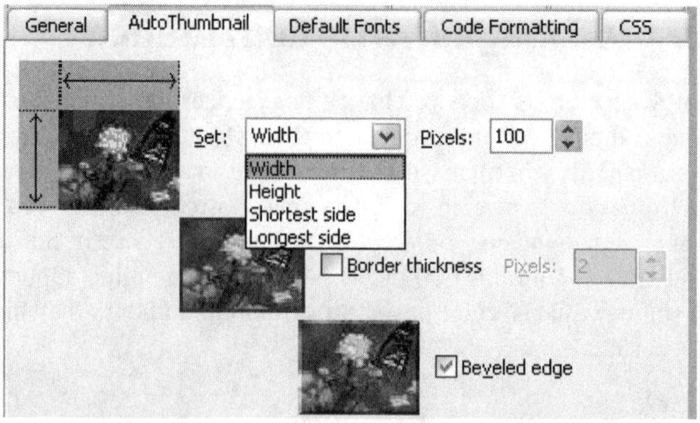

FIGURE 3-7 Choose appearance options for thumbnails.

Specify the options for the thumbnail:

- Click the Set drop-down arrow and choose an option for configuring the thumbnails. You can base thumbnail size on the width, height, or shortest or longest side of an image. Specify the pixel dimension to use; the default is 100 pixels.
- Select the Border Thickness check box to use a border around the image, identifying the thumbnail as hyperlinked. The default value is 2 pixels.
- Select the Beveled Edge check box to frame the thumbnails.

Click OK to close the dialog box.

Save the web page before testing the thumbnail. Expression Web 2 produces a duplicate of your original image at the thumbnail size and displays it in the Save Embedded Files dialog box prior to saving. The thumbnail image is saved in the same folder as the original by default. Click OK to embed the file and save the web page.

Tip Read more about embedding in the earlier section, "Embed Image Files."

To test the file, display it in your browser (press F12 to open your default browser). Click the thumbnail on the page to replace it with the full-size image.

Crop an Image to Fit

One of the most common edits is *cropping*, or removing content from the edges of an image. Not only can cropping off parts of an image correct an unbalanced composition, it can also define an area of importance

Expression Web 2 offers a Crop tool on the Pictures toolbar. Cropping hides the content but doesn't delete it, which lets you resize the crop or remove it as necessary.

To crop an image, follow these steps:

1. Select the image on the web page and click Crop on the Pictures toolbar to display a cropping frame over the graphic, shown below.
2. Drag the resize handles to define the content you want to use.
3. Click Crop on the Pictures toolbar again to complete the process.

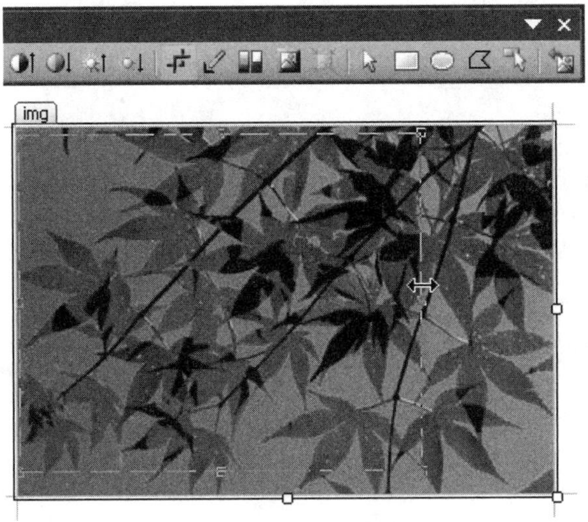

Tip Decide beforehand if you need to use a cropped image where bandwidth is a concern. In an Expression Web 2 web page, the cropped content is hidden, not removed from the image. As a result, the web page carries the extra content unnecessarily. If bandwidth is a concern, crop your image in an image editing program, and then use the cropped version in your web page.

Rotate and Flip Graphics

Sometimes an image looks better on the page if you can reorient it. For example, a landscape with hills rising into the distance may look better with the hills at the edge of the page, rather than snuggled up to the text.

Expression Web 2 offers tools to either rotate or flip images on the Pictures toolbar. Select the appropriate tool to Rotate Right 90 Degrees (clockwise), Rotate Left 90 Degrees (counterclockwise), Flip Horizontally 180 Degrees, or Flip Vertically 180 Degrees.

Bevel an Image Edge

In the younger days of the visual browser, image bevels were a big deal, often sprinkled liberally on any site considered cool. Now, beveled images can date a web page, but they still offer an interesting effect if used judiciously.

Did You Know?

You Can Reverse Graphic Edits

If you edit a graphic and then change your mind, click Restore on the Pictures toolbar to revert to the file's state when you last saved the page. Keep in mind that only the changes made since the page was saved are reversible.

If you can't revert to an appearance you like, delete the image and reinsert it. For big editing jobs, consider using an image editor before placing the image in your web page.

Bevels create a dimensional appearance to the edges of an image. Select the graphic on the page and click Bevel on the Pictures toolbar. Keep clicking until the desired bevel depth is achieved. You can't reverse the process, but you can undo it by clicking Undo on the Common toolbar.

Create Low Resolution Graphics

Expression Web 2 lets you associate a low resolution image with a high resolution image on a web page. To attach a low resolution alternative, right-click the image on the web page, and click Picture Properties from the shortcut menu to open the Picture Properties dialog box.

On the General tab, click Browse to locate and select the image. Click OK to close the dialog box.

Position Images on a Page

There are two ways to use image placement features in Expression Web 2. In this chapter, you'll see how to work from the Design view and make the placements right on the page. In Part II of the book, you'll learn how to code the placements yourself using CSS.

Regardless of the approach, Expression Web 2 lets you work with a tracing graphic, usually a mockup of a web page that you can use for placement.

Insert a Tracing Graphic

The layout of a web page is often based on a sketch or mockup created in another program, such as Adobe Fireworks. Use the Trace Image feature to define a background picture and its placement to use as a guide for creating the web page. The traced image is stored as an embedded file with your other web site content.

Open the web page and follow these steps to insert a tracing image:

1. Select View | Tracing Image | Configure to open the Tracing Image dialog box. Click Browse to locate and select the image for the background (Figure 3-8).

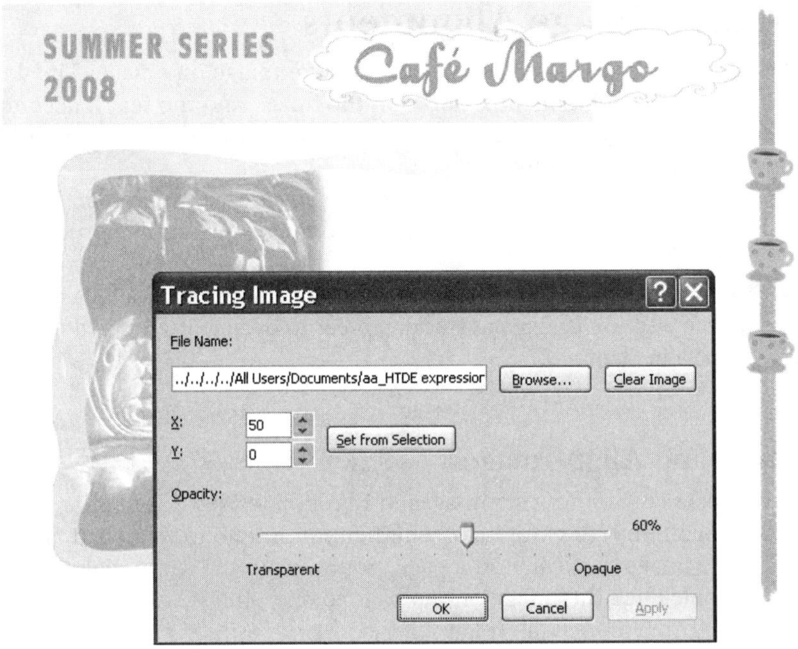

FIGURE 3-8 Select and configure a tracing image for the page background.

Tip Adjust the image anytime by reopening the Tracing Image dialog box.

2. Specify the location for the image by typing values in the X (distance from the left margin in pixels) and Y (distance from the top margin in pixels) fields, or click Set from Selection.
3. Drag the Opacity slider to specify the image's visibility. The default is set at 75 percent.
4. Click Apply to display the image on the page. Make adjustments to the settings as required, and click Apply after each change. Click OK to close the dialog box.
5. Choose View | Tracing Image | Show Image to toggle the image's visibility on or off.

Note Tracing images are often used in conjunction with layout tables. Read how to use layout tables in Chapter 9.

Specify Image Alignments

There are a variety of ways you can place an image on a page. The default options include simple relationships between the image and the text it accompanies, such as placing the image at the baseline or center of a row of text. Or, use different wraps to flow text around a graphic.

Expression Web 2 lets you control the space surrounding an image on the page. Margins are outside of the border and padding is inside the border.

Note In addition to using features to position images horizontally and vertically, you can also use layers and stacking order to overlay images and text on a page. Read how in Chapter 8.

Wrap and Align Images

The process of configuring images in Expression Web 2 is similar to the process in Word documents. Regardless of whether you intend to wrap text around an image or align the image vertically on a page, you work in the same dialog box.

Double-click the image on the page to open the Picture Properties dialog box. Click the Appearance tab (Figure 3-9).

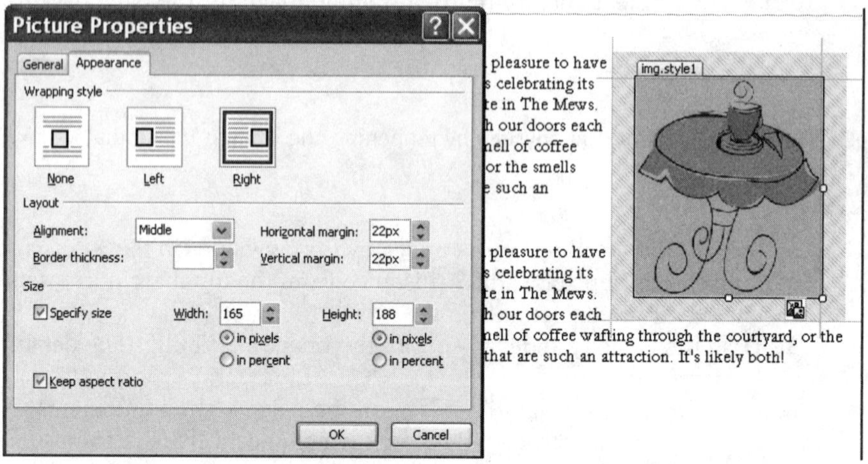

FIGURE 3-9 Configure text and image placements using wrapping.

Note You may be familiar with text wrap from other programs. As you'll see in Part II, CSS refers to text wrap as a float. In Figure 3-9, for example, the style is `"float:right"`.

In the dialog box, choose options for the image's layout and click OK to close the dialog box and apply the settings. Choices include:

- **Specify the text wrap** The default text wrap style is None. Click Left to align the image with the left margin and wrap text around the right side of the image. Click Right to align the image with the right margin and wrap text around the left side of the image, as in Figure 3-9.
- **Specify a vertical alignment** Click the Alignment drop-down arrow to open a list and choose an alignment option. Choose from several choices for aligning with the page or the text.
- **Specify a border** Click the Border Thickness arrows to define the width of the border, or type the value in pixels. The image in Figure 3-9 doesn't include a border.
- **Specify margins** Click the arrows or type values in both the Horizontal and Vertical Margin fields. On the page, you'll see the margin areas identified with a hatched border.

Note The left and right margins can't be different values, nor can the top and bottom margins. In the next sections, read how to configure margins and borders further.

Define Space and Edging Options

Sometimes, adding a border to an image enhances its appearance on the page. Use settings in the Borders and Shading dialog box to customize borders and define *padding*, the amount of space between the border and the image itself. By default, an image doesn't use borders, padding, or shading. You can apply any combination of these options in the dialog box.

Select the image on the page and choose Format | Borders and Shading to open the dialog box, which displays the Borders tab by default. As you see here, borders, padding, and shading are all applied to the image, which shows both in the Preview on the dialog box and on the page.

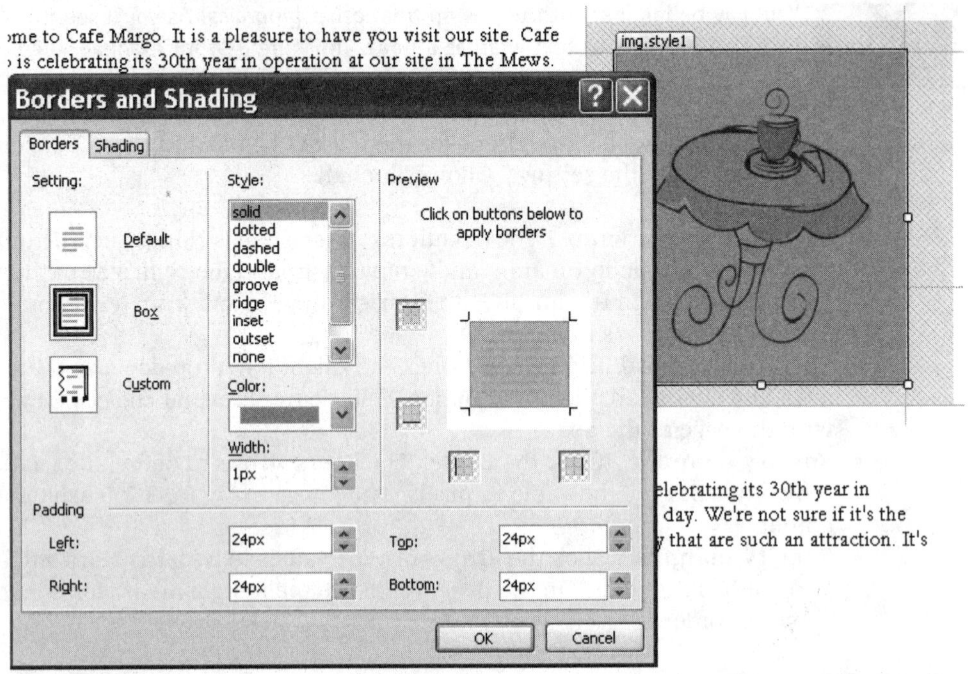

Click a Setting option. The default option is without borders. As you select an option, you see it applied in the Preview. Choose a style from the list, a color from the drop-down list options, and a width by clicking the arrows to display a value in pixels.

Click the appropriate buttons on the Preview to add or remove a border from one or more sides of the image. Finally, type a padding value in pixels for each edge of the image, or use the arrows to define the values.

Click the Shading tab to apply colored fills and patterns. In this tab of the dialog box, you can do the following:

- Specify a fill color for the background and foreground by clicking the appropriate drop-down list and choosing a solid color.
- Click Browse to locate and select a pattern to use as a background picture. Once the picture is selected, identify the position vertically and horizontally and specify whether to repeat the image to tile it, or whether to attach it in a fixed location in the image space.

Tip The background specified applies only to the image. Read about adding a background to a page in Chapter 2.

When you've made your choices, click OK to close the dialog box and apply the settings.

Tip To configure basic border settings, click the Border drop-down arrow on the Common toolbar and choose an option.

Adjust Margins and Padding in Design View

In Design view, you can adjust an image's margins and padding on the page and see the changes as you make them. As you reposition the settings, the margin or padding size in pixels displays in a screen tip (Figure 3-10).

Note You can't display both margin and padding options simultaneously; the illustration is a composite image.

- **Adjust margins** Select the graphic on the page to show the hatched colored frame identifying the margin surrounding the image. Drag the margin lines to the desired width.
- **Adjust padding** To display the padding lines, click the image and press SHIFT to toggle the blue padding lines' visibility. With the SHIFT key pressed, drag a padding line to reset the width.

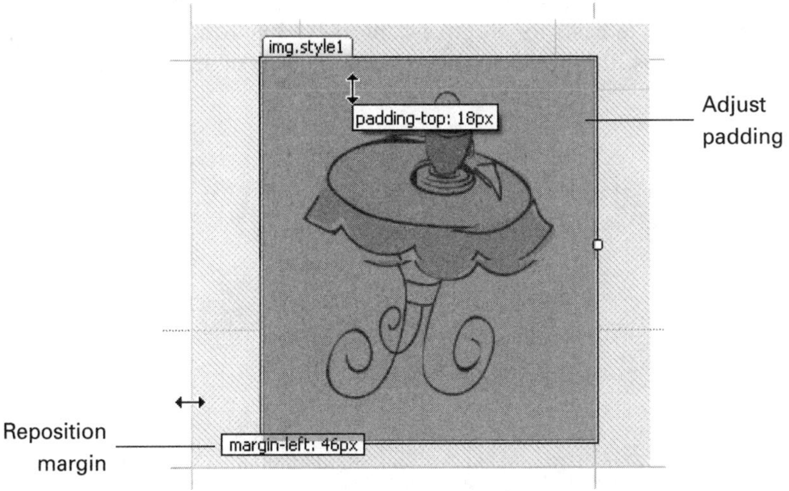

FIGURE 3-10 Adjust margins and padding on the page.

Did You Know?

Files Shown in This Chapter Are Available Online

Flipping through pages in a book or reading topics here and there is one thing—getting to work with the source materials is another. For your experimenting pleasure, check out the book's Spotlight Project. The project includes the pages used in several chapters for designing the Café Margo web site.

Summary

This chapter introduced you to the Expression Web 2 graphic features. There are several methods of adding images to pages, including using Photoshop images.

To help edit and work with the images for your pages, Expression Web 2 offers the Pictures toolbar. You can edit image characteristics such as color intensity and transparency or modify the visual attributes by cropping, rotating, or flipping the image.

As with text, there are many ways to modify the appearance and display of images on pages. You can apply and modify the display features without writing styles, although Expression Web 2 defines the styles based on the choices you make. Many features, such as specifying image size, margins, and padding, can be adjusted on the page as well as in the dialog boxes.

In the next chapter, read how Expression Web 2 helps you configure and define hyperlinks, the basis for web page interactivity. You'll discover how to use text links, use images as links, and define specific regions of an image as a *hotspot*, or active link location.

4

Link Content in Your Site

HOW TO...

- Create basic hyperlinks
- Link pages together
- Link to external sources
- Customize link appearances
- Link from images and image maps

Hyperlinks are the basis of online activity. Links lead from page to page in your site, or from area to area among pages on your site. You link to external sites, which then link to other sites, and so on, and so on. In your site, you can also link to other types of files for your visitors to download or view.

Links don't have to be attached to text. Expression Web 2 offers tools to use images as links, using the entire image or predefined areas on the image.

Hyperlink Basics

Regardless of the method you use to write a web page—whether you work in Expression Web 2, code by hand in Notepad, or use another web design program—hyperlinks work the same way. Fortunately, Expression Web 2 does a lot of the work for you, but it's important to understand basic information about links when you're trying to determine why a link is broken.

Hyperlink Paths

A hyperlink path follows one of three patterns, depending on the content being linked:

- **Absolute URL** Includes all components of the address for a link, such as `http://www.website.com/images/logo.jpg`. Read how to add an absolute URL in the sidebar, "Read a Web Address."
- **Relative URL** Doesn't include all the path components since it is usually used for linking content within a site. However, a browser can find the page using the missing protocol and server path components from the page's URL. Many relative URLs reference only the file path, folder, and linked filenames such as `/images/logo.jpg`.

  A relative URL is more convenient to use than an absolute URL. Maintaining relative URLs lets you move your site content when necessary without requiring you to restore all the links in your site. For example, if you store your web site's files in the folder named `my_site` on your web server, as long as the files' relationships are maintained, your links are preserved.

Note If you maintain your site within the Expression Web 2 web site folders and paths, Expression Web 2 is able to update your links automatically using the site's metadata. Read more in Chapter 1.

- **Anchor URL** An anchor URL is used to navigate within a single page. A location on the page is named using a *hypertext reference*, commonly called an *anchor* or *bookmark*, and is included with the page's name. For example **/default.html#message** opens the web page and displays the page location where the message reference is located.

Tip Read more on anchors, or bookmarks, in the section "Link to Specific Locations."

Define Different Link Types

Links of different types are easy to insert and customize in Expression Web 2 using the Insert Hyperlink dialog box. Later, you can return to revise or edit any link using the same commands and features in the Edit Hyperlink dialog box.

Regardless of the link type, begin in the same way. Select the text or object on the page to serve as the hyperlink. Right-click and select Hyperlink to open the Insert Hyperlink dialog box (Figure 4-1).

Add Internal Links between Pages

Offer your visitors a convenient path through your web site using internal links among pages and content on your pages.

To link your pages or to link a file to a page, follow these steps:

1. Select Existing File or Web Page at the left of the dialog box.
2. Locate and select the file using the options in the Look In section of the dialog box:
   - Click Current Folder and select a file from the list of documents.

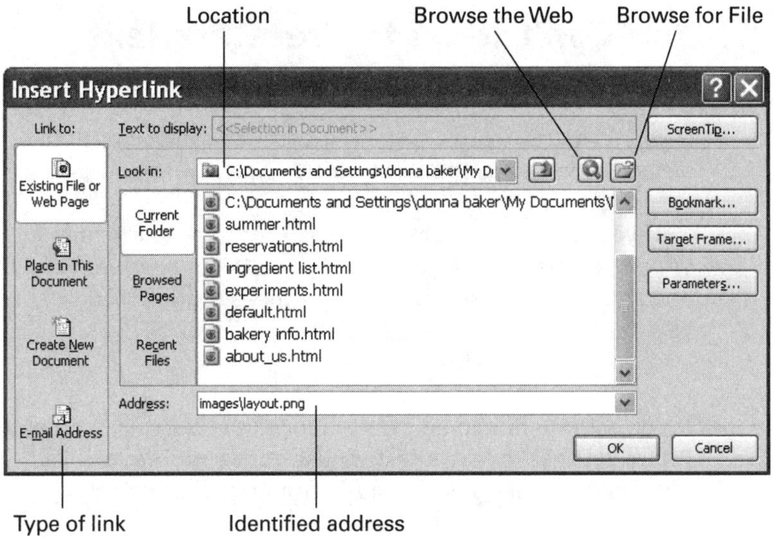

FIGURE 4-1 Configure links in the dialog box.

How to...

Read a Web Address

A hyperlink links to a destination address for a document or other types of data on the World Wide Web. Just as your home address follows a specific pattern, or *syntax*, so does a destination's URL (Uniform Resource Locator).

An absolute, or full web address, such as http://www.big-dog-motors.com/html/default.html, follows these syntax rules:

```
scheme://host.domain:port/path/filename
```

The address components include:

- The *scheme* identifies the type of service, such as `http` or `ftp`.
- The *domain* specifies the Internet domain name, such as `big-dog-motors`.
- The *host* states the location where the domain is supported. The default host for `http` is www.
- The *:port* (often omitted) names the port number used by the host. The default port for `http` is `80`.
- The *path* shows the subdirectory at the server that points to the file. If the document is at the root directory of the web site, the path can be omitted.
- The *filename* defines the document by name and a file type, such as `default.html`.

Did You Know?

You Don't Need to Preselect Text on a Page to Create a Link

If you select text on the page, you'll see it when you open the Insert Hyperlink dialog box in the Text to Display field. Type new text in the field if you want to change the text for the link.

If you have a new blank page and want to get some links into place before starting the design, simply right-click on the page where you'd like to insert a link to open the shortcut menu and choose Insert Hyperlink to open the dialog box. Then type text in the Text to Display field.

- If you want to link to an external location that you've recently visited, click Browsed Pages to load a history list from your browser and select the file.
- Click Recent Files to select a file from those you've edited recently in Expression Web 2.

3. Click OK to close the dialog box and complete the link.

Tip

To test a link on a page, press and hold the CTRL key and click the link to open the destination in your browser.

Link to a Page Online

Web sites usually link to online resources. In Expression Web 2, it's easy to locate and select a page online to link to your site's pages. From the Insert Hyperlink dialog box, follow these steps:

1. Click the Browse the Web button to open your web browser. Locate and open the page to be linked.
2. Press ALT + TAB to switch back to Expression Web 2. The web page's address is shown in the Address field at the bottom of the dialog box.
3. Click OK to close the dialog box and finish the link.

Link and Build Pages Simultaneously

If you're starting a new site or adding a component to an existing site, you can add a link and a new page at the same time in the Insert Hyperlink dialog box. Follow these steps:

1. Click Create New Document from the options at the left of the Insert Hyperlink dialog box. You'll see the main content area change to a different set of options.
2. Type a name for your new file in the Name of New Document field.
3. Select an editing time from the When to Edit radio buttons. If you are adding a single page, click Edit the New Document Now to move into the Editing window when you save the new link. Otherwise, click Edit the New Document Later if you're adding a few files, as you see next.

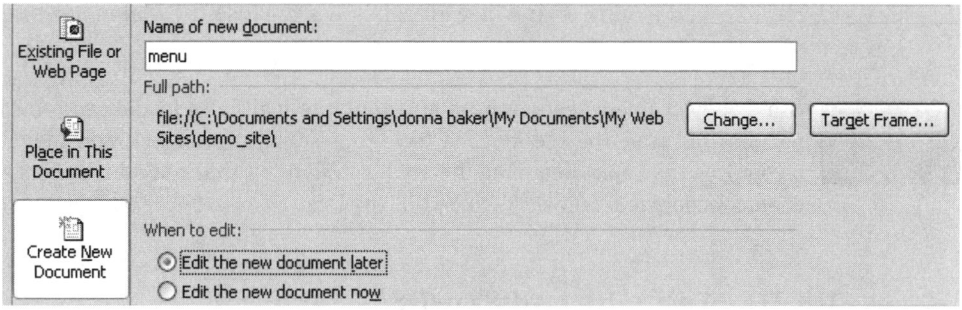

4. Click OK to close the dialog box and finish the link.

Tip If you want to change the location of the new file, click Change to open a Browse dialog box. Locate and select the folder where you want to store the files and click OK.

Offer Direct E-mail Links

Nearly every web site you visit offers a way to contact people connected with the site, whether corporate executives, the webmaster, or Tony at Tony's Toolshed. To add an e-mail link, select E-mail Address from the link locations at the left of the Insert Hyperlink dialog box to show the fields for e-mail addressing.

Type the address in the E-mail Address field. As you click the field and start typing, the program automatically adds the `mailto:` attribute to the link before displaying the typed text. If it's available, choose the address from the list of recently used addresses (Figure 4-2).

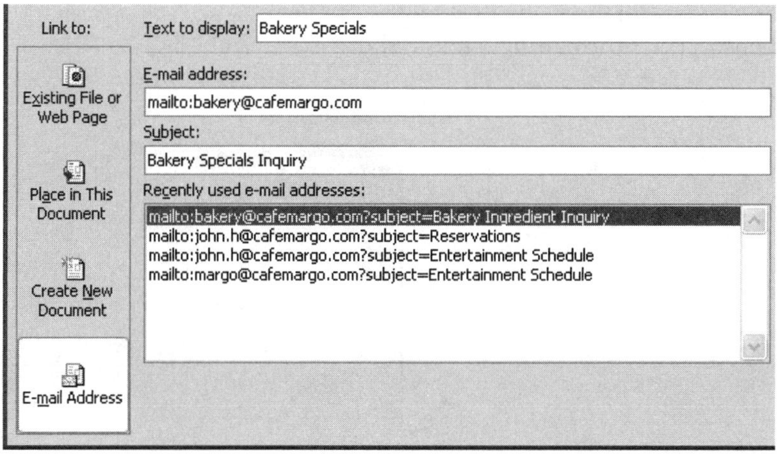

FIGURE 4-2 Add e-mail addresses and subjects quickly.

If you like, add a Subject line as well. Click OK to close the dialog box and finish the link.

Tip Use a Subject line when you have a variety of e-mail links leading to the same person. That way, the user doesn't have to describe the subject, and the recipient recognizes the topic area immediately. Keep in mind that not all browsers or e-mail clients recognize a Subject included in the link.

Link to Specific Locations

Expression Web 2 offers a tool to identify a specific location on a page to use as a link's destination. The destination is called a *bookmark*, also called an *anchor*.

Like a regular hyperlink, a bookmark uses an absolute or relative URL. The bookmark is identified with a named tag, appended to the end of the URL.

Using bookmarks requires several steps:

1. Add the bookmark to the page location.
2. Link to the page and the specific location.
3. View and test the link.

Create the Bookmarked Content

You have to identify the name and location on a page before you can use it as a link target. Select the text or object on the page to use as the bookmarked content. Choose Insert | Bookmark to open the Bookmark dialog box, and type a name (Expression Web 2 allows multiple words and spaces). Click OK to close the dialog box. Continue adding and naming other bookmarks as required.

On the page, bookmarked text is shown with a dashed underline. You can attach a bookmark to a blank area of a page as well. As you see here, the bookmark is associated with the blank line and has a name. To see the bookmark on the page, choose View | Formatting Marks | Show.

Tip If you want to remove a bookmark, click its name in the Other Bookmarks on This Page area of the Bookmark dialog box and click Clear.

Link to a Bookmark

Bookmarked locations are considered link targets, configurable in the Add (or Edit) Hyperlinks dialog box. To link to a bookmark, follow these steps:

1. Select the link text on your page and right-click to open the shortcut menu. Choose Hyperlink to open the Insert Hyperlink dialog box.
2. Click Existing File or Web Page on the Link To list at the left of the dialog box to display the settings.
3. Select the file containing the bookmarks. You'll see the page's URL in the Address line at the bottom of the dialog box.
4. Click Bookmark to open the Select Place in Document dialog box. Click the bookmark to use as the destination, and click OK to close the dialog box. On the Insert Hyperlink dialog box, the selected bookmark is written as part of the page's URL (Figure 4-3).

You can also use bookmarks as link targets on the same page. Select the text and open the Insert Hyperlink dialog box. Click Place in This Document from the list at the left side of the dialog box. Click the bookmark you want to use as the target from the list of inserted bookmarks shown on the dialog box.

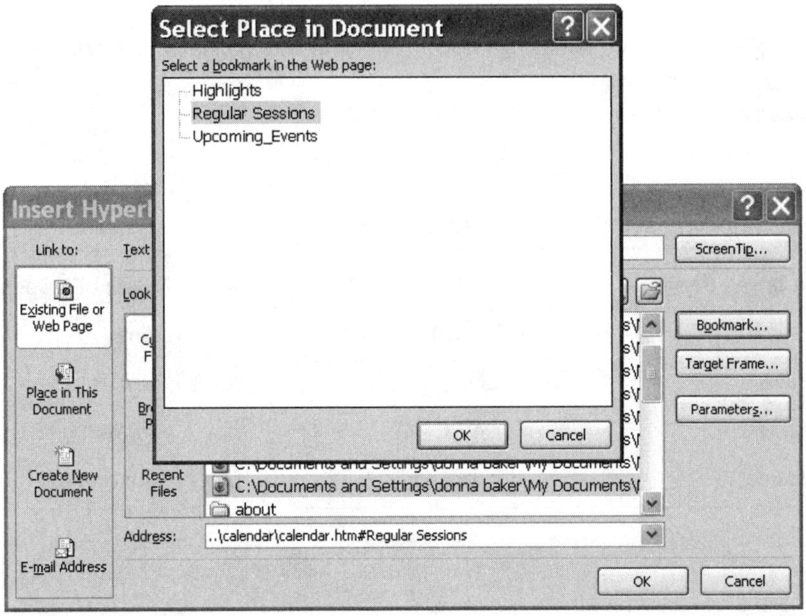

FIGURE 4-3 Choose a bookmark as a link target.

Note Expression Web 2 uses the `name` attribute to identify the bookmark. In upcoming versions of XHTML, the `id` attribute replaces the `name` attribute. To display properly in older browsers, it's best to use both attributes. You'll have to type the `id` attribute on your page's Code view manually as Expression Web 2 doesn't offer that customization.

Choose a Target Frame

By default, when you click a hyperlink on a web page the linked page opens in the current browser window. You can substitute one of several options, referred to as a *target frame*.

Set the target frame as you are configuring the rest of your link's characteristics. In the Insert Hyperlink dialog box, click Target Frame to open the Target Frame dialog box.

Click New Window in the Common Targets list at the right of the dialog box. In the Target Setting, the option is shown as `_blank`. Click OK to close the dialog box, and return to the Insert or Edit Hyperlink dialog box. Click OK to close the dialog box and return to the program.

In Code view, you'll see the target attribute is included with the rest of the link information. For example:

```
<a href="http://www.cafe_margo.com" target="_blank">Café Margo</a>
```

The target options are listed in Table 4-1.

Note Read about using frames for displaying web pages in Chapter 9.

TABLE 4-1 Specify a Target Frame to Display for a Followed Hyperlink

Common Target Option	Target Code	Where Target URL Opens
New Window	*_blank	new window
Whole Page	*_top	full window
Same Frame	*_self	frame containing clicked link
Parent Frame	*_parent	parent frameset

How to... **Redirect Links**

If you move a page on your site and correct your links internally, anyone visiting your site will find the page. On the other hand, external links from other web sites to that page won't be able to find it. Instead of producing a message that the file isn't found, use the Expression Web 2 feature that automatically transfers visitors to the new location.

Follow these steps to redirect a URL:

1. Choose Task Panes | Behaviors to display the Behaviors panel.
2. Open the page you want to redirect and click the <body> tag on the Quick Tag Selector at the top of the Editing window.
3. In the Behaviors task pane, click Insert to open a list and select Go to URL.
4. In the Go To URL dialog box, type the URL for the new page or file location and click OK to close the dialog box and set up the behavior.

Customize Link Appearances

Links are highly configurable page elements that are part of the <body> tag. In Part II, you'll see how styles are used for customizing link appearances to match the rest of your site's color and font schemes. Without writing styles, you can customize link appearances using settings in the Page Properties dialog box or add a screen tip to give viewers more information.

Specify Link Text and Color

A hyperlink shows different states or conditions that relate to your recent activity. The point of using different states is to give your page visitors some feedback and a history of their recent activity on your site. A hyperlink has four states:

- **Default state** A normal, unclicked state of the hyperlink, written as `a:link`
- **Active state** A hyperlink that has been clicked and currently being displayed by the browser, written as `a:active`
- **Visited state** A hyperlink that has been visited recently, written as `a:visited`
- **Hover state** The hyperlink under the mouse pointer, written as `a:hover`

Work from Design view for simple changes. Choose Format | Page Properties to open the Page Properties dialog box. Click the Formatting tab.

In the Colors section on the dialog box, click any of the hyperlink drop-down arrows to open color selection panels and select an alternate color. As you see here, you can select from the Standard Colors, Custom Colors, Document Colors you've selected elsewhere in the program, or click More Colors to open a color picker to specify a Custom Color.

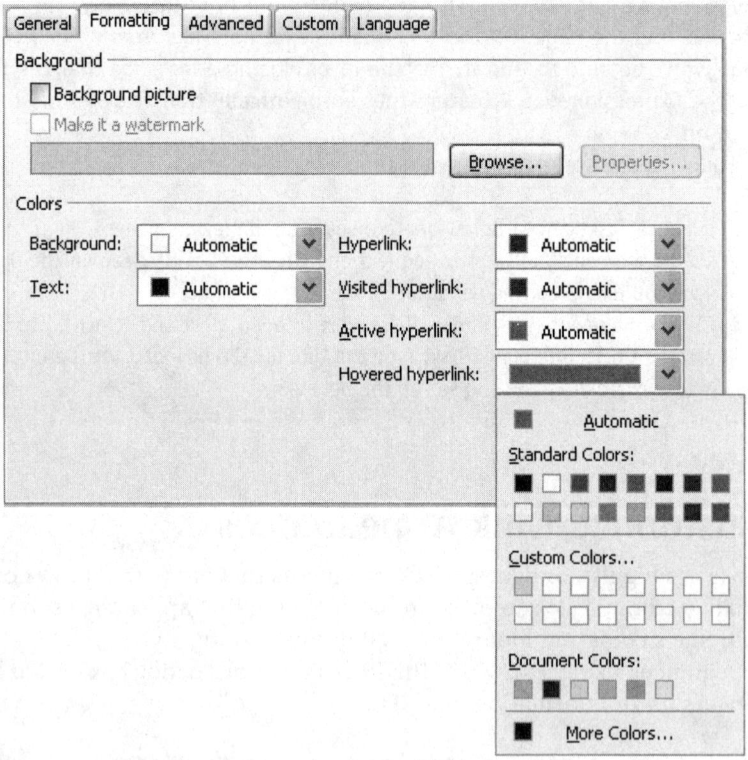

Insert ScreenTips

Sometimes links on a page are self-explanatory. If a button or link states "Home," it's probably safe to assume that clicking the link takes you to the site's home page. On the other hand, some links may be more obscure, or you might want to add a bit of information the viewer can read before clicking the link.

Expression Web 2 lets you configure a message, or *ScreenTip*, that displays in a pop-up box when the mouse is over the hyperlink. You can either set the ScreenTip as you configure the hyperlink, or at any time following these steps:

1. Right-click the link to open the shortcut menu and choose Hyperlink Properties to open the Edit Hyperlink dialog box.
2. Click ScreenTip at the upper right of the dialog box to open a small dialog box containing a text field.
3. Type the text for the ScreenTip and click OK; click OK again to close the Edit Hyperlink dialog box.
4. Press F12 to view the page in your default browser. When you move your mouse over the link, you'll see the text (Figure 4-4).

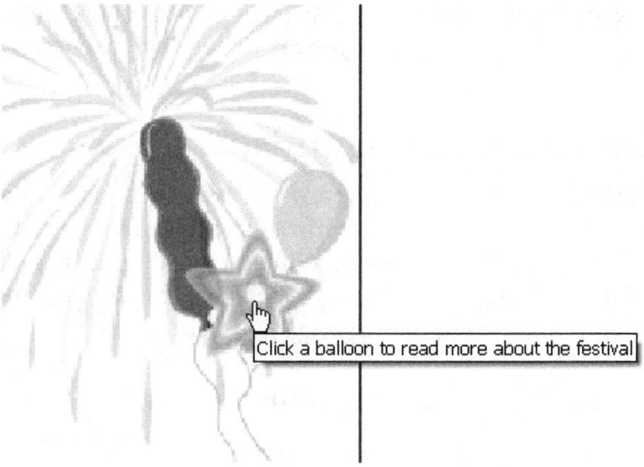

FIGURE 4-4 Use visible text to prompt or guide users.

Remove a Link from a Page

You often have to make changes to your site's contents, including links. If you want to edit the content of a link, select the text on the page, right-click to open the shortcut menu, and choose Edit Hyperlink. The resulting dialog box is the same as the Insert Hyperlink dialog box.

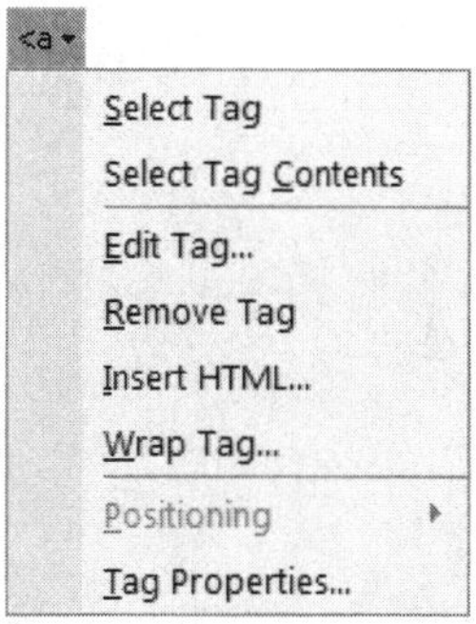

You can access several commands for working with your links from the Editing window when you're in Design view. Move your mouse over the appropriate <a> tag on the Quick Tag Selector bar at the top of the web page, and then click the arrow next to the <a> tag to open the menu shown here. Select Remove Tag to delete the hyperlink.

Design Object Hyperlinks

Links aren't confined to text. Often, you see links attached to individual images as buttons. You may also see an image map, an image with defined coordinates used as links over the image.

Use Images as Links

Many sites use both text and image links on their pages. Hyperlinking from an image is less complex than using a button. A button is image-based as well but offers several button states showing image variations based on behaviors and mouse actions. (Read about configuring image states using CSS in Chapter 6; read about behaviors in Chapter 10).

Select the image on the page and right-click to open the shortcut menu. Click Hyperlink to open the Insert Hyperlink dialog box, discussed in previous sections.

Create Hotspots on an Image

Image maps are another use of images for hyperlinking on a web site. Unlike a simple image link, where the hyperlink is attached to the entire image, an *image map* attaches links to specific areas of the image based on its coordinates.

Working in Design view, define each area, or *hotspot*, using commands on the Pictures toolbar. Hotspots can be rectangles, circles, or polygons.

Insert a Rectangular or Circular Hotspot

Both rectangles and circles are drawn in one step. The point you click serves as the edge for the hotspot.

Follow these steps to add a rectangular or circular hotspot to an image:

1. Open the web page, and select the picture on the page.
2. Click one of the hotspot tools on the Pictures toolbar, for example, the Rectangular Hotspot (Figure 4-5). Click the picture and drag to create the rectangle shape. Release the mouse to define the coordinates; the Insert Hyperlink dialog box opens.

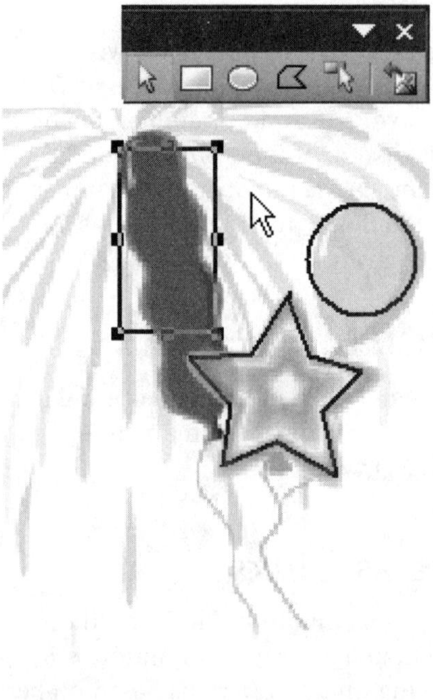

FIGURE 4-5 Use the tools on the Pictures toolbar to insert a hotspot.

3. Specify the hyperlink using options and settings described in previous sections. Click OK to complete the link and close the dialog box.
4. Repeat with other areas as required. Save the file and test the links in your browser.

Note To set a hyperlink for all other areas on the image outside of the hotspots, select the image and add a hyperlink to it.

Drawing a Polygonal Hotspot

To draw an irregular shape, select the Polygonal Hotspot tool, click to set each point of the shape, and double-click the starting point to complete the shape. As shown in Figure 4-5, the shape can mimic any object in the image.

Modifying a Hotspot

When you're checking your web pages, it's important to check all the links carefully. Hotspots are invisible, but Expression Web 2 offers a tool to help you keep track. Click the Highlight Hotspots button on the Pictures toolbar to show them on the page; click the button again to toggle off the highlight.

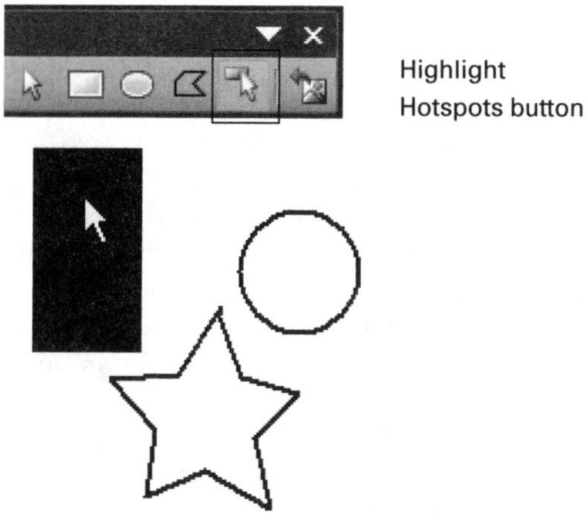

Did You Know?

Hotspots Are Based on Geometry

Nearly everything on a web page is based on grid coordinates, including hotspots. The position of an object on a page is defined in relation to the left upper edge of the page—hotspots on an image are related to the left upper edge of the image.

The positions of several points in each hotspot tell your browser where to place the hyperlink area.

If you want to change the location or configuration of the hotspot, click the Select button on the Pictures toolbar. Click and drag the hotspot to reposition it, or drag a point on the hotspot to change its configuration.

If you want to modify the link, double-click the hotspot to open the Edit Hyperlink dialog box. Adjust the settings and click OK to close the dialog box and apply the changes.

Test and Evaluate Links

Hyperlinks are easily evaluated in Expression Web 2. You can test and generate reports on all your links, including hyperlinks and references to images and other files like download files and CSS files. Check out Chapter 16 for in-depth information on testing and preparing a site for use.

Note See Chapter 16 for details on Hyperlinks reports. There are a number of reports available, including All Hyperlinks, Unverified, Broken, External, or Internal hyperlinks.

Work with the Folder List, Web Site view on the Editing Window, and the Hyperlinks panel to review your site's hyperlinks.

To check the link structure in your pages, select the page's name in the Folder List. In the Editing window, click Web Site above the Quick Tag Selector bar. You'll see a diagram of the selected page with the links that lead from and to the page (Figure 4-6).

In the diagram, look for these features:

- Unverified or unbroken links show a solid shaft.
- Broken links show a split shaft.
- A page containing a set of links shows a plus sign (+); click to display the page's link sub diagram; click (-) to collapse the subdiagram.
- To show links to images, right-click the diagram and choose Hyperlinks to Pictures.
- To show page titles instead of filenames, right-click the diagram and choose Show Page Titles.
- To show multiple links from one page to another page, right-click the diagram and choose Repeated Hyperlinks.

How to... Pinpoint Unused Files

Before you finish working on a site, it's a good idea to check for unused files. That way, it's easier to keep track of the content for the pages, not to mention decrease the size of your site.

Choose Site | Reports | Problems | Unlinked Files. Check the list for stray files and delete them. On the other hand, you may find that you've missed files that should be linked.

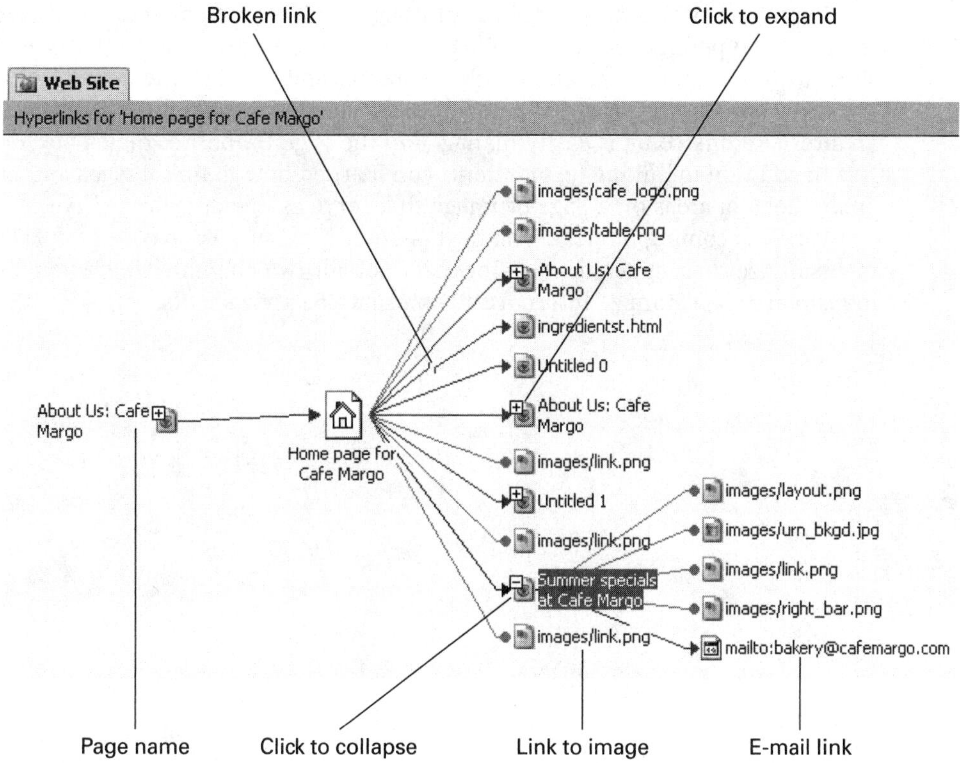

FIGURE 4-6 Review your pages' links as a diagram.

Tip If you'd like to diagram a different page's links, right-click the icon and choose Move to Center to redraw the display.

Note The three pages for the Café Margo example site are available online and contain a variety of links using techniques described in this chapter. Look for the readme04 .html file for more information and a complete list of assets.

Summary

This chapter discussed the ubiquitous hyperlink, the basis for online activity and interaction. You saw how web addressing works and how hyperlinks address locations in different ways.

Expression Web 2 offers multiple linking activities and configurations through the Insert Hyperlink dialog box. While there, you can link between pages, to external sites, within a single page, and to other content, and you can add e-mail links.

Links are often configured using CSS. However, simple styling, such as choosing an alternate link color, is easily managed in the Page Properties dialog box.

In addition to linking text content, you learned how to link images and how to create hotspot areas on a page or image that serve as links.

Part II is coming up next. The next chapter looks at how to configure HTML styles to customize their appearance. After that, look for two chapters where you'll see how to fashion and customize internal and external CSS style sheets.

PART II

Style Your Site with Cascading Style Sheets

Visual configuration of page elements like text, images, positioning, and so on became popular earlier in the development of the Internet. As time passed and browsers became more sophisticated, web pages bloated with descriptions for displaying the content on a page. A fairly simple tag, such as a `<tr>` identifying a table row, could contain multiple attributes defining the appearance of the table row, which detracted from the primary purpose of the table: to show tabular information.

Flash forward to today: Present day web pages separate content from display by using the web page for code and information and style sheets for visually presenting the web page.

In this part, you'll see how content is styled using Expression Web 2. First, you'll see how to use Code view to view and edit HTML code. Then you'll see how to work with Cascading Style Sheets (CSS). You'll be introduced to the concept of styles and learn how to use the different CSS tools Expression Web 2 offers.

5

Take Care of Code and Tags Manually

HOW TO...

- Work in Code view
- Use tag writing tools
- Define tag attributes
- Generate tag styles

You don't have to read this chapter to use Expression Web 2, or to create and build a great web site. On the other hand, if you are the sort of person who likes to look "under the hood," then read on.

Expression Web 2 is a terrific learning tool as you can split the view to show Code and Design views at the same time. Select an image or text on your page, and you see the corresponding code selected. Select a block of code in the Code view and see what's selected in the Design view.

In this chapter, see how the code and script tools work together, and how they can help make your web page design and development more streamlined.

Note Throughout the chapter, commands are applied using toolbar tools or shortcut keystrokes. In all cases, the commands are available from the program menu.

Work in Code View

The Code view is an alternate view displayed in the Editing window. Expression Web 2 offers a number of tools and features that work in conjunction with the Code view, as you'll discover throughout the chapter. Some tools are tailored to view code, others for writing, and still others for reviewing and editing.

Check Out Code View Features

Some of the tools are visible in the program interface, while others appear in response to your code writing activities. Open a web page in Expression Web 2, and click Split at the bottom of the Editing window to show Design/Code view (Figure 5-1).

A number of features coordinate to show you information, provide assistance, and list tools to add code. In the program window, look for these code-oriented features:

- **Status Bar** If there are errors in the code on a page, you'll see an icon on the Status Bar. Move your mouse over the icon to read a description of the issues.

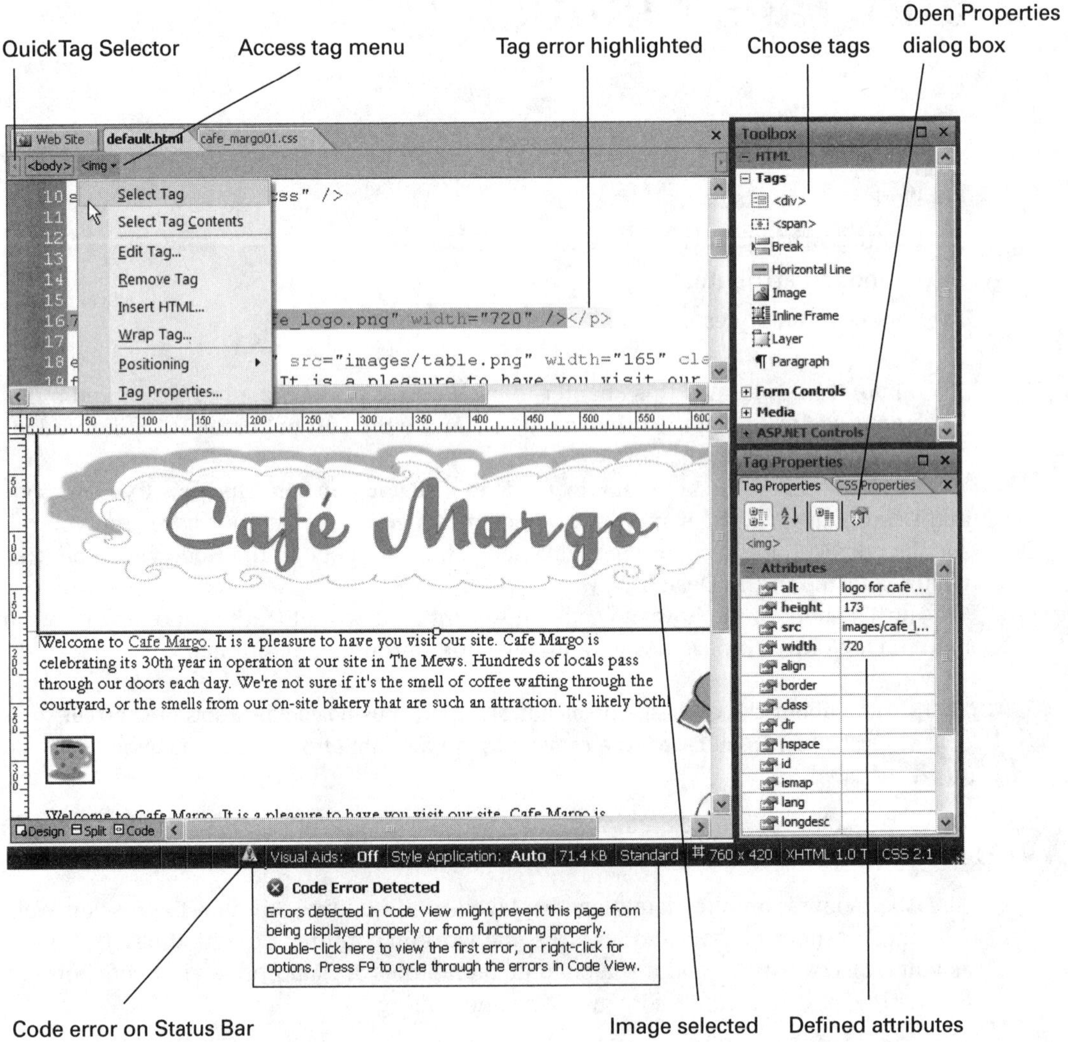

FIGURE 5-1 Use coding features in the program window.

- **Code view** The Code view of a web page displays the directly-editable code that makes up a page. With the Split view, you can see the Design and Code views of your web page simultaneously.
- **Tag Properties task pane** The properties for a selected tag are shown in the Tag Properties task pane, where you can modify or change the values.
- **Quick Tag Selector** The Quick Tag Selector bar helps you to view, select, remove, or edit tags while working in either Design view or Code view. The bar also enables you to open the Quick Tag Editor dialog box and various Properties dialog boxes and to quickly set the positioning style of a tag.

Expression Web 2 offers numerous other features that aren't shown in Figure 5-1. You'll see how the features work as you read through the chapter.

Insert Comments and Code

You have several choices for writing HTML elements in Expression Web 2. Of course, you can type everything manually, or you can use the Code View toolbar to insert code elements to get your structure organized.

The Code View toolbar combines commonly used features from the Code Formatting options and commands from the Code View and IntelliSense submenus, which appear on the Edit menu.

When your code is written, check it for compatibility with your chosen standards.

Add Tags and Comments

Use commands from the Code View toolbar to add HTML comments, empty tags, and common HTML tags. Click the page in Code view to place the insertion point where you want to insert the code. Choose View | Toolbars | Code View to open the toolbar.

Tip Click Options on the toolbar to open a list of display features you can choose for the code display, such as lines, a wider margin at the left of the page, wrapping lines, and so on.

Click one of the self-named insertion options according to your coding requirements. For example, click Insert Start Tag to add an opening tag for an HTML element, click Insert End Tag to add the closing tag, or click Insert Comment to include the structure for an HTML comment, as shown here.

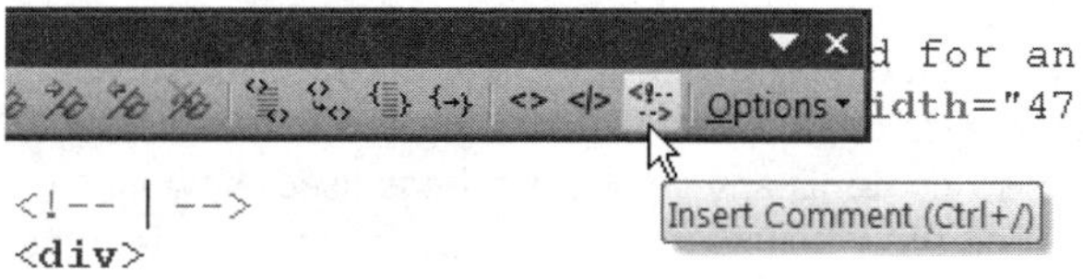

Quick Tag Selections

There are two great tools on the Code View toolbar for selecting items in Code view. Click in the area where you want to make selections. Then, click Select Tag to highlight the tag pair and its contents.

If you need to select just the tag, click Find Matching Tag to highlight one tag of the pair as you see next; click again to highlight the other tag.

Options
<div>
Find Matching Tag (Ctrl+;)
<img alt="sketch of coffee cup for links" height="38"
src="images/link.png" width="40" class="style1" /></div>

While that may not seem like a big deal when you can see both tags on the page, it certainly helps when you're looking for a closing tag that's hundreds of lines of code later.

Check for Compatibility Issues

Suppose you are rebuilding your site and want to modify the pages to comply with a different XHTML or CSS standard. Instead of making changes manually, you can turn to the Compatibility task pane. Use the results to view a list of all code errors and incompatible code in one or more web pages or an entire web site. Follow these steps to run a check:

1. Choose Task Panes | Compatibility to display the pane horizontally below the Editing window.
2. Click the right arrow (it's green on the program) at the upper left of the pane to open the Compatibility Checker dialog box.
3. Choose what pages to check, such as all open pages, your entire site, or the current page. Also, choose options for HTML and CSS, or leave the default check box selected to run the check based on the DTD (document type declaration) in the page.
4. Click Check to close the dialog box and test the pages.
5. The results are shown on the Compatibility pane (Figure 5-2). Click the left and right arrows to move through the list and evaluate the page.

Note Click Generate HTML Report—the bottom tool on the Compatibility pane's toolbar—to open a web page listing the features in your page. The list includes `<meta>` content, any styles, headings used, how many pages were checked, and so on. If you like, you can save the file for future reference.

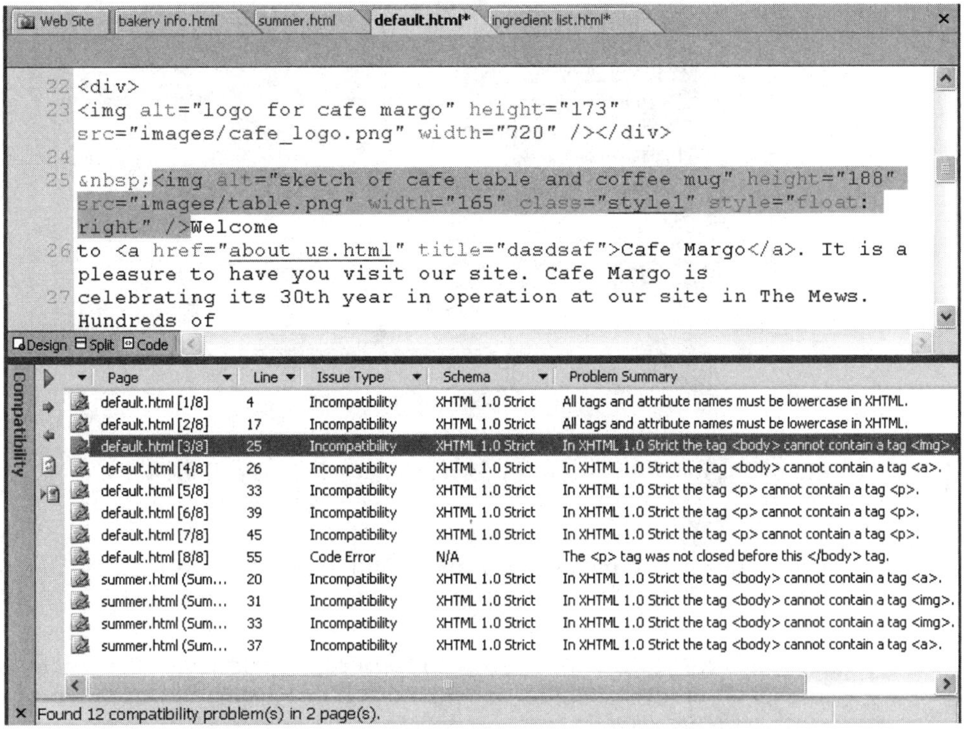

FIGURE 5-2 Check for potential problems using different standards.

Customize Code Display Options

Many people accustomed to hand coding develop a layout pattern to keep track of their development and make the code simpler to troubleshoot. For example, you may prefer to use a particular amount of indenting, or place a closing brace on a blank line. Whether you code by hand or not, it's useful to use a consistent layout. Fortunately, you can use options in Expression Web 2 to specify how code is formatted and color-coded.

To set Code view preferences to suit your work habits, choose Tools | Page Editor Options to open the Page Editor dialog box.

Set Formatting Preferences

Click the Code Formatting tab to specify how tags are written and displayed on the page. Many of the options are self-explanatory, such as specifying the depth of a tab (Figure 5-3).

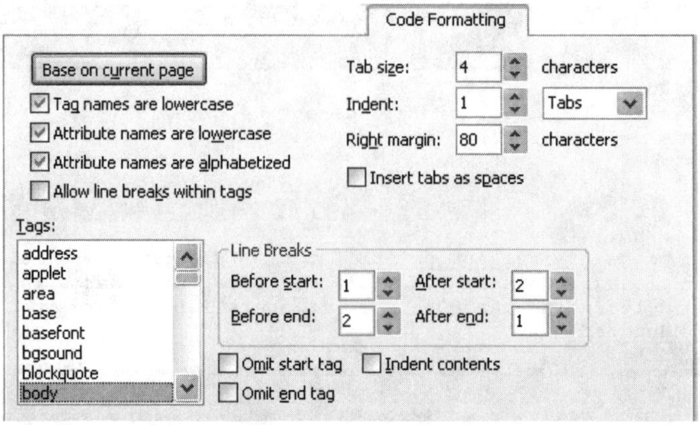

FIGURE 5-3 Specify options for formatting code in the Code view.

There are a few items you may find useful in the Code Formatting preferences, including:

- If you have written code by hand and spaced it according to your preferences, instead of setting individual options, click Base on Current Page to transfer your settings to the program options.
- Leave the default options to use lowercase for tags and attributes to comply with XHTML standards. One option, Attribute Names Are Alphabetized, may or may not be useful for you. Some like to consider attributes alphabetically, while others have their own methods for writing and remembering to include attributes.
- Be careful using the Allow Line Breaks within Tags option. If you intend to use a lot of JavaScript, for example, line breaks interfere with parsing the code.

Tip If you want lines to wrap to make reading the Code view easier, click Options on the Code View toolbar, and click Word Wrap.

- Click through the Tags list and check the Line Breaks options for tags you regularly use. Some tags, such as <body>, activate additional options to omit start or end tags, which is contrary to XHTML standards.
- Most tags let you indent contents, which can help you keep track of your code as you develop it.
- The lower part of the dialog box (not shown in Figure 5-3) deals with CSS formatting, indenting, and shorthand properties—read how to choose these options in Chapter 6.

Track Content Using Color

Click the Color Coding tab to specify colors for code elements. You can select color schemes for text written in Code view and display items shown in Design view.

Click Code View Settings to see the list of Display Items. The list is categorized according to the type of content, such as CSS, HTML, PHP, Script items, and so on. Click an item to activate the Item Foreground and Item Background color fields and to show a colored example in the Preview area. Additionally, if you choose a text item, such as HTML Element Name, you can choose font styles.

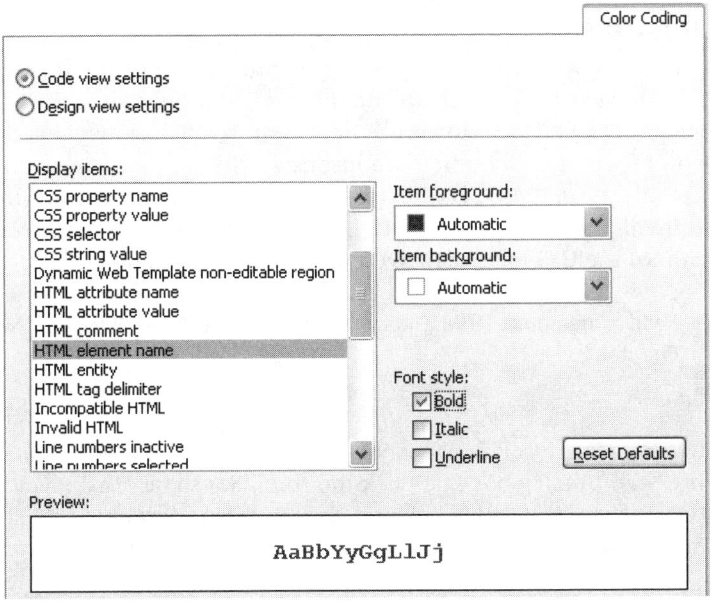

Unless you need a particular color scheme to stimulate your thought processes, you probably won't need to change the settings.

Note You can set the color for code bookmarks either in the dialog box or from the Code View toolbar. Read how in the sidebar, "You Can Change the Color of Code Bookmarks," later in the chapter.

Click Design View Settings to show a list of Display Items that overlay your page. Sometimes you need to change colors based on the items you use and your page's color scheme. For example, the Dynamic Web Template items show in pale yellow, which disappear if your page uses a pale yellow background.

The Display Items are listed in groups, including Dynamic Web Template Features, Layout Tables, Other Layout Positioning Items, Master Pages, and so on.

Note Other preferences apply to writing and working with the Code view, as described throughout the chapter.

Use IntelliSense to Prompt Your Code Writing

Expression Web 2 includes the IntelliSense feature that gives you context-sensitive assistance as you write code. Use IntelliSense to insert code automatically as you type, look up code elements, or follow code hyperlinks.

Configure IntelliSense Shortcuts

If you're starting on your hand coding adventures, the default settings are probably enough. However, if you are an adept hand coder but like using IntelliSense to make coding quicker, you can customize the way IntelliSense displays the shortcut menus and how tags and punctuation are inserted.

In Code view, the DTD (document type declaration) defines the options available in the IntelliSense shortcut menu. Likewise, the CSS Schema specified for the page determines the CSS level displayed in the shortcut menu.

Note Read more about DTDs and schemas in the section, "Create a New Page," in Chapter 2.

To customize IntelliSense, choose Tools | Page Editor Options to display the Page Editor Options dialog box and click the IntelliSense tab. Make your selections, and click OK to close the dialog box and change the preferences.

In the dialog box, all auto features are selected by default as you see here.

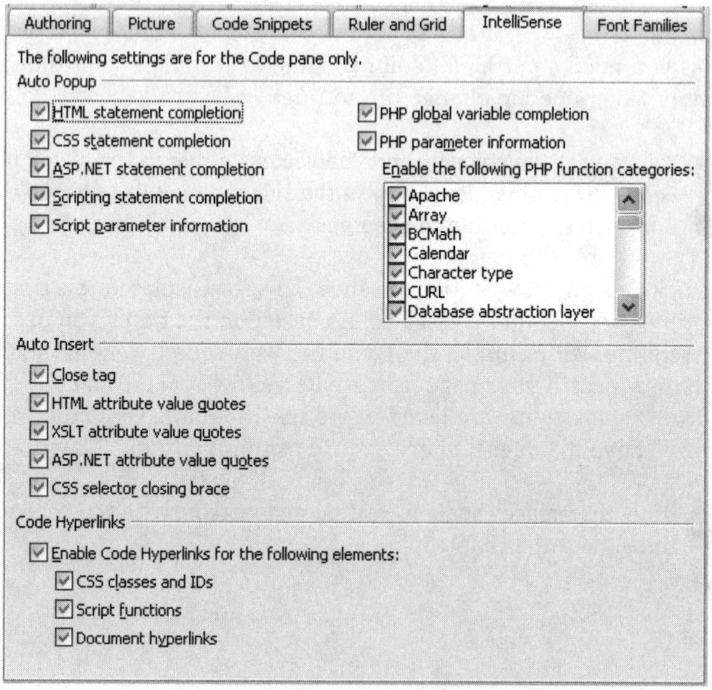

Although you'll probably leave the default options, you can make changes in three categories, including:

- **Auto Popup** Shows content for completing HTML, CSS, and ASP.NET statements, as well as script statements and parameters
- **Auto Insert** Automatically closes tags, braces, and quotes
- **Code Hyperlinks** Let you follow a link by using the CTRL-click shortcut

Note The options include settings for PHP. Read about PHP in Chapter 13.

Write Code Using IntelliSense Prompts

IntelliSense is an interactive partner in your code writing efforts. Along with HTML, you can use IntelliSense for CSS and script functions. Read about using CSS in Chapters 6 and 7 and script functions in Chapter 10.

You can access the features from the Edit menu, but it's far simpler to work from the Code View toolbar. To write code for your page using IntelliSense assistance, follow these steps in Code view:

1. Choose View | Toolbars | Code View to display the toolbar.
2. Click on the page in Code view where you want to insert a tag or tag property. The choices available depend on what you type or where you click; if clicking doesn't reveal any assistance, check your cursor location:
   - To show a list of tags, type an opening angle bracket < or click within an empty pair of brackets < > and click List Members on the Code View toolbar (Figure 5-4).

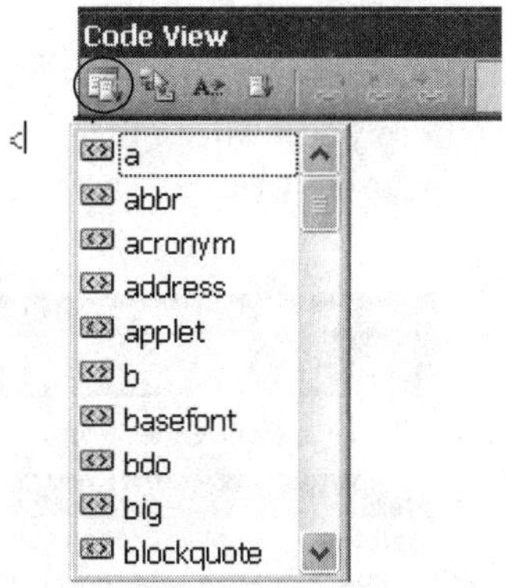

FIGURE 5-4 Use IntelliSense to offer code completion options.

How to... **Get Used to Having Help**

As you start writing code yourself, it's surprising how you come to rely on IntelliSense prompts. Keep in mind that items are automatically closed, including tags, braces, and quotes. So, if you have been writing code manually before you started working with Expression Web 2, it takes some time to adjust.

- To show a list of tag properties, click in an opening tag after the HTML element and press SPACEBAR or click List Members on the Code View toolbar.

3. Scroll through the list to find the item you want to use, and double-click (or press TAB or ENTER) to insert it in the Code view. If you decide you don't want to use any assistance, press ESC to close the list.

The Quick Tag Editor uses some IntelliSense features. As you type in the editor, you'll see a pop-up list of tags, properties, or values display. Read more on the Quick Tag Editor later in the chapter.

Use Code Snippets for Speedier Coding

A code snippet is a string of code or text you can reuse as you like. Use one of the code snippets preloaded in Expression Web 2, or create your own. Access the code snippets using keywords for even faster coding.

The point of using code snippets is to save time and prevent errors when hand coding. For example, if you use the same `<meta>` tags in the `<head>` tag for your web pages, type them once, and then save them as a snippet until you write the next page. If you work with any pay-per-click or other site advertising, paste the advertising code on a page, then copy it and create a snippet.

Insert a Code Snippet on a Page

Insert a code snippet in Code view, in another file such as a text file, or on a web page. Click the cursor where you want to insert the code snippet. To activate the Code Snippet menu shown here, press CTRL-ENTER or click List Code Snippets on the Code View toolbar.

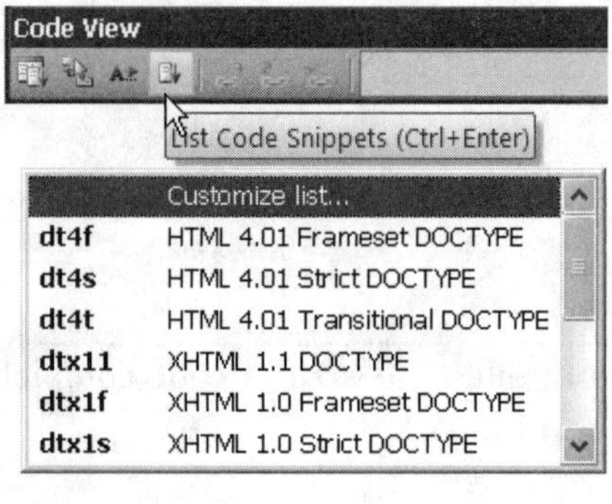

Scroll through the list to locate the snippet you want to use, or type its keyword. Press ENTER or TAB or double-click the listing to insert the code.

Customize Code Snippets

Modify, add, and delete snippets according to what you need and how you work. Choose Tools | Page Editor Options, and click the Code Snippets tab.

Tip If you have the Code View toolbar and the Code Snippets list open, double-click Customize List at the top of the Code Snippet menu to open the Page Editor Options dialog box.

Make any or all of these customizations:

- Click a snippet in the list and click Remove to delete it.
- Click Add to open the Add Code Snippet dialog box, identical to the Modify Code Snippet dialog box.
- Click a snippet in the list and click Modify to open the Modify Code Snippet dialog box (Figure 5-5). Change the keyword if you like, type or modify the description listed with the snippet, or type or change the code for insertion.

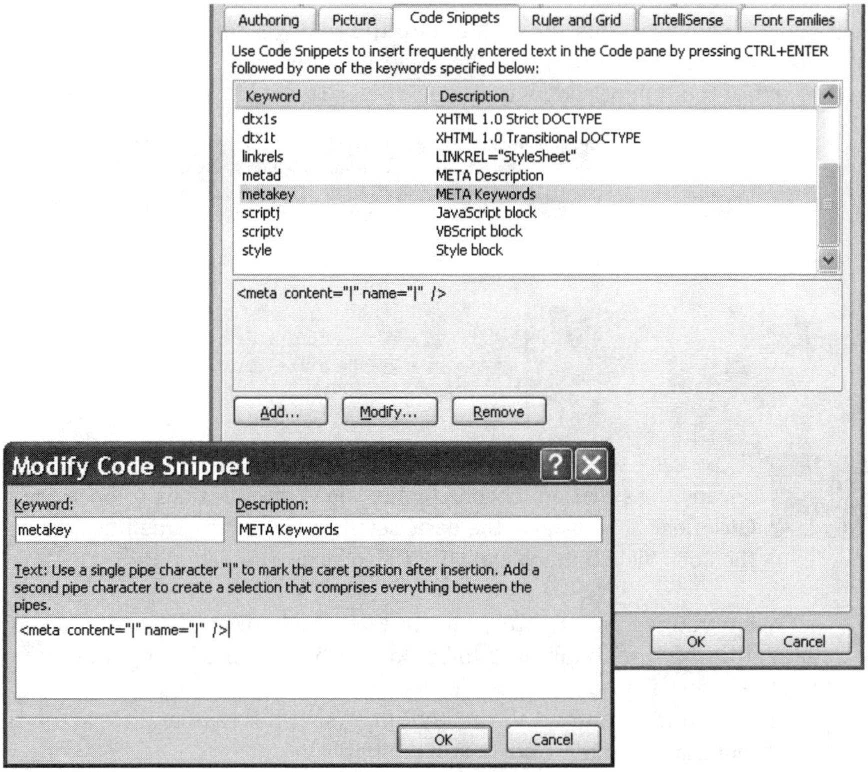

FIGURE 5-5 Modify an existing snippet or write your own.

How to...

Use Pipes in a Snippet

Use a pipe character (|) in the snippet's text to identify a location to place the insertion point when the code is added to the page. If you add two pipe characters (| |), the code content between the characters is selected. In the example shown in Figure 5-5, the code is modified from the default `metakey` snippet and reads:

```
<meta content= "|" name="|" />
```

When the snippet is pasted into a page, the cursor sits at the location of the first pipe character, and the content from the first to second pipe characters is selected. It doesn't need selection; its purpose is to give you two attributes to customize. Adding the pipe character inserts a space in the code and serves as a reminder to add values for both attributes.

Keep Track with Bookmarks

During a work session, you can add temporary bookmarks to the code in your web page. The code bookmarks are temporary—when you close the page, the code bookmarks are removed.

In Code view, click the location on the line where you want to add a bookmark and click Toggle Bookmark on the Code View toolbar. A colored rectangle displays to the left of the line of code where you've inserted a bookmark, as you see here.

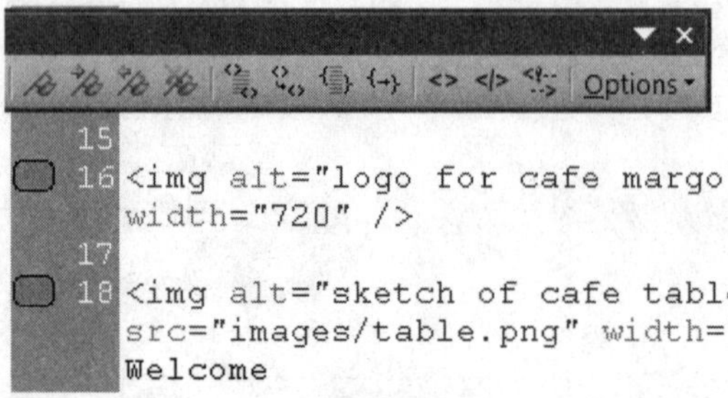

Tip If you can't see the bookmark, it's likely that you're not showing line numbers. To remedy the situation, choose Tools | Page Editor Options to open the dialog box. Click General to display the basic settings. Select the Line Numbers check box in the Code View Options and click OK to close the dialog box.

When you're editing your page, and using a bookmark system to keep track of changes, jump from bookmark to bookmark by clicking Next Bookmark or Previous Bookmark on the Code View toolbar.

If you want to remove all the bookmarks, either save and close the file, or click Clear Bookmarks on the Code View toolbar.

Did You Know?

You Can Change the Color of Code Bookmarks

You don't need to use the default colors for bookmarks, just as you don't need to keep default fonts and colors for your code. If you want to customize the look of bookmarks, choose Tools | Page Editor Options and click the Color Coding tab.

Choose the Code View Settings radio button, and click Bookmarks in the Display Items list. You'll see the default Bookmarks color is aqua. Click the color drop-down arrow and choose another color from the Color Panel options. Your only choice for custom color is the foreground, as the bookmarks are a solid color.

Access More Code Assistants

Whether you're working in Code or Design view, Expression Web 2 offers more assistants—or is that assistance? The Tag Properties task pane lets you instantly add a tag. The Quick Tag Selector and its editor help you locate and check out your content.

Use the Tag Properties Task Pane

The Tag Properties task pane is a quick way to view attributes and specify values for a selected tag. Typing the attribute/value pair in the code displays the setting in the Tag Properties task pane; specifying a value for an attribute in the Tag Properties task pane is reflected in the page code. Where you choose to work depends solely on your personal preference.

Choose a Display Option

Customize the layout of the Tag Properties task pane based on how you like to work. Examples of the same tags using different configurations are shown in Figure 5-6:

- **Show Categorized List** Displays the properties in alphabetical order divided into Attributes and Events categories. Use this option when you want to concentrate on one aspect of your coding.
- **Show Alphabetized List** Displays all properties in a list. Use this option when you want to apply or check both events and attributes for an object.
- **Show Set Properties on Top** Moves the defined attributes to the top of the list, followed by the remainder. You can show properties at the top of the list, regardless of which list option you choose.
- **Show Tag Properties** Displays the Properties dialog box for the selected tag.

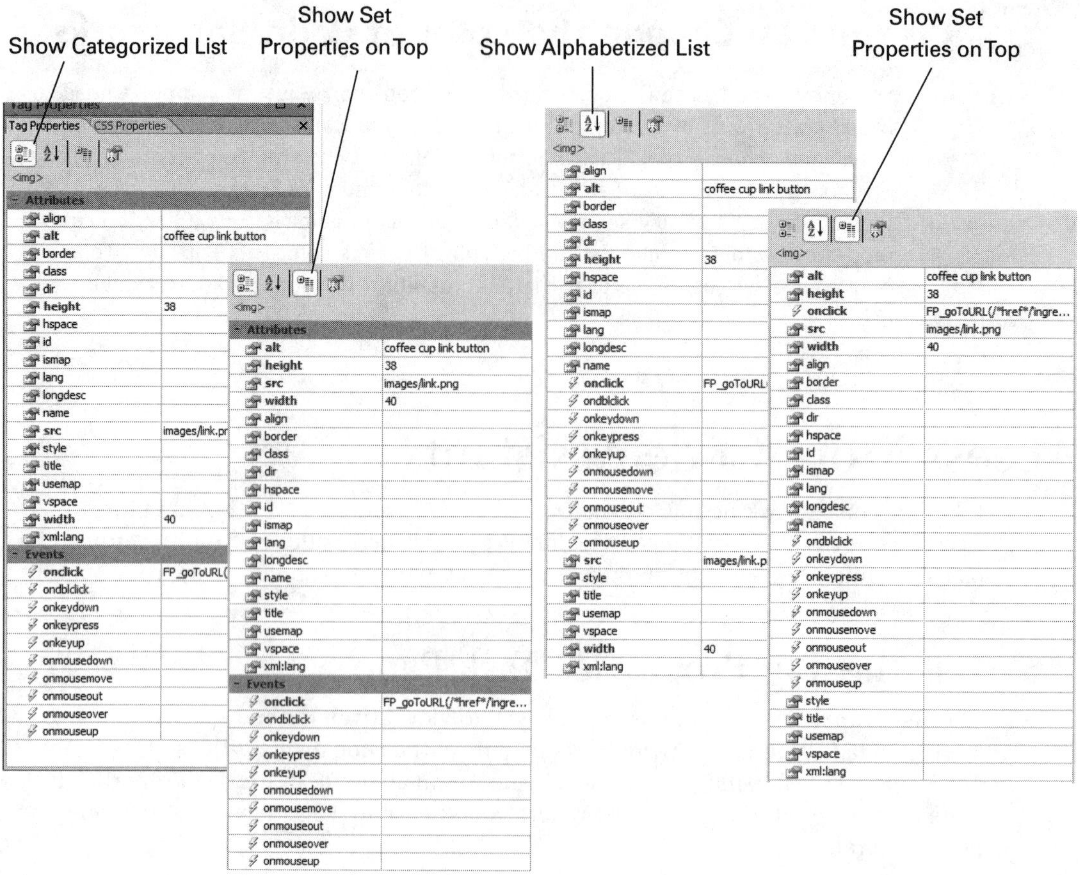

FIGURE 5-6 Display properties for tags in different configurations.

View and Edit Tag Properties

In other chapters you've seen different properties dialog boxes for objects such as pages and images. You can access the properties dialog box pertaining to a selected tag through the Tag Properties task pane or through the main program menu. If your coding is simple, the common attributes available in the dialog boxes are all you need.

However, it's a good idea to get accustomed to working in the Tag Properties task pane instead. You'll save time since the values are shown next to the Editing window, and all the attributes for a tag are available.

Follow these steps to edit tag properties:

1. Activate the tag by clicking in the code in Code view or the object in Design view. In the Tag Properties task pane, you'll see the tag shown below the Show Categorized List button and the list of available attributes for the selected tag listed in a table on the task pane.

2. Click a box to the right of the attribute you want to change to display selection options that vary according to the attribute (Figure 5-7).
3. Type or select a value for the attribute, including:
   - A drop-down list offering the possible values, such as the align attribute shown in an expanded view in Figure 5-7.
   - A text field to type a value, such as the `id` value `intro` shown in the figure.
   - An ellipsis to open the Modify Style dialog box where you can customize the tag further.

Speed Things Up with Quick Tags

Use the Quick Tag Selector bar, located at the top of the Editing window, to work with tags in Code or Design view. Click on the page in Design view or within a line of code in Code view to activate the tags. As you see here, the tag is highlighted on the Quick Tag Selector bar, the tag's content is highlighted in the Code view, and its object is selected on the Design view.

Some of the tag's menu items open the Quick Tag Editor dialog box, where you can type or edit code.

Manage Content Using the Quick Tag Selector

The Quick Tag Selector displays the hierarchy of tags from `<body>` (or `<head>` depending on your page location) through subsequent nested levels with the selected tag at the right of the bar. Tags that nest or wrap around the current tag appear to the left of the current tag, such as the `<div>` tag in Figure 5-8.

Tip To see a list of tags wider than the Editing window, scroll horizontally using the arrows at either end of the bar.

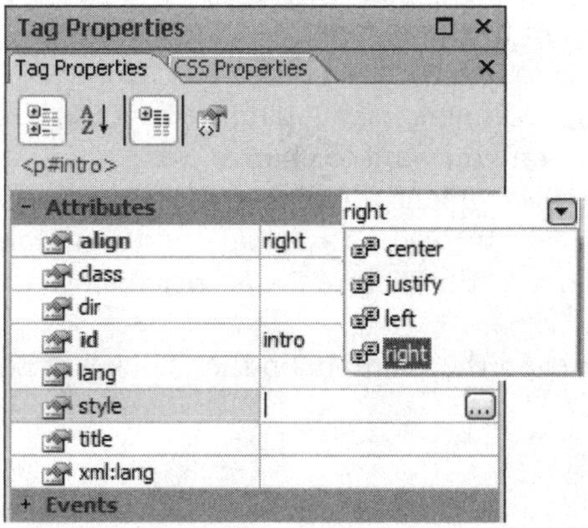

FIGURE 5-7 Choose values for the tag's attributes.

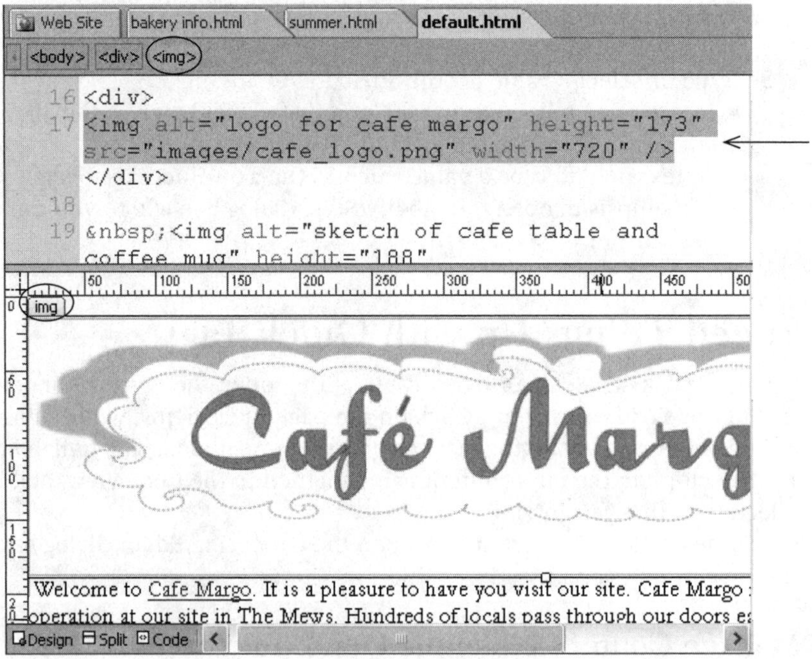

FIGURE 5-8 Tags are identified in multiple locations.

Click the tag's drop-down arrow to open a list of commands. To modify tag structures, choose one of these options:

- **Select Tag** Selects a tag's contents and its surrounding tags. Of course, clicking the tag on the Quick Tag Selector selects the content and tags, so you won't use the command often.
- **Select Tag Contents** Selects the text inside the pair of tags. Use this command when you want to move content to another location on the page or to copy and paste content to use within a different tag.
- **Remove Tag** Deletes the tag pair, leaving the content on the page. Use this command when you want to change a tag.
- **Tag Properties** Opens the dialog box containing properties applicable to the tag. For example, if you select a `<p>` tag, the Paragraph Properties dialog box opens; an `<img>` tag opens the Picture Properties dialog box, and so on.

Other choices on the menu open the Quick Tag Editor.

Edit Content with the Quick Tag Editor

The Quick Tag Editor opens in response to selecting one of three options from a tag's drop-down menu on the Quick Tag Selector. The choices include:

- **Edit Tag** Edits the selected tag and its attributes or adds additional tags.
- **Insert HTML** Adds additional code to the page.
- **Wrap Tag** Wraps the selected tag within another tag, such as a `<div>` tag.

Follow these steps to use the Quick Tag Editor:

1. Click the location where you want to modify the tag.
2. Click the drop-down arrow next to the tag associated with your selected location and choose Edit Tag, Insert HTML, or Wrap Tag to open the Quick Tag Editor dialog box.
3. Type the code to insert and click Enter. The dialog box closes, and your edits are made.

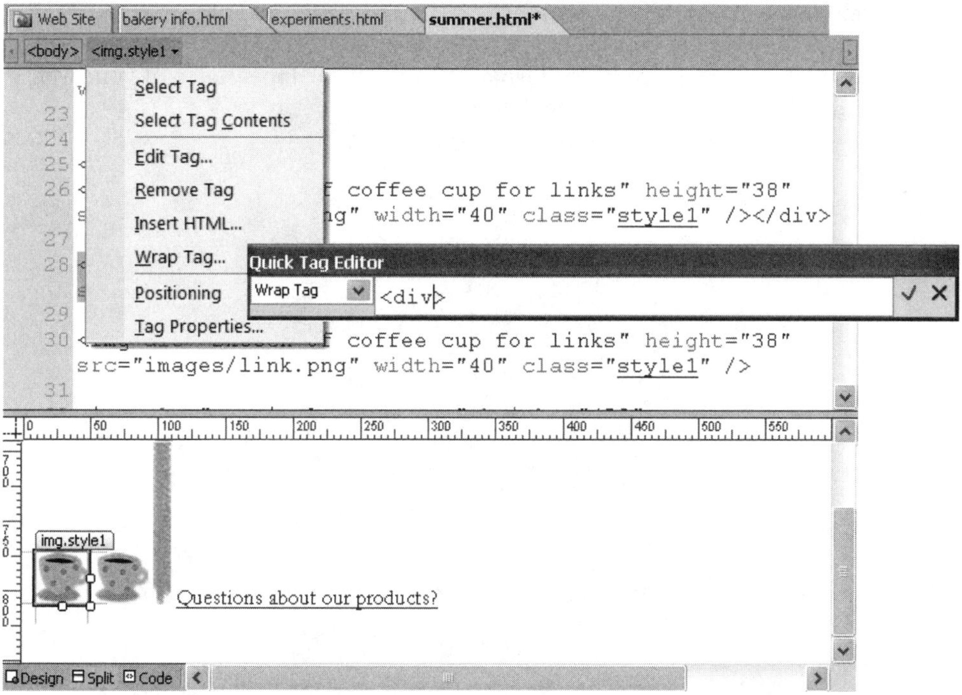

Note The illustration is a composite image, showing both the tag's menu and the Quick Tag Editor. In the program, the menu closes as the Quick Tag Editor opens.

Summary

In this chapter, you discovered a variety of Expression Web 2 features for writing and customizing code in Code view. If you are strictly the WYSIWYG type, you won't likely venture too far into the code side of things. However, it's important to have an understanding of how what you see relates to the page's code.

You saw how to customize preferences for writing and formatting code and learned some tips on when to use the settings. Expression Web 2 offers several interrelated tools and features accessible from the Code View toolbar. One of the biggest tools is IntelliSense, a context-sensitive tool that offers code prompts based on your cursor location.

You can save code that you use repeatedly, like the `<meta>` tags in the `<head>` of a page, or your copyright information, and then insert it automatically using code snippets. Not only does inserting prewritten code save time, it also prevents error.

Expression Web 2 includes several tools accessible from the program window to help in your code writing efforts. The Tag Properties task pane lets you click an option to add a tag instantly. Quick Tags—both the Quick Tag Selector and Quick Tag Editor, help you zero in on your content.

In the next chapter, we'll look at code of another sort as we look at CSS. Cascading Style Sheets are the basis for formatting the visual appearance of your web site, and offer a lot of great timesaving features.

6

Create and Manage Styles in Expression Web 2

HOW TO...

- Understand the CSS structure
- Design styles
- Customize tag styles
- Work in Expression Web 2 style panels

HTML was originally designed to identify the content in a document, such as a heading or an image. A browser read the tag and displayed the contents using the formatting defined by the tag. During the latter part of the 1990s, browsers allowed for more and more new HTML tags, and attributes for those tags.

The World Wide Web Consortium (W3C) specified both HTML and style standards with the release of HTML 4.01, released a week before the turn of the millenium in December 1999. All major browsers support CSS. In addition to separating presentation from content, style sheets save a lot of time. For example, changing a style's settings in an external style sheet globally changes that style for all pages using the style sheet throughout your web site.

Styles and style sheets require their own written expressions and formatting. Expression Web 2 offers several ways to design, configure, and integrate styles and style sheets into your web pages and sites.

Note Two sidebars in the latter part of this chapter demonstrate an example workflow using the program's task panes to apply and control styles. Part I explains how to set preferences and create styles. Part II continues with sorting and naming the set of styles.

Understanding CSS

CSS stands for *Cascading Style Sheet*. The *cascading* term refers to building styles based on a sequence of rules. As the rules are applied, the styles cascade into a final style displayed on the page. Styles apply to text as well as *block elements*, standalone content like headings and paragraphs; or `<div>` tags, block elements you define in the page's code to lay out page content like columns.

Note Read more about positioning, block and inline elements, and other features in Chapter 7.

Apply Inheritance to Page Contents

Inheritance is an important part of the cascade and explains how a heading knows what font to display. Paragraph tags inherit certain properties from body tags, for example. Bullet lists in turn inherit certain properties from paragraph tags, and so on.

Here's an example rule for the `<body>` tag on a page:

```
body {font-family: Geneva; font-style: italic; }
```

All the paragraph text on the page will use Geneva font in italics. Bullet lists and other content that inherits properties from the paragraph tag use Geneva font in italics because the paragraph tag inherited the font characteristics from the body tag. In order to display content like bullet lists using other fonts or font styles, you would need to write a more specific rule that overrides the inherited characteristics.

Whether you rely solely on the Expression Web 2 CSS tools to automatically apply styles for you, use the Manual Style Application mode, or write CSS in another program or as a text file, having a basic understanding of CSS and how styles work makes designing your pages simpler and more efficient.

Note The first parts of this chapter deal with the structure and application of CSS. The remainder describes the CSS tools offered in Expression Web 2. Chapter 7 continues with Expression Web 2 CSS tools and also focuses on manual CSS design.

How to Write a CSS Statement

CSS follows a specific pattern, or *syntax*, with requirements for punctuation, wording, and other elements.

Write a Style Declaration

A style description, also called a *rule set*, includes three parts, written as:

```
selector {property: value}
```

- The *selector* refers to the HTML tag, such as `<h2>` or `<blockquote>` that you want to style. You can use other selectors as well, described in the upcoming section, "Specify a Type of Selector."
- The *property* is an attribute of the HTML tag. Different types of tags, such as paragraphs or tables, may have different attributes. For example, both tables and paragraphs can have text attributes, but you can't use a table-layout property for a paragraph.
- The *value* is the specific setting you want to apply to the property, such as a background's color or a heading's alignment.

Pay Attention to Syntax

There are several syntax requirements to keep in mind to successfully style a web page. The basic requirements include:

- Write the standard syntax as the property and value separated by a colon, surrounded by curly braces. An inline style, written within an HTML tag on a page, doesn't include curly braces.
- If the value has more than one word, such as many font names, enclose the value in quotes, such as `h4 {font-family: "Lucida Sans"}`
- Selectors can be grouped if the same property and value applies to them all. For example, `h1,h2,h3 {font-family: "Lucida Sans"}` means all the Heading 1 through Heading 3 tags use the Lucida Sans font.
- You often use more than one property, each of which must be separated by a semicolon. For example, `h1,h2,h3 {font-family: "Lucida Sans"; color: teal}` means the three heading tags use teal green Lucida Sans text.

Tip If you are designing a complex style sheet or writing one by hand place each property on a single line to make it easier to read.

Specify a Type of Selector

CSS style application depends on the selector's definition. Whether you write styles in a page's internal style sheet or a linked external style sheet, the outcome is the same. CSS allows for three categories of selectors.

Element Selectors

Element selectors apply a style to an existing HTML tag. Whenever that tag is used, the content always displays the same characteristics on the page. When you write the style declaration, use the tag as the selector:

```
h3 {color: teal; background-color: #E9E9E9}
```

This means, on a web page, all Heading 3 tags are a teal green color on a pale gray background.

Heading 3 text always has a pale gray background and teal green text.

There aren't any changes made in the page's code to reflect a custom appearance for the heading tag. Your browser recognizes that any <h3> tag it encounters is to be teal green with a gray background.

Class Selectors

Class selectors describe a style that you can apply to different items, such as a font color for a heading, blockquote, table heading, and so on. If you change the style, the contents of your page automatically update.

Expression Web 2 uses class selectors as the default method for defining styles.

```
<style type="text/css">
.style2 {
    border: 0px solid #E9E9E9;
}
.style6 {
    border: medium solid #C0C0C0;
    background-color: #99CCFF;
}
.style7 {
    border: medium solid #C0C0C0;
    background-color: #CCFF99;
}
.style8 {
    border: medium solid #C0C0C0;
    background-color: #CC99FF;
}
.style9 {
    font-family: "Adobe Garamond Pro",
"Century Schoolbook", serif;
}
```

Preface a class selector by a period (.) when writing the style; the page's code uses the style without the period. Expression Web 2 numbers class selectors sequentially. The CSS is correct, but it isn't easy to identify one style from another.

Tip Fortunately, you can customize numbered selectors, as you'll see later in the chapter.

Figure 6-1 shows an example style using a class selector. The style may apply to any page element you like, such as a heading, column heads in a table, or a paragraph.

This example shows how the style is specified the <h3> tag:

```
<h3 class="customer">Ingredient List </h3>
```

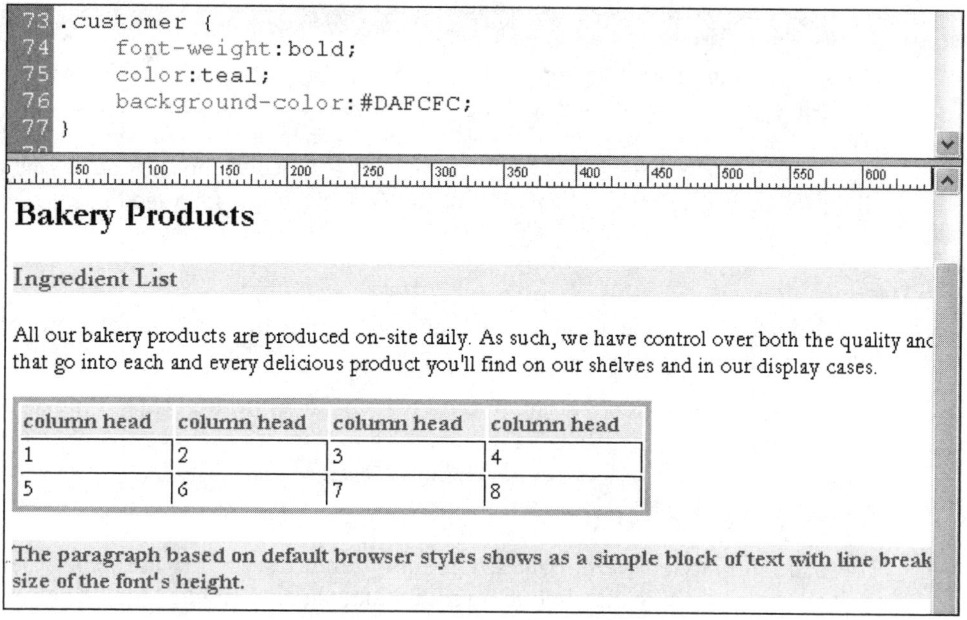

All our bakery products are produced on-site daily. As such, we have control over both the quality anc
that go into each and every delicious product you'll find on our shelves and in our display cases.

The paragraph based on default browser styles shows as a simple block of text with line break
size of the font's height.

FIGURE 6-1 Apply the same class-based style to different tags.

On the page's HTML, the tag specifies the style as an attribute and value for the <h3> tag.

ID Selectors

An ID selector is a named style used to define properties for a specific item on a page or across your site. For example, you may have an ID style defined for the copyright information on your pages.

Preface an ID selector by the number sign (#) on the style sheet. In this example, the style at the top produces the content shown below it:

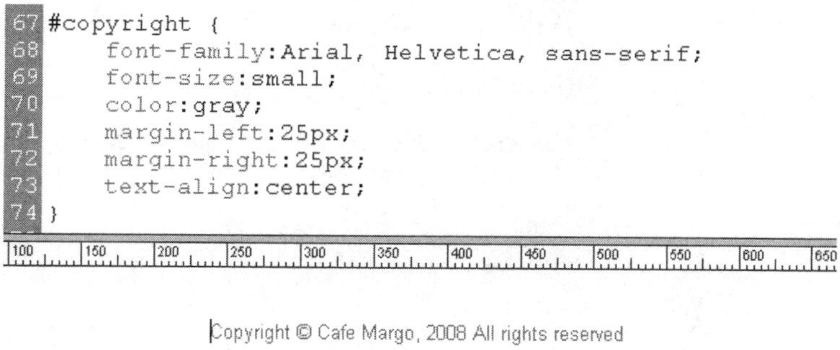

#copyright {
font-family:Arial, Helvetica, sans-serif;
font-size:small;
color:gray;
margin-left:25px;
margin-right:25px;
text-align:center;
}
Copyright © Cafe Margo, 2008 All rights reserved

Every Web Page Has Styles

Every web page has styling applied to it to display HTML code because browsers contain built-in styles. That's why you'll always see a layout on a web page. As you see in Figure 6-2, even without adding styles, the main headings look different, the text separates into paragraphs, and the hyperlink has a blue underline. If you clicked the link, the color changes to a magenta underline indicating a followed link.

To display the style, the `<p>` tag includes the `id` attribute and the `copyright` value, written as:

```
<p id="copyright"> Copyright © Cafe Margo 2008, All rights reserved </p>
```

Apply Style Rules

There are four style levels or *rules*. The most generic styles are at the browser level, with the most specific attached to an individual tag on a single page. Each rule level

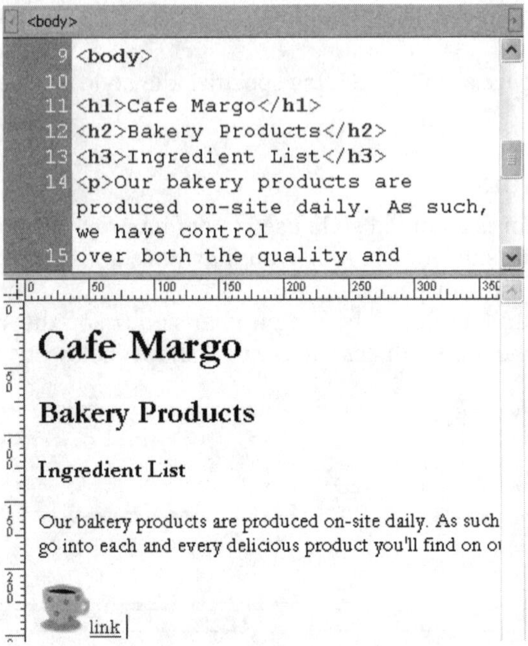

<body>
<body>
<h1>Cafe Margo</h1>
<h2>Bakery Products</h2>
<h3>Ingredient List</h3>
<p>Our bakery products are produced on-site daily. As such, we have control
over both the quality and
Cafe Margo
Bakery Products
Ingredient List
Our bakery products are produced on-site daily. As such
go into each and every delicious product you'll find on o
link

FIGURE 6-2 Code elements display default appearances due to the browser's built-in styles.

inherits characteristics from the previous level. Expression Web 2 works with external and internal style sheets and inline styles only.

Link to an External Style Sheet

The most useful way to use styles for a web site is with an external style sheet. The styles are listed in a file saved with the .css (cascading style sheet) extension. The style sheet is then attached to each web page in your site by adding a `<link>` tag within the `<head>` tag, such as:

```
<link href="cafe_margo01.css" rel="style sheet" type="text/css" />
```

You can use and attach different external style sheets for different parts of your site, or use multiple style sheets linked to the same page. For example, you may have a style sheet for general site pages, another style sheet for online ordering or catalog pages, and another style sheet for information or data sheet pages.

Tip The cascading concept is applied to multiple style sheets linked to the same page. If a page uses multiple style sheets, the browser processes the styles in their order of appearance on the page.

Write Styles for a Specific Page

If you look at your Expression Web 2 pages, you'll see the styles attached to the individual pages by default. The styles are contained as an *internal* style sheet and written within the `<head>` tag of the page. You write styles for both internal and external style sheets the same way.

Using an internal style sheet is inefficient when looking at the overall site styling. On the other hand, if you are designing a single page for a single purpose, like a newsletter you send via e-mail or a big company announcement, then an internal style sheet is the way to go. Rather than plain text, your readers can view a publication with an attractive layout.

Note Read how to modify the default methods for handling styles using the Page Editor options in the section, "Specify Styling Preferences."

Insert a Style for a Single Tag

The final style rule is an *inline* style where the style is attached as an attribute to an HTML tag as in this example:

```
<p style="font-weight: bold; color: #FF5050"> text for paragraph </p>
```

Use an inline style for a specific purpose, such as a paragraph designed to announce your big company press release. In the example, the paragraph is written in bold, salmon-colored text.

Note Don't overdo the use of inline styles. They are hard to troubleshoot and difficult to control if you later decide to use an internal or external style sheet.

Use Expression Web CSS Tools

Expression Web 2 offers several task panes designed to coordinate and manage your styles and style sheets. The features include:

- **New Style and Modify Style dialog boxes** Design new styles or edit existing styles. You'll see a preview of your style as you specify its characteristics.
- **Apply Styles task pane** Lists style types and specifies what styles are used in your current page or in a selection. Here you can also add and edit styles, apply or remove styles, and attach or detach an external style sheet.
- **Manage Styles task pane** Functions like a subset of the Apply Styles task pane. You can move styles back and forth from internal to external style sheets or to inline styles.
- **CSS Properties task pane** Lists the style details for a current selection on a page. You'll see a list of the properties and *order of precedence*, or application sequence depending on the style hierarchy.

Note This list identifies those CSS program features used for Auto Style Application mode. Chapter 7 discusses additional tools and toolbars available for Manual Style Application mode.

Specify Styling Preferences

Expression Web 2 uses Auto Style Application mode, which predetermines many of the style features, such as their selectors and whether styles are inline or included in an internal spreadsheet. You can specify how styles are formatted based on choices made in a variety of dialog boxes.

Switch Style Application Modes

To switch from manual to auto design, right-click Style Application on the status bar at the bottom of the Expression Web 2 program window to display a menu. Choose Mode | Manual to change modes. On the menu, click CSS Options to display the Page Editor Options dialog box, showing the CSS tab, or choose Tools | Page Editor Options and click the CSS tab (Figure 6-3).

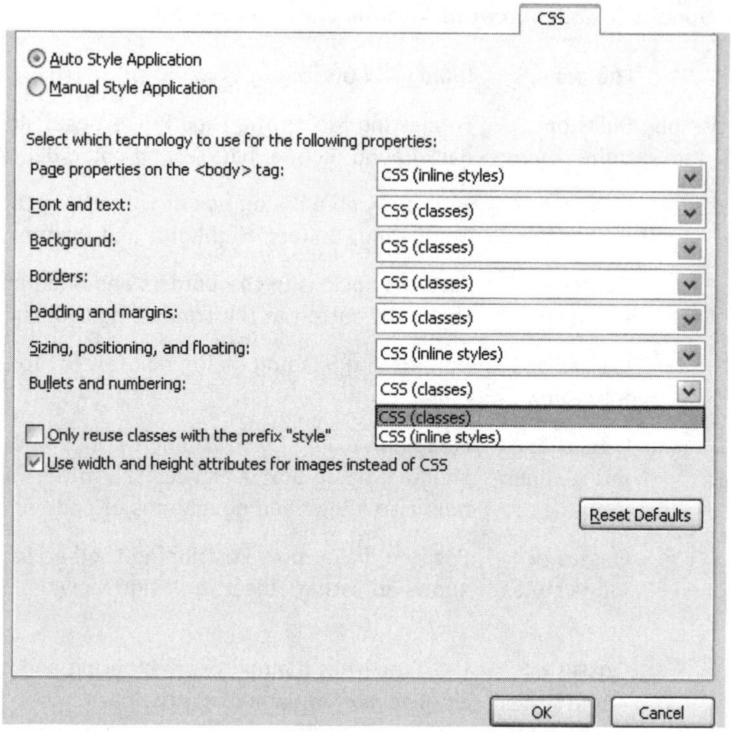

FIGURE 6-3 Specify the formats for CSS properties.

Configure CSS Property Choices

In the dialog box, click either Auto Style Application or Manual Style Application to show alternate panes for setting styles. The dialog box shows the style application mode shown on the status bar by default. The choices are nearly identical regardless of the chosen application mode. The properties, choices, and style options are listed in Table 6-1.

Note The same settings apply to configuring the program for Manual mode. You may not need to make any changes from the defaults depending on how you work in Manual mode. For example, writing your styles using IntelliSense in Code view bypasses style rules established or written by Expression Web 2.

TABLE 6-1 Specify Management of Various CSS Properties

Property	Choices	Dialog Box Options
Page properties on the `<body>` tag	Rules or inline styles	Formatting tab on the Page Properties dialog box: set background picture, background color, default text color
Font and text	Classes or inline styles	Font or Symbol dialog box or Formatting toolbar (except for Numbering, Bullets, Highlight, and Borders buttons)
Background	Classes or inline styles	Patterns options in the Borders and Shading dialog box or the Highlight button in the Formatting toolbar
Borders	Classes or inline styles	Borders and Shading dialog box (except for Padding options)
Padding and margins	Classes or inline styles	Paragraph dialog box, Padding options in the Borders and Shading dialog box, Advanced tab in the Page Properties dialog box; also allows adding margins or padding in Design view
Sizing, positioning, and floating	Classes or inline styles	Position dialog box, Positioning toolbar, Layers task pane; also allows adjusting object in Design view
Bullets and numbering	Classes or inline styles	List Properties dialog box, Numbering and Bullets buttons on the Common or Formatting toolbars

In addition to defining style formats for different properties, you can also specify these features:

- The option Only Reuse Classes with the Prefix "Style" is deselected by default and available only in Auto mode. Expression Web 2 writes default styles using a sequentially numbered `.styleN` name. You can select the option to restrict changing styles to those inserted automatically by the program.
- The option Use Width and Height Attributes for Images Instead of CSS is selected by default. Expression Web 2 sets size attributes as part of an `<img>` tag in the HTML rather than using CSS properties. Leave this setting selected, and use CSS for setting sizes only where necessary, such as defining uniform sizes for thumbnail images or static background images. Otherwise, you'll have to write styles for each image of different sizes you use on your site.

Tip If you've made some changes and want to make more adjustments but can't remember what you've done, click Reset Defaults to start again.

How to...

Use a Workflow, Part I: Design CSS Styles

In previous chapters, you saw how easy it is to configure the appearance of content on your web pages using the toolbars, dialog boxes, and commands offered by Expression Web 2. You saw how Expression Web 2 then takes those settings to create a whole range of styles named *.styleN* (*N* is a number from one to infinity!).

If you aren't a CSS whiz and aren't interested in dealing with the actual CSS code, you can use a simple workflow to keep track of your styles with a minimum of confusion.

Follow these steps to style your site:

1. In the Page Editor Options dialog box, on the CSS tab (described in the previous section), make these two changes, then click OK to close the dialog box:
   - Click the Page Properties on the `<body>` Tag drop-down arrow and choose CSS (Rules).
   - Click the Sizing, Positioning, and Floating drop-down arrow and choose CSS (Classes).
2. Start your first page. Add the content, images, links, and so on. Be sure to use the proper tags for items like headings, bullet lists, numbered lists, and so on to make it easier to manage styles later.
3. Using the dialog boxes and toolbars, change the layout and appearance of the page as you like. Take the time to make sure you are satisfied with the appearance of the different features on the page.
4. Carefully evaluate each change before you make it to see if there's already an existing style. If you click on page content, the style is highlighted in the Apply Styles task pane. As you see here, selecting Heading 2 text selects both the `h2` contextual selector at the bottom, and the `.style7` style.

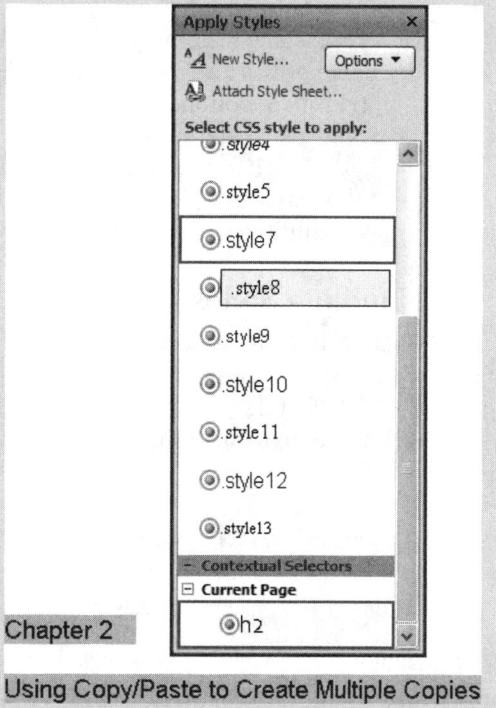

Tip In the sidebar "Use a Workflow, Part II: Sort Out Your Styles," learn how to remove extra styles and evaluate and rename the styles added to the page.

Work with Styles in the Apply Styles Task Pane

Use the Apply Styles task pane to work with the styles for your web pages. Here you'll find tools to apply or modify styles, attach or detach external style sheets, select all instances of a style's use in a web page, and view the code for the style's rule set.

Viewing the Styles

The Apply Styles task pane lists each style according to its rules, making it simple to identify the style you want to apply. The source, selector, and use of the styles for your page are identified with icons in the task pane (Table 6-2).

You'll see the styles associated with a web page organized in different ways (Figure 6-4).

The styles display according to their type:

- Styles using class or ID selectors display according to their external style sheet's name or Current Page if the styles are written to an internal style sheet (both style sheet options are shown in Figure 6-4).
- Styles using element or tag selectors are listed under the Contextual Selectors heading when the cursor is within the tag's content (h2 in Figure 6-4).
- Inline styles display in the Contextual Selectors heading as well when your cursor is within the content using the style.

Handling Styles

Click Options to open a menu where you can sort your styles by category or filter the styles list according to the current page or selection.

Not all styles include a background color, of course. Expression Web 2 shows a default green color, which is hard to see with lighter colored text. To change it, click

TABLE 6-2 Key to the Apply Styles Task Pane Icons

Icon	Description
Red dot	ID selectors
Green dot	Class selectors
Blue dot	Element selectors
Yellow dot	Inline styles
Circle	Identifies styles used in the active page
@ symbol	Imported external cascading style sheets

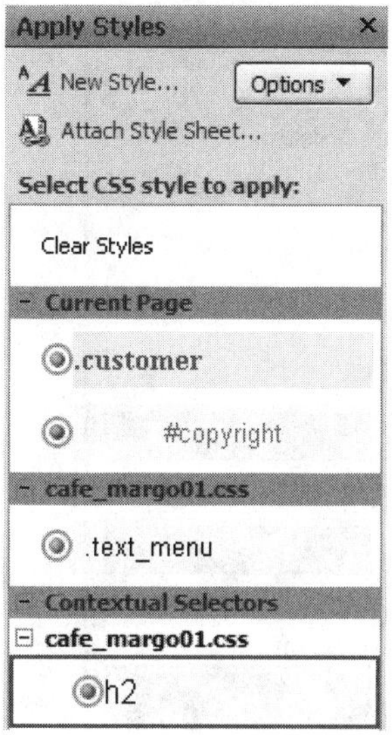

FIGURE 6-4 Styles display according to various criteria.

Options | Preview Background Color on the Apply Styles task pane. Select a color in the More Colors dialog box, click OK and you can see your styles (Figure 6-5).

Tip To review a style's rules, hold your cursor over the style's name to display the rules in a pop-up window, also shown in Figure 6-5.

On an individual style basis, click the style to display a menu containing a range of commands from modifying and renaming the style to changing the style sheet links.

Two commands you'll use frequently on the Options menu include:

- **Go To Code** This command lets you jump to a style on a long style sheet. Expression Web 2 automatically opens an external style sheet and conveniently places the cursor at the start of the style's code.
- **Select All** *x* **Instance(s)** Whether a style is used once or ten times on a page, this command highlights the code containing the style, and also highlights the content on the page. You might want to use this style to assist in making design decisions, such as changing text size or modifying a margin depth.

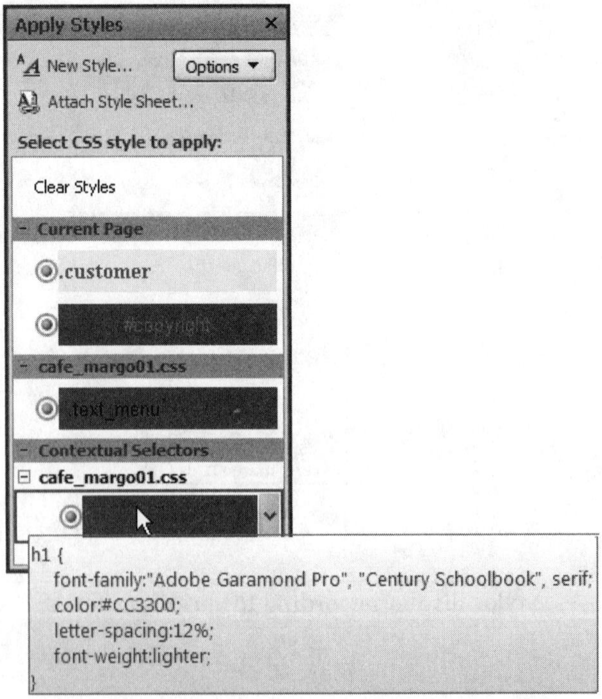

FIGURE 6-5 Change the background color for easier viewing.

How to...

Use a Workflow, Part II: Sort Out Your Styles

Once you've added the styles for your page and ensured you're not using multiple styles for the same text, it's time to sort and rename them. Along the way, you may find you have styles that aren't necessary, or that could be substituted with another style.

Follow these steps to evaluate the styles for duplicates, missed content, and so on:

1. In the Apply Styles task pane, hold your mouse over the first `.styleN` (probably *.style1* unless you've culled extraneous styles) to see the style properties in a pop-up for reference. Viewing the properties gives you an idea of the style's purpose.

Note The properties are shown in the CSS Properties task pane as well, which we'll look at later in the chapter.

2. Right-click the style name to open the shortcut menu, and choose Select All *x* Instance(s). You'll see the content selected on the page.

How to...

3. Scroll through the page and check that the correct content has the selected style. In the example shown here, *.style2* is applied twice in the file, when it should be applied three times. Scrolling through the content and selecting the next instance of the text that should use the style shows *.style9* is applied.

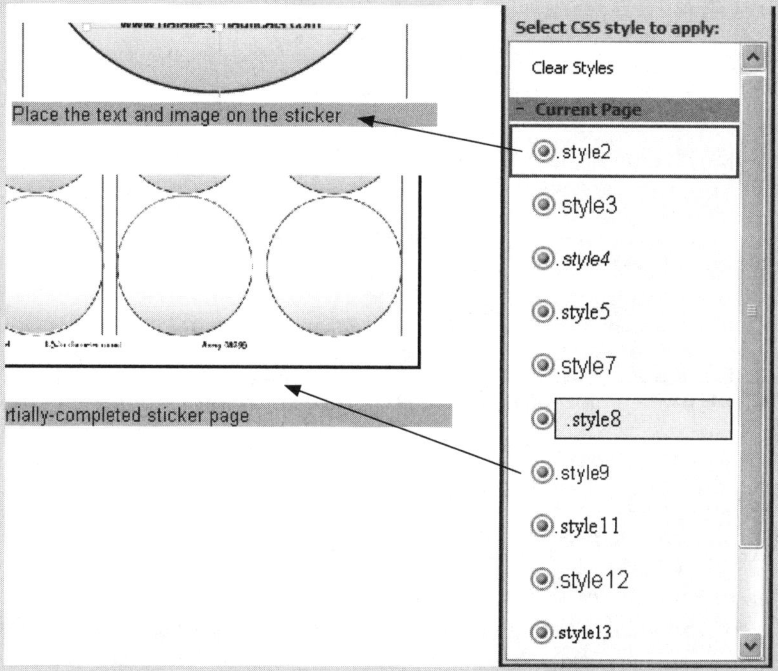

4. To repair the style, right-click the style for removal on the Apply Styles dialog box, and click Delete from the shortcut menu. Click Yes in the confirmation dialog box, and the style is removed. The text to which it was applied is selected on the web page, without a style. Click the correct style to apply, in this case *.style2*.
5. Right-click the style name to open the shortcut menu again, and check the correct number of instances is listed. With the shortcut menu open, click Rename Class "style2" to open the Rename Class dialog box.
6. Type a descriptive name in the field; in the example, the style is named *caption* as it styles image captions. Leave the check box Rename Class References in This Page selected to have Expression Web 2 automatically update the page for you. Click OK to close the dialog box and change the name.
7. Click anywhere on the page to deselect the selected content. Otherwise, the selected content takes on the next style you select to work with.
8. Continue with the remainder of your styles, checking them for completeness, removing any duplicates, and renaming them (Figure 6-6).

Note You may need to make changes to the styles (likely if you delete a style wrapped around another style). See how to use the Modify Style dialog box in the next section.

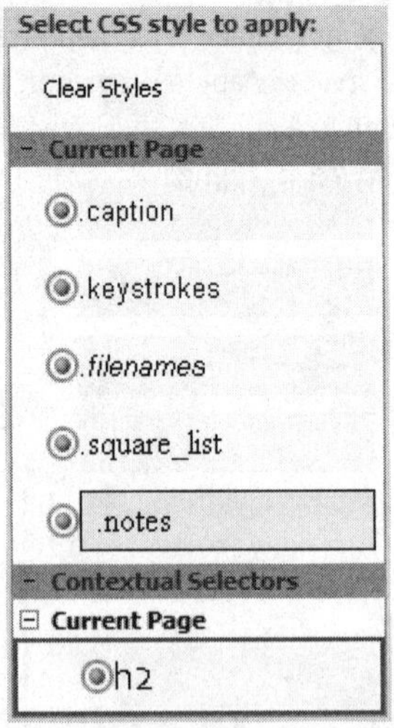

FIGURE 6-6 The revised list of styles are complete and use meaningful names.

Keep Track of Styles in the Manage Styles Task Pane

The Manage Styles and Apply Styles task panes have a number of common features for convenience, although they have different purposes. The icons for both task panes are the same (refer to Table 6-2 for a description of the style icons). You'll also find the details of a style in a pop-up box if you hover your mouse over its name.

Both panes offer a list of styles. The Apply Styles task pane shows examples of the style, making it simpler to select a style to apply. On the Manage Styles task pane, you'll find the styles listed simply by name, although you'll see a preview if you click the style's listing. Unlike the Apply Styles task pane (shown here, on the left), the Manage Styles task pane (shown on the right) shows the *contextual selectors*, that is, the HTML elements that you've modified from their default appearances.

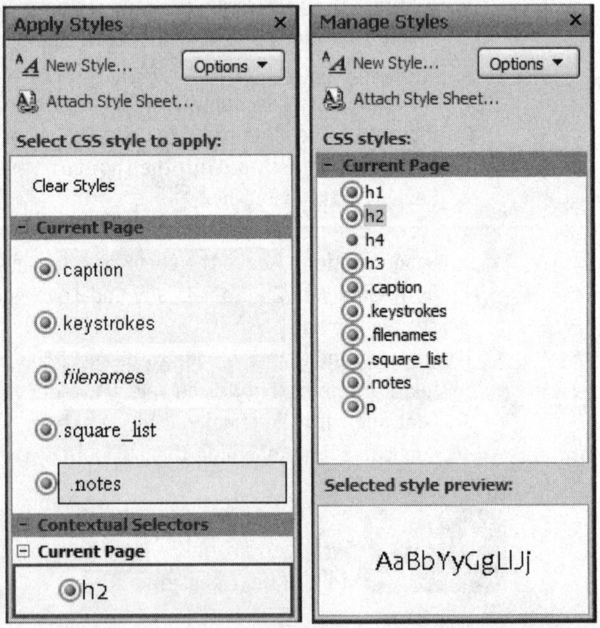

It's easy to keep track of a page's styles when there are only a few. On a well-developed site with dozens of pages, you may have a few dozen styles. Keeping track is where the Manage Styles task pane comes in (Figure 6-7).

Write a New Style

For some features, such as changing a font color or size, it's easy to work in the Editing window with the toolbars and Apply Styles task pane. You may have an existing style that needs modification, or you may want to start a more complex style from scratch. You use the same process to create a style for an internal or external CSS.

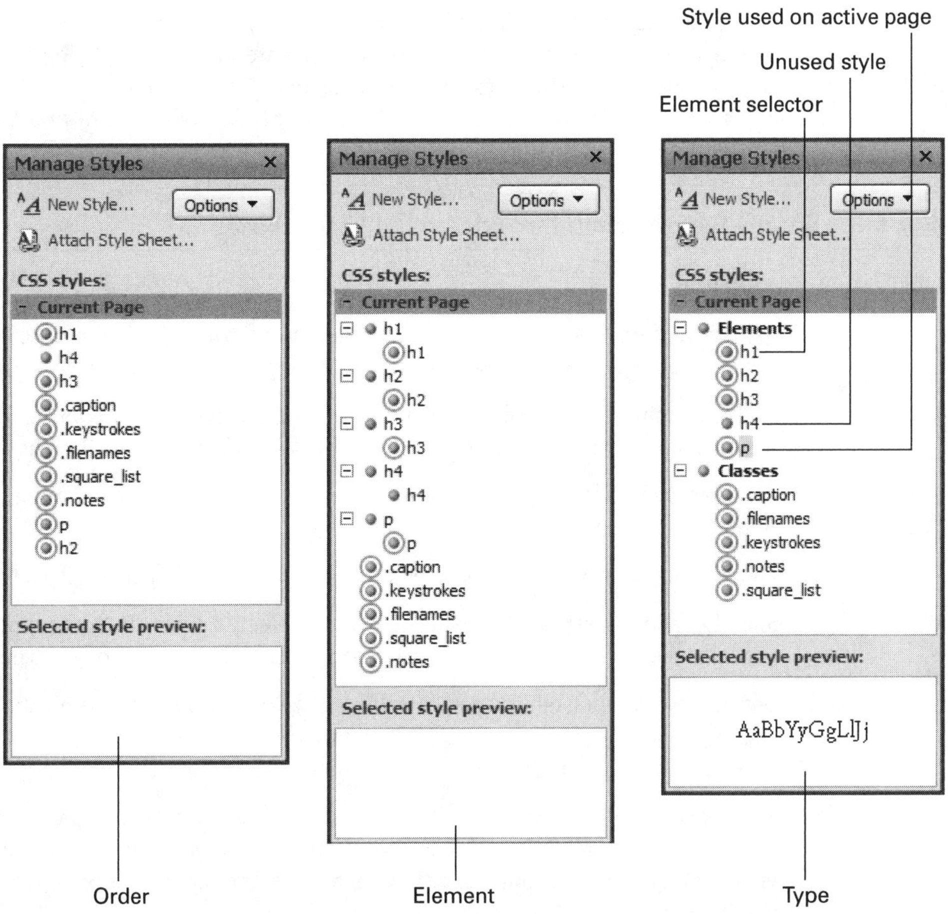

FIGURE 6-7 Choose a sort method to show styles on the task pane.

Construct a New Style

To design a new style or change an existing one, use the New Style or Modify Style dialog box. Both dialog boxes offer identical settings.

Follow these steps to put together a new style:

1. Click New Style on either the Apply Styles or Manage Styles task pane to open the New Style dialog box.
2. Click the Selector drop-down arrow and choose an existing HTML element to configure, or type a name for the new style in the field. To define a new class selector, type a period (.) and the name without spaces. To define a new ID selector, type a number sign (#) followed by the name without spaces.
3. Click the Define In drop-down arrow and choose a location if you want to save the style in a style sheet rather than in the page you're working on. If you choose a style sheet option, click Browse to locate an existing style sheet.
4. Choose settings from the various categories listed on the dialog box, described briefly in Table 6-3. Category names shown in bold (such as Font and Border in Figure 6-8) contain chosen properties.

TABLE 6-3 Specify Basic Settings for Styles in the Dialog Box

Style Category	Properties
Font	Set the features for text in a style, such as the font family, size, and color. Also set decorations such as underlines, strikethroughs, and blink.
Block	Define spacing and alignment settings for tags and properties. Choose settings for word and letter spacing, text indent and alignment, and line height.
Background	Set characteristics for backgrounds such as color, images, repeats, and positions. Apply a background to any element on a page.
Border	Choose settings for border color, width, and style; specify which edges to apply.
Box	Specify padding and margin values for all or selected sides. The dialog box contains a diagram of the CSS box model reference to help choose settings.
Position	Define how content related to the selected style uses positioning on the page, such as absolute (based on page coordinates) or relative (in relation to other objects). Specify stacking order of elements, set absolute sizes.
Layout	Specify settings for tags and properties controlling placement of page elements. Specify height and width, a float (how other content wraps or floats around an element), or how to display overflow text that's too large for a resized browser window.
List	Set the appearance of bullets or numbers and bullet size or type for list tags, including imported image bullets.
Table	Set table display characteristics, such as whether to show empty cells or collapse borders for empty areas, and where to place a caption in relation to the table.

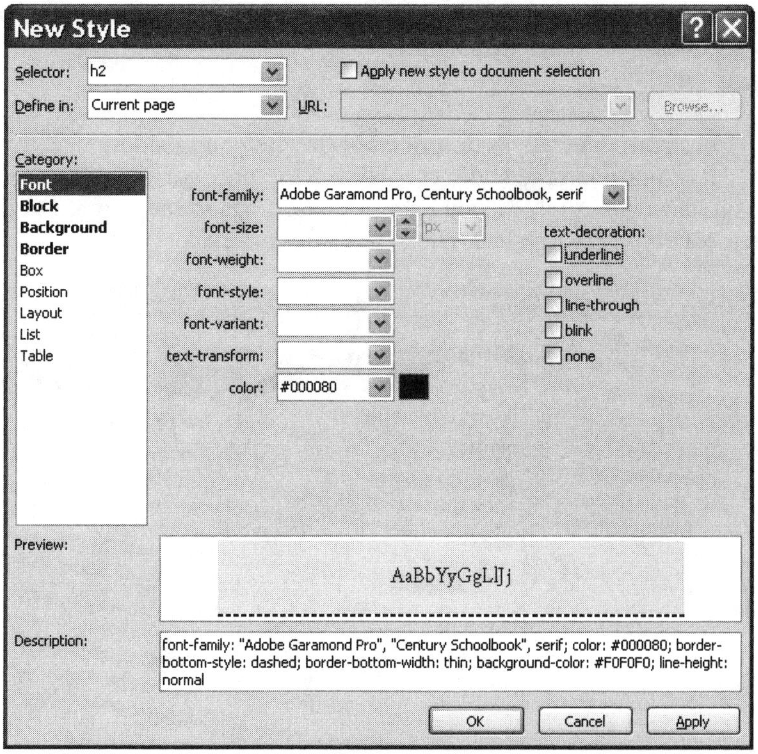

FIGURE 6-8 Configure or modify settings for a style in the dialog box.

5. Configure or modify settings for a style in the dialog box.
6. Watch the Preview and read the Description at the bottom of the dialog box as you choose your settings. If you like, click Apply as you choose the settings to see how the style looks on the page.
7. Once you're finished the configuration, click OK to close the dialog box and add the style to your page's style sheet.

Note Read more about building styles using the different style categories in Chapter 7. For a full list of CSS styles, turn to Appendix B at the back of the book.

Create an Inline Style

To define a new inline style on a page, select the content and then click New Style on the Apply Styles or Manage Styles task pane to open the dialog box. Click the Selector drop-down arrow and choose (inline style), located at the top of the list.

Note The other selection options at the top of the dialog box are disabled when you choose an inline style option.

Configure the style as described in the previous section.

As you develop the style, you can see the preview at the bottom of the dialog box. If you like, click Apply as you choose the settings to see how the style looks on the page. When you're finished, click OK to close the dialog box.

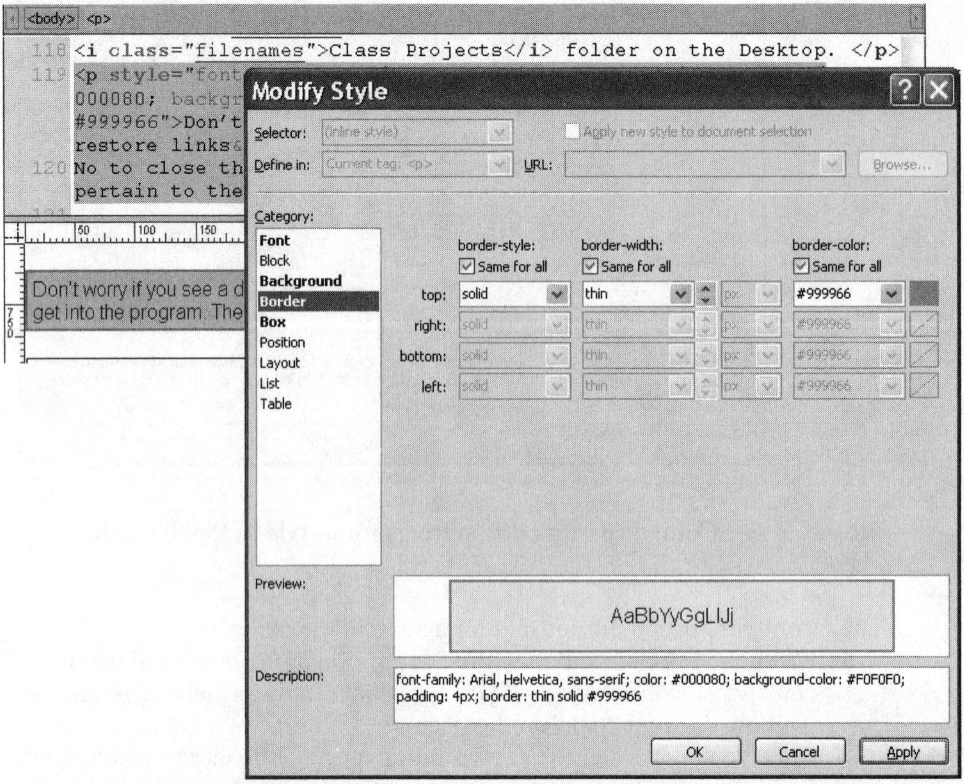

In the program, you'll see the inline style on the Apply Styles task pane when your cursor is within the content containing the style (Figure 6-9).

Once you click off the area, the Inline Style heading on the dialog box disappears. You don't see an inline style listed on the Modify Styles task pane.

Create a Style Sheet

Although Expression Web 2 doesn't offer an automatic way to produce a separate style sheet from your existing pages, it's a simple two-part task. First, create the style sheet from your existing content, and then attach it to the HTML page.

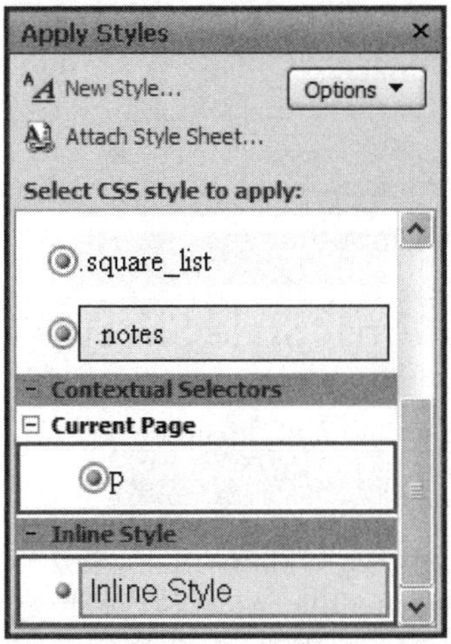

FIGURE 6-9 An inline style is listed with other page styles only when the content is active.

Move Styles to an External Style Sheet

The structures of internal and external style sheets are the same, making it simple to move to a separate document. Follow these steps to create an external style sheet from an internal style sheet:

1. Choose File | New | CSS to open a blank style sheet. The sheet is named *Untitled_1.css* by default.
2. Open your HTML page with the internal style sheet you'd like to use, and click Code at the bottom of the Editing window to display the Code view.
3. At the top of the page's HTML code, select everything between the `<style type="text/css">` and `</style>` tags, including the `<style>` tags. Press CTRL-C to copy the content from the page.
4. Click the tab for the blank CSS page. You'll see the cursor active at Line 1. Press CTRL-V to paste the styles on to the CSS page.

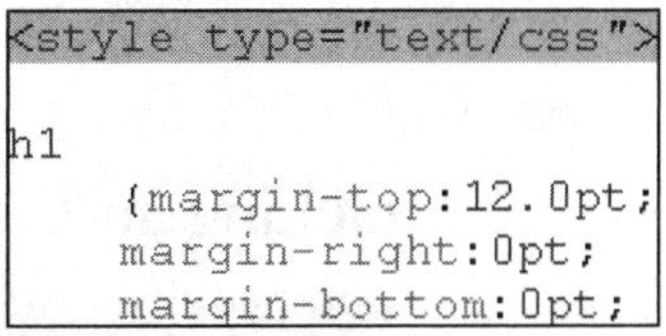

5. Delete the opening `<style>` tag on Line 1 of the style sheet shown here and the closing `</style>` tag on the last line of your code.
6. Choose File | Save As to open the Save As dialog box, showing the current web site in the Save In field.
7. Type a name for your style sheet in the File Name field; click the Save As Type drop-down arrow and choose CSS Files. Click Save to create the style sheet and close the dialog box.

Tip Although you started with a CSS page, the Save As dialog box defaults to saving as a web page.

The styles are contained in an external style sheet you can attach to any pages you like, or even use it for other sites.

Attaching an External Style Sheet

For any page on your site, you simply attach the style sheet using the task panes. Follow these steps to attach a style sheet:

1. Click Attach Style Sheet on either the Manage Styles or Attach Styles task pane to open the Attach Style Sheet dialog box.
2. Click Browse to open the Select Style Sheet dialog box for you to locate and select your file. Click OK to close the dialog box and insert the style sheet's URL on the Attach Style Sheet dialog box, as you see here.

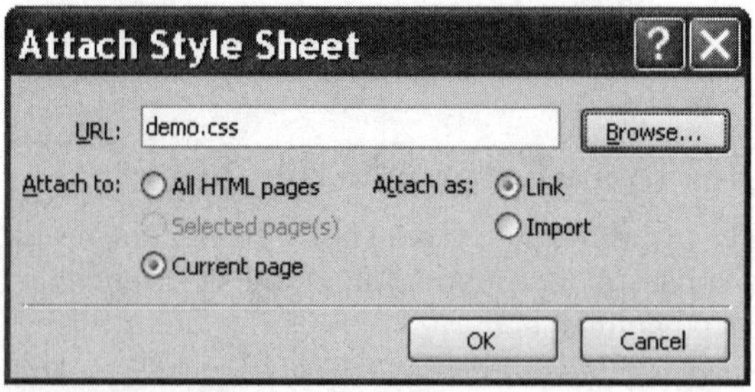

3. Choose an attachment option. If you are working with a specific page, the Current Page option is selected by default. You can also attach the style sheet to all open HTML pages or to a selection of pages.
4. Choose how to attach the file. The default choice is Link. If you want to place the style sheet internally, click Import.
5. Click OK to close the dialog box and attach the style sheet. In the Code view, you'll see the reference to the style sheet at the end of the <head> tag:

```
<link href="demo.css" rel="stylesheet" type="text/css />
```

Attaching an External Style Sheet to the Original HTML Page

If you've copied a style sheet from an internal location on a web page to create an external style sheet, don't delete the styles instead of copying them to form the new CSS page. If you do, all the styles on your page will need to be reapplied.

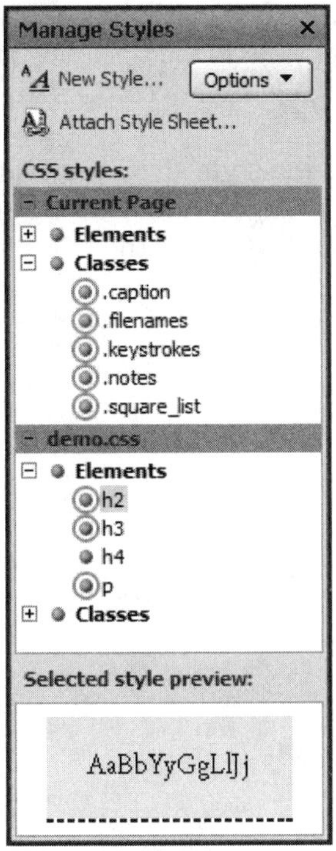

FIGURE 6-10 Both internal and external style sheets are attached.

Instead, attach the external style sheet first. You'll see both the internal and external style sheets listed in the Apply Styles and Manage Styles task panes (Figure 6-10).

Finally, select the internal style sheet content on the code page and delete it.

Summary

Styles give your web pages personality, presence, and ease of reading. Imagine how boring a web page containing an unending stream of text would be to read!

In this chapter, you learned how Cascading Style Sheets got their name from the way styles inherit their characteristics from the default level (browser styles) to the tag-specific inline style. You saw how to work with the three types of selectors used to define a style, including element, class, and ID selectors. Two "Use a Workflow" sidebars clarified the application and sorting of styles.

The latter part of the chapter explained how to use the Expression Web 2 CSS tools for creating and applying styles in the program. Most of the work takes place in the

Apply Styles and Manage Styles task panes, which contain methods for displaying and handling styles. You saw how to create a new style using the New Style dialog box. Finally, you discovered how to move styles to a style sheet, and then how to attach a style sheet to a page.

In the next chapter, the style sheet saga continues with discussions on how to write your own CSS. It's not as difficult as it appears! You'll see how to use more Expression Web 2 CSS tools, such as the CSS Properties task pane, IntelliSense, and various CSS reports.

7

Design CSS-Based Layouts

HOW TO...

- Start a style sheet using prebuilt content or from scratch
- Use IntelliSense to help write styles
- Create special styles for links
- Design unique paragraph styles
- Modify styles using Find/Replace
- Create CSS reports

When you are new to web design and Expression Web 2, writing styles yourself seems like a daunting task. Although it can be intimidating, you'll find yourself checking out the Code or Split view more and more as you work, until you readily recognize the elements that make up your styles. If you're at that stage—or would like to be—this chapter's for you.

Chapter 6 explained how to use the task panes and dialog boxes to create and apply styles. This chapter picks up where Chapter 6 left off, showing you more tools available in Expression Web 2 to help write and manage styles.

Create CSS Layouts from Scratch

Using the Expression Web 2 Automatic Style Application mode for writing styles doesn't require you to track and follow styles. Regardless of how many styles named `.styleN` are listed in your document, it probably works visually, and probably validates as well.

Note Read about cleaning up automatic styles in Chapter 6.

Moving to Manual Style Application mode is a whole new ballgame. You control and manage your styles as you develop them. That way, when you want to add another property to a style or create a style applicable to several elements, the configuration is up to you. Of course, that freedom comes with responsibility: you must know what you're doing! Fortunately, Expression Web 2 offers tools like IntelliSense for CSS and task panes like CSS Properties, which help you construct styles.

Use a Supplied Style Sheet

Many people find a blank page intimidating. If you're one of them, you can start your design using one of the preconfigured Expression Web 2 style sheets. The preconfigured style sheets include fonts and colors.

Select a Style Collection

Expression Web 2 offers a number of choices to start your style sheet. Follow these steps to make a selection and get your design underway:

1. Choose File | New | Page to open the New dialog box displaying the Page tab.
2. Click Style Sheets in the left column to display a list of options in the center column. Make a selection to see a thumbnail in the Preview area and a note on the font family and color scheme used.
3. When you've found an appropriate style sheet, such as one of the following samples, click OK to close the dialog box and create the new style sheet.

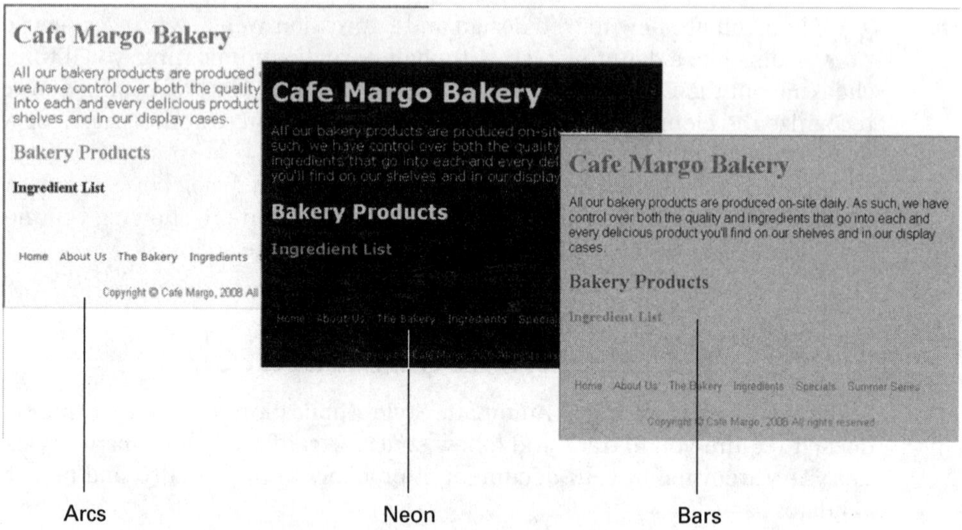
Cafe Margo Bakery
Bakery Products
Ingredient List
Home About Us The Bakery Ingredients
Cafe Margo Bakery
Bakery Products
Ingredient List
Cafe Margo Bakery
All our bakery products are produced on-site daily. As such, we have control over both the quality and ingredients that go into each and every delicious product you'll find on our shelves and in our display cases.
Bakery Products
Ingredient List
Arcs
Neon
Bars

Review the Style Rules

The style sheet is quite basic, but gives you a starting point. You can review the contents of the style sheet using the CSS Properties panel (Figure 7-1).

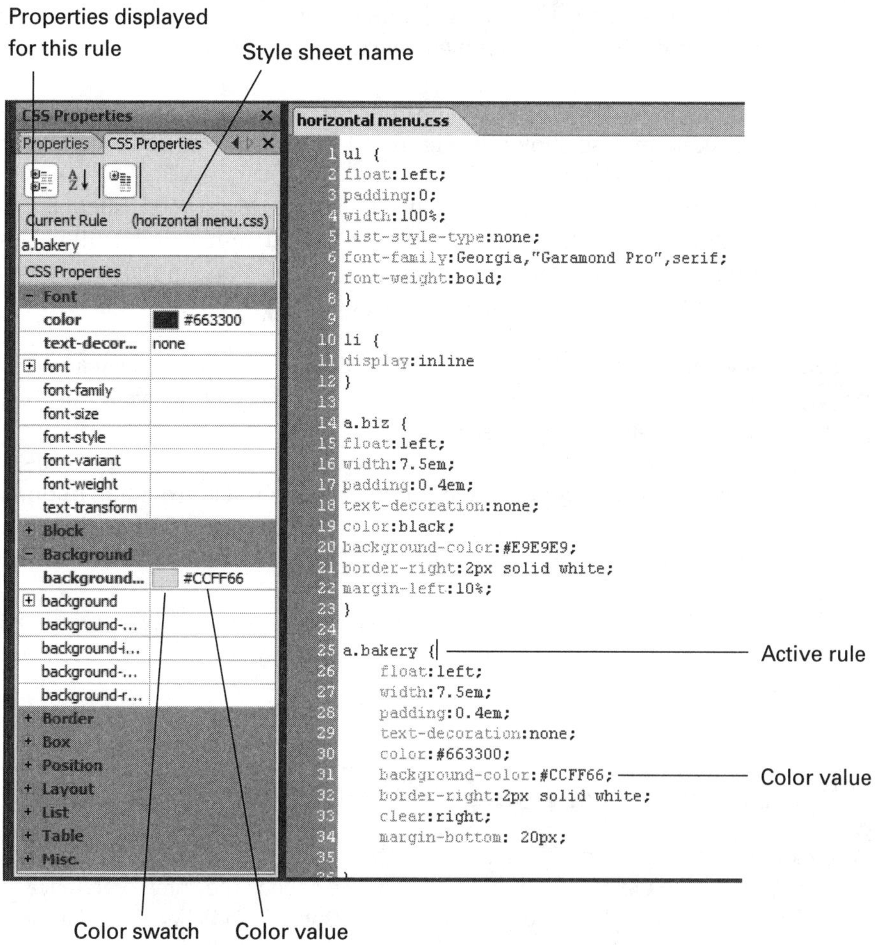

FIGURE 7-1 Start from a preconfigured set of basic styles.

Note The default style sheets offered in Expression Web 2 define colors with RGB (Red/Green/Blue) color values, rather than the more common hexadecimal (hex) values. You can use hex color values, RGB (the default color space for monitors), or named colors, such as `color:white`.

In the example shown in Figure 7-1, typical of the preconfigured style sheets, notice that the styles contain:

- Three link styles for different link states (read about designing custom links later in the chapter)
- A body style using the fonts and background color described in the dialog box

- One style to declare the fonts for the headings
- Six styles for each of H1 through H6 specifying a text color for the heading

You can check out and change the styles on the page, or take advantage of the CSS Properties task pane, also shown in Figure 7-1. You can view details of the styles in the task pane and make changes if you like.

Click the style sheet somewhere within a style's declaration, such as body. At the top of the CSS Properties task pane, you'll see the Current Rule heading shows that the properties displayed are for the body style rule. The name of the style sheet is listed to the right of the Current Rule heading for reference.

Tip Seeing the style sheet's name isn't a big deal in this case since you're only working with one style sheet. For some sites you may have multiple style sheets, in which case it's useful to see the name.

Click any displayed property to open a drop-down list providing options. Color thumbnails are one of the most convenient features of the CSS Properties task pane. For example, the body style uses a peach background, as you can see in the CSS Properties.

The style sheet lists the value for the color. Unless you're extremely familiar with color systems, you're not likely going to recognize `rgb(255,204,153)` as a light peach color.

How to... Choose IntelliSense Preferences

You can change program preferences rather than using the default IntelliSense functions to assist in writing CSS, although it is not recommended. The three preferences are quite useful and save time. Choose Tools | Page Editor Options and click IntelliSense to show its tab.

You'll find three options specific to writing and working with CSS:

- **The CSS statement completion in the Auto Pop-up section** Controls the pop-up list display as you write CSS code. It takes a bit of time to get used to working with the lists, but they help make your writing more efficient.
- **The CSS selector closing brace in the Auto Insert section** Inserts the right curly brace (}) in a style declaration automatically. If you are accustomed to hand coding, you may want to deselect this option.
- **The CSS classes and IDs in the Code Hyperlinks section** Hyperlinks styles on a page to their originating CSS. This is a terrific feature, and deselecting it is not recommended. All you have to do is press CTRL and click a style name in a web page to display the style's rule set in the associated style sheet.

Read more about preferences in the section, "Use IntelliSense to Prompt Your Code Writing," in Chapter 5.

Note Read more about using the CSS/Tag Properties task panes in Chapter 5.

Write with IntelliSense

One of the best code-writing features offered in Expression Web 2 is IntelliSense. As you develop a style, an IntelliSense shortcut menu displays offering you completion options. Not only does it make for quick style development, it helps you remember proper terms for properties or values and lists existing items in your style sheet, such as classes or ID names.

Define the Style Rule

Here's an example IntelliSense workflow using an element selector (Figure 7-2). The process is nearly the same with class and ID selectors, aside from having to type the entire selector's name.

Follow these steps to develop a style rule:

1. In Code view, click where you want to start the style.
2. Start to type an HTML element's name and an IntelliSense pop-up listing HTML elements displays.
3. Scroll through the list to the selector you want to use and double-click to insert the selector and close the list.

Note If you use either a class or ID selector, you have to type the full name and the opening curly brace ({) to prompt IntelliSense.

4. Add the opening curly brace ({) for the style, and a property list opens. Scroll to find a property, and double-click to insert it and close the list.
5. Add the punctuation, and another list opens. Scroll to find a value and open a color swatch dialog box or other selection option.

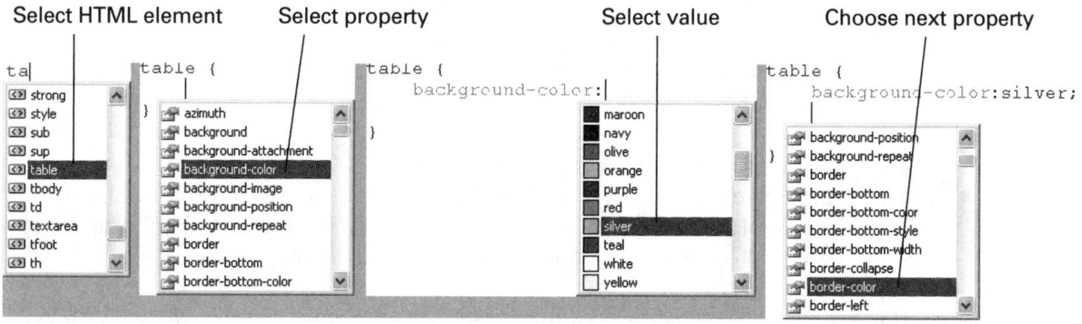

FIGURE 7-2 Take advantage of IntelliSense prompts.

6. Type a semicolon (`;`) when the property is finished. When you start a new line or insert a space, the IntelliSense menu opens again.
7. Repeat adding properties and values until you're finished.

Note IntelliSense works the same way in either external or internal style sheets. If you want to write an inline style, click the end of the element's name and press SPACEBAR to add a space and prompt the IntelliSense menu to open.

Define a Property with Multiple Values

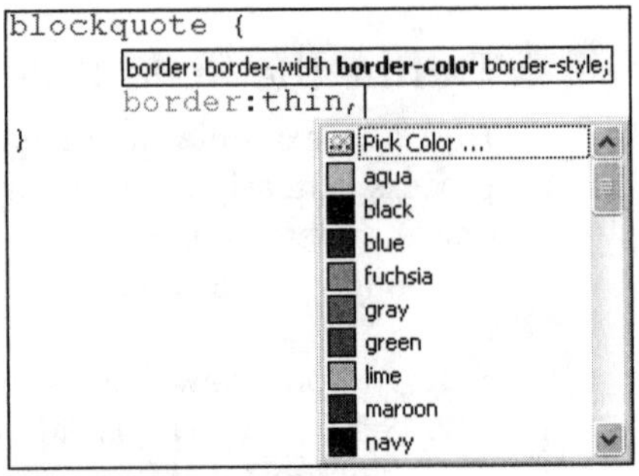

If you choose a property that offers multiple values, such as the `border` property, the components that make up the property are shown in a tooltip. The active property in the pop-up menu is shown in bold in the tooltip.

Double-click to make the selection. The IntelliSense pop-up menu closes; type a comma (`,`) to reopen the tooltip and pop-up menu and continue. Notice the properties in the tooltip shows a semicolon (`;`) at the end of the string identifying how many choices you can make for the particular property. In this `border` example, you can specify three values for the single property.

Handle the Pop-ups

To take advantage of how IntelliSense works, keep these tips in mind when you're writing styles:

- If you don't see an IntelliSense shortcut menu when you want to insert an element, class, ID, property, or value, check your cursor location. It may not be in a usable location.
- There are several actions in the Code view that initiate the IntelliSense feature depending on the part of the style rule you're writing.
- At each stage, use the lists to select a style component, or keep typing to close the list until the next IntelliSense prompt is triggered.
- Once the IntelliSense pop-up displays, you can position the cursor on the page using ENTER or TAB to line up your property-value pairs as you select them.
- If you type outside the IntelliSense pop-up, the box closes. To reopen it, delete the last character you typed on the page and retype.
- To get IntelliSense started, type the first letter of the HTML element (element selector). For an ID selector, type a number sign (#), ID name, and opening curly brace ({); for a class selector, type a period (`.`), class name, and opening curly brace ({) (Figure 7-3).
- In the pop-up, scroll through the list with your mouse, use keyboard arrows, press PAGE DOWN or PAGE UP to move one screen at a time, or type the first letter to move to that part of the list.

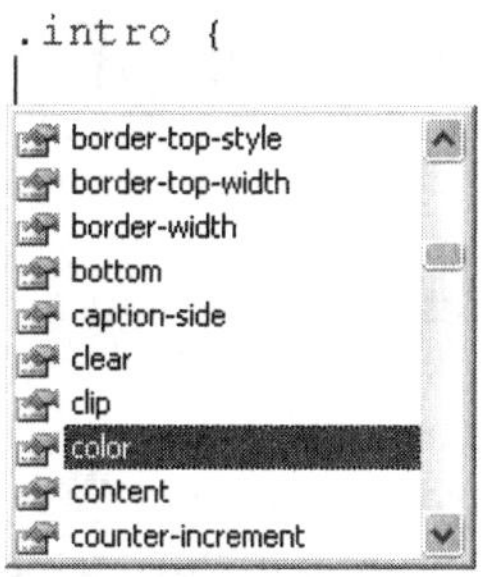

FIGURE 7-3 Type specific content on the page to trigger the IntelliSense feature.

Did You Know?

You Can Write Styles in Shorthand

When designing your own styles, you can either write each property and its value individually, or write an abbreviated syntax called *shorthand CSS*. For example, you can write a style for text using font-style, font-variant, font-weight, font-size, line-height, and font-family properties on separate lines:

```
p.special {
font-style: italic;
font-weight: bold;
font-size: larger;
font-family: Georgia;
}
```

Or, in the shorthand version, list the comma-separated values in a single line, such as:

```
p.special {italic, bold, larger, Georgia;}
```

If you have the same styles defined in multiple locations, such as an embedded style sheet and an external style sheet, watch out for property changes. If you use both short and long syntax formats, omitted properties in a shorthand rule can override properties defined in another rule.

For example, if your shorthand syntax for the <body> tag doesn't include a background color, even if your longhand syntax assigns a color for the background color property, the shorthand may reign supreme and show a default white background.

Write Different Types of Styles

Have you ever seen something on a web page and wondered how it was done? Or would you like to create a specific look on your page but aren't sure where or what to write? If your answer is Yes, this section is for you.

You'll find a reference to the different style categories and information about properties and values important for writing clean and complete CSS. We've added a few style examples to illustrate different CSS categories and properties. You can use the examples to add some punch to your pages.

You can work directly in Code view to write your styles. If you feel more comfortable starting from a prompt, refer to the methods described in Chapter 6.

Note Basic information on using type, font, and block properties and styles isn't included in this chapter. For that information, check out Chapter 2 and Chapter 6.

Start a Paragraph with a Bang

CSS lets you use a *pseudo-element*, the name given to a style sheet selector identifying a specific component of an element. You can use these special selectors to create a drop-cap letter for a paragraph or display the first line of a paragraph differently from the rest. Pseudo-elements are written as:

```
selector:pseudo-element {property: value}
```

Configure the First Line

Use the *first-line* pseudo-element to style the first line of text in a selector, such as a paragraph. You can only use the first-line pseudo-element for block-level elements. For example:

```
p:first-line {color:#0000ff;font-variant:small-caps;}
```

In this example, the browser displays the first line in italics in gray text. The length of the line depends on the size of the browser window.

You can use any of these properties to write a first-line pseudo-element:

background	clear	color
font	letter-spacing	line-height
text-decoration	text-transform	word-spacing
vertical-align (if `float:none` is used)		

Add a Distinct First Letter

Add a special style to the first letter of the text in a selector using the first-letter pseudo-element as in this example:

```
p:first-letter {color:#ff0000; font-size:xx-large;}
```

You can use most of the properties listed for the first-line pseudo-element except word spacing and letter spacing, since you're styling a single letter. In addition, you can use border, float, margin, and padding properties.

Save the Special Effects for Special Paragraphs

Suppose you've faithfully recreated the code in this section for your latest web page development session. When you preview the page, each and every paragraph uses the special styles. To specify a particular paragraph, create a class for it, like this example:

```
p.intro:first-line {font-style:italic; color:#CD5C5C;}
```

When the `intro` style is applied to a paragraph, the first line is italics in medium red.

You can configure the same appearance in a paragraph using separate `<span>` tags to differentiate the first letter or first line, although the first line won't change the number of words using the style as the browser window resizes.

The simplest way to use both ideas in one paragraph is to use the pseudo-element for the first line (written above), and a `<span>` tag and class for the first letter. Like this:

```
span.first {float:left; font-size:200%; line-height:80%; width:0.95em;}
```

Check out the effect in your browser.

Welcome to Cafe Margo!
We are pleased to have you visit our site! Cafe Margo is celebrating its 30th year in operation at our little shop in The Mews. Hundreds of locals pass through our doors each day. We're not sure if it's the smell of coffee wafting through the courtyard, or the smells from our on-site bakery that are such an attraction. It's hard to choose!
On our site, you'll find information about us, our bakery products, daily specials, and even the

Tip You'll have to experiment to make the appearance come together correctly. As the font size is set larger, narrow the width to prevent a gap before the text of the paragraph and lower the line height to keep from pushing the first letter down into the paragraph.

Include Special Background Image Styles

Do you think only of pages when you think of background styles? While you can certainly use an image or color background for your pages, you can also use background properties for styling text, a table, an image, and so on.

Choosing background images and colors are discussed in several locations in previous chapters. There are other properties you can use to add detail and a customized appearance to your page.

Specify Background Repeats

If you've ever seen a page with multiple copies of an image on the background, you've seen the `repeat` property in action.

There are several ways to define background image repeats:

- **`no repeat`** Displays the image once at the beginning of the element, although you can specify its location.
- **`repeat`** Tiles the image horizontally and vertically.
- **`repeat-x` or `repeat-y` values** Display a horizontal or vertical band of images, respectively.

Assign Attachment and Position

You can specify how the background is attached (see Figure 7-4). The default scrolls the background along with the page content. Sometimes you'll see a background on a page, such as a business logo, that stays in position as the content scrolls over it. To create that effect, use `background-attachment:fixed`.

Your background image doesn't have to cover the entire page. Instead, you can define where it is located on the page both vertically and horizontally.

Note If the attachment is defined as `fixed`, the position of the image is relative to the browser window, not to the element.

Here's an example using properties to define a vertical band style of repeat. The `background-position` identifies how far from the left the vertical band displays.

```
{ background-image: url('images/right_bar.png');
background-repeat: repeat-y;
background-position: 88%; }
```

Construct a Horizontal Menu

Horizontal menus are common on web pages, often below the logo and header message. It's simple to create a menu in a one-row table, but it's much more interesting (and challenging) to design the menu using CSS.

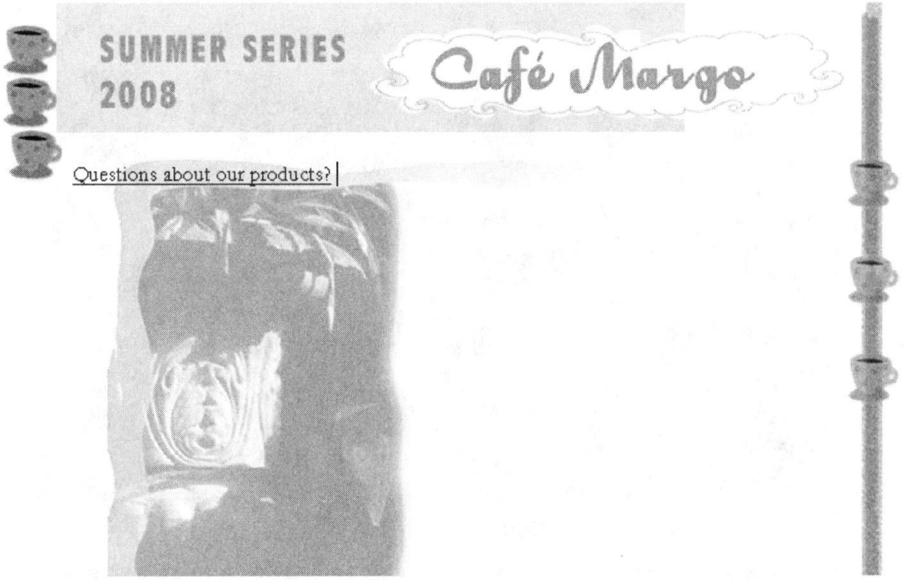

FIGURE 7-4 Place a background into a specific area of the page.

A horizontal menu uses settings from a variety of style property categories (as listed in the Expression Web 2 New Style dialog box), including:

- Box properties
- Border properties
- List style properties

Note Read about using the New Style dialog box in Chapter 6.

Define CSS Box and Border Properties

Box properties define what you'd assume from the name—the edges around a box object, which can be any block element. Border properties define the characteristics of the border edging an element, such as the style, color, and width. Apply settings to individual sides of an element or use the same settings on all sides.

Most of the properties are self-explanatory, such as `width` and `height`, or easy to understand based on a visual model (Figure 7-5).

Padding, Margins, and Borders In Figure 7-5, the edging surrounding the text is the *padding*. Padding is the amount of space between the content and the outer edge, or the space between the content and the border. The *border* is the frame surrounding

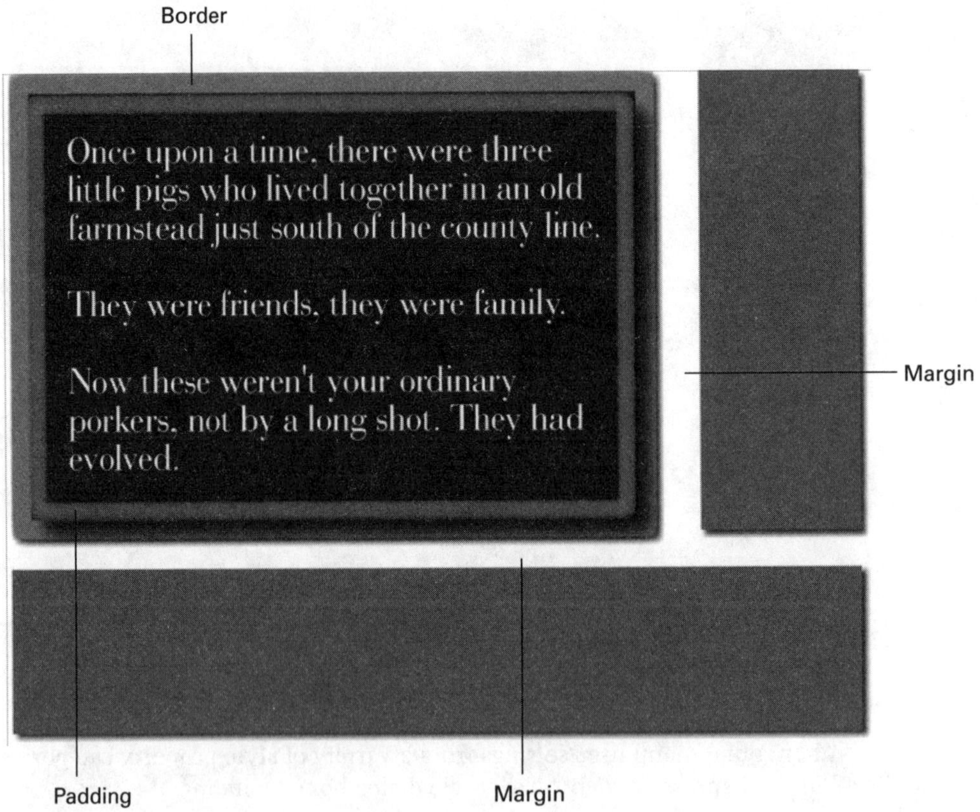

FIGURE 7-5 Specify properties for a boxed object.

an object and its padding. A *margin* is the amount of space between an object and another object. Define the margin's dimensions from the border, or from the margin if your object doesn't use a border.

Note An *outline*, another category of element edging, is a line drawn outside the border edge within the margins. Since outline properties don't display in Internet Explorer, Expression Web 2 doesn't offer their configuration settings in the program.

Float Objects Floats are commonly used to specify the location for items like images or pull quotes. Use a float to define the side where other elements will float around the element. Margins are often set to specify the amount of space left between the object and other content. In this example, the top margin is 10px, while the right and bottom margins are 24px.

On our site, you'll find informat
products
kinds of
you'll fin
question
drop us
and ask
Yum!
Ov
people h
goods. W
cinnamo
of our amazing onion and cheese Dan
about our recipes.

Clear Objects Use the `clear` property to specify a location where floating objects aren't allowed. For example, using the property `clear:left;` prevents any floating objects from displaying to the left of the object.

Configure a List

The List style category specifies the appearance of a list either bulleted or numbered. You can specify a bullet image and define its position or choose not to use a visible character, as in the horizontal menu example coming up.

There are two position options related to placement and wrapping of text. An outside position is *indented* and the text wraps, while an inside position is *outdented* and text wraps to the left margin (Figure 7-6).

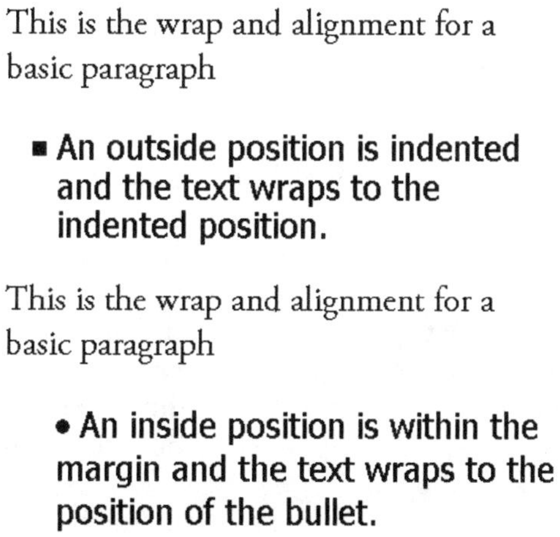

This is the wrap and alignment for a basic paragraph
■ An outside position is indented and the text wraps to the indented position.
This is the wrap and alignment for a basic paragraph
• An inside position is within the margin and the text wraps to the position of the bullet.

FIGURE 7-6 Set indents and outdents for lists.

Bring the Pieces Together

Now you've read about most of the style elements required in a horizontal menu.

Note In the upcoming section "Write Anchor Pseudo-Classes," read about using pseudo-classes to define different link states. In the menu's CSS, you'll see the `a:hover` style, which defines the appearance of the link when your mouse is over the text.

Here's what goes into the menu's CSS:

```
ul {
float:left;
padding:0;
margin-left:10%;
list-style-type:none;
font-family:Georgia,"Garamond Pro",serif;
font-weight:bold;
}

li {
display:inline
}

a {
float:left;
width:7.5em;
padding:0.4em;
text-decoration:none;
color:black;
background-color:#E9E9E9;
border-right:2px solid white;
}

a:hover {
background-color:#FF5050;
color:white;
}
```

There are four styles that make up the menu. Many of the properties are familiar and easy to understand. There are a few properties that you might not be familiar with, or you may not understand why the settings were chosen:

- **`ul` (unordered list)** Specifies the horizontal width of the list, its float status, and the type of bullets, in this case, `list-style-type:none;` or no bullets.
- **`margin-left:10%;`** Moves the menu 10 percent of the page's width from the left edge. As you'll see in the next section, the margin helps the menu placement on the page with the logo.
- **`li` (list item)** Forces a list to a single line using the `display:inline;` property. That way, the usual line breaks before and after items in a list are removed.

- **a (anchor)** This tag for the hyperlink includes many of the properties that give the menu its appearance, including the text and background color, padding, and a right border that shows as a separator between the links. Notice that the style includes the `width:7.5em;` property, which means the width of each link is seven and one half times the width of the font used for the link.
- **`a:hover`** This style defines the color of the link's text and background when you move the mouse over it.

Attach the Styles

When the style sheet is attached to the HTML page, the links are placed in an unordered list following the logo image, written as:

```
<img src="images/cafe_logo.png" alt="logo for cafe margo" />
<ul>
<li><a href="#">Home</a></li>
<li><a href="#">About Us</a></li>
<li><a href="#">The Bakery</a></li>
<li><a href="#">Ingredients</a></li>
<li><a href="#">Specials</a></li>
</ul>
```

On the web page, the menu and logo align well horizontally. Moving the mouse over a link shows the `a:hover` background and text color (Figure 7-7).

Customize Links without Writing JavaScript

A basic hyperlink is just that—basic. The default link shows as underlined blue text; a visited link shows as underlined maroon text. If you've wondered about links on pages that look very customized, they're either scripted links or use pseudo-classes.

The previous example showed one pseudo-class for the `a:hover` state—when the user mouses over the link, the background and text change color; moving the mouse away from the link returns it to its default text and background.

FIGURE 7-7 Add a horizontal menu across the top of a web page.

By far the simplest way to change link appearances on your site is using an external style sheet and attaching it to your pages.

Tip For a single page using specialized layouts different from the rest of your site, either build a separate external style sheet, or use an internal style sheet on that page. If you have a large site and use several layouts and schemes, consider building separate style sheets to keep the different sections organized.

Write Anchor Pseudo-Classes

An *anchor*, or hyperlink, on a page has several states based on the response to mouse actions. Style each of the four mouse responses using a pseudo-class in this order:

1. An unvisited link as it appears on the page initially, written as `a:link`
2. A link that has been visited during the current browser session, written as `a:visited`
3. A link responding to a mouse in its location, written as `a:hover`
4. A link clicked on the page, written as `a:active`

You don't need to use all link states all the time. For example, you might want to use just an `a:hover` pseudo-class. However, you must use the sequence of styles in the order listed here. Otherwise, you won't see the links' styling on the web page.

Combining Link States and Classes

You can combine a pseudo-class with a CSS class. In the example, the menu on the home page works on other pages of the site in a slightly different form when separate classes are defined.

A class named `biz`, written for the menu on the home page and other business-related pages, uses this style:

```
a.biz {
    float:left;
    width:7.5em;
    padding:0.4em;
    text-decoration:none;
    color:black;
    background-color:#E9E9E9;
    border-right:2px solid white;
    margin-left:10%;
}
```

Note You can see an example of the style's output in Figure 7-7. The menu's styles were reconstructed slightly to use in multiple locations. For more, read the sidebar "Plan Ahead to Simplify Writing Styles."

Another class, named bakery, written for the menu on the food-related pages, uses this style:

```
a.bakery {
   float:left;
   width:7.5em;
   padding:0.4em;
   text-decoration:none;
   color:#663300;
   background-color:#CCFF66;
   border-right:2px solid white;
   clear:right;
   margin-bottom: 20px;
}
```

On the web pages, the pseudo-classes appear the same but the basic menu looks slightly different, as you see here. Although you don't see the menu in color on this page, on the web page the menu using the a.bakery class uses brown text on a green background as the default for the menu.

All our bakery products are produced on-site daily. As such, we have control over
ingredients that go into each and every delicious product you'll find on our shelves and
Pastry
Danish
Cookies
Pies
Bakery Products

The pseudo-class styles are used regardless of the class specified for the <a> tag, so you'll see the same hover and visited links colors.

How to... Plan Ahead to Simplify Writing Styles

The examples in this section on pseudo-classes are a case in point for good planning. If you refer to the earlier description of the <a> tag's style, you'll recall there are properties setting the margin to align better with the logo on the web page. That's fine if that's the only type of <a> tag in use.

But what if there are multiple anchor styles combined with pseudo-classes? Well, the styles need changing, and you may need a <div> tag to wrap another menu to make sure the other menu looks good on its page.

Or, you can plan ahead. For the example web site, rather than including properties like margins in the ul style, include items that can pertain to a particular circumstance (like the alignment with the logo) in a class specific to that menu location.

Design Quick Column Layouts

If you do an impromptu survey of some random web sites, you'll find a strong move toward positioning content in columns on pages. In the past, columnar page layouts were usually controlled by placing the contents in tables. To comply with current standards, page layouts are accomplished using `<div>` tags and setting properties such as margins and floats to make everything align properly.

Lay Out Pages with Positioning Properties

Designing a page using resizable columns takes time. Fortunately, Expression Web 2 offers a series of different columnar layouts you can use as a starting point for your web site's development.

Select the Layout

Follow these steps to start a CSS layout:

1. Choose File | New | Page to open the New dialog box, displaying the Page tab.
2. Click CSS Layouts to show a list of options, as well as a short description and a preview. As you see here, there are nine choices.

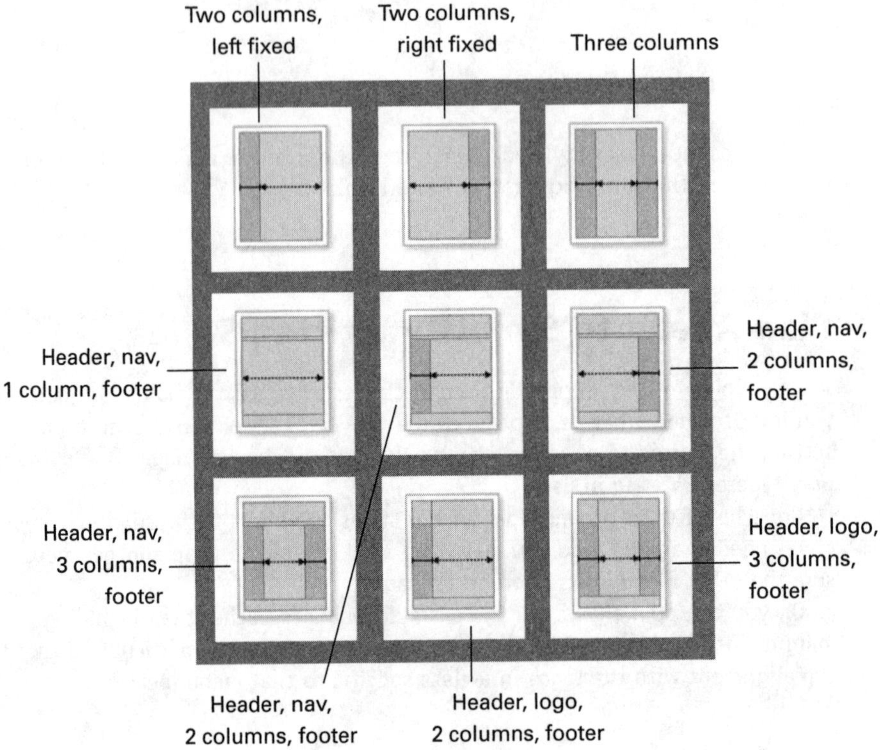

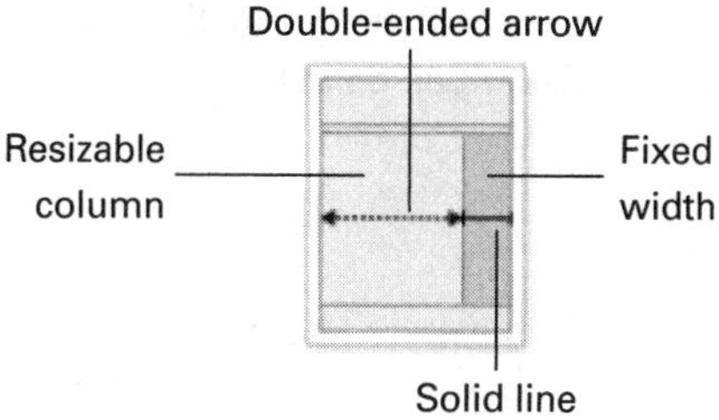

FIGURE 7-8 Preview the features for each page layout option.

3. Choose an option closest to your planned page design. As you click through the list, you'll notice the previews share some common features (Figure 7-8). Fixed-width columns are darker gray than resizable columns and show a solid line as opposed to the double-ended arrow shown on a resizable column.

Note All automatic resize windows (those shown in light gray) specify a minimum width of 600px. The header and footer areas aren't resizable.

4. Click OK to close the New dialog box. You'll see two new files: an HTML web page and a corresponding CSS page. The example layout uses the *Header,nav, 2columns,footer* option.
5. Choose View | Visual Aids to open the submenu. Select options to display content areas on the page, including Show, Block Selection, Visible Borders, and Empty Containers. Select Margins and Padding if you intend to customize the page layout further.
6. Choose View | Formatting Marks and select Aligned Elements and Tag Marks. On the page, you'll see the structure of the <div> tags, as well as an indicator identifying the right-aligned `div#right_col`.

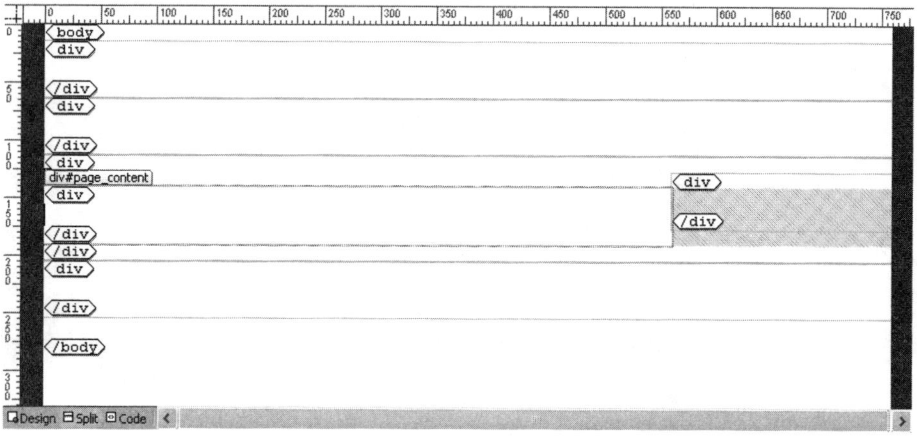

7. Save the HTML and CSS files.

Note When you save the style sheet, manually choose CSS from the Save As Type drop-down list, as the dialog box defaults to saving files as web pages.

Review the CSS

Expression Web 2 generates a style sheet automatically for the layout. The style sheet includes a style for each <div> created, as well as one for the <body>. Figure 7-9 shows the CSS and inserted comments for the page.

```
/* The browser styles include 8px margins;
set to 0 for precise layout control */
body {
    margin: 0;
    padding: 0;
}

/* Add properties as you develop your site */
#masthead {
}

/* The top nav div is unstyled as well */
#top_nav {
}

/* The container wraps the next two styles, and
ensures a mimimum amount of page content
displays regardless of browser window size */
#container {
    min-width: 600px;
}

/* The right column aligns with the right side
of the page, and has a constant width*/
#right_col {
    width: 200px;
    float: right;
}

/* Setting the right margin allows for proper
display of the right column */
#page_content {
    margin-right: 200px;
}

/* The clear property prevents the right column
from extending into the footer so it can extend
across the page  */
#footer {
    clear: both;
}
```

FIGURE 7-9 The layout includes a style sheet.

Specify Precise Positions and Display Using CSS

Use positioning properties to specify content positioning and display on the web page. Expression Web 2 positioning styles include position type, z-index, and placement on the page.

Position Objects Exactly

The default positioning for content on a web page is `position:static`. By default, the content flows along with the text and other content on the page.

Did You Know?

You Can Make It Easier to View the Blank Layout Page

Even showing tag marks and visual aids on the HTML page using the multiple `<div>` layout isn't simple to view. Take a minute to define the layout more clearly, at least until you add your page content.

There are different ways to select the `<div>` tags and then alter their corresponding styles. You can scroll through your CSS page, select the existing color, and then replace it with another color number. Or, you can use one of the Expression Web 2 task panes for quicker style updates.

Here's the simplest way to make similar changes to a batch of styles:

1. Right-click the style's name in the Apply Styles or Manage Styles task panes to open the shortcut menu. Choose Modify Style to open the dialog box.
2. Click Background from the category list at the left of the Modify Style dialog box. Then click the Background-color drop-down arrow and select a color, or click the blank swatch to the right of the drop-down arrow and select a color from the More Colors dialog box (click OK to close the dialog box).
3. Click Apply to set the color for the style.
4. In the Selector field at the top of the dialog box, type the name for the next style.

Note As the styles are IDs, you won't find them listed in the Selector drop-down list.

5. Set the background color and then click Apply. Don't click OK or the dialog box will close. You should change all the styles first before ending the task.
6. Repeat for as many selectors as you need to modify. Finally, click OK to close the dialog box.

(Continued)

Did You Know?

In one task, you've made changes to multiple styles and saved time and mouse clicks. As you see, it's simple to identify the components on the page.

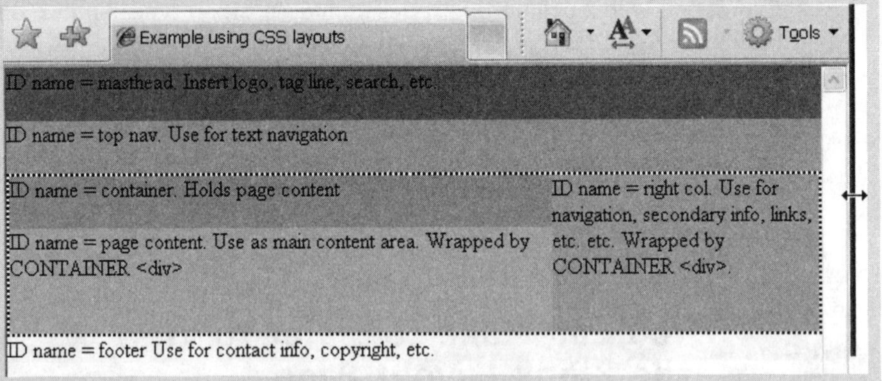

Tip

When you use <div> tags that are parents to nested <div> tags, such as the page contents and right column in the example, add a border to the parent tag as well as a colored background. This way, when you're setting margins and padding you'll have a better indication of the layout when you see a border.

There are three more properties for precise content placement, including:

- **Absolute positioning** places the content relative to the upper-left corner of the page or relative to the coordinates of an absolutely or relatively positioned parent.
- **Relative positioning** places the content using coordinates relative to the content block's position in the text flow of the page.
- **Fixed positioning** places the content block using coordinates relative to the top left corner of the page. The page content scrolls, while the content block remains stationary. You'll often see fixed positioning for background images such as logos.

Stack Objects Using Z-index

The z-index refers to a 3D coordinate that defines the sequence that a page's content is layered, also called its stacking order. The higher the z-index number (or Layer number), the higher the element in the stacking order. Inversely, the lower the z-index (or Layer number), the lower the element in the stacking order, which can be a negative number. For example, in Figure 7-10, the image of the cup has a z-index of 2, shown as Layer 2, and the courtyard image is on Layer 1.

Note

You'll use z-index as part of the code for defining layers in Chapter 8.

FIGURE 7-10 Stacked layers using absolute positions.

Did You Know?

There Are Numerous Ways to Specify a Size

The default unit for location and size is pixels (px) since that's how web content on a screen is measured. Whether pixels or other units, the abbreviation for the unit must follow the value without a space.

- `cm` (centimeters), `mm` (millimeters), and `in` (inches) are basic units of measurement used in everyday activities.
- `em` (ems) refers to the size of the letter *M* in a font. `Em` is a relative measurement and often used in web pages.
- `ex` (exes) refers to the height of a lowercase *x* in a font. Use `ex` to set the size of content based on the size of surrounding content. For example, in a list bullet, you could use the `height: 0.5ex` property to show the bullet at half the size of the text.

(Continued)

Did You Know?

- `pc` (picas) are printing measurements; 6pc=1in.
- `pt` (points) are printing measurements; 72pt=1in.
- `%` (percentage) is a relative measurement based on the parent's value. For example, tables are often sized as a percentage of the page's width.

Note There's one exception to the unit of measurement rule: If the value is 0, you don't need to specify a unit, since 0 is 0 whether you're describing millimeters or miles.

Specify Content Placement

You can define a content block's size and location. However, size values are overridden by the actual size of the content. Refer to the sidebar "There Are Numerous Ways to Specify a Size" for information on choosing sizing values.

Generate CSS Reports

As part of your site building process, Expression Web 2 offers a number of CSS reports pertaining to the CSS in your web site. The reports deal with links, style compatibility, errors, and usage.

If your site is simple—for example, it uses one external style sheet and a few inline styles—running reports helps to confirm that all is well. On the other hand, if you've got several external style sheets as well as inline styles and embedded style sheets, tracking down an error in a paragraph style can be a time-consuming process.

Note Read about the Compatibility task pane in Chapter 5 in the section, "Check for Compatibility Issues."

Check Your Styles' Locations

Style Sheet Links is a site report shown in the Reports view of the Web Site tab. The report lists the web pages in your web site that either import or link to an external cascading style sheet. If you're using multiple style sheets, you'll appreciate this report option!

To run a report, choose Site | Reports | Shared Content | Style Sheet Links. You'll see a list of the pages in your site, their titles, and style sheet links (Figure 7-11).

Tip You can easily make changes to a page's title and style sheet link directly from the report window. Double-click the field on a page's row of the report to open the page at the position where the content is located. When you've made your change, click the Web Site tab to return to the Reports view.

Name ▼	Title ▼	Style Sheet Links ▼	In ... ▼
bakery info.html	Untitled 0	cafe_margo01.css	
experiments.html	Untitled 1	cafe_margo01.css	
contact_us.html	About Us: Cafe Margo	cafe_margo01.css	
specials.html	Bakery Specials - Sp...	cafe_margo01.css	
summer.html	Summer specials at ...	cafe_margo01.css	
default.html	default.html	cafe_margo01.css	
ingredient list.html	Bakery-Ingredient Lists	cafe_margo01.css, horizontal ...	
CSS_layout_eg.html	Example using CSS l...	CSS_layout_eg.css	
horizontal menu.html	Home	horizontal menu.css	
demo_workflow.html	After you click the link		
showandtell.html	Untitled 1		images...

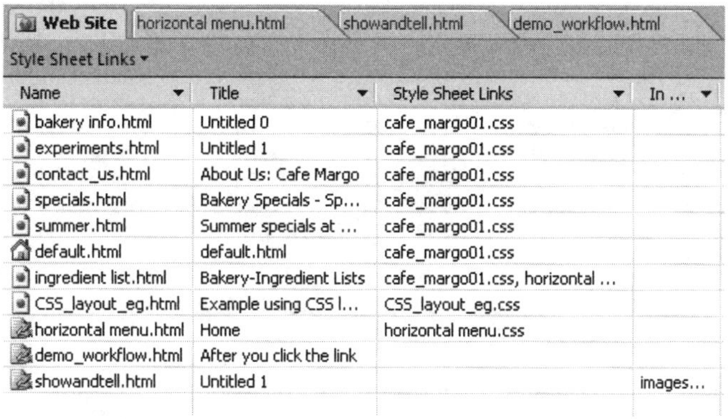

FIGURE 7-11 Generate reports on the style sheets used in your site.

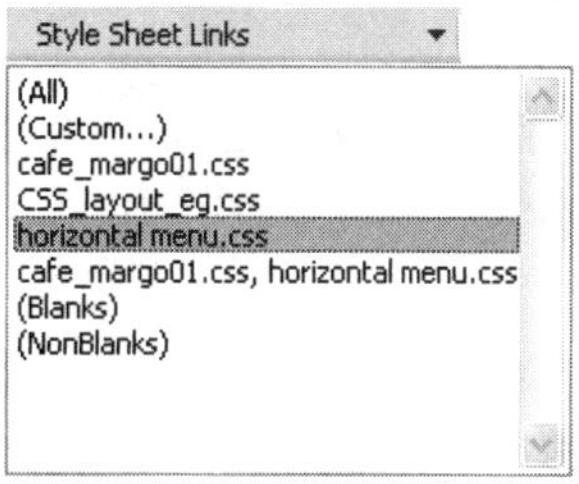

If your site is large, be sure to take advantage of the Style Sheet Links report's filter feature. To use it, click any column heading's arrow to display a list of options. You'll find each list starts with (*All*), which is the default display that shows all the returns. Next is (*Custom...*), which lets you customize the filter, followed by a list of the entries for that column.

Click the item to use for filtering, and the rest of the report's returns are hidden. Click the column heading again and click All to remove the filter.

CSS Reports

When you're finishing work on a site (even if only for the day), check for errors and style usage by running the CSS Errors and CSS Usage Reports. To generate either type of report, follow these steps:

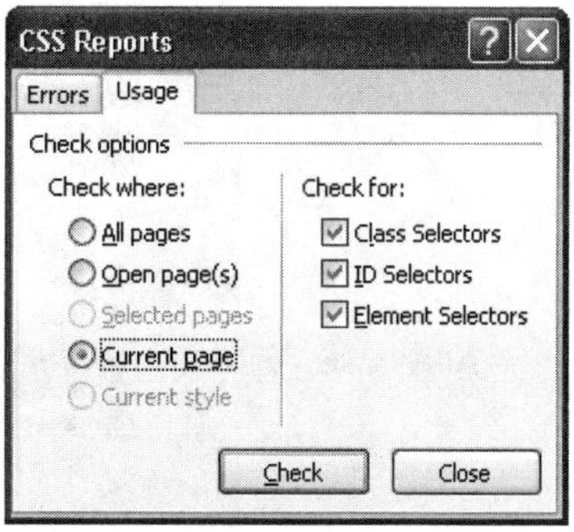

1. Choose Task Panes | CSS Reports to open the CSS Reports task pane horizontally below the Editing window. Click the green menu arrow at the upper left of the task pane to open the CSS Reports dialog box shown here.
 - Click Errors to show the CSS Errors Report options. Specify where to check and what errors to look for.
 - Click Usage to show the CSS Usage Report options. Specify where to check and what selectors to check for.

2. Click Check to close the dialog box and run the test. The results are shown in the CSS Reports task pane.

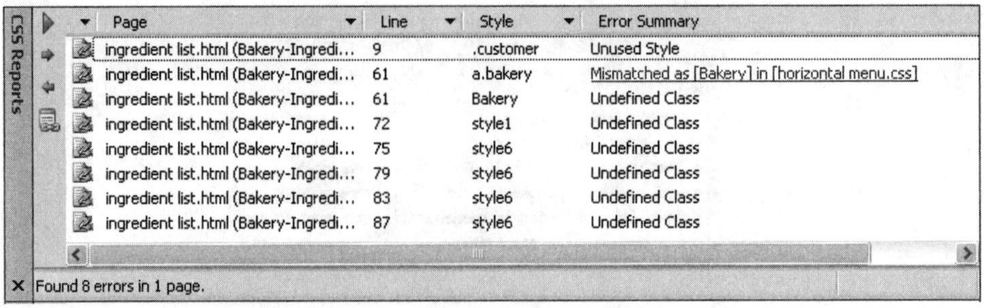

CSS Reports
Page
Line
Style
Error Summary
ingredient list.html (Bakery-Ingredi... 9 .customer Unused Style
ingredient list.html (Bakery-Ingredi... 61 a.bakery Mismatched as [Bakery] in [horizontal menu.css]
ingredient list.html (Bakery-Ingredi... 61 Bakery Undefined Class
ingredient list.html (Bakery-Ingredi... 72 style1 Undefined Class
ingredient list.html (Bakery-Ingredi... 75 style6 Undefined Class
ingredient list.html (Bakery-Ingredi... 79 style6 Undefined Class
ingredient list.html (Bakery-Ingredi... 83 style6 Undefined Class
ingredient list.html (Bakery-Ingredi... 87 style6 Undefined Class
Found 8 errors in 1 page.

FIGURE 7-12 Track style errors from the report.

Check for Errors

Use the CSS Errors Report to pinpoint a number of style and style sheet features, including:

- **Unused Styles** Class selectors referenced in a web page that aren't defined in a style sheet
- **Undefined Classes** Class, ID, and element selectors defined in a style sheet and not used in your web site
- **Mismatched Cases** Mismatched case use in Class and ID selectors. As shown in Figure 7-12, using a class named `bakery` in the style sheet and referencing it as `Bakery` in the web page returns the error. Click a hyperlink to show the source of the style in your style sheet.

Check for Style Usage

Like the CSS Errors Report, the CSS Usage Report displays in the CSS Reports task pane. Use this report to track what styles are used where. The report shows a list of CSS selectors, which pages use the styles, and where the style rules are located.

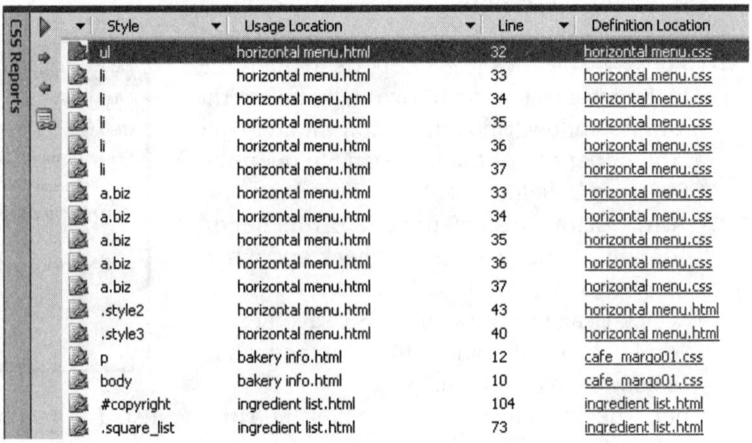

CSS Reports
Style
Usage Location
Line
Definition Location
ul horizontal menu.html 32 horizontal menu.css
li horizontal menu.html 33 horizontal menu.css
li horizontal menu.html 34 horizontal menu.css
li horizontal menu.html 35 horizontal menu.css
li horizontal menu.html 36 horizontal menu.css
li horizontal menu.html 37 horizontal menu.css
a.biz horizontal menu.html 33 horizontal menu.css
a.biz horizontal menu.html 34 horizontal menu.css
a.biz horizontal menu.html 35 horizontal menu.css
a.biz horizontal menu.html 36 horizontal menu.css
a.biz horizontal menu.html 37 horizontal menu.css
.style2 horizontal menu.html 43 horizontal menu.html
.style3 horizontal menu.html 40 horizontal menu.html
p bakery info.html 12 cafe_margo01.css
body bakery info.html 10 cafe_margo01.css
#copyright ingredient list.html 104 ingredient list.html
.square_list ingredient list.html 73 ingredient list.html

Note Most of the report's contents are self-explanatory, with the possible exception of the Status column, where you'll find an icon identifying the type of file containing an error and its status.

Two of the report's results let you track content:

- Double-click a row to open the file containing the style reference listed in the Usage Location column. You can double-click anywhere except over the Definition Location column.
- Click the file name in the Definition Location column to open the referenced style sheet.

Working with the Results

It's all well and good to see a list of issues, but time-consuming to flip back and forth between the report and the web pages or style sheets containing errors. Fortunately, you can access a number of commands from a shortcut menu, accessible when you right-click a row in either the CSS Errors or CSS Usage Reports.

Choose from these options:

- Click Go to Page to open the web page and highlight the issue or style on the page (Figure 7-13).
- Select the files you want to track down in the report results and choose Select Resulting Files in Folder List from the shortcut menu to highlight the files in the Folder List task pane.
- While you can't export a formatted file from Expression Web 2, you can copy results to reuse elsewhere, such as a task list. Select the rows to copy, and choose Copy Results from the shortcut menu.

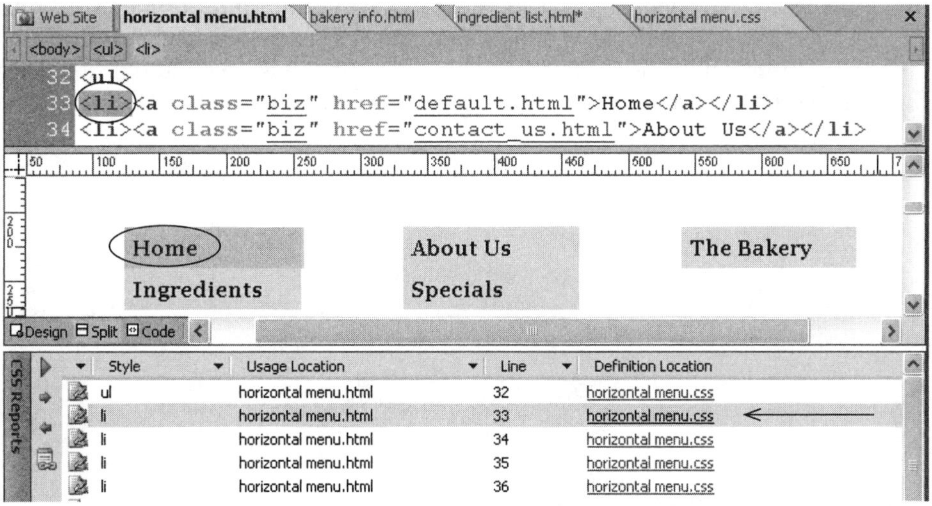

FIGURE 7-13 View the source of an error or a style's location automatically.

Summary

From adding a simple background color to the page to stacking several images for a composition using positioning properties, Cascading Style Sheets bring your web pages to life. In this chapter, you learned about writing styles yourself. Coding CSS isn't for everyone, although it's important to have some familiarity with the structure of a page to help plan and create pages that look and function correctly.

Expression Web 2 offers IntelliSense for CSS, which is a terrific tool that provides prompts as you write styles. The feature offers a list of possible rules, shows you properties, and then offers a selection of values. You can even write a shorthand version of a style using IntelliSense.

Much of this chapter focused on using different categories of styles to create specific page elements that are popular in web pages. You learned how pseudo-elements might add interest by inserting a special first letter or first line style. You also saw how you could specify the precise location for an element on the background of a page—no more simple tiled image backgrounds for you!

You discovered how to design a horizontal menu, which is another popular style feature. The menu is constructed using a combination of a list, links, and pseudo-classes for the link tags. The menu appears quite active, although there isn't any JavaScript involved.

Positioning is an important aspect of CSS, as you learned in the chapter. Expression Web 2 offers a number of column layouts to use for assigning page areas to different features and functions. The layouts are easily customizable for whatever your particular site's requirements may be.

Finally, you learned how to create different CSS-related reports. In addition to locating styles, you checked out error and usage reports.

Part III is up next. There you'll see how to add a number of different types of content and structure ranging from tables to templates, JavaScript to Silverlight.

Be sure to check out the Spotlight project in the center of the book. You'll find a web site design project for Café Margo, the site used to produce some of the examples and images in the book. The Spotlight shows you how to build the site, design the structure using a CSS column layout, and then build a variety of styles to customize the pages.

PART III

Give Your Site Structure and Pizzazz

Now that you know the basics of creating web pages, we're going to bring it together. In Part III, we'll talk about the tools that Expression Web 2 offers to give your web applications consistency. The consistency is more than just the visual appearance. It's also things such as consistent navigation elements. This part talks about techniques that will not only give you consistency, but save you time.

Expression lets you easily add JavaScript behaviors. This provides functionality that ranges from opening custom windows to checking for required form data to fancy image processing. You can also extend it way beyond the basics that Expression provides by adding your own custom code.

You'll also learn about advanced techniques that make your applications sizzle. These include using media such as MP3, WMA, and Flash files. With these additional items, you can take your web application into a whole new realm of richness.

8

Lay Out Pages with Dynamic Web Templates and Layers

HOW TO...

- Create dynamic web templates
- Attach dynamic web templates
- Create real-life web sites with dynamic web templates
- Use free dynamic web templates
- Create layers
- Use layers

In this chapter, we'll talk about saving you time, giving your web site consistency, and giving you more flexibility. Dynamic web templates (DWTs) can save you time by providing a way to easily duplicate work in the future. If you spend sufficient time to create a dynamic web template that can be used as a framework for later pages, then when you create the later pages you may save a significant amount of time. If it's your web page, it's nice to save time. But if you are working on web sites for which you charge by the hour, then saving time will make your services much more competitive since you can charge less.

Layers also give you the ability to save time, but they give you an even bigger advantage than the time saving: greater flexibility. Layers are components that you create and can use over. They can also be placed anywhere in the rendered part of your HTML document. So a reminder in the lower right corner on one page can be the same reminder in the lower left corner of another page.

Web page consistency is an extremely important goal. It gives users a homogenous experience. If your pages fluctuate wildly, then users can become confused or disoriented. In the early days of web development, page inconsistency was fairly common. That's because everyone wanted to try all of the new techniques they had learned.

We had an independent study student once who turned in an assignment that she was very excited about. She spent a lot of time on it and thought it was great. But each page was totally different. It didn't glue together. The entire web site was so disturbing that if we found it on the Web we would not have looked at more than three or four pages before leaving for good.

Create Dynamic Web Templates

Dynamic web templates give you the ability to easily keep all of your pages looking the same. With DWTs, you can create one page that sets the standard for all of your other pages. It can include a color scheme, navigation selectors, copyright information, contact information, and anything else that must remain consistent. All of your other pages can then inherit the work that you did on the DWT.

There are two ways to create dynamic templates: by creating a blank dynamic template and by saving an HTML file as a dynamic template. We'll cover both methods because they are both useful in different situations.

Create Blank Dynamic Templates

Creating a blank dynamic template is easy. These steps walk you through the process and adding an editable region. Editable regions are the ones that the attached pages can edit. Noneditable regions are the HTML areas that are only edited in the DTW and not in the attached pages.

1. From the File menu, select New Page. A dialog box will appear as shown in Figure 8-1.
2. Select Dynamic Web Template and click OK.
3. To make working with dynamic templates simpler, make sure that the Dynamic Web Template toolbar is opened. (If it is not, select Dynamic Web Template from the Toolbars submenu in the View menu.)

Did You Know?

You Should Enable Metadata

Expression Web uses metadata to manage interpage relationships. This includes the relationships between DWTs and the attached pages. Before using DWTs in Expression, you should make sure that metadata is enabled. On the Site menu, choose Site Settings. When the Site Settings dialog box appears, click on the General tab. The Manage the Website Using Hidden Metadata Files check box must be selected in order for Expression to use metadata to manage the relationships.

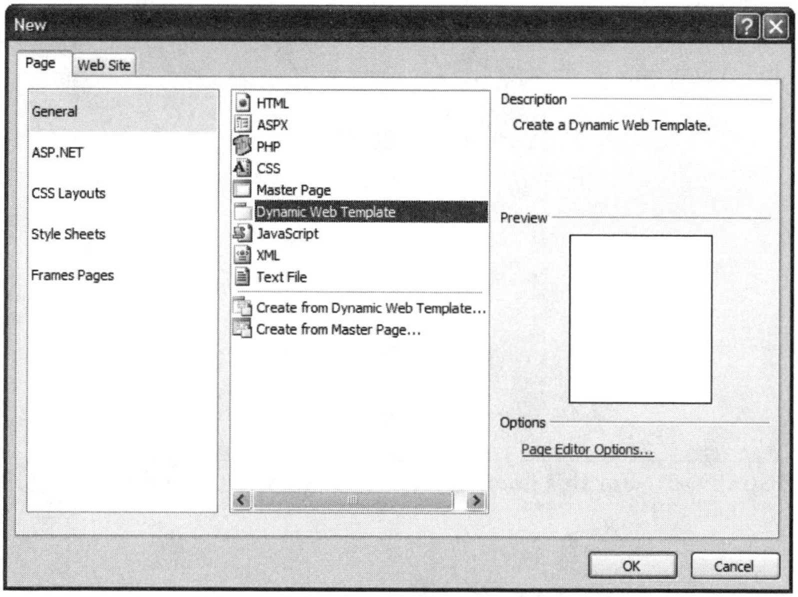

FIGURE 8-1 You can create a new dynamic template from the New dialog.

4. By default, Expression creates editable body and editable title regions.
5. Make sure that you are in Design view.
6. Click the mouse below the editable body region.
7. Type the word **TEST** and it will be part of a newly added paragraph.
8. In the Dynamic Web Template toolbar, click the Manage Editable Regions button as indicated in Figure 8-2. The Editable Regions dialog appears.
9. Enter **TESTREGION** in the Region Name field as shown in Figure 8-3.
10. When you save the file, it will be saved with a .dwt extension.

We'll talk more about using DWTs later in this chapter in the section entitled "Use Dynamic Web Templates." After that, several real-life examples are created in the section "Create Real-Life Web Sites with Dynamic Web Templates."

FIGURE 8-2 The Manage Editable Regions button

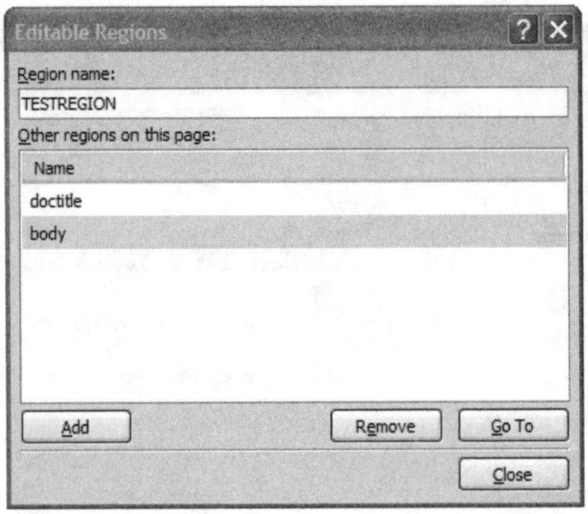

FIGURE 8-3 For this example, name the new region TESTREGION.

Convert HTML Documents to Dynamic Web Templates

You can convert any HTML page to a DWT. This is helpful when you have HTML pages that already exist and you want to use them as a template for a web site. To create a DWT from an HTML page, follow these steps:

1. Open the HTML page that you want to turn into a DWT.
2. Select the object that you want to be an editable region.
3. Click on the Dynamic Web Template toolbar and click the Manage Editable Regions button.
4. You will be prompted to save the HTML document as a Dynamic Web Template as shown in Figure 8-4.
5. Click Yes, and a file selector dialog will appear in which you can save the HTML file as a DWT.
6. The Editable Regions dialog box will appear and allow you to create an editable region in the template.

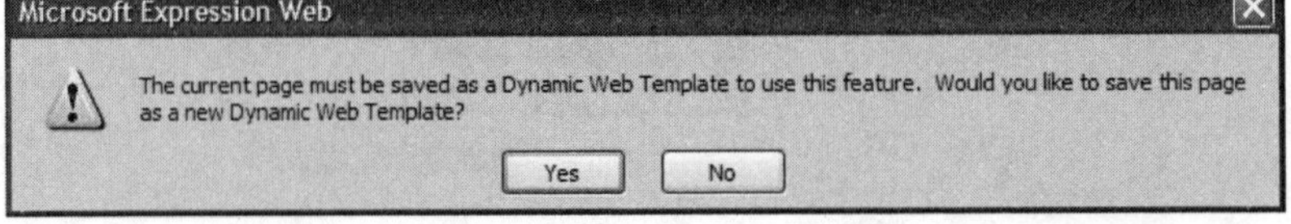

FIGURE 8-4 You will be prompted to save the HTML file as a DWT file.

Use Dynamic Web Templates

Once you have your DWTs created, you can use them. It's a simple process—all you need to do is attach the template to any HTML files that you want to conform to the template.

Let's say that you are getting ready to create a web site with ten pages. You might want to start by creating a DWT on which the pages will be based. You could then create ten HTML pages and attach the DWT to them.

There's an example DWT file that's posted on the Chapter 8 page at http://rickleinecker.com/HTDE/Chapter8.aspx and also posted on www.mhprofessional.com. The file is named example1.dwt. Follow these steps to use the file as a template for HTML files.

1. Download Example1.dwt from the Chapter 8 page.
2. Save Example1.dwt into your web directory.
3. Open Example1.dwt from Expression Web.
4. Look at the file in Code view and notice that there are two editable regions: one named doctitle and one named body. These are the only two regions that can be edited.
5. Go back to Design view.
6. Create an HTML file.
7. Save the newly created HTML file as Example1.html.
8. From the Format menu, select Dynamic Web Template | Attach Dynamic Web Template. The Attach Dynamic Web Template file selector appears, as shown in Figure 8-5.

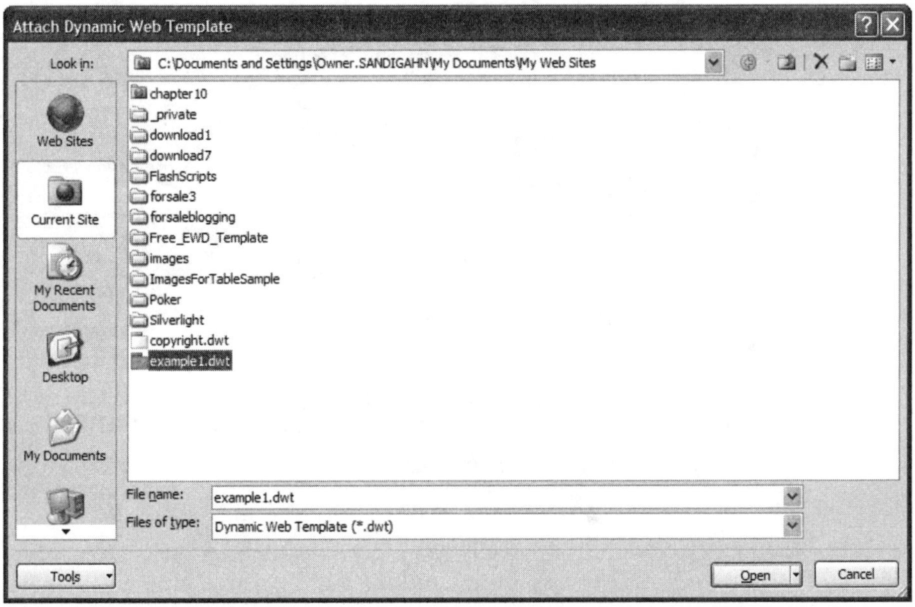

FIGURE 8-5 You must select the DWT that you want to attach.

9. Choose Example1.dwt and click Open.
10. You will get a notification that the file has been updated.

You will notice that the Example1.html file looks almost identical to the Example1.dwt file. Also notice that the mouse cursor is only enabled to indicate editing in the middle section, where the editable region is named body. Using Design view, you won't be able to edit anything except the body region in the middle as shown in Figure 8-6.

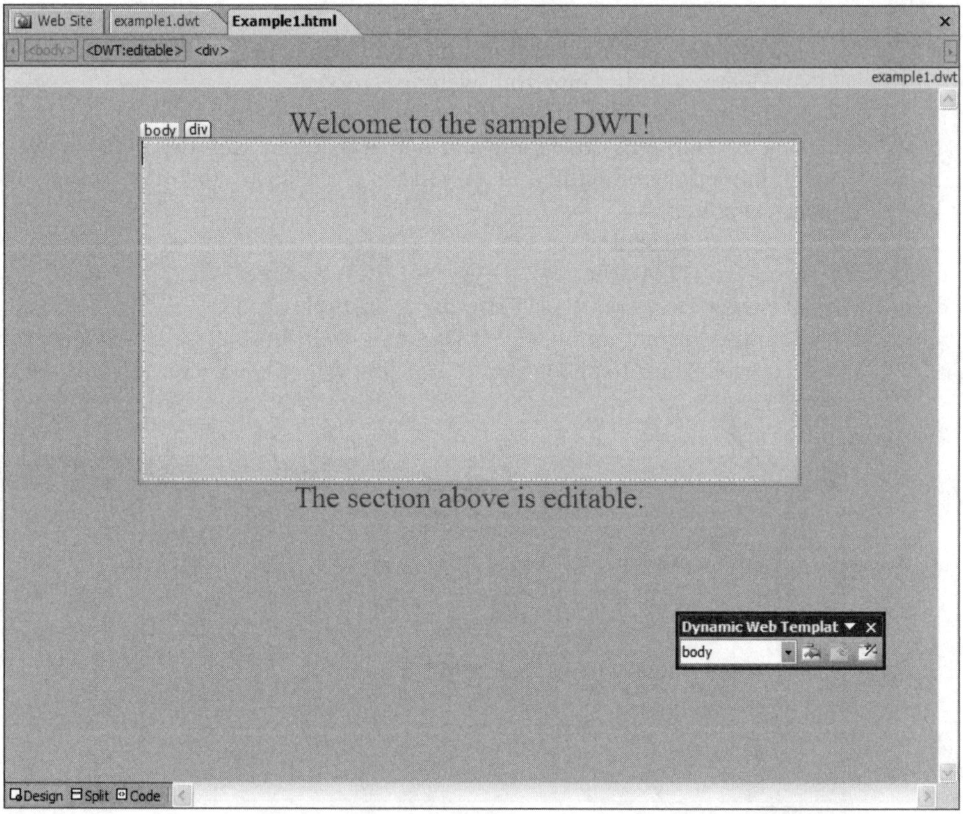

FIGURE 8-6 Only the center of this page is editable once the DWT file is attached.

Cafe Margo: You Can Almost Smell the Coffee

Cafe Margo is a well-established local bakery and coffeehouse, offering a variety of drinks and in-store baked goods. The cafe is a family-owned business, currently managed by Kelly Banks, granddaughter of the original owner. In her three years as manager, Kelly has introduced new bakery items and started offering special events like summer coffeehouse entertainment.

Kelly decides it's time to take their business online. She is a business person, not a programmer or web designer, and she turns to Expression Web 2 as her tool of choice. Kelly is an experienced Microsoft Office user and likes that some of the features are already familiar to her.

Tackling Phase 1

Kelly intends to build the web site in phases. To start, she needs to produce an example of the pages and content to illustrate the site to her family. In the sample phase, she'll design the structure for the site and its appearance to display basic information about the business.

Although she intends the prototype to be a sample, she doesn't want to repeat work later, and she'll take advantage of some Expression Web 2 features that help design a site more efficiently. Kelly decides the first stage includes:

1. Designing the structure of the pages using a CSS Layout option.
2. Creating folders and pages to hold the web site's contents.
3. Starting, naming, and saving the web pages.
4. Importing and placing images on the pages.
5. Placing imported content and creating new content for the pages.
6. Adding basic styles using Design view and task panes.
7. Tweaking and customizing styles in Code view.

The Start

As you learn in the sidebar below, you'll find the files to do this project on the McGraw-Hill web site. The first folder is named cafeR and contains the "raw" files, including images, HTML, basic CSS files, and source text files.

In this folder, you'll find these items:

- A subfolder named images, containing the images used in the site's pages.
- menu.css, a style sheet used for the horizontal menus in the site.

How To...

Build the Site Yourself

The site in this Spotlight is fictitious. If you like, you can download the files used to construct the Spotlight project and recreate it yourself. There are two sets of files available. For convenience, both the raw and finished sets of files contain duplicate sets of images. That way, you won't have to worry about changing references.

Here's what you do to find the project files. First, go to http://www.mhprofessional.com/. On the main page, click Computing to open the McGraw-Hill Professional page. Scroll down the page to the Downloads link at the left of the page. Click Downloads Section to open a list of books. Scroll down the list, or click G-I in the index to find the book's title.

The site is by no means complete, as you'll read in the sidebar "There's a Long Way to Go" at the end of the chapter. Rather, it illustrates how to start a site using a variety of features and workflow options in Expression Web 2.

- cafe.text, the text used on the pages.
- cafe_margo.css, the partially completed style sheet for the site.

The Finish

The second folder contains the finished HTML and CSS pages along with a duplicate image set. The second folder, named cafeF, contains the finished site. In this folder, you'll find:

- The images subfolder, containing the site's images
- cafe_margo.css and menu.css style sheets
- default.html, bakery.html, and summer.html web pages
- cafe.txt, the original text file

> **NOTE**
>
> If you start the site from scratch, Expression Web 2 recreates the metadata folders and contents automatically.

The Images

The images subfolders contain duplicate sets of images for convenience. The image named color palette.jpg includes color swatches and names for the site's color scheme. As you'll see later, having a set of color swatches makes it easy to specify colors in Expression Web 2. The image files include:

cafe_logo.png	link.png	red_mug.png
color palette.jpg	logo2.png	table.png
courtyard.jpg	page_name.png	

Build the Structure

Kelly's site construction starts with defining the site and its folders. Then, rather than simply adding a number of blank pages, she puts one page together and makes copies for the page sites. Of course, when she convinces her family (and business partners) that a web site is the way to go, she'll define a template to streamline page building.

Start the Site

First things first. Kelly defines the site, following these steps:

1. Choose File | New | Web Site to open the New dialog box. Click General to display the options. Choose Empty Web Site.
2. Click Browse at the bottom of the dialog box to open the New Web Site Location dialog box. Browse to the storage location, click New Folder on the dialog box's toolbar and type a name for the folder in the pop-up field. Click OK to create the folder.

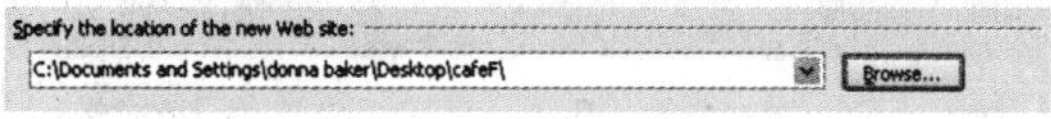

3. Click Open to select the new folder and close the dialog box, returning to the New dialog box. You'll see the location string on the dialog box. Click OK to close the dialog box and configure the site.

> **NOTE**
>
> Read about starting a web site in Chapter 1.

Bring in the Content

Kelly decides to bring in the content for the site now, rather than waiting until she's ready to start page assembly. To do that, follow these steps:

1. Choose File | Import to open the Import dialog box.
2. Click Add Folder to open a browse dialog and locate the cafeR folder.
3. Open the cafeR folder, and select the images folder. Click Open to include the list of files in the Import dialog box.
4. Click Add File in the Import dialog box to reopen the Browse dialog. Browse to the cafeR folder and open it.
5. Select the three individual files listed. These include cafe_margo.css, menu.css, and cafe.txt. Click Open to return to the Import dialog box. You'll see 13 files for the project listed (Figure 1).

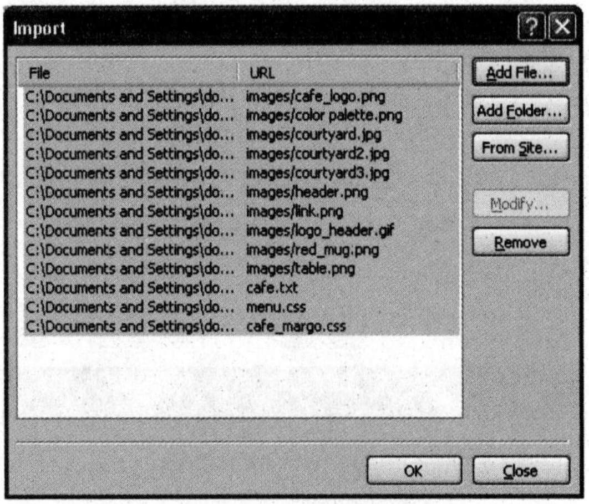

Figure 1. Select the folder and files for the site.

6. Click OK to close the dialog box and import the files. You'll see the images folder and three files listed in the Folder List.

NOTE

Read about importing files in Chapter 1.

Choose a Layout

Rather than start a blank web page, Kelly's going to use a preconfigured layout so she'll have the structure of the page to use as a starting point.

Start the First Page

Choosing a page structure adds an HTML and a CSS page to the site automatically. To get underway, follow these steps:

1. Choose File | New | Page to open the New dialog box, displaying the Page tab.
2. Click CSS Layouts to show the options. Select Header, Nav, 1 Column, Footer. In the Preview area, you'll see the page split into four <div> areas.

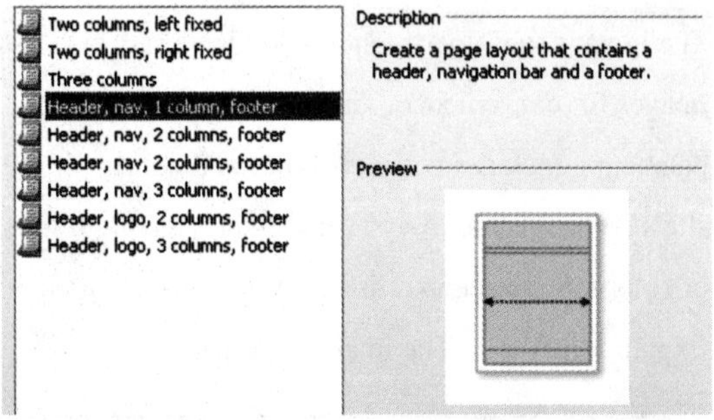

3. Click OK to close the dialog box and add the web and CSS pages, both named Untitled_1 by default.

4. Select Untitled_1.html and choose File | Save As to open the Save As dialog box. The page is renamed default.html by default. Click Save to save the file.

5. Select Untitled_1.css and choose File | Save As to open the dialog box again. Name the file cafe.css and click Save to rename and save the style sheet.

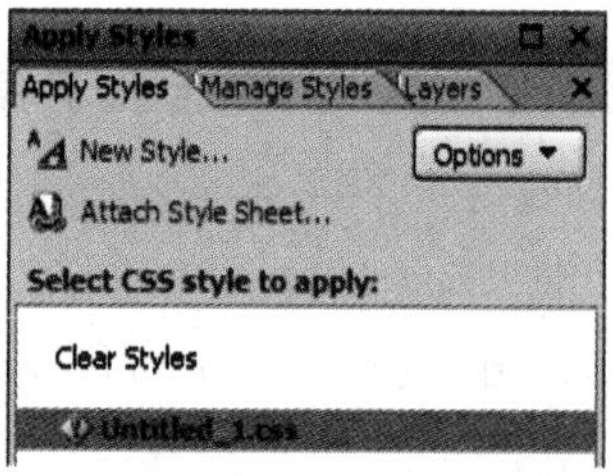

Figure 2. An error notification indicates the style sheet is missing.

2. In the Folder List, right-click Untitled_1.css Page and choose Delete from the shortcut menu. In the confirmation dialog box, click Yes to remove the page from the site.

3. In both the Apply Styles and Manage Styles task panes, you'll see an error notice regarding the deleted style sheet (Figure 2).

4. On either task pane, click Attach Style Sheet to open the dialog box. Click Browse to open the site's folder and select cafe_margo.css. Click Open to attach the style sheet. You'll see the list of styles currently active for the default.html page listed in the task panes.

5. Right-click the Untitled_1.css label on either task pane and choose Remove Link, or select the link's tag on the Code view, as shown below, and press DELETE.

6. Save the default.html page.

NOTE

Read about choosing and using CSS layouts in Chapter 7.

Combine Styles

The Untitled_1.css page contains four styles for the layout. Rather than using multiple style sheets, it's easy to combine them. Follow these steps to reorganize the styles:

1. Select the contents on the Untitled_1.css page and copy it. Then paste it at the top of the cafe_margo.css file. Save the cafe_margo.css file with the added styles.

TIP

Include the comment as well. It takes a minute to add comments to a style sheet but can save a lot of time later trying to figure out how and where to use the style.

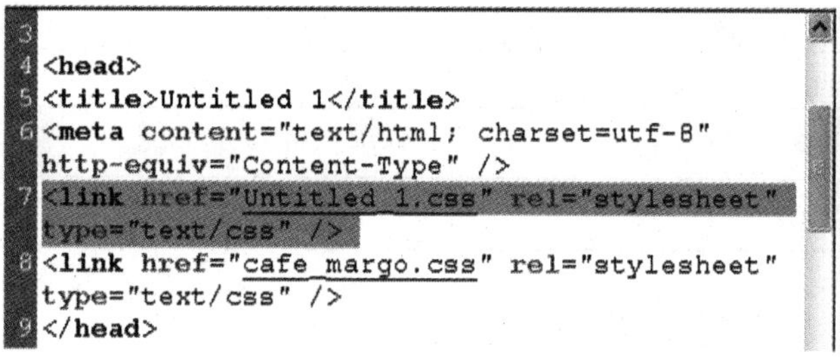

3
4 <head>
5 <title>Untitled 1</title>
6 <meta content="text/html; charset=utf-8"
http-equiv="Content-Type" />
7 <link href="Untitled_1.css" rel="stylesheet"
type="text/css" />
8 <link href="cafe_margo.css" rel="stylesheet"
type="text/css" />
9 </head>

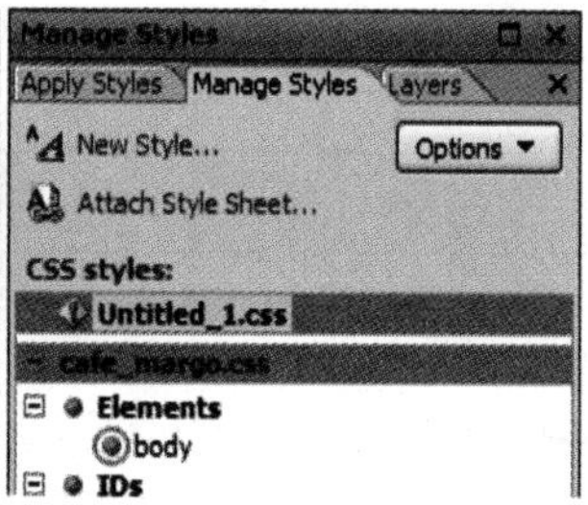

Assemble the Default Page

The site files are brought together into the web site folder, and there's a default.html page to serve as the home page for the site. Rather than duplicating the page now for the rest of the pages, Kelly is going to add the basic content to the default page and then create duplicates for the remaining pages.

The CSS layout uses four <div> tags to differentiate the page content. Table 1 lists the tags, how Kelly intends to use the areas, and comments.

Kelly plans her work based on the contents of her site's pages. She decides to:

- Define the size for the <masthead> area based on the logo and header sizes.
- Insert the <top_nav> and <footer> areas' contents on the default.html page.

Once Kelly has those areas configured, she can make the other pages for the site.

Add the Logo Header

Kelly plans on two different headers for her pages. One is the full Cafe Margo logo, and the other is the central part of the logo and another block of text with the page's name. She'll add the first logo now and the others when she creates additional pages.

Follow these steps to visualize the page areas and add the first image:

1. Double-click the Visual Aids label on the status bar at the bottom of the program window to toggle the aids to On. You'll see the striped areas on the Design and Split view of the page indicating the locations of the <div> tags.
2. Click the top stripe, which shows the div#masthead label. If you look in the Code view, you'll see the cursor is within the first <div> tag.
3. From the images folder in the Folder List, click and drag the cafe_logo.png file to the page and drop it into the first <div> tag's stripe.
4. The Accessibility Properties dialog box opens. Type a description in the Alternate text field. Kelly types **Cafe Margo logo**. Click OK to close the dialog box and place the image (Figure 3).

Page Area	Content	Comment
<masthead>	logo and page headings	differences among pages
<top_nav>	horizontal navigation menu	common on all pages
<page_content>	information about business	different on each page
<footer>	copyright and contact info	common on all pages

Table 1. Contents for Cafe Margo Web Site

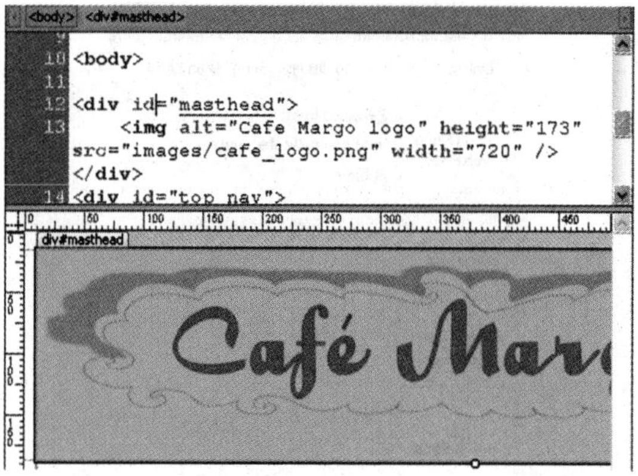

Figure 3. Place the logo image in its designated location.

Insert the Navigation Menu

Kelly intends to use the same navigation menu for all her pages. She's going to attach a separate style sheet she created for the menu. She created a text menu while experimenting with the program, which she copied into a text file along with some text from the cafe's marketing material she'll add into the web pages later.

Attach the Navigation Menu

Kelly doesn't have to integrate all the styles into one sheet, so she decides to simply attach the navigation menu's style sheet to her page, following the same steps as earlier when she attached the main style sheet.

That is, with the default.html page active in the Editing window, click Attach Style Sheet on the Apply Styles or Manage Styles task panes to open a dialog box. Click Browse to locate and select the menu.css style sheet, and click OK. The dialog box closes, and the style sheet is attached.

Add the Menu Code

Kelly spent some time learning how to work with Expression Web 2, and read how to build a horizontal menu using styles in Chapter 7 of a delightful book called *How To Do Everything: Microsoft Expression Web 2*. She's planning to try that herself, and already typed the code in a text file.

To add the menu to the page, follow these steps:

1. Double-click the cafe.txt file in the Folder List to open it in the Editing window. Select and copy the code written in Lines 1-8 for the `<ul>`.
2. Click the default.html page's tab to display it in the Editing window.
3. In the Code view, click after the `<div id="top_nav">` opening tag, and paste in the code.
4. On the Design view, you'll see the set of links added within the `<div>`.

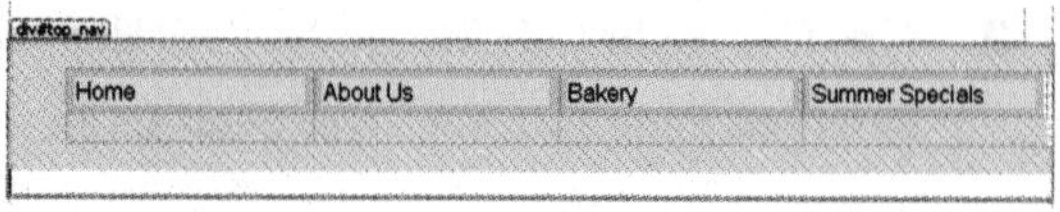

5. Save the file, and press F12 to view the page in your browser. Move your cursor over a link to see the hover state (Figure 4). At this point, there aren't any linked files so nothing changes if you click a link.

Figure 4. View the menu in your browser.

NOTE

The menu can be configured in a table. Read about using tables in Chapter 9.

Complete the Page Footer

The final common element for every page is the copyright notice and e-mail contact at the bottom of the page. Kelly plans to type the text directly on the page and create a style embedded in the page. Then she'll add a style for the `<div>` itself.

Add the Text and Link

In addition to the text, the footer includes a symbol. Follow these steps to add the text and symbol to the page:

1. In the Design view, click inside the `div#footer` area at the bottom of the page to display the area's frame.
2. Type **Copyright Cafe Margo 2008 All Rights Reserved**. Press TAB. Then type **Send Us an Email.**
3. Place the cursor in the space after "Copyright." Choose Insert | Symbol to open the Symbol dialog box. Look for the copyright (©) sign. Click the sign, and then click Insert. Click Close.
4. Select the Send Us an Email text and right-click to open the shortcut menu. Click Hyperlink to open the Insert Hyperlink dialog box.
5. Click E-mail Address in the Link To column at the left of the dialog box to display the e-mail settings.

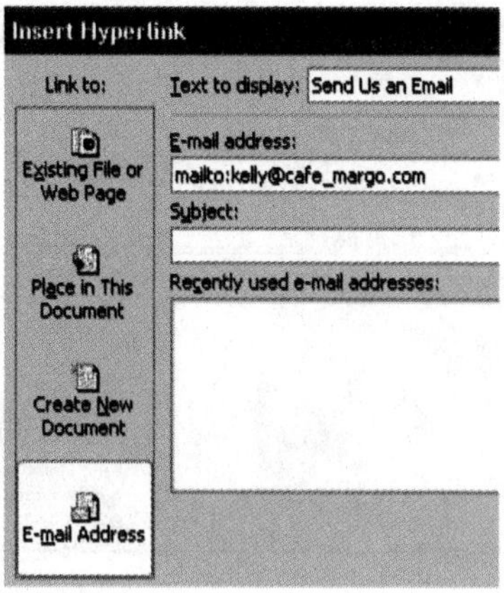

6. Type an e-mail address in the field following the `mailto:` tag, which is inserted automatically. Click OK to close the dialog box and complete the link.

NOTE

Read about using different types of hyperlinks in Chapter 4.

Style the Copyright Text Appearance

Once the link is completed, you'll see the text for the copyright notice looks different than the link (Figure 5). If you look at the Elements list in the cafe_margo.css styles in the Manage Styles task pane, you'll see there's a style for the `<a>` tag, applied to the e-mail link.

To take care of the appearance of the copyright notice, Kelly creates a new style following these steps:

1. Select the text on the Design view or in the Code view to apply the style directly to the text.

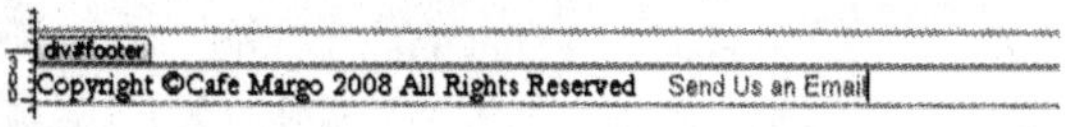

Figure 5. The text and link use different styles.

How To…

Get Ready for Some Color

One of the images included for the project is named color palette.png. You'll use it periodically throughout the rest of the project for defining colors for the site. Open the Images folder in the Folder List, and then double-click the color palette.png file to open it in your system's default image viewer.

If you're not sure what program to use, right-click the color palette.png file in the Folder List to open a shortcut menu. Click Open With to display a submenu listing programs on your system that can show the image, such as Microsoft Office Picture Manager, Paint, and so on. Choose a program from the list to open the image, and leave the file sitting open on your desktop.

You can choose a color in Expression Web 2 by sampling it from the desktop, as you'll see in upcoming section, "Style the Copyright Text Appearance".

2. Click New Style on the Apply Styles or Manage Styles task panes to open the New Style dialog box.

3. Click the Selector drop-down arrow to open a list of tags, and choose (inline style), shown at the top of the list.

TIP

When you make the selection, the other options at the top of the dialog box are grayed out as the style is placed within the tag on the page only.

4. In the Font category, click the Font-Family drop-down arrow, and choose Arial, Helvetica, Sans-serif.

5. Still in the Font category, click the Color drop-down arrow, and choose More Colors to open the More Colors dialog box. Click Select to activate the Eyedropper tool. Move the tool over the color palette.png image, and click the pale brown color swatch, second from the top in the right column to specify the color. You'll see the color show in the New Color Swatch on the More Colors dialog box. Click OK to close the dialog box and return to the New Style dialog box.

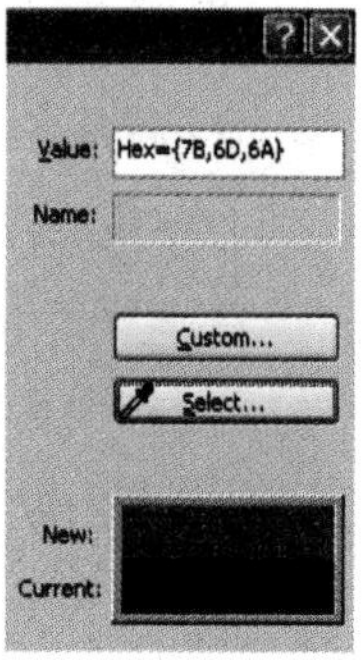

6. Click OK to close the New Style dialog box and return to the program. On the Apply Styles task pane, you'll see a new Inline Style added (Figure 6). On the Design view you see the styled text, and in the Code view you'll see the settings chosen.

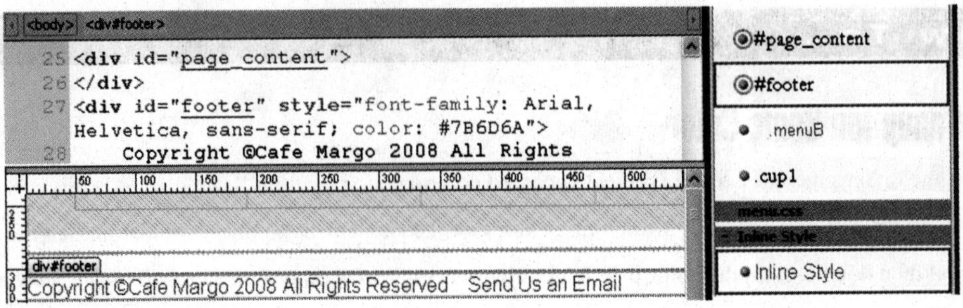

Figure 6. Configure a style for a single element inline.

NOTE

All but three of the color swatches in the color palette.png image show a color value that's two or three shades different from the values written on the figure when sampled in Expression Web 2. For example, the color selected in Step 5 is defined as #7D6F6C in Photoshop, and #7B6D6A in Expression Web 2. We've always noticed a slight difference between Microsoft color definition and Adobe color definition (used to create the color palette image).

Space the Text on the Page

For the final bit of styling on the page, Kelly adds a style for the <div> tag itself. Although the style hasn't been configured in any way, it was established when the CSS layout was defined at the start of the project. Read more about working with border and box styles in Chapter 7.

Follow these steps to specify the spacing on the page and add a border above the text:

1. In the Apply Styles or Manage Styles task panes, right-click the #footer ID to open the shortcut menu, and choose Modify Style to open the Modify Style dialog box.
2. At the top of the dialog box, you'll see the Selector is #footer; the rest of the items are grayed out. This means the new style is added to your attached style sheet, cafe_margo.css.
3. Choose these options for the style:

Category	Property	Value
Block	text-align	center
Border	border-top-style	dashed
Border	border-top-width	thin
Border	border-top-color	#3DA7B0 or #3CA5AE
Box	padding	Same for all, 12px
Padding	margin	Same for all, 12px
Position	width	720px

NOTE

The border color is the center swatch in the right column of the color palette.png image. The position is given the same width as the logo at the top of the page, which aligns the content visually.

Figure 7. The previewed page shows the completed footer.

4. Click OK to close the dialog box.
5. Press F12 to test the style. You'll see an embed dialog box open first asking if the style sheet should be updated. Click OK to save the updated style sheet and view the page (Figure 7).

TIP

You can save the style sheet first before previewing, but starting the preview command prompts to save the style sheet anyway, saving you one step.

Duplicate the Page

The common material in the first web page is finally finished with one exception. In Code view, type a title for the page in the `<title>` tag, shown in Line 5 of the default page layout.

To create the second and third pages for the site, choose File | Save As to open the Save As dialog box. Save the file as bakery.html, and click Change Title to activate a field to type a page title. Click Save to close the dialog box and save a copy of the file.

Repeat for the summer.html page—the third web page. Again, change the title.

TIP

Each time you save the page with another name, the newly named file is shown in the Editing window. Check you're using the correct page as you add and customize content.

Add Content to the Home Page

Now the three pages are created, Kelly adds the images, text, and completes the links on the default, or home page.

Insert and Tag the Text

The text in the cafe.txt file contains content Kelly assembled from other marketing material. The text pasted into the web page is raw text. That is, it hasn't been defined in any block tags such as headings or paragraphs.

Follow these steps to add the text to the default.html page:

1. Double-click the cafe.txt file in the Folder List to open the file containing the text for the pages in the Editing window.
2. Select and copy the text for the home page from the cafe.txt page, listed on lines 11 through 14.
3. Reopen default.html to display it in the Editing window.
4. In Design view, click the page content `<div>`, located between the links and the copyright areas.
5. Paste the text into the page content area.

6. Select text in Design view and assign tags using the Style List on the Common toolbar. The page layout is fairly obvious—apply <h1> to the first line; and break up the remainder of the text into three <p> tags.

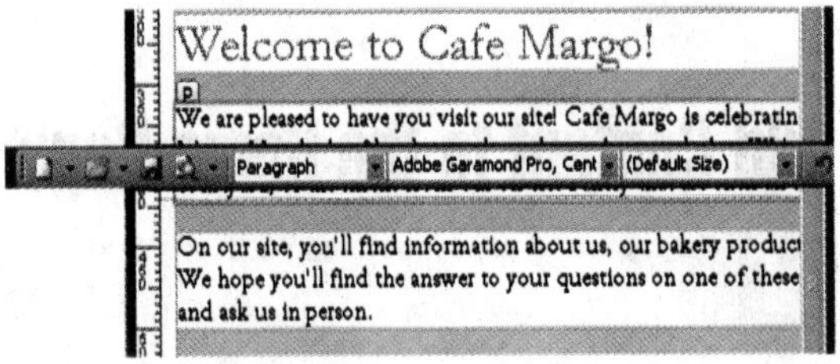

NOTE

Read about using text in Chapter 2.

Add and Style an Image

On the home page, Kelly intends to place a sketch of a table used on their menu. Once the image is on the page, she'll write a style to place it in a specific location with the text wrapping around it.

Place the Image

In the Folder List, open the Images folder, and drag the table.png file to the page at the start of the second paragraph. Once the mouse is released after dragging the file, the Accessibility Options dialog opens. Type a short text label for the image. Kelly types **sketch of table with dishes and napkin**. Click OK to close the dialog box and insert the image on the page.

Writing the style is up next, but to test the placement as you develop the style, add an ID to the <img> tag first. On the Quick Tag Selector at the top of the Editing window, click <img> to open the menu, and choose Edit Tag to open the Quick Tag Editor.

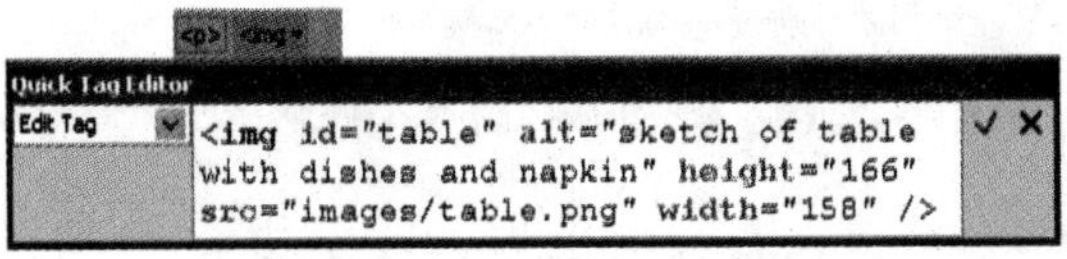

Figure 8. Add an ID for the image's style.

Type **id="table"** after the opening <img> tag, and click the check mark to close the dialog box and change the code (Figure 8).

Write the Positioning Style

The new style for the table image placement can be placed inline or on the current style sheet. To add it to the style sheet, click New Style in the Apply Styles task pane to open the New Style dialog box.

At the top of the dialog box, make these selections:

- Type **#table** in the Selector field.
- Choose Existing Style Sheet from the Define In drop-down list.
- Select the Apply New Style to Document Selection check box
- Click the URL drop-down list and choose cafe_margo.css.

Make the choices shown next for the style properties and values:

Category	Property	Value
Box	Margin	Same for all; 10px
Position	position	relative
Layout	float	right

Click Apply to see the changes on the page as you configure the style, then click OK to close the dialog box and complete the style. Before going on to adding links, press F12 to view the page in a browser. As you see here, the image anchors the bottom of the page.

Finish the Menu Links

There is no page for linking from the About Us text in the horizontal menu at the top of the page. Kelly isn't sure how she wants to handle that information and decides to wait for input from her family. In the meantime, she simply links to the default.html page.

The links for the horizontal menu and their destinations include:

- **Home** Links to default.html
- **About Us** Links to default.html
- **Bakery** Links to bakery.html
- **Summer Specials** Links to summer.html

Café Margo
Home
About Us
Bakery
Summer Specials
Welcome to Cafe Margo!
We are pleased to have you visit our site! Cafe Margo is celebrating its 30th year in operation at our little shop in The Mews. Hundreds of locals pass through our doors each day. We're not sure if it's the smell of coffee wafting through the courtyard, or the smells from our on-site bakery that are such an attraction. Drop in, and decide for yourself!
On our site, you'll find information about us, our bakery products, daily specials, and even the kinds of coffee we brew. We hope you'll find the answer to your questions on one of these pages. If not, drop us an email, or stop in for coffee and ask us in person.
We bake all our goods onsite daily. Some of our recipes are heirlooms and family secrets, so we won't be sharing them! On the other hand, we do have plenty of recipes we'd love to share. Check out the Summer Specials page for information on upcoming baking demonstrations. You won't want to miss them!
Copyright ©Cafe Margo 2008 All Rights Reserved
Send Us an Email

Complete and Test Links

Kelly's final task for the default.html page is to add the links. For each link, select the text for the link, right-click, and choose Hyperlink Properties to open the Hyperlink dialog box. Select the Existing File or Web Page category in the column at the left of the dialog box to display the pages in the site. Double-click the hyperlink's page to apply the link and close the dialog box.

Add Links from the Home Page

Kelly also adds a few links within the body of the page, including:

- In the last sentence of paragraph 2, attach an e-mail link to the phrase "drop us an e-mail"
- In the first sentence of paragraph 3, attach a link from the phrase "onsite daily" to the bakery.html page.
- In the second to last sentence of paragraph 3, attach "Summer Specials" to the summer .html page.

Style the Links on the Page

The links on the page use the <a> tag's appearance as included in the style sheets. To make the links appear more consistent with the text on the page, Kelly's written a simple style using the page's fonts, a custom color, and removed the text decoration from the link, which is an underline by default.

To attach the style, select each link's text again, and click .body in the cafe_margo.css list of styles on the Apply Styles task pane. On the final page, the text matches the contents of the page without interfering with the links in the menu at the top or the e-mail link in the footer of the page (Figure 9).

Design the Bakery Page

The bakery page is intended to show visitors a sampling of what Cafe Margo has to offer. At some point, Kelly intends to provide links to nutritional information for each of their products, but that's in the future. For now, she wants to show the layout of the page.

From top to bottom, here's what needs to be done on the bakery.html page:

- Replace the logo and write a style for one of the two replacement logo images.
- Finish the links for the horizontal menu.
- Insert tags to define the page content.
- Add a static background image for the page.
- Insert bookmarks and internal links on the page.

TIP

The page uses the heading styles included in the cafe_margo.css style sheet.

Change the Page's Logo

Kelly plans to have a smaller logo on the item pages on her site to differentiate them from the home page. She wants to use the logo stacked atop a block of color showing the page's name.

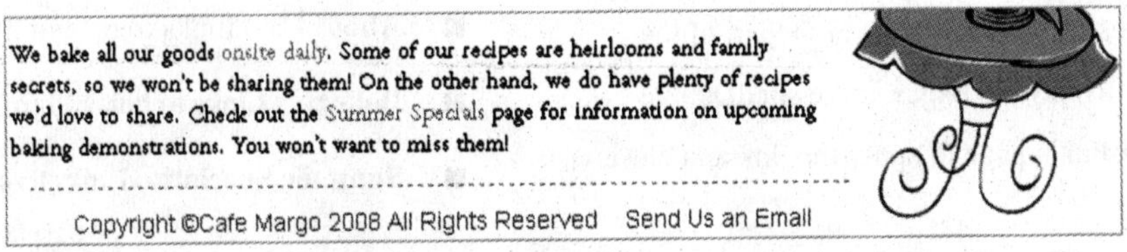
We bake all our goods onsite daily. Some of our recipes are heirlooms and family secrets, so we won't be sharing them! On the other hand, we do have plenty of recipes we'd love to share. Check out the Summer Specials page for information on upcoming baking demonstrations. You won't want to miss them!
Copyright ©Cafe Margo 2008 All Rights Reserved
Send Us an Email

Figure 9. The final page uses multiple link appearances.

Swap the Logo Image

Kelly has a slightly different version of her logo, as well as a block of text that she'll modify for her pages.

Here's how to change the logo:

1. Select the cafe_logo.png image in the <div#masthead> area of the page and delete it.
2. From the images folder in the Folder List, drag the page_name.png file to the empty <div> space. In the Accessibility Properties dialog box, type <alt> text, such as **page name color bar**, and click OK to close the dialog box and add the image.
3. Drag the logo2.png file from the images folder in the Folder List and drop it after the image inserted in the previous step. Add <alt> text, such as **cafe margo logo2**, and click OK to close the dialog box and insert the image.

On the page, you'll see the color block with the smaller logo image below. It's not quite right yet.

Define a Layer for the Layout

Kelly wants the logo to overlay the color block. To do that, she'll define a new style, named .logo2, to configure the logo image as a layer and position it over the color block.

Figure 10. Position the logo image to overlap the color block.

Using the steps described in several earlier sections, define a new style having these characteristics:

- Name the Selector.logo2, defined in the cafe_margo.css style sheet
- In the Position category, specify `position:absolute; top:25px; left180px`

Now, when you look at the page, you'll see the logo image overlaps the color block (Figure 10).

Save a Code Snippet for Future Use

Kelly intends to use the same logo arrangement for other pages, including the summer.html page she's already designed. To save time, she makes a code snippet, following these steps:

1. Click the <div#masthead> tag on the Quick Tag Selector above the Editing window to select all the tag's contents. Copy the code.
2. Choose Tools | Page Editor Options | Code Snippets to display the Code Snippets tab.
3. Type a keyword, such as **logo2**, and add a description if you like.
4. In the Text area of the dialog box, paste the copied code, and click OK to close the dialog box.
5. Click OK again to close the Page Editor Options dialog box.

NOTE

Since she's finishing the page from top to bottom, Kelly checks and finishes the links from the horizontal menu to the appropriate pages. For more, check out the earlier section "Complete and Test Links."

Define the Page Content with Tags

The bakery.html page is made up of an introductory set of paragraphs and then two blocks of content that are formatted in the same way. You can add tags using whichever method you prefer, such as selecting the text on the Design view and choosing the tag from the Common toolbar.

Here are the page's tags:

1. Apply <p> tags to each of the four sentences in the introduction to the page.
2. Apply <h2> tags to the "Danish Pastry" text and the "Magnificent Muffins" text.
3. Apply <p> tags to the intro sentence following the <h2> text lines.
4. For each of the pastry and muffin lists, apply <h3> tags to the product name and <p> tags to the product descriptions.

When you're finished, all the text on the page is tagged in small, discrete sections, like you see here.

TIP

If you want to see the tags on the Design view, as shown here, choose View | Formatting Marks | Tag Marks.

Place a Background Image on the Page

Kelly plans to add a sketch of a coffee cup from her menu to the background of the bakery page. She'll design an embedded style, using the steps described in several earlier sections:

1. Select the <body> tag from the Quick Tag Selector to apply the style to the entire page.
2. Click New Style in the Apply Style task pane to open the New Style dialog box; name the Selector .bakery_bkgd, embedded in the *current page*.
3. In the Background category, click Browse to open a dialog box, and select the red_mug.png image as the background.
4. Choose these other properties in the Background category:

```
background-repeat: no-repeat;
background-attachment: fixed;
(x) background-position: right;
(y) background-position: center;
```

5. Click OK to close the dialog box and apply the style. In the browser, you'll see the coffee cup image stays in the same location as you scroll the page (Figure 11).

> **NOTE**
>
> Read more about using background styles in Chapter 6.

Insert Bookmarks and Links

The bakery.html page needs some internal links, or bookmarks, to identify content positions on the page. The bookmarks will then be used to link content from the top of the page to the pastry and muffin lists.

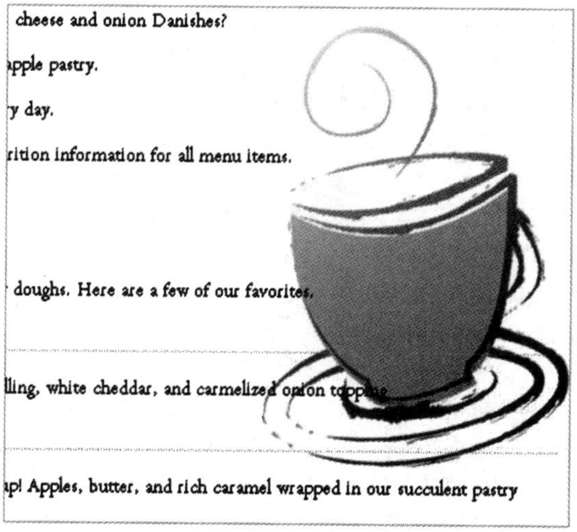

Figure 11. The image is fixed in position on the background.

Use a Graphic as a Bookmark

Kelly decides to use a small graphic as the bookmark destination and apply an existing style to the images. To insert graphics and apply bookmarks, follow these steps:

1. From the images folder in the Folder List, click the link.png image and drag it to the start of the "Danish Pastry" heading. In the Accessibility Properties dialog box, type `<alt>` text such as **image for pastry link** and click OK to close the dialog box and place the image.
2. Repeat with another copy of the image, placing it at the start of the "Marvelous Muffins" heading.
3. One at a time, click the images on the page in Design view, and click .cup1 in the Apply Styles task pane to apply the style. The style includes a margin and vertical positioning for the image in relation to the heading text.
4. Click the image next to the "Danish Pastry" heading and choose Insert | Bookmark to open the dialog box. Type a name for the bookmark, such as **danish**, and click OK.
5. Repeat with the second image next to the "Marvelous Muffins" heading, and name the bookmark **muffins**.
6. At the top of the page, select the phrase "fresh pumpkin muffin" in the second paragraph. Right-click and choose Hyperlink from the shortcut menu to open the Insert Hyperlink dialog box (Figure 12).

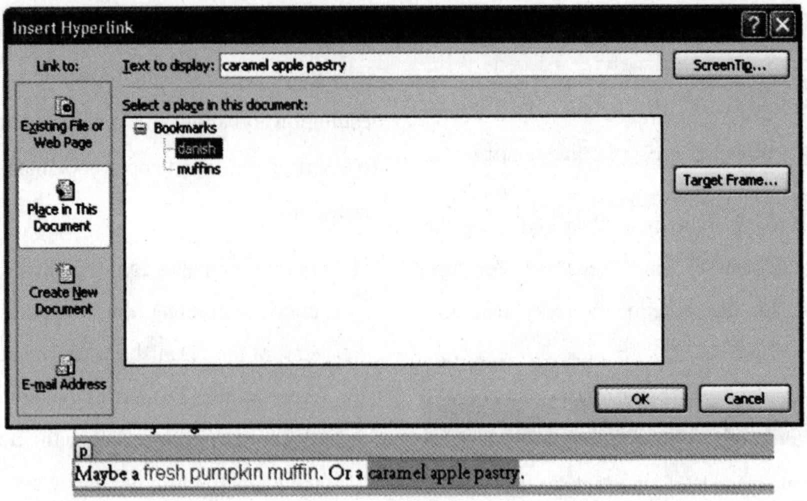

Figure 12. Create links from text to locations on the page.

7. Click Place in This Document in the column at the left of the dialog box to display the Bookmarks. Click Muffins to set the link destination, and then click OK to close the dialog box.

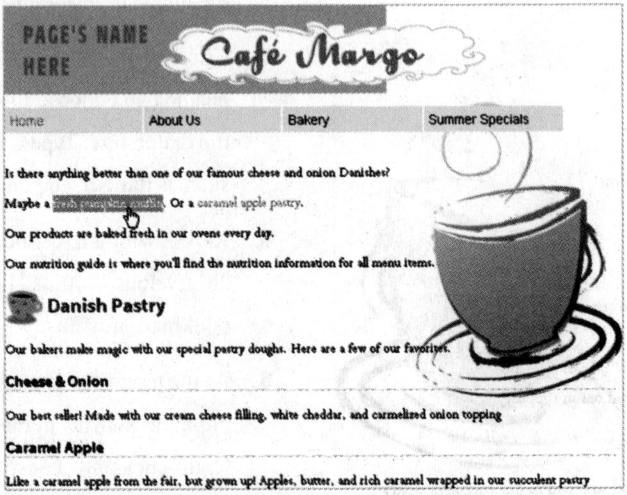

8. Repeat with the second phrase on the same line, "caramel apple pastry." This time, click the Danish bookmark.

9. Select each of the two phrases again, and click .body in the Apply Styles task pane to configure the links' appearances to match the pages, as you see next.

The bakery.html page is done.

Configure the Summer Specials Page

Summer specials at Cafe Margo are Kelly's pet project. So far, she's introduced a weekend evening coffeehouse complete with entertainment. She's also convinced her head baker (and aunt) to offer some baking demonstrations. On this page of the site, Kelly intends to provide an overview of the special events, which she'll expand in the future.

From top to bottom, here's how Kelly plans to complete the page:

1. Replace the logo with the two-image logo using a code snippet saved from the bakery.html page.
2. Finish the menu's links.
3. Add tags to configure the text on the page.
4. Insert and style an image.

Modify the Top Elements on the Page

When she modified the bakery.html page, Kelly created a code snippet to use for the two-image logo for her secondary pages. Now, all she has to do is apply the code snippet.

Apply the Replacement Logo

To apply the snippet and change the code for the page's logo, follow these steps:

1. In Design view, select the <div#masthead> tag in the Quick Tag Selector. Click Code to switch to Code view, with the tag selected.

> **TIP**
>
> You can select the code directly in the Code view, but it's easy to select the tag and then switch views.

2. With the cursor somewhere in the <div> tag code, press CTRL-ENTER to open the code snippet list, shown here.

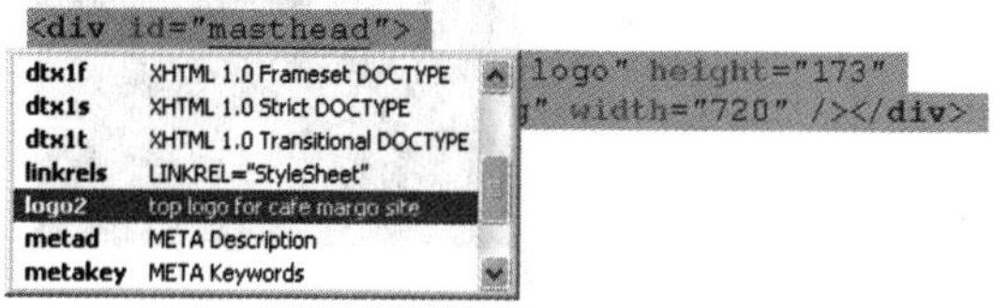

3. Scroll through the list to find the logo2 snippet. Double-click logo2 to replace the code and close the list.

> **NOTE**
>
> Read about code snippets in Chapter 5.

Adjust the Navigation Links

Once again, Kelly has to complete the links for the horizontal navigation menu on the page. Follow the same process as for the preceding two pages' configurations.

By the way, she could create links to nonexistent pages at the beginning of the project rather than amending them as she comes to the pages, or create a code snippet for the menu as well.

Wrap up the Summer Page Design

There's not a lot of configuration required for the summer.html page, as Kelly isn't sure how extensive

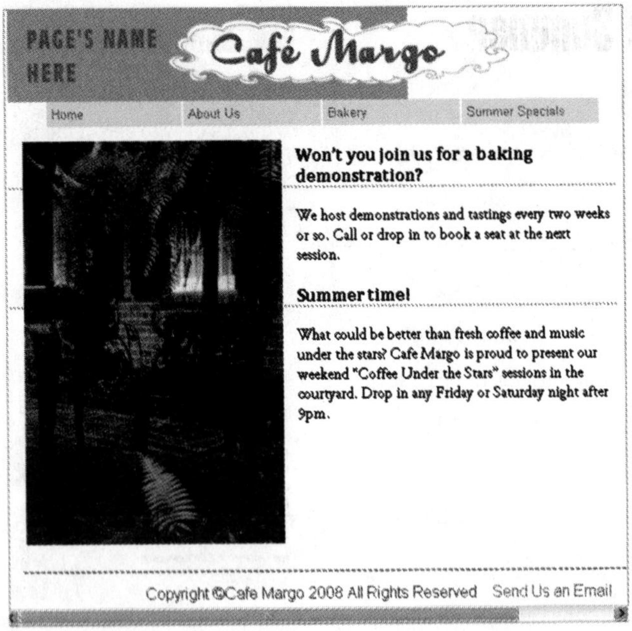

Figure 13. The final summer programs page

the design should be for the demonstrations and coffeehouse evenings. All she configures for the summer.html page are some simple text styles and one image.

Tag and Style the Page Text The text on the summer.html page is simple to tag. The text is comprised of four paragraphs—assign `<h3>` tags to the first and third paragraphs, and `<p>` tags to the second and fourth paragraphs.

Insert and Style an Image The page needs an image of some sort, and Kelly has some interesting shots of their courtyard. She decides to add one image for now, placing it at the left side of the page. Insert the courtyard.jpg image at the start of the `<div>` tag for the page content.

Kelly types **courtyard iron table and chair** for the `<alt>` text for the image. In the Code view, she types the style for the image manually. The final tag for the image reads:

```
<img alt="courtyard iron table and
chair" src="images/courtyard.jpg"
style="float: left; margin: 15px;" />
```

The summer.html page has a simple but attractive layout as you see in Figure 13.

Summary

This Spotlight project outlined a way for a small business person to use Expression Web 2 to build a web site.

Kelly started out by constructing the site's folders and importing the images and other files she had prepared. She used a CSS Layout option provided by Expression Web 2 as the starting point for her page layouts. The Cafe Margo logo fit into the top <div> of the page, followed by a horizontal menu.

Before creating the separate site pages, Kelly inserted a common copyright and e-mail block into the footer `<div>` on the page.

Kelly then moved into configuring the separate pages. She pasted text from a file where she'd assembled content from other marketing materials on to the three pages.

On her site's default.html home page, Kelly added tags and styles to the text pasted on to the page. She included one image positioned using a style and added a new style to make the text links appear more like the body text.

She got creative on the bakery.html page, using a sketch of a coffee cup as a static background behind the text. She also added links from text on the page to bookmarks attached to small graphics next to page titles.

The final page, the summer.html page, used basic heading and text styles for an attractive layout. Kelly added one photograph of the Cafe Margo courtyard for interest.

During the course of the project, Kelly used many Expression Web 2 features, worked in Code and Design views, and attached styles to separate style sheets, embedded style sheets, and wrote inline styles as well.

It's a great beginning.

Did You Know?

There's a Long Way to Go

The content added to Kelly's site in this project is a simple prototype to illustrate what she wants to do in the site. There are many, many features she can add in addition to the few included in this Spotlight. For example:

- Kelly can design a template to use for updating her site, and creating consistent new pages (as described in Chapter 8).
- She can add pages containing tables listing nutritional information about her bakery products (check out Chapter 9).
- She can add some interactivity to the pages using behaviors and JavaScript. Kelly might want to have images that swap out on pages describing bakery products, for example, or open pop-up windows describing information about different products (read more in Chapter 10).

Did You Know? (Cont.)

- There are many ways to use media on a website, and the Cafe Margo site is no exception. For example, Kelly could include video from the summer coffeehouse sessions, Flash files to show baking techniques, or video clips from her bakery classes (and more, as you can read in Chapter 11).
- When Kelly puts her next phase of business expansion into effect, she'll need an online ordering system to ship her topping and seasoning mixes. (Read about designing and using forms in Chapter 12).
- Adding PHP pages and scripts to her site could let visitors know the special of the day automatically, or how many days until the next coffeehouse session (get the scoop on PHP in Chapter 13).
- To simplify advertising specials and upcoming events on her site, Kelly could add ASP.NET controls like AdRotators and Calendars (read about ASP in Chapter 14).
- Kelly might want to evaluate and test her pages from an accessibility standpoint. Although Kelly uses basic accessibility features such as alternate text for images, she could add more compliant features like `<longdesc>` tags and files for any video or Flash included on her site (read about accessibility issues in Chapter 15).

How to...

Avoid DWT Pitfalls

There are some gotchas that you need to be aware of when attaching DWTs.

Failed Updates

There are times when pages might not update, especially for a Windows SharePoint server. To fix this problem, follow these steps.

1. Make your changes.
2. Choose Recalculate Hyperlinks from the Site Settings dialog box.
3. From the Format menu, select Dynamic Web Template, and choose Update All Pages.

Some DWT-Related Commands Are Unavailable

Sometimes after you make a change to a DWT, the Update All Pages and Update Attached Pages menu commands are unavailable. Only the pages that are opened in Expression will be updated. If you find yourself in this situation, you will have to open all of the other attached pages and update them.

Script Inside of the Body Tag

There are many times when you need some script inside of the body tag such as the following:

```
<body onload="MyFunction();">
```

When you attach a DWT, this code will be lost since the body tag is considered a noneditable region. The best way to overcome this is by rescripting the functionality and putting it inside a scripting editable region.

You may need to add the following to the appropriate place in your DWT:

```
<!-- #BeginEditable "scripting" -->
<!-- Scripting area here -->
<!-- #EndEditable -->
```

CSS Linking Issues

Expression Web does not allow you to link a CSS file to HTML pages that are attached to a DWT. The solution is to link the CSS to the DWT file.

You can add content to the middle section so each attached page has its own unique content. In this way, you save time since you don't have to fuss with the layout each time. You also have a much easier mechanism for web site consistency.

While in Code view, the noneditable regions are clearly demarcated by a light yellow color. This gives you a visual cue that you should not be editing these sections. However, there might be times when you absolutely must make a change. Expression will allow you to make a change, but it will ask you how to handle the edits that you performed in the noneditable regions, as shown in Figure 8-7.

The first choice means that you probably made a mistake and don't want to keep the changes you made in the noneditable regions. The second choice means that you want to keep the changes you made to the noneditable regions, and that you realize the DWT file and all attached HTML files will be updated, too.

So far, we've created an HTML file and then attached a DWT file, but you can do both steps at once. From the File menu, select New | Create From Dynamic Web Template. This creates a new HTML file that is already attached to a specified DWT file.

There are some standard DWT region names. You can name your editable regions many things, but these standard names can make it easier for other developers to understand the purpose of the editable regions. Table 8-1 shows these standard names along with their descriptions.

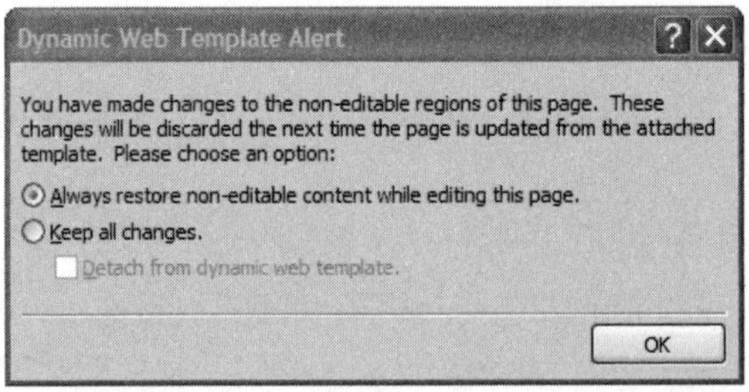

FIGURE 8-7 You will be prompted when you make changes to the noneditable regions while in Code view.

TABLE 8-1 Standard DWT items

Region Name	Region Characteristics
doctitle	The title of the page. This is what appears in the uppermost left status bar of the published page. To edit this and the following two regions, right-click over the body of the page and select Page Properties. Fill in your own information for the Title, Page Description, and Keywords fields. You will want to do this on each page.
keywords	Keywords for your page/site; important for search engine spidering purposes. To edit, follow the preceding instructions for doctitle.
description	Description of your page/site; important for search engine spidering purposes. To edit, follow the preceding instructions for doctitle.
scripting	Location for any coding (ASP, JavaScript, and so on) that requires placement within the `<HEAD> </HEAD>` tags of the web page.
banner	Name of the page being viewed. You may either use the text banner provided with FrontPage or type in the title manually.
sub_menu	Secondary navigation. Uses FrontPage navigation structure link bar; depending on the location of the page in the FrontPage navigation structure, this will be set to either Child or Same level. Default is Child level.
body1	Main content. In a 2- or 3-column layout, this content will appear in the widest content column. In a 1-column layout, it will appear first.
body2	Secondary content. In a 3-column layout, this content will appear in the left column. In a 2-column layout, it will appear in the smaller of the two columns. In a 1-column layout, it will appear directly beneath the body1 editable region's content.
body3	Third level content. In a 3-column layout, this content will appear in the right column. In a 2-column layout, it will appear directly beneath the body1 editable region's content. In a 1-column layout, it will appear directly beneath the body2 editable region's content.
special1	Place for an applet or anything else.
special2	Place for an applet or anything else.

Create Real-Life Web Sites with Dynamic Web Templates

In this section we'll create some more complete DWTs and web pages. We'll use CSS to provide style information. The first example in this section is a small business web site for a company named ACME.

Our approach for this walkthrough is to add one thing at a time and test. This is what we teach our programming students, who tend to write a lot of code, try it out, and then struggle to fix the problems. It's easier, however, to fix the problems as you go so that you don't get to the end with hundreds of lines of code to weed through.

1. Create a new web site. The example is named Walkthrough1.
2. Create an images directory and a css directory inside of your new web directory.
3. Create a DWT named ACME.dwt.
4. Create a CSS file named ACME.css and save it into the css directory.
5. Create an image for the top of the pages that is 660 ×120 pixels and save it into the images directory. The example is a sunset image named Sunset.jpg.
6. Create Default.htm from the ACME.dwt file.
   Now you have the basic files that you need to get started. From this point, you're going to add the code that will allow the pages to display the masthead. Once this is done in the DWT, all of the derived pages will benefit from your development. There are two classes to add to the CSS file and some stylistic changes for the body. The container class determines the look and feel of the main content section. The masthead determines the look and feel of the masthead, which uses the 660 × 120 image.

Note This entire project can be downloaded from the Chapter 8 page. However, we suggest that, if possible, you work through this walkthrough on your own; you will learn much more!

7. Add the following code to the ACME.css file. (If your image is not named Sunset .jpg, you will need to change it in this code.)

```
body
{
   margin: 0;
   padding: 0;
   border: 0;
   background-color:#E6FFFF;
}
#container
{
   width: 660px;
   margin: auto;
   padding: 0;
   border: 0;
```

```
    border-right: 2px solid #8c8c8c;
    border-bottom: 2px solid #8c8c8c;
    border-left: 2px solid #8c8c8c;
    background-color: #f1f1f1;
}
#masthead
{
    width: 660px;
    overflow: hidden;
    margin: 0;
    padding: 0;
    border: 0;
    text-align: right;
    background-color: #336699;
    background-image: url('../images/Sunset.jpg');
    background-position: top;
    background-repeat: no-repeat;
    height: 120px;
}
h1
{
    color:#FFFFCC;
}

h3
{
    color:#FFFFCC;
}
```

8. In ACME.dwt, add the following link inside the <HEAD> section.

```
<link rel="stylesheet" type="text/css" title="CSS"
     href="css/ACME.css" media="screen" />
```

9. In ACME.dwt, edit the code within the <BODY> section as follows:

```
<body>
<div id="container">
  <div id="masthead">
    <h1>ACME Corporation</h1>
    <h3>The Greatest Company</h3>
  </div>
<!-- #BeginEditable "body" -->
<!-- #EndEditable -->
</div>
</body>
```

10. Save all files and preview the default.htm file. It will appear similar to the one in Figure 8-8.

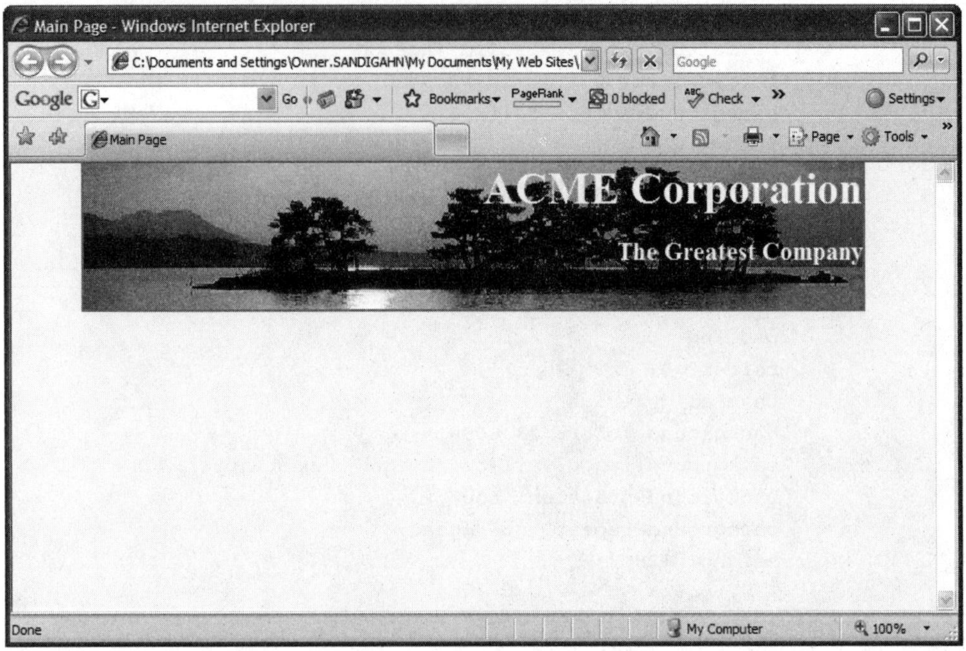

FIGURE 8-8 So far, this template provides a masthead with company information.

Now the page is starting to take shape. The next several steps will create the rest of the pages for the site and add a foot object with navigation and copyright information. We'll also need to add more information to the CSS file to describe the new <DIV> tag that we'll be adding; then we'll add the <DIV> to the DWT file.

1. Add the following to ACME.css.

```
#footer
{
   width: 100%;
   overflow: auto;
   clear: both;
   margin: 0;
   padding: 0;
   border: 0;
   text-align: center;
   padding-bottom: 10px;
}
a
{
   color: #c55;
```

```
    text-decoration: underline;
}
a:hover
{
    color: #9c9;
    text-decoration: none;
}
#footer p
{
    font-size: x-small;
    color: #c77;
}
```

2. Add the following to the ACME.dwt file before the close of the container <DIV> tag:

```
<div id="footer">
    <p><a href="default.htm">Home</a> | <a href="About.htm">About</a>
    | <a href="Contact.htm">Contact</a> | <a href="Links.htm">Links</a> </p>
    <p><a href="http://www.ACME.com/">
    &copy;www.ACME.com - 2008</a></p>
</div>
```

3. From the ACME.dwt file, create the HTML files About.htm, Contact.htm, and Links.htm.
4. In order to temporarily make the page look normal, there are a bunch of <BR /> tags above the footer. This prevented the footer from being immediately below the masthead. Next, take these out and add content to the middle of the page.
5. Save all files and preview. They should look similar to what you see in Figure 8-9.
6. The next thing we'll do is add a navigation bar at the top. This will be another <DIV> tag that will be contained within the container <DIV> tag. Add the following to ACME.css.

```
#navigation ul
{
    list-style-type: none;
    width: 100%;
    margin: 0;
    padding: 0;
}

#navigation li
{
    float: left;
}
```

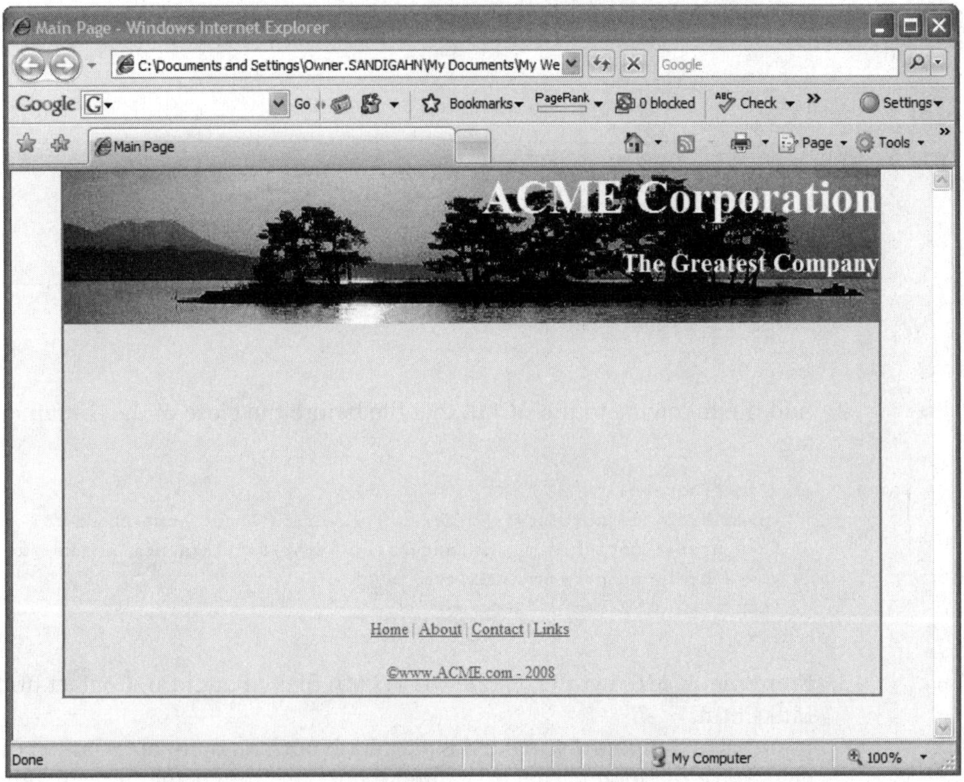

FIGURE 8-9 Now the page has a footer.

```
#navigation a
{
   font-weight: bold;
   text-decoration: none;
   color: #000;
   display: block;
   padding: 5px;
   border: 1px solid #cdc;
}

#navigation a:hover
{
   font-weight: bold;
   text-decoration: none;
   color: #fff;
   border: 1px solid #c77;
   background-color: #c77;
}
```

7. Add to ACME.dwt the following inside the container <DIV> tag, right below the masthead.

```
<div id="navigation">
   <ul>
      <li><a href="default.htm">Home</a></li>
      <li><a href="About.htm">About</a></li>
      <li><a href="Contact.htm">Contact</a></li>
      <li><a href="Links.htm">Links</a></li>
   </ul>
</div>
```

Now your page is relatively complete. All you need to do is add content to each page. There are actually two projects on the web site. One has no content and is blank so that you can more easily add content. The second has sample content. You can see the main page in Figure 8-10 with sample content.

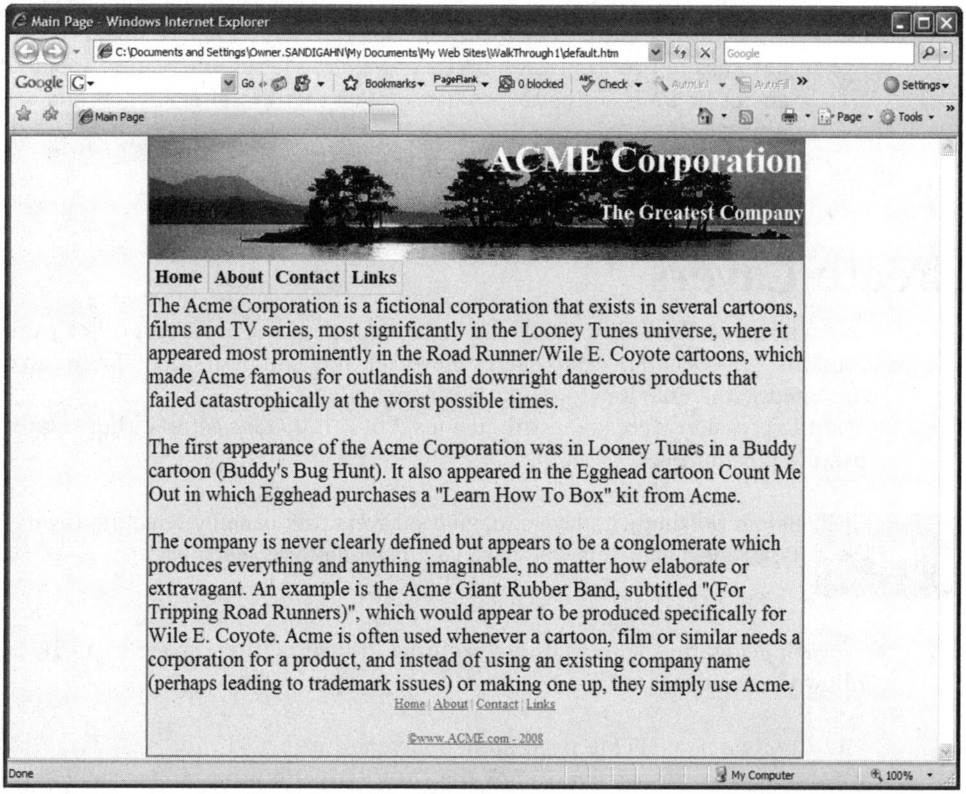

FIGURE 8-10 This page has the three elements that we added along with sample content.

Did You Know?

You Can Use Free Dynamic Web Templates

There are a lot of web sites that have free Dynamic Web Templates. Most of these sites offer fairly simple DWTs in the hope that you'll buy their fuller and more complex DWTs. We've used a number of the free templates in the past with great success. It's a great way to get up and running in a short amount of time.

The page at http://by-expression.com/samples/ has several very cool yet simple free DWTs. Be careful, though, since some of the templates on this page are FrontPage templates and won't work correctly with Expression Web 2.

The page at http://www.templatehappy.com/free-frontpage-expression.html also has some very nice DWTs that you can download. You can use them free of charge, but they have copyright notices that you are not allowed to remove until you pay for them. The great thing is that you can try them and develop with them before you have to pay for them. If you navigate to http://www.freewebsitetemplates.com/forum/, you will see some links to their free Expression Web templates. What's really good about this site is that you can get some help on their forums. Many people who use the templates go to the forums for help, and the questions that you might ask may have already been answered.

The page at http://www.outfront.net/tutorials_02/fp_techniques/dwt-1.htm has links to free Expression DWTs, as well as a lot of information about creating and using DWTs. This site also has a forum that can offer support and answer your questions.

Create Layers

Layers give you flexibility. They can hold text, graphics, and most other page elements. Layers can overlap each other, and they can be hidden. They can also be combined with behaviors for some very cool effects.

In Expression Web, layers are just a set of <DIV> tags set to either relative or absolute positioning.

Note Before working with layers, open the Layers task pane by selecting Layers from the Task Pane menu. This will make your layering tasks much easier.

We'll get started with a simple example. It inserts three layers in an HTML page. Follow these steps.

1. Create a new HTML page named Layers.htm.
2. In the Layers task pane, click the Insert Layer button. A layer will appear in the HTML document.
3. Move the layer lower and to the right.

4. As an alternative method of adding a layer, click the Draw Layer button in the Layers task pane.
5. Position the mouse in the HTML document, hold the left mouse button down, and draw the layer.
6. Add a third layer to the HTML document.
7. Position the three layers so that they all overlap as shown in Figure 8-11.
8. Go to Code view.
9. Add background color to each style element as follows.

```
<div id="layer1" style="background-color:aqua; position: absolute;
   width: 164px; height: 152px; z-index: 1; left: 37px; top: 46px"></div>
<div id="layer2" style="background-color:fuchsia; position : absolute;
   left: 145px; top: 137px; width: 145px; height: 136px; z-index: 2"></div>
<div id="layer3" style="background-color:gray; position: absolute;
   left: 239px; top: 238px; width: 174px; height: 136px; z-index: 3"></div>
```

10. Save the document.
11. Preview the document. The three overlapping layers will all be different colors.

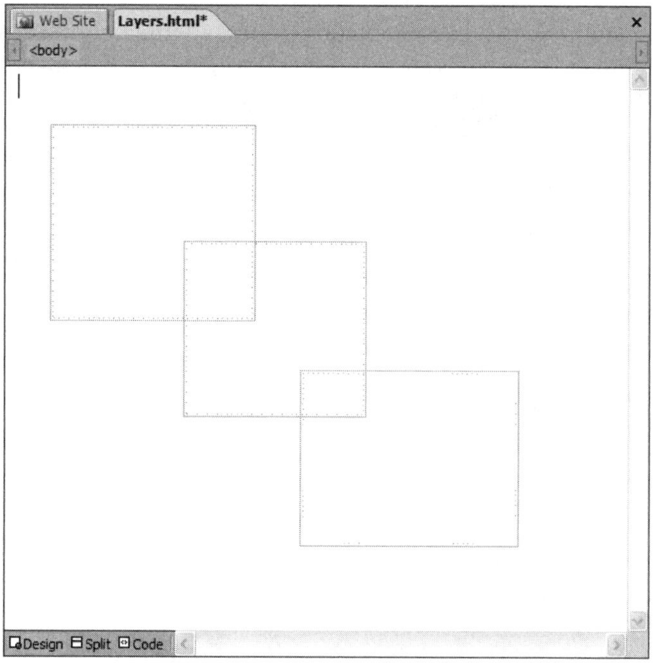

FIGURE 8-11 This HTML document has three overlapping layers.

You can also create behaviors for layers, which is covered in Chapter 10. Behaviors allow HTML items to respond to mouse events and other dynamic events.

You can add text inside of the layers. To do this, type text in either Design or Code view. The text attributes such as the size and color can be set in the normal ways while in Design mode. Just highlight the text and choose a font size and color.

You can also center the text in the usual ways, or you can add a text alignment attribute to the layer's style as the following example shows:

```
<div id="layer1" style="text-align:center; background-color:aqua;
   position: absolute; width: 164px; height: 152px; z-index: 1;
   left: 37px; top: 46px"></div>
```

It's also easy to add a background image to a layer by adding a background-image attribute to the style. The following example shows a layer that has a background image:

```
<div id="layer2" style="background-image: url('Moon.jpg');
   position : absolute; left: 448px; top: 77px; width: 286px;
   height: 284px; z-index: 2"></div>
```

Summary

In this chapter you've learned about dynamic templates and layers. Expression makes both of these tools easy to use and implement. And when you do, your web application will be much more consistent and it will be much easier to maintain.

You will become adept at dynamic templates and layers with a little practice. And once you have added the extra skill to your arsenal, your web applications will go to a new level.

9

Organize Content in Tables and Frames

HOW TO...

- Create tables
- Format tables
- Layout web pages with tables
- Use frames

This chapter is about HTML tables and frames. Both offer mechanisms that allow you to format your pages. Their flexibility gives you options that let you show tabular data, lay out web pages, and perform advanced formatting.

Almost every HTML page uses tables, and many of them use multiple tables. Frames aren't used nearly as often as tables, but still add a powerful tool to your arsenal. In this chapter you will learn how to use tables and frames to give your pages a professional look.

Expression Web 2 makes using tables easier than ever. It has a number of table layouts that you can add to your HTML pages.

Create Tables

The first thing you need to learn is the basics of tables. This section shows you the essentials you need to get started.

Create Rows, Columns, and Headings

A table, very much like an Excel spreadsheet, has rows and columns. A row goes right and left while a column goes up and down. At any given row or column position is a cell, and cells contain the information, or data. Figure 9-1 shows a table with its rows, columns, and cells labeled.

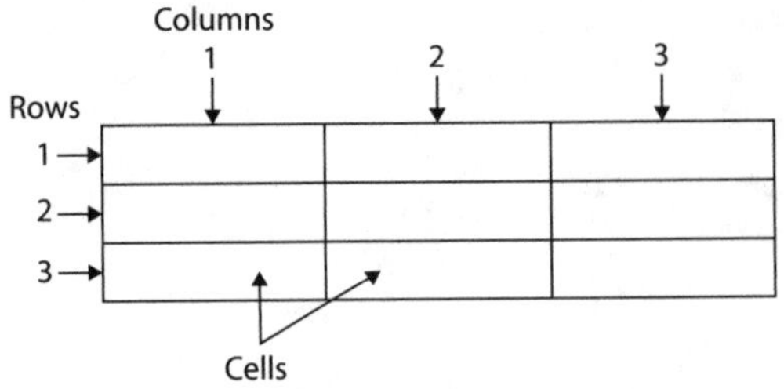

FIGURE 9-1 A table with its rows and columns labeled

There are two ways to add tables to your HTML pages: by using Expression's table inserter, or by manually adding HTML code to your page. In most cases you let Expression Web 2 do the work of inserting tables. To do this, follow these steps:

1. Position the cursor where you want a table inserted.
2. Select Insert Table from the Table menu.
3. When the Insert Table dialog appears, edit the number of rows and columns and any other options you desire. The table will then be a part of your HTML page.

Figure 9-2 shows the Insert Table dialog box. It has a number of options that we'll talk about in the section "Format Tables" later in this chapter. For now, simply note that this table has three rows and three columns.

Once the table has been inserted into the HTML document, you will see it in Design view, as shown in Figure 9-3. This isn't necessarily how it will appear when it is rendered in a browser, but it is intended to let you see where it falls within the document.

You can easily change the number of rows and columns once a table has been inserted. Right-click anywhere inside the table to bring up a pop-up menu, then select Table Properties. The Table Properties dialog box will appear and allow you to change the table's attributes. The Table Properties dialog is almost identical to the Insert Table dialog box.

The code for the table needs some explanation. No matter how good an application's editing dialogs are (and Expression's are very good), there are many good reasons to use Code view. The following code is behind the 3 × 3 table that we inserted.

```
<table style="width: 100%">
    <tr>
        <td> </td>
        <td> </td>
        <td> </td>
    </tr>
```

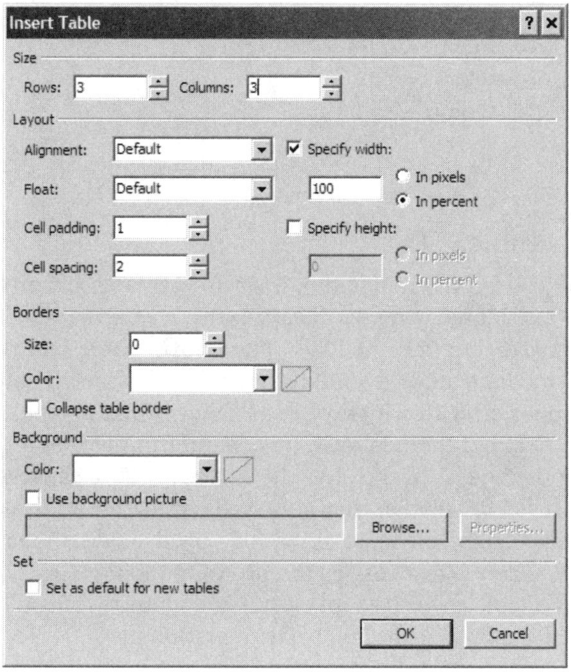

FIGURE 9-2 The Insert Table dialog is set to insert a table with three rows and three columns.

FIGURE 9-3 Once inserted, the table appears in the HTML document so that it's clear where it fits into the document.

```
<tr>
     <td> </td>
     <td> </td>
     <td> </td>
</tr>
<tr>
     <td> </td>
     <td> </td>
     <td> </td>
</tr>
```

```
        <tr>
                <td> </td>
                <td> </td>
                <td> </td>
        </tr>
</table>
```

Use the <table> Tag

In the table code you'll notice that it starts with a `<table>` tag and ends with a `</table>` tag. More correctly, it starts with a `<table>` tag which includes the attribute `style="width: 100%"`. The `<table>` tag indicates the start and the `</table>` tag indicates the end of the table construct. There are quite a few attributes that are supported with which you can determine the look and appearance of a table. We'll get to many of them later in this chapter in the section "Format Tables".

Setting the width (in the style attribute) to 100% causes the table to occupy as much width as is available. In other words, if the browser is 800 pixels wide, the table will be almost 800 pixels wide; if it's 1000 pixels wide, the table will be almost 1000 pixels wide; when a user resizes the browser, the table will resize accordingly. While you can set a table's width as an exact pixel value, we usually use percentage values so that our tables adjust according to the situation.

<tr> Tag Explained

Within the `<table>` and `</table>` tags are `<tr>` and `</tr>` tag pairs. These indicate the start and end of each table row. If a table has five rows, you will have five pairs of `<tr>` and `</tr>` tags. It is essential to note that once you start a `<tr>` tag, you must have a `</tr>` tag before starting another row with a `<tr>` tag. In other words, the following code is incorrect.

```
<tr>        Start of Row 1
</tr>       End of Row 1
<tr>        Start of Row 2
</tr>       End of Row 2
<tr>        Start of Row 3
<tr>        Start of New Row (Incorrect)
</tr>       End of Row 3
</tr>       End of the Incorrect Row
```

The best way to avoid any incorrect syntax with `<tr>` and `</tr>` tags is to use the Page Properties dialog box to edit them. It will make sure that your rows start and end correctly and that there isn't any improper nesting.

Note *Nesting* refers to items within items. For instance, tables within tables are often referred to as nested tables.

<td> Tag Explained

Within the `<tr>` and `</tr>` tags are `<td>` and `</td>` tag pairs. These indicate the start and end of each column within a row. If a row has five columns, then you will have five pairs of `<td>` and `</td>` tags. As with the row tags, once you start a `<td>` tag, you must have a `</td>` tag before starting another column with a `<td>` tag.

The data that appears in each cell is the data that can be found within each column tag. For instance, if a table lists different automobiles, then the following would cause Porsche to appear in one of the cells:

```
<td>Porsche</td>
```

You don't have to go to Code view to put data into a cell. All you need to do is type what you want in each cell from the Design view, and Expression places it in the code. Cells need at least one character in order to render correctly; a blank space in the code between the `<td>` and `</td>` tags doesn't count. That's why Expression puts the ` ` special symbol in each cell: it causes a blank space to be rendered in the cell. If this wasn't there, the cell would not render correctly.

Note A space in Design view will automatically give you the ` ` symbol in the code, but a space entered into the code is just a space.

Let's try an experiment. In the 3 × 3 table, insert an automobile make in each cell. Have Expression render it by pressing F2 or selecting the Preview button. You will see a simple table with automobile types in it. Now go to Design or Code view and remove the content from one of the cells and re-render it. Depending on your browser, the cell with no content might appear to be malformed rather than simply empty.

For examples of using tables go to http://rickleinecker.com/HTDE. (You can also find the table example files from McGraw-Hill Professional's web site at www.mhprofessional.com in a file named TableDemoSamples.zip.) The specific link for this chapter's examples can be found at http://rickleinecker.com/HTDE/Chapter9.aspx. Figure 9-4 shows a comparison of the 3 × 3 table where all cells have content, and the 3 × 3 table where one cell has no content.

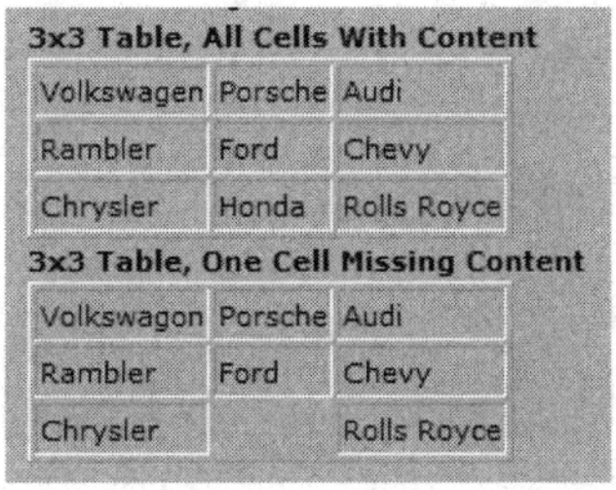

3x3 Table, All Cells With Content

Volkswagen	Porsche	Audi
Rambler	Ford	Chevy
Chrysler	Honda	Rolls Royce

3x3 Table, One Cell Missing Content

Volkswagon	Porsche	Audi
Rambler	Ford	Chevy
Chrysler		Rolls Royce

FIGURE 9-4 A comparison of a table where all cells have content with a table that has one cell with no content

In general, tables have the same number of columns for each row, so a table with 15 rows and 5 columns will have normally have five columns in all rows. However, this restriction can be overcome by setting a column span for any cell.

Let's say that all of the rows have five columns, but you want one row to have just one column. You can set its column span to 5, and that particular row will have only a single column that spans five columns.

You can use Expression to set the column span, or you can do it in HTML code. To set column span, right-click on any cell and select Cell Properties from the pop-up menu. The Cell Properties dialog box will appear as shown in Figure 9-5.

If you set the Columns Spanned field to a value greater than 1, its span will increase. Note that all cells to the right of the expanded cell will shift to the right. You may have to delete cells that get shifted out of the table. Figure 9-6 shows a table with shifted cells followed by a table where the cells outside of the table have been deleted.

You can also change the span for any cell in the HTML code. To do this, just add the colspan attribute to any <td> tag. Here are two examples:

```
<td colspan="2">
<td colspan="5">
```

You can let Expression set your header cells instead of editing the HTML code. First, select the cells you want to transform to header cells, then right-click and select Cell Properties from the pop-up menu. Now select the Header Cell check box. The selected cells will become header cells and their text will be bold and centered.

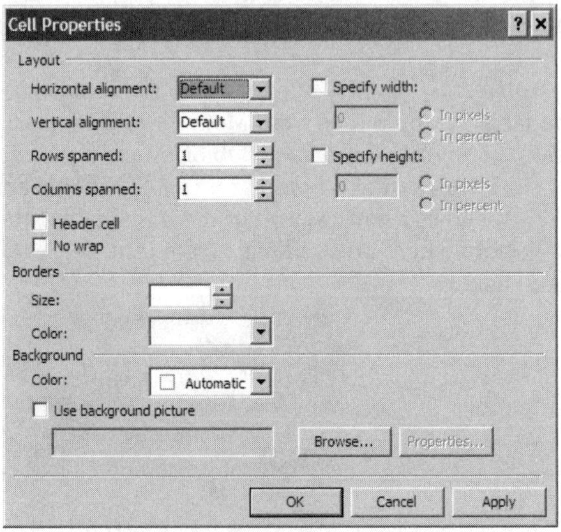

FIGURE 9-5 The Cell Properties dialog box allows you to set the column span.

Table with cell shifted out of table.

Volkswagen	Porsche	Audi	
Camaro		Road Runner	Charger
Rambler	Ford	Chevy	
Chrysler		Rolls Royce	

Table with shifted cell deleted.

Volkswagen	Porsche	Audi
Camaro		Road Runner
Rambler	Ford	Chevy
Chrysler		Rolls Royce

FIGURE 9-6 You might get cells that shift out of the table if you increase the column span of a cell.

Tags Inside Table Cells

So far, the examples in this chapter have used simple text as the data inside of each cell. If you limit your tables to this, they won't contain that much useful functionality. Fortunately, table cells can contain any HTML data or tag, including other tables. Yes, you can have tables within tables.

How to...

Add Special Table Headings

There is a special version of the column <td> tag: the <th> and </th> tag pair. These are normally used for the table header row (usually the first row of data in the table). These tags function exactly as the <td> and </td> tag pair do except for two things. The first is that the text in them is bold. The second is that the data in them is centered. This saves you from having to use the bold (or strong) and center tags within each cell of the table header row. The following example shows a simple table with a header row:

```
<table style="width: 100%" border="1">
     <tr>
          <th>Header 1</th>
          <th>Header 2</th>
          <th>Header 3</th>
     </tr>
     <tr>
          <td>Camaro</td>
          <td>Road Runner</td>
          <td>Charger</td>
     </tr>
</table>
```

Let's start by creating another 3 × 3 table into which we'll insert images. The next thing we'll do is collect nine images in a folder. First, create a folder named ImagesForTableSample within the current project. If your project is in a different location than this, your path will be different from the example. We named the nine image files for this example Sample1.jpg through Sample9.jpg. You can name them whatever you wish, but again, your path will be different from the example if you change the name. The path for your nine collected images should be My Documents\My Web Sites\ImagesForTableSample. By default, Expression works from My Documents\My Web Sites, and by using the folder within our web project, we will be safe using relative paths. When we move the web project to another location such as a web server, the links won't be broken since they are relative.

Now that you have a 3 × 3 table, the working folder inside of your project's folder, and the nine sample images, you can insert the images into the table. Insert images into each cell with the following process.

1. Select a single cell into which you wish to place an image.
2. From the Insert menu, select Picture | From File.
3. Find the image file by clicking the Current Site button and opening the new folder (ImagesForTableSample for the demo), as shown in Figure 9-7.

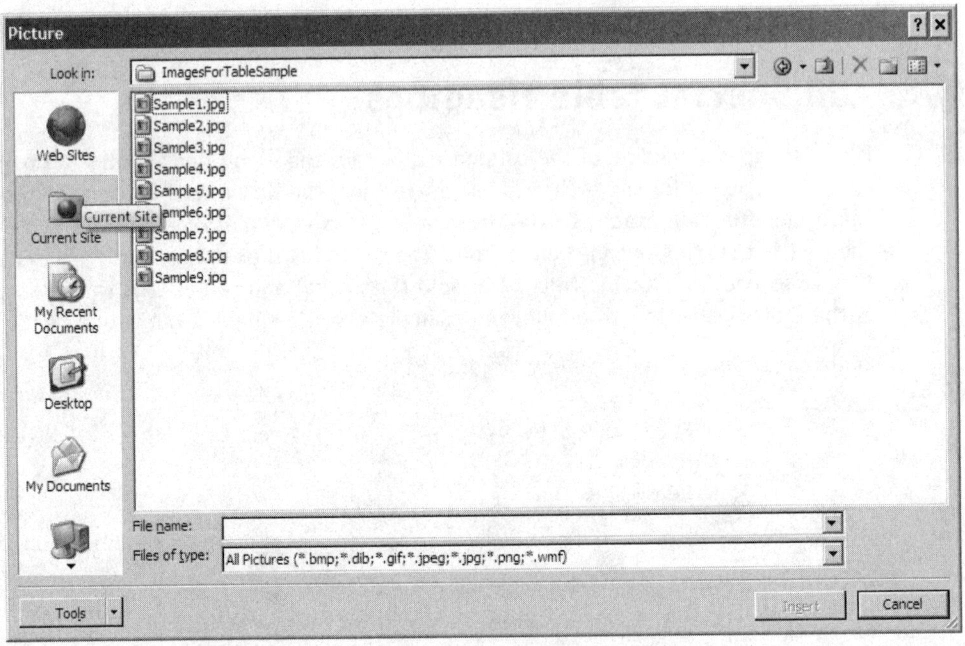

FIGURE 9-7 Find your Current Site folder and open the newly created folder within it.

4. Select the image you want to insert in the selected cell.
5. Add any desired information such as Alternate Text in the Accessibility Properties dialog box that appears. Your image will appear in the selected cell of the table.

If you examine the HTML that Expression created, you'll see <img> tags inside of the cells. The following is code from one of the cells that Expression created.

```
<td><img alt="" src="ImagesForTableSample/Sample3.jpg"
    width="159" height="104" /></td>
```

Note that the image width and height were added. Doing this manually is a time-consuming process, and having the size attributes automatically added saves you a lot of time. It's also convenient that the HTML for the image is created and inserted into the cell, and all you had to do was use a file selector, find the images, and click the Open button.

Note Expression will allow you to insert an image from anywhere on your hard drive by using the Insert from File dialog. When you save the page, you will be asked what folder to put the image into. You will need to select a folder that's inside of your web somewhere. If the image is not within your web, then when you upload to the server the image won't be found. We once had a student who worked on a project from home. Even after we harped on him about this point, many of his images were references to his hard drive with paths such as C:\My Documents\figure.jpg. When we accessed his web site, the images could not be found. It looked fine from his computer because the path was valid for him. Just make sure that all of your image references are within your web directory.

There is a collection of nine sample images posted on http://rickleinecker.com/HTDE/Chapter9.aspx that you can download for this demo. You can also see the demo right below the download link.

The last basic table skill is to put a table within a table. This can get confusing when you're developing a web page. Some students blow a fuse trying to keep it straight. If your tags don't match, for instance, you use a <td> without a matching </td>, or you have incorrect nesting, it can be difficult to get back on track. In spite of those caveats, though, tables inside tables are powerful tools.

We'll start with a 2 × 2 table that contains four ice cream flavors: vanilla, chocolate, strawberry, and cookie dough. However, there are four varieties of chocolate that we need to specify. To do this, insert a 2 × 2 table inside of the cell where we want the chocolate varieties. Figure 9-8 shows a page with three tables: the first with nothing in the chocolate cell, the second with a table in the chocolate cell, and the third with the "table within a table" populated with four chocolate varieties.

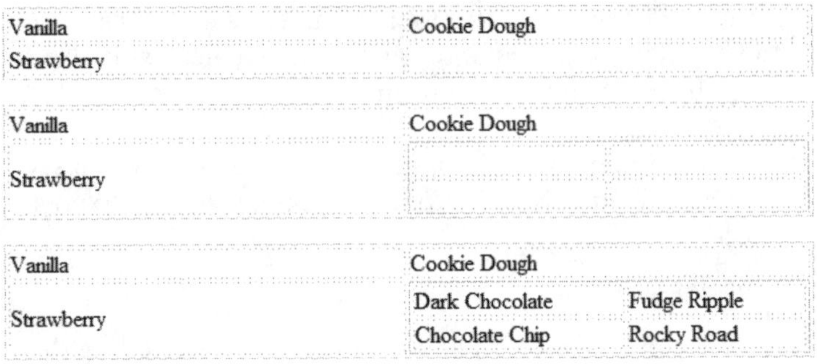

FIGURE 9-8 A progression of tables, whereby the final result is a table within a table containing four varieties of chocolate.

Format Tables

Now that you know the basics of tables, we can turn our attention to their formatting. Tables can be formatted in many ways, thus providing you with a way to get the look and feel you want. This section shows you how to format the various elements of tables.

Set the Background Color

One of the first things we usually do to a table is change the background color of the entire table, a row, or a single cell. To change the background of the entire table, right-click on the table and select Table Properties from the pop-up menu that appears. The Table Properties dialog box will appear. In the Background section of the dialog box, click the Color drop-down and select a color for the entire table.

There is no HTML attribute that can be inserted into the `<table>` tag that changes the color of the table. But Expression does a very smart thing to change the background color of the entire table. It gives the table a unique class name and then defines the

Did You Know?

The Numeric Color Values Are Made of Red, Green, and Blue Values

Many HTML colors have names such as Cyan and Red. But many colors are numbers. The format of the colors is a six-digit hexadecimal number. The first two digits (ranging in value from 0 to 255) represent the red component of the color, the next two the green component, and the last two the blue component.

Depending on the red, green, and blue values that are specified, a color results. You can use programs such as PC Paint or Paint Shop Pro to help you figure out custom colors.

background color of the unique class's style in the head section of the HTML. Following is the code for a table with the unique class of style1. The table code was created when we used the Insert Table dialog to insert a table into a page. The class attribute was added when the table color was changed with the Table Properties dialog.

```
<table style="width: 100%" class="style1">
```

In the head section of the page the style is inserted that sets the background color of the table as follows:

```
<style type="text/css">
.style1 {
	background-color: #FF00FF;
}
</style>
```

Expression doesn't have a mechanism for setting the background color of an entire row. However, if you select an entire row, you can set the color for each individual cell in the row with the Cell Properties dialog box. There is also a way you can manually set the color for an entire row in the HTML code, by adding a bgcolor attribute to a <tr> tag as follows:

```
<tr bgcolor="red">
```

Add Background Images

You can easily set the background of a table to an image instead of a color. To do this, open the Table Properties dialog box. Under the Color drop-down, select the Use Background Picture check box and browse for an image to use as the background of the table, as shown in Figure 9-9.

You can set the background picture of a single cell in a similar manner. Just right-click on a cell, select Cell Properties from the pop-up menu, and the Cell Properties dialog box appears. Select the Use Background Picture check box and browse for the image you want to use as the cell's background image.

Insert Borders

About half of the time we need a border around the tables we use. Borders are especially desirable when a table contains information that's being presented to page readers. You can specify the border size (width in pixels) and its color from the Table Properties dialog box in the section labeled Borders. In addition, you can set the border for any cell. To do this, open the Cell Properties dialog box. Use the Borders section to set the size and color of the cell border.

There is also a way to add code to the HTML so that the table and all of its cells have borders. In the <table> tag you can add a border attribute as follows:

```
<table style="width: 100%" border="3">
```

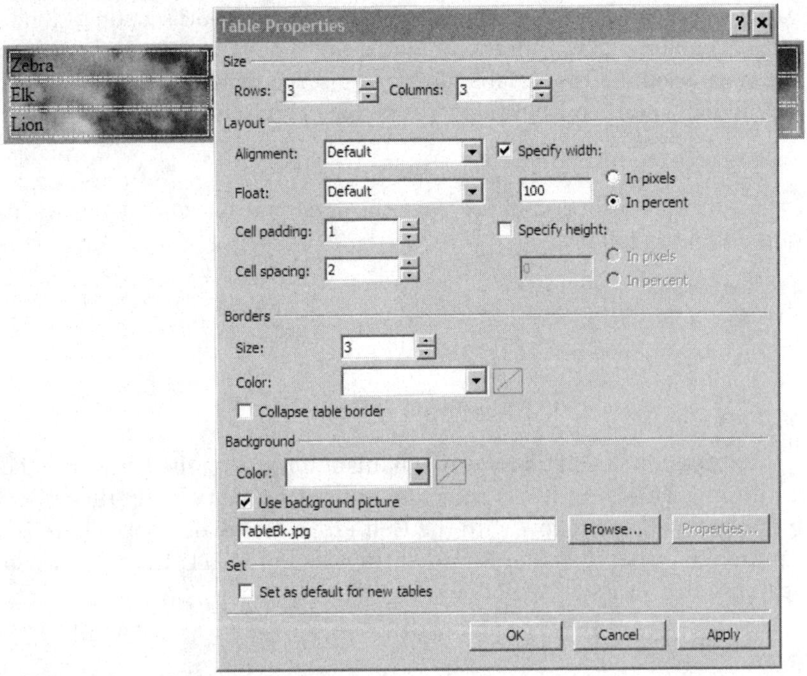

FIGURE 9-9 A table with a cloud picture as background and the Table Properties dialog

Use Cell Padding and Cell Spacing

Tables have two values that can be changed to fit a variety of situations: `cellpadding` and `cellspacing`. By default the `cellpadding` value is 1 and the `cellspacing` value is 2.

The `cellpadding` value determines the number of pixels between the border of a cell and the content. For instance, if the `cellpadding` value is set to 10, there will be 10 pixels between the cell border and the content such as text or an image.

The `cellspacing` value determines the number of pixels between the cells. For instance, if the `cellspacing` value is set to 15, there will be 15 pixels between all of the cells in the table.

To set the `cellpadding` and `cellspacing` values, open the Table Properties dialog box and adjust the Cell Padding and Cell Spacing numeric controls to change the `cellpadding` and `cellspacing` values for the table. You can also directly add attributes to the HTML `<table>` tag as follows:

```
<table style="width: 100%" cellpadding="20" cellspacing="20">
```

Figure 9-10 shows three tables. The first has the default `cellpadding` and `cellspacing` values. The second has a `cellpadding` value of 20. The third has a `cellspacing` value of 20. Since the tables have borders, you can easily see how the `cellpadding` and `cellspacing` values affect their look.

Adjust Content Alignment

Just as with word processors, you can align text within cells in a number of ways. Table text can be aligned left, center, and right, and cells can each have their own alignment that overrides the table alignment. Horizontally you can align cells left, center, right, and justified. With no justification specified, the text will normally align left by default for a table or cell.

To align text, open either the Table Properties dialog box (if you want to set the alignment for the entire table) or the Cell Properties dialog box (if you want to set the alignment for a cell). The Table Properties dialog has an Alignment drop-down, and the Cell Properties dialog has a Horizontal Alignment drop-down. Use these to set to the desired alignment.

You can also align text within a cell vertically. The default setting is for the text to be centered vertically. Changing the vertical alignment is especially useful if cells

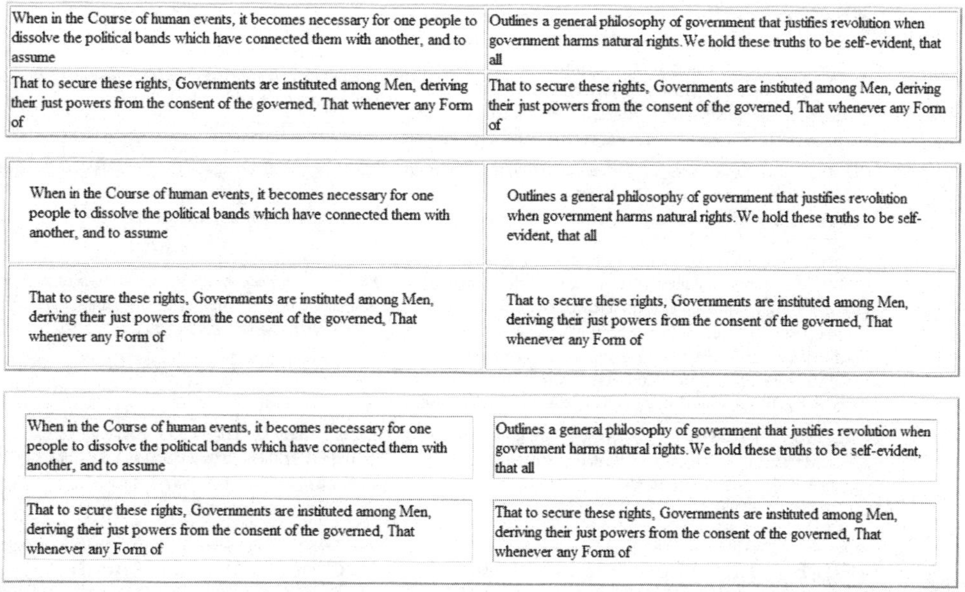

When in the Course of human events, it becomes necessary for one people to dissolve the political bands which have connected them with another, and to assume	Outlines a general philosophy of government that justifies revolution when government harms natural rights. We hold these truths to be self-evident, that all
That to secure these rights, Governments are instituted among Men, deriving their just powers from the consent of the governed, That whenever any Form of	That to secure these rights, Governments are instituted among Men, deriving their just powers from the consent of the governed, That whenever any Form of

When in the Course of human events, it becomes necessary for one people to dissolve the political bands which have connected them with another, and to assume	Outlines a general philosophy of government that justifies revolution when government harms natural rights. We hold these truths to be self-evident, that all
That to secure these rights, Governments are instituted among Men, deriving their just powers from the consent of the governed, That whenever any Form of	That to secure these rights, Governments are instituted among Men, deriving their just powers from the consent of the governed, That whenever any Form of

When in the Course of human events, it becomes necessary for one people to dissolve the political bands which have connected them with another, and to assume	Outlines a general philosophy of government that justifies revolution when government harms natural rights. We hold these truths to be self-evident, that all
That to secure these rights, Governments are instituted among Men, deriving their just powers from the consent of the governed, That whenever any Form of	That to secure these rights, Governments are instituted among Men, deriving their just powers from the consent of the governed, That whenever any Form of

FIGURE 9-10 These three tables have different `cellpadding` and `cellspacing` values.

that are horizontally adjacent have different amounts of data. When this happens and the default vertical alignment is centered, the cells with the least content will have a gap at the top. Our senses are usually okay when there is a gap at the bottom, since many pages have some blank space at the bottom and we're used to this. But when there is space at the top, we perceive a problem. For this reason, we usually align cells to the top vertically. Figure 9-11 shows two tables. The first has the default vertical alignment and the second is aligned at the top vertically.

Adjust the Size

We've already talked about setting tables to occupy the entire browser window width by setting the table width to 100 percent. You can also set the table's vertical height to a percentage of the available browser window width. We almost always use a percentage value when we set a table size because the table size adjusts as the browser window is resized. To set the table width and height, open the Table Properties dialog box, select the In Percent radio button, and enter the percentage value that you want.

There are times, however, when setting a table's width or height to a specific pixel value is best. When this is the case, select the In Pixels radio button, and enter the pixel value that you want.

When in the Course of human events, it becomes necessary for one people to dissolve the political bands which have connected them with another, and to which have connected them with another, and to which have connected them with another, and to which have connected them with another, and to which have connected them with another, and to assume	Outlines a general philosophy of government that justifies revolution when government harms natural rights. We hold these truths to be self-evident, that all
That to secure these rights, Governments are instituted among Men, deriving their just powers from the consent of the governed, That whenever any Form of	That to secure these rights, Governments are instituted among Men, deriving their just powers from the consent of the governed, That whenever any Form of

When in the Course of human events, it becomes necessary for one people to dissolve the political bands which have connected them with another, and to which have connected them with another, and to which have connected them with another, and to which have connected them with another, and to which have connected them with another, and to assume	Outlines a general philosophy of government that justifies revolution when government harms natural rights. We hold these truths to be self-evident, that all
That to secure these rights, Governments are instituted among Men, deriving their just powers from the consent of the governed, That whenever any Form of	That to secure these rights, Governments are instituted among Men, deriving their just powers from the consent of the governed, That whenever any Form of

FIGURE 9-11 These two tables show the effect of vertical alignment.

You can also specify the width and height of a cell in the same way you do a table's, except that you use the Cell Properties dialog box.

Use Style Sheets to Format Tables

You can apply style changes to all of the tables in a page very easily by creating a style that applies to tables. Follow these steps:

1. Select New Style from the Format menu.
2. Choose Table from the Selector drop-down.
3. Choose Current Page from the Define In drop-down.
4. Select each table attribute you want to change from the Category list.
5. Set the values in the items that appear in the main part of the dialog box.
6. Choose and edit additional categories if you want.
7. Click OK.
8. Look at the HTML code in the head section and you'll see the newly created style code.

Once you create the new style for the tables in a page, all of the tables will change appearance. Any styles that are applied to individual tables or cells will override the style settings that you just created.

You can save a table style to an external style sheet. To do this, select New Style Sheet of Existing Style Sheet from the Define In drop-down. The benefit to saving these in an external style sheet is that many pages in your site can be attached to the style sheet, allowing you to change attributes in all your pages with only one change in the style sheet.

Lay Out Web Pages with Tables

So far, we've used tables to present content. Tables can also be used very effectively to lay out a web page. If, for instance, you want a web page with a header and footer, a contents pane to the left, and a main content area, then you can create a table into which all of these elements will fit. Many web sites have a header with three content columns in the middle. Without a table it's very difficult to maintain this type of web page structure.

Fortunately, Expression has a number of ready-made tables that can be inserted into your web page to provide the appropriate layout. Let's say you want a page in which you'll present three historical documents such as the Declaration of Independence, some historical facts, and the Preamble to the Constitution. You could use a page layout based on one of the table patterns that are built into Expression to do this.

The following steps will walk you through this process.

1. Start by creating a new web page in your project.
2. From the Tables menu, select Layout Tables; the Layout Tables window will open, as shown in Figure 9-12.
3. In the Table Layout section of the Layout Tables task pane, select the design that has a header, three content sections, and a footer.
4. In the design window, right-click on the table and select Table Properties from the pop-up menu.
5. Set the width to 100 percent. (See the "Adjust the Size" section earlier in this chapter for more help in setting the size of a table.)
6. Enter text into the header and footer sections and format it.

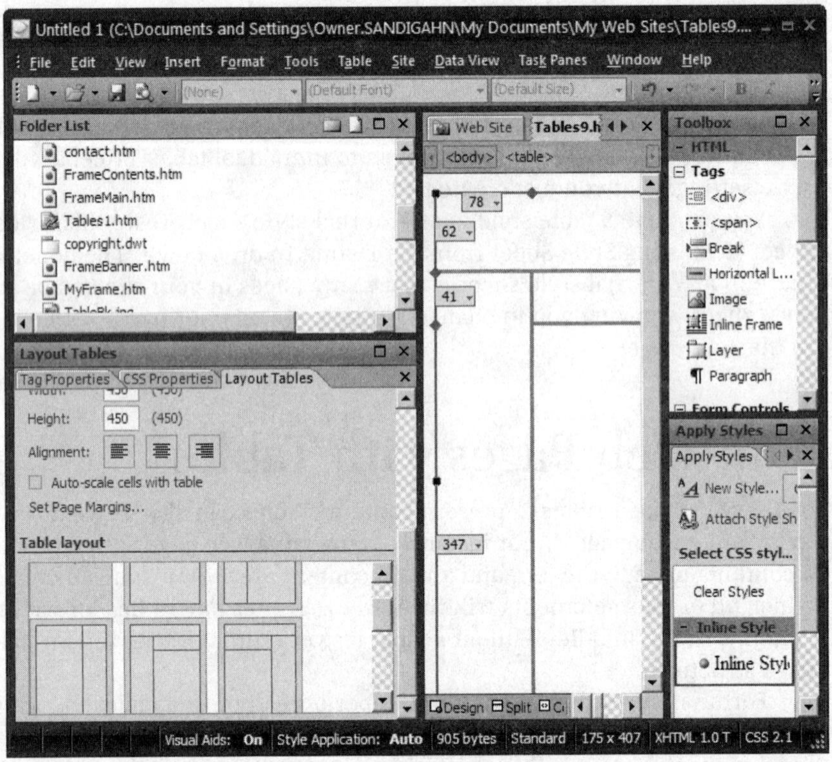

FIGURE 9-12 A Layout Tables window opens.

7. Enter content into the three sections in the middle.
8. When you render the page, it will be similar to what you see in Figure 9-13.

One of our favorite available layouts has a header and footer, a link column on the left, and a main content area. A tooltip appears when you hover over it in the Layout Tables window with the text "Header, Left, Top Right, and Body." Just to prove how easy the creation of a web page is when using the provided layouts, we timed the creation of a web page. It took 6 minutes and 22 seconds, and the page can be seen in Figure 9-14. This page can also be viewed in the Chapter 9 web page at http://rickleinecker.com/HTDE/Chapter9.aspx.

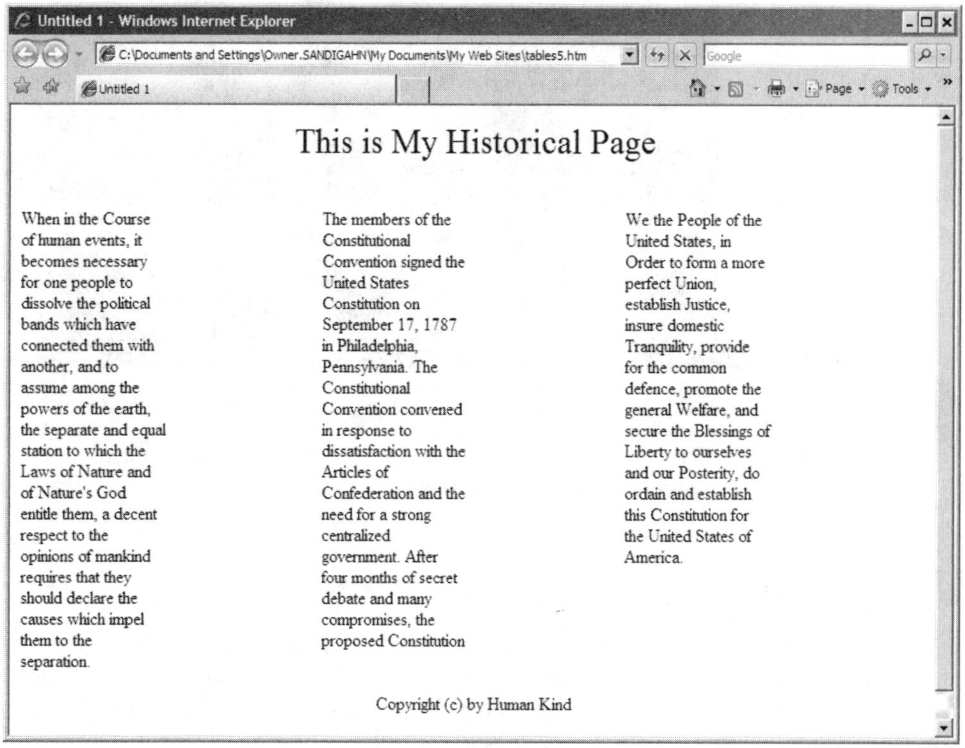

FIGURE 9-13 It took almost no time to create this formatted web page by using one of Expression's layout tables.

FIGURE 9-14 This web site might look complicated, but with Expression's table layouts it is easy to create.

Use Frames

Similar to layout tables, frames give web designers a way to organize page content into multiple regions of the screen. Frames add some functionality to layout tables that may make them a better choice than layout tables in certain situations.

Frames are an aggregation of several web pages into an organization unit known as a frameset. In order to use frames, there must be a controlling page that specifies the frameset. This controlling page rarely displays anything to the user, but it lets the browser know which pages are contained in the frameset and how to display them. Frames divide the page into multiple rectangular areas and display a separate document in each area. Each of the rectangles in which a document is contained is called a frame.

One advantage to frames is that you can edit each of the frames within a frameset on its own. This can make it easier than using tables since the content for that particular frame is encapsulated within its own document. It is simpler to create and maintain than a large document, and some of the complexities such as shared and overlapping style sheets might be avoided.

Another big advantage to frames is that you can change the content in a frameset's frame without changing the content in the other frames, which can make for smoother navigation and information presentation. For instance, one of the frames can have several links. Each time a link is selected, the content in another frame can change while the rest of the frameset remains the same.

Some web developers never use frames. Their reasons range from HTML aesthetics to theoretical arguments. If you want to use frames, don't let these naysayers deter you. There is a time and place to use frames, regardless of any negative ideas you might read.

To get started with frames, from the File menu select New | Page. The New dialog box will appear in which you can specify the type of new page you want to create. When you select Frames Pages, a number of design types will appear in the middle window. Choose the design you want, as shown in Figure 9-15.

Framesets all need different HTML files for each frame in the set. You can edit the frameset file and manually set these files, but Expression makes it very easy. When you first create a frameset, Expression places two buttons inside of each frame. One of the buttons lets you insert an existing HTML file into the frame, and the other lets you create a new HTML file into the frame. Figure 9-16 shows a newly created frameset with two buttons in each frame.

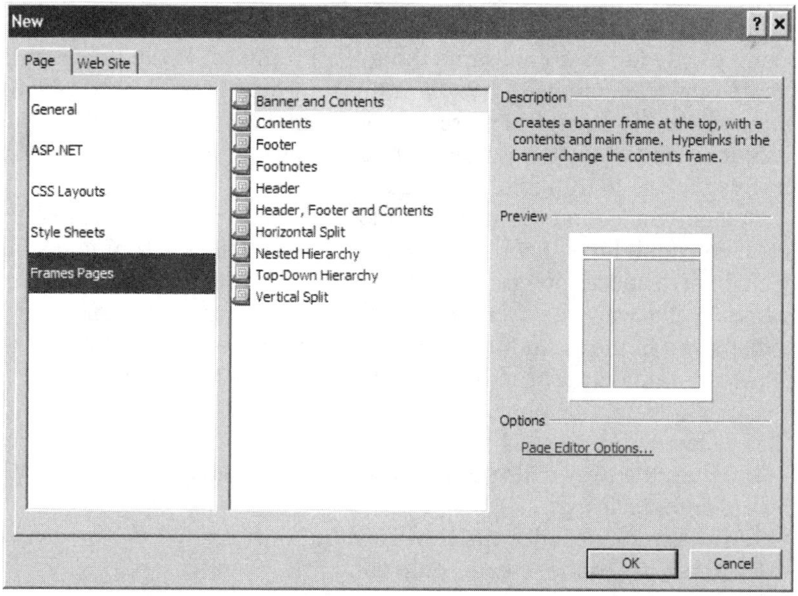

FIGURE 9-15 Frames pages can be created in a number of design patterns.

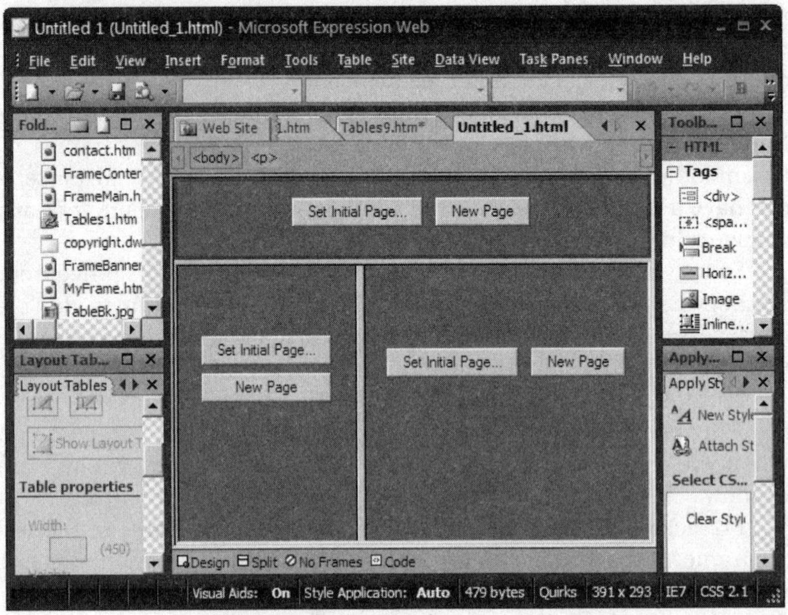

FIGURE 9-16 Expression makes it easy to specify HTML files for each frame.

In the last section, we created a table layout page and timed how long it took. It seemed only fair to do the same thing for a frameset to see how easy it would be. We created the frame files so that the frameset would look like the table layout page, and you can see the result in Figure 9-17. Creating the frameset and frame files took a little longer than the 6 minutes and 22 seconds it took for the table layout: from start to finish it was 10 minutes and 14 seconds.

When you look at the frameset in Figure 9-17, you'll notice that the frame on the left has several links. Each of these links has an HREF attribute just as a normal link does, but we added a target attribute so that the link target is loaded into the main frame. In this way, the user's selection in the left frame determines the content that is displayed in the main frame. To create a frameset and get links in the left frame to cause content to appear in the main frame, follow these steps:

1. Select File | New.
2. When the New dialog box appears, select Frames Pages and use the Banner and Contents design.
3. In each frame, click the New Page button.
4. In the top frame, create some content.
5. In the main frame, create some content.

FIGURE 9-17 This frameset web page looks similar to the table layout page in the earlier part of the chapter.

6. In the left frame, create three links: link1.htm, link2.htm, and link3.htm, respectively.
7. To create the links in the left frame:
   a. Type in the link text.
   b. Select the link text.
   c. Press CTRL-K or select Hyperlink from the Insert menu.
   d. Type in the target HTML filename: for example link1.htm, link2.htm, and link3.htm.
   e. Click the Target Frame button and select the target frame as shown in Figure 9-18.
8. Make sure that you have the HTML files for each link (for example link1.htm, link2.htm, and link3.htm), then save all pages and test the frameset.

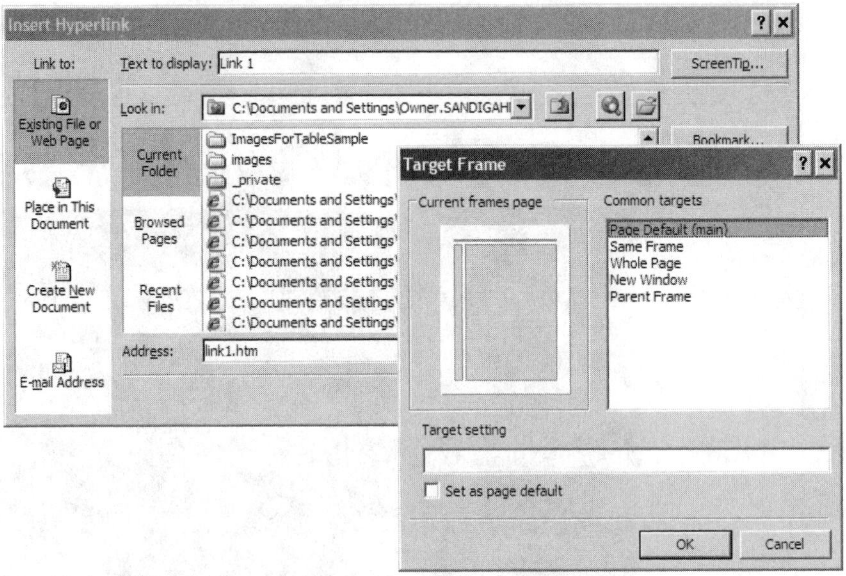

FIGURE 9-18 This dialog allows you to set the target frame.

Summary

Tables are a great way to format your web pages. There are plenty of preconfigured table layouts that Expression Web 2 offers. You can also create your own custom table layouts.

Frames are a more controversial layout mechanism, and many web developers avoid them at all costs. However, we have found several places where they are the best option, so frames are a good tool to have available.

10

Use Behaviors for Action and Interaction

HOW TO...

- Understand JavaScript
- Create JavaScript code with Expression Web 2: Add Behaviors
- Use active buttons

In the beginning there was static HTML.

Of course, that statement is not completely true, but it did get your attention. It's more accurate to say that the Web in the early to mid-1990s contained *mostly* static HTML. *Static HTML* is made up of a markup file and its assets (such as image files) that were created with an editor, uploaded to a server, and viewed by web browsers in the same way each time. There is no interaction or variance in the static HTML presentation. In this chapter we'll talk about how Expression Web 2 gets us beyond static HTML.

Web developers soon employed a wide variety of techniques to activate pages and provide interactive experiences. These fell into three major categories: server-side dynamic HTML creation, embedded applications such as Java and ActiveX, and client-side dynamic HTML.

- **Server-side HTML creation** This was done with technologies such as ASP (now ASP.NET), Cold Fusion, PHP, and JSP. There are many more of these server-side technologies today.
- **Embedded applications** These are executable binaries that are embedded within HTML documents. Java is a safe technology that consists of pseudo-code that a Java Virtual Machine interprets. ActiveX is an unsafe technology that can potentially damage a computer. There are also many other technologies such as Flash.
- **Dynamic HTML** This technique is often referred to as DHTML, for dynamic HTML, and it is accomplished using JavaScript—code that is part of the HTML document and interpreted at runtime. JavaScript is theoretically safe and should cause no security risks. It has, unfortunately, been compromised over the years. In spite of the small number of JavaScript issues, we still view it as safe.

Understand JavaScript

JavaScript may seem daunting at first, but in the next section, "Create JavaScript with Web Expression 2," you'll see how Expression makes it all easy by injecting the JavaScript for you.

Java is an object-oriented programming language that was developed in the 1990s. There is a lot of folklore that goes with it, including the notion that it was written in less than 24 hours. The syntax of Java is similar to the C and C++ languages and also to the modern C# (C Sharp) language. JavaScript's implementation of the Java language is simpler than the Java language that's used to create applets on the Web. It's more forgiving, especially because it doesn't require each line to end with a semicolon. It also offers variant variables similar to Visual Basic. In short, it's an easy language to learn and use.

There are some great tutorials online. Rather than listing them here in the hopes that they remain valid, we have listed them on a web page that can easily be updated: http://rickleinecker.com/HTDE/Chapter10.aspx.

With JavaScript there are three major programming aspects: code, data, and events. The code performs the actions. Think of code as the verb—it does stuff. The data is usually variables that contain state information. Think of data as adjectives—they contain attributes such as brown, large, and numbers such as 5 and 17. Lastly, think of events as external things that happen—user interactions are the most common that JavaScript deals with. Here are some simple examples.

```
var counter;
for( counter=0; counter<15; counter++ )
{
    document.writeln("This is line " + counter + "<br />");
}
```

In the previous example you can see data and code. The data is the variable named counter, and the code is what's known as a `for` loop that counts and outputs text. The document.writeln( ) method is built into the browser Document Object Model (DOM). There are many classes and methods that are available to JavaScript programmers. The next example shows you event handling:

```
<span id="testyou" onmouseout="this.style.color='black'"
                   onmouseover="this.style.color='red'">This is a test</span>
```

In the previous example, you can see two events being handled: code that fires in response to the event, and data that is used in the process. The two events are onmouseover and onmouseout. They fire off when the user hovers the mouse over the text (onmouseover) and when the user moves the mouse out of the text area (onmouseout). The code is `this.style.color=` followed by the data `'black'` or `'red'`.

Did You Know?

JavaScript Functions Are Sometimes Better Than Inline JavaScript Code

There are times when embedded code is limiting, as in the examples where the onmouseover and onmouseout events are triggered. You might want to perform a number of tasks that would be extremely awkward as inline code. When this is true, you should create and call functions as follows:

```
<script language="javascript">
function MakeBlack(obj)
{
  obj.style.color='black';
}
function MakeRed(obj)
{
  obj.style.color='red';
}
</script>
<span id="testyou" onmouseout="MakeBlack(this);"
                   onmouseover="MakeRed(this);">This is a test
</span>
```

Create JavaScript with Expression Web 2: Add Behaviors

Now we get to the easy part. In this section we'll let Expression do the work for us. It can easily create JavaScript code governing HTML behaviors. All you need to do is use Expression's design windows to specify the behaviors that are applied to HTML objects.

Start by opening the Behaviors task pane by selecting Format | Behaviors. The Behaviors task pane appears, as shown in Figure 10-1.

On the Behaviors task pane, you'll see an Insert button. This button offers you the behaviors that Expression can insert. Figure 10-2 shows you the list that's available.

We'll take time now to use the behaviors: we'll go through each one and use it to alter some HTML code.

Most of the examples mentioned in this chapter can be seen at http://RickReinecker.com/HTDE/Chapter10.aspx.

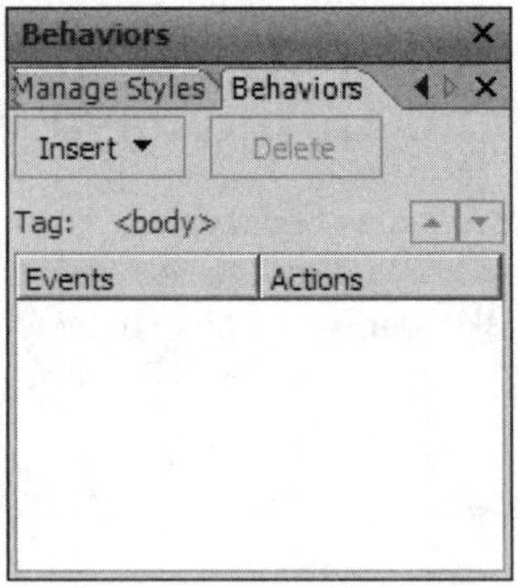

FIGURE 10-1 The Behaviors task pane gets you started in creating behaviors for your HTML page.

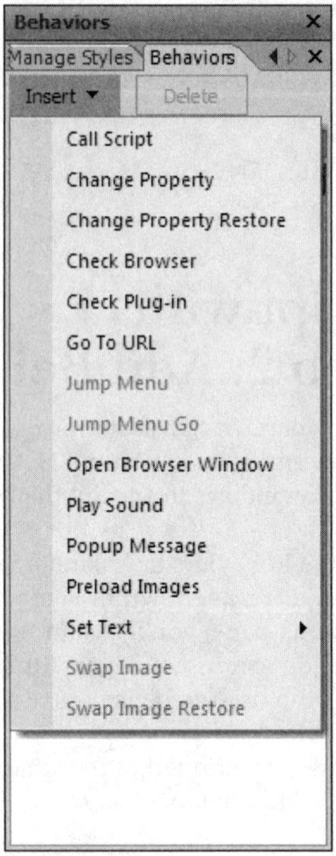

FIGURE 10-2 Expression offers many behaviors that it can insert for you.

Use the Change Property and Change Property Restore Behaviors

The first behavior we'll use is the Change Property behavior, which allows you to change the property of an HTML object in response to an event. The properties that change usually correspond to style changes that can be made such as a font color or a border width. The event that fires the property change is usually the onmouseover event. You can use another event instead of onmouseover for the property change if you want.

There are quite a few reasons for changing properties in response to an event:

- To provide a response to users
- To call attention to an HTML object
- To provide information about an HTML object and what it represents

There are quite a few properties that can be changed including the following:

- Fonts, including size, color, and style
- Position, including alignment and exact x/y position
- Borders, including size, style, and color
- Visibility

Let's start by changing the color of several paragraphs. We started by creating an HTML page with three paragraphs. For each of the paragraphs we did the following:

1. Click in the paragraph.
2. Click the Insert button in the Behaviors task pane.
3. Select Change Property; the Change Property dialog box appears.
4. Click the Font button.
5. Change the color, as shown in Figure 10-3.
6. Select the Restore on Mouseout Event check box (which causes the object to be restored upon an onmouseout event).
7. Click OK.

When you view the page in a browser, the text in each paragraph will change colors.

The Change Property Restore behavior is a related behavior. If you forget to use the Restore on Mouseout Event button to restore the objects, you can add this and it will do the same thing.

Use Check Browser and Check Plug-in Behaviors

We all know that web browsers are platform independent, right? Actually, although that is the goal, it doesn't happen to be true. Anyone who has ever developed a sizable web application knows that Firefox and Internet Explorer render HTML differently in subtle, if not in downright exaggerated, ways. And of course, there are plenty of other

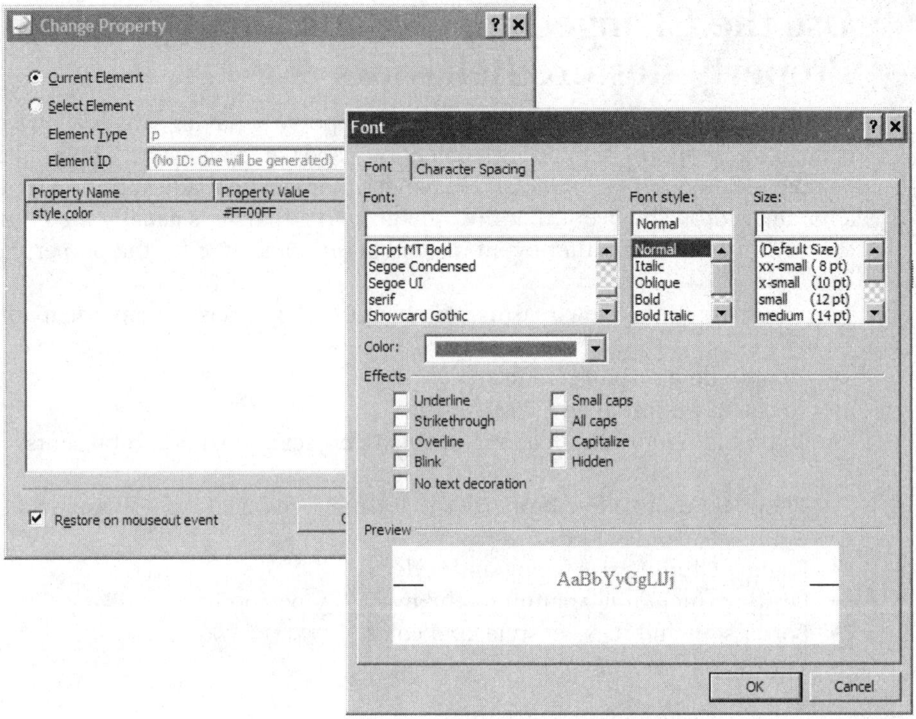

FIGURE 10-3 You can set many properties, including the color.

browsers such as Safari, Opera, and AOL only to name a few. It can be difficult to get HTML code to work perfectly with all browsers.

Here are the reasons you might need to check for the browser version:

- Some critical presentation HTML doesn't render the same in all browsers.
- You need to use different plug-ins for different browsers.
- Your web application requires a minimum version number.

You can use JavaScript to identify the browser type that is accessing your web page. It's easy to do and you can find the code in hundreds of places on the Internet. However, you won't know if the code you're downloading works correctly, and you won't know if it supports a wide variety of browsers—most only support detection of Firefox, Internet Explorer, and Opera.

Expression solves this dilemma for you by offering a Check Browser behavior that looks for various browser versions. It supports seven browser types, which is almost always enough to make sure that your web page looks the same for everyone. Let's say that you have a page that looks great in Internet Explorer, but Firefox doesn't render correctly. You can create two sets of HTML code, one for Internet Explorer and one for Firefox. Then you can use Expression's behavior so that the correct HTML code is used.

To get started, follow these steps.

1. Create three HTML pages: CheckBrowser.htm, YesIE.htm, and NotIE.htm.
2. Enter some simple text into YesIE.htm and NotIE.htm so that you can easily see which one is currently being rendered.
3. Open the CheckBrowser.htm file.
4. Make sure that the body object is selected in the HTML document.
5. Open the Behaviors task pane. Click Insert and select Check Browser.
6. Select a browser type in the If the Current Browser Type Is combo box.
7. In the Version combo box, leave it set to Any or choose a specific browser version.
8. You must choose one or both of the Go to URL check boxes; select both for this demo.
9. In the first text box enter **YesIE.htm**; in the second enter **NotIE.htm**, as shown in Figure 10-4; then click OK.
10. When you preview the CheckBrowser.htm file, it will redirect to YesIE.htm or NotIE.htm.

You might find it somewhat limiting to have the Check Browser behavior redirect to a URL. Sometimes you need to perform tasks within the HTML page rather than redirecting. Here's how we solved this problem. First, we added two variables in the JavaScript code block that Expression inserted. Then, we copied the FP_checkBrowser( ) method, renamed it FP_checkBrowserModified( ), and modified it to set the newly added variables instead of redirecting. Next, we called the new method from the body tag's onload event. Last, we added code to output the browser type. The point is, you can use Expression's behaviors for your purposes, even if they don't exactly match your needs. The code that Expression injects is well-written and therefore easily modified.

Since the modified code is large, it is available at http://rickleinecker.com/HTDE/Chapter10.aspx. You can get the code there and see how it works.

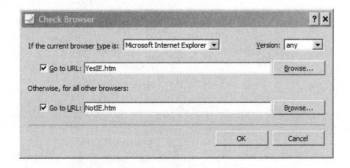

FIGURE 10-4 Redirect to the two HTML files that you created.

Checking for browser plug-ins is almost identical to checking for browser types and versions. To check for a browser plug-in, click the Insert button from the Behaviors task pane. Then select Check Plug-in, select the plug-in you want from the combo box, and specify the URLs to redirect to.

Use the Go To URL Behavior

This is a simple behavior; it simply redirects the page to another URL. It's more flexible than a link because a number of events can trigger it, as shown in Figure 10-5.

Here are some reasons you would use this behavior:

- To provide an easier navigation method for users who have disabilities
- To offer a keypress for navigation
- To require users to double-click to prevent accidental selection
- To examine the state of HTML objects to determine if the redirect is allowed

Using the behavior is easy. Follow these steps:

1. Select an HTML object in the design window (this will be the object whose events trigger the behavior).
2. Click the Insert button in the Behaviors task pane.
3. Select Go To URL.
4. Enter the URL in the text box and click OK.
5. By default, the trigger event is the onmouseover event. To change the event that triggers the behavior, click the item in the Events part of the Behaviors task pane and select the desired event.

When you add the Go To URL behavior, a JavaScript small function is inserted. Inside this function you can add code to check other HTML objects. For instance, if you have some radio buttons and the second button must be selected before a redirect is allowed, you can perform the check in the function.

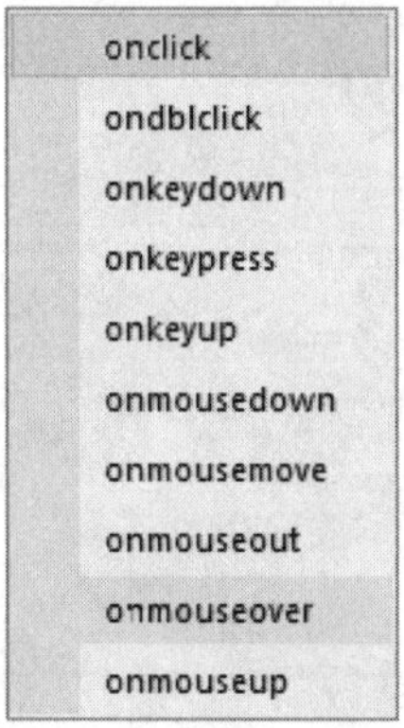

FIGURE 10-5 This behavior responds to a number of events.

The following example has a paragraph with a behavior that responds to an onmouseover event and redirects to yahoo.com. We added two radio buttons in a form. We then edited the FP_goToURL() method that Expression created. If the first (and default) radio button is selected, then the behavior will not happen. Following is the modified JavaScript code; you can also see this as an example at http://.rickleinecker.com/HTDE/Chapter10.aspx.

```
function FP_goToURL(url)
{

 if( document.forms[0][0].checked )
 {
   return;
 }
 window.location=url;
}
```

As you've already seen, you can enhance Expression's behaviors by editing the code that it injects into the HTML. This gives you a foundation upon which you can build some very useful functionality.

Use Open Browser Window Behavior

There are lots of sites that open up those pesky pop-up windows that annoy everyone. But there are many legitimate occasions when you need your web pages to open up additional windows.

Expression has a behavior that allows you to open browser windows. You might say you can already do that by adding a target attribute to a link. While that is true, Expression's Open Browser Window behavior injects JavaScript into your HTML code, which is far more flexible than a simple link with a target attribute.

Here are situations in which you might want to use the Open Browser Window behavior:

- You need to respond to events other than a mouse click.
- You want to set the size of the new window.
- You want to set the user interface items in the new window.
- You want to customize the injected JavaScript.

Let's start off with the simplest usage of the behavior. Select an HTML object (we used a newly created paragraph), click the Insert button in the Behaviors task pane, select the Open Browser Window behavior, enter a URL, then click OK. When you view your HTML page and hover over the object, a new window will appear that hosts the URL that you specified.

You'll see that by default there are no user interface items such as a navigation toolbar or a status bar. Those are selectable when you create or edit the behavior. The Open Browser Window dialog box has check boxes that allow you to choose these, as shown in Figure 10-6.

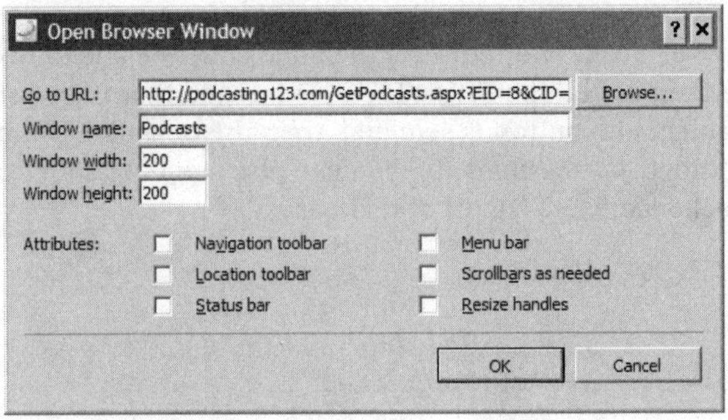

FIGURE 10-6 Turn user interface items on in the Open Browser Window dialog box by selecting check boxes.

In the example at http://rickleinecker.com/HTDE/Chapter10.aspx you can double-click on some text and a window with podcast links for this book will appear.

Use Jump Menu Behavior

There are quite a few times when you need an easy way for users to select a destination from many targets. But regular hyperlinks can take up a lot of space, and screen real estate is something that can be in short supply. This is the main reason to consider using a Jump Menu behavior. It allows you to put a large number of choices using a small amount of the available screen.

Follow these steps to add a Jump Menu behavior to your web page:

1. Select the location in your web page where you want the jump menu to appear. (This way of starting is different from many of the other behaviors since you don't select an object.)
2. In the Behaviors task pane click the Insert button.
3. Select Jump Menu, and the Jump Menu dialog box appears.
4. For each item that you want in the menu, do the following.
   a. Click the Add button.
   b. Type the text that will appear in the Choice text box.
   c. Type the URL in the Value text box.
5. Your choices will show in the list box in the Jump Menu dialog box, as shown in Figure 10-7.
6. When you are done, click OK.
7. The jump menu appears in the HTML page.

Some sites use this technique very effectively. If you want to see the best example we've encountered thus far, go to http://bodybuilding.com/store/index.html. This web site crams a lot of targets into three jump menus, and it makes the user experience much better since there's lots of room for information.

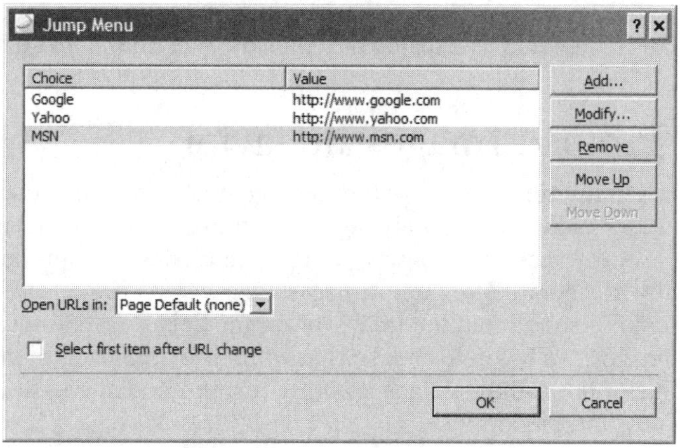

FIGURE 10-7 The items that you add will appear in the Jump Menu list box.

Use Play Sound Behavior

One of the Expression behaviors allows a web page object to play a sound when the page loads or in response to a user-generated event. We've never been a fan of music and sounds in web pages—probably because we almost always have web radio playing in another browser window, and web pages that play music and make sounds interfere with that music.

There are times when sound is appropriate, however. Many children's sites can benefit from sound effects when kids take certain actions. It adds another modality of reinforcement to the graphics on the screen.

The following are some places you might want music or sound in your web page:

- On pages that are games
- Where it is important to provide feedback and reinforcement for user interaction
- On a specialty site where music is important for the ambience

Adding music is simple. Start by selecting an HTML object in the page. Click the Insert button in the Behaviors task pane and select Play Sound. Enter the sound in the text box and click OK.

Expression supports a number of sound formats including WAV, MID, RAM, AU, and SND. Try not to use uncompressed formats such as WAV or SND, as the load time will be long.

Use Popup Message Behavior

This may be the simplest behavior that Expression has to offer. When this behavior is fired off, it displays a message box with a text message. To use it, select an HTML object in the document. Click the Insert button in the Behaviors task pane and select Popup Message. When the dialog box appears, type in the text that you want to appear.

Use Preload Images Behavior

There are many times when web pages dynamically change the image source (src attribute) for pictures. The web page can exhibit noticeable delays and slowdowns during user interaction if the new images are retrieved from the server. This is especially exaggerated for larger images.

There is a solution to the image swapping delay. JavaScript has a mechanism with which images can be preloaded so that when they are used there is no delay. The technique of preloading images is highly recommended any time images are swapped during user interaction.

Expression makes it easy to preload images with its Preload Images behavior. To use this behavior, follow these steps:

1. Select the HTML body object.
2. Click the Insert button in the Behaviors task pane.
3. Choose Preload Images from the menu.
4. In the Preload Images dialog box, as shown in Figure 10-8, use the Image Source File text box to enter or browse for each file you want to preload.
5. You will see the selected files in the Preload Images list box.
6. Click OK.

The example has two changing images. The first image preloads and the second does not. You can easily see the difference in delay when you initially hover the mouse over the Porsche images. Once the second image in the right pair of images has been loaded, it will perform as well as the pair of images on the left.

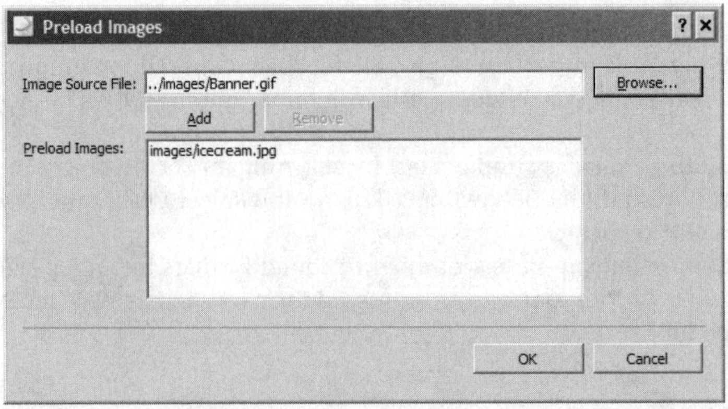

FIGURE 10-8 Your selected images will be in the Preload Images list box.

Use Call Script

Expression provides a behavior that lets you call your own JavaScript code. It is easy to use and allows you to use existing code or special code that you need. There are many reasons why you would want to use this behavior, including:

- To use code from other HTML pages
- To use code from third-party vendors
- To use code that you downloaded from a source
- To create and utilize code that is far more complex than the JavaScript that Expression behaviors provide

To use this behavior, you'll need a JavaScript function. You can get a set of functions and variables at http://rickleinecker.com/HTDE/Chapter10.aspx. You can copy the code and paste it into your HTML document, or you can create your own JavaScript code. The main function for this code is named MyScript.

Once you have a JavaScript function, you can use Expression to call it as a behavior. To do this, follow these steps:

1. Select the HTML object that you want to add the behavior to. If you use the code that was provided on the web page, you need to add a paragraph as follows:

```
<p>Double Click to Call a Script Here <span id="ColorText"
    style="color: #ff0000">This text is red.</span></p>
```

2. Click the Insert button in the Behaviors task pane.
3. Choose Call Script from the menu and the Call Script dialog box appears.
4. Enter the script function. For instance, if you use the code that was provided on the web page, you will enter **MyScript();** in the text box. If your function is named YourScript() then you would enter **YourScript();** in the text box.
5. Click OK.
6. Select the event trigger from the menu. For this example we'll use a double-click event.
7. When you save and preview the web page, the selected event trigger will fire off the code.

If you used the provided code, when you preview the page and trigger the event the red text will gradually change to black. When you trigger the event again it will gradually change back to red. If you wrote your own code, then that will be called.

Use Set Text

There is a very useful behavior that lets you set text in a number of objects including form text fields, the status bar, frame text, and layer text. One of our students recently used this to provide a large amount of information to users about a book bibliography. For the web site that the student created, hovering over a book title sets the text in an HTML document with a description of the book. In this way, users can get all of the information without a screen that is crowded or that scrolls forever. You can see the page at http://thelionspawonline.com/biblio.htm.

There are many reasons you might use this behavior, including the following:

- To provide extended information about an item on the page
- To fill in form data based on user interaction
- To display messages to users based on user interaction
- To set the text in the status bar

It's easy to add this behavior to your HTML page. Follow these steps to create an example:

1. Create a paragraph with text in it that says "Double-click to Set The Text".
2. Add a form text input box to an HTML page and make sure it is placed inside of the paragraph.
3. Name the text input box MyTextBox.
4. Select the paragraph.
5. Click the Insert button in the Behaviors task pane and choose Set Text.
6. Select Set Text of Text Field, and the Set Text of Text Field dialog box appears.
7. In the Text Field drop-down, select the form text field named MyTextBox.
8. Add some text in the New Text box.
9. Click OK.
10. Set the trigger event to Double-click.

When you save and preview the page and double-click the Double-click to Set The Text text, whatever text you entered in the New Text box will be placed in the input text box.

Rollover Images and Active Buttons

Rollover images change when the mouse hovers over them. Rollover images (or *rollovers*) are popular because they give the image a live feeling. They indicate that something will happen when you click it. For example, the rollover in Figure 10-9 changes from a grayscale picture to a color picture when the mouse is over it. You can also see this in the Chapter 10 demo web page.

Rollovers are really two images: the image when the mouse is over, and another when it's not. JavaScript swaps between them when the mouse moves over and when it leaves being over. Expression makes it easy to create rollover images with its Swap Image behavior. Follow these steps to create a rollover image:

1. Create two images of the same size (we'll refer to them as Rollover1a.jpg and Rollober1b.jpg).
2. Insert Rollover1a.jpg in a web page.

FIGURE 10-9 These two images are used for a rollover behavior.

3. Select the image and click the Insert button in the Behaviors task pane.
4. Choose Swap Image and the Swap Images dialog box appears, as shown in Figure 10-10.
5. Enter the URL for the new image in the Swap Image URL text box or click the Browse button to find it.
6. Click the Restore on Mouseout Event check box.
7. Click OK.

When you save and preview the page, the images will swap when the mouse enters and leaves the image area. This behavior can be used for all image buttons. It's a very effective technique for activating pages.

How to... **Find and Create Custom Image Effects**

There is a great tool at http://dynamicdrive.com/dynamicindex4/filter/index.htm that allows you to experiment with custom image effects. Once you find exactly what you're looking for, it will even create the code for your page.

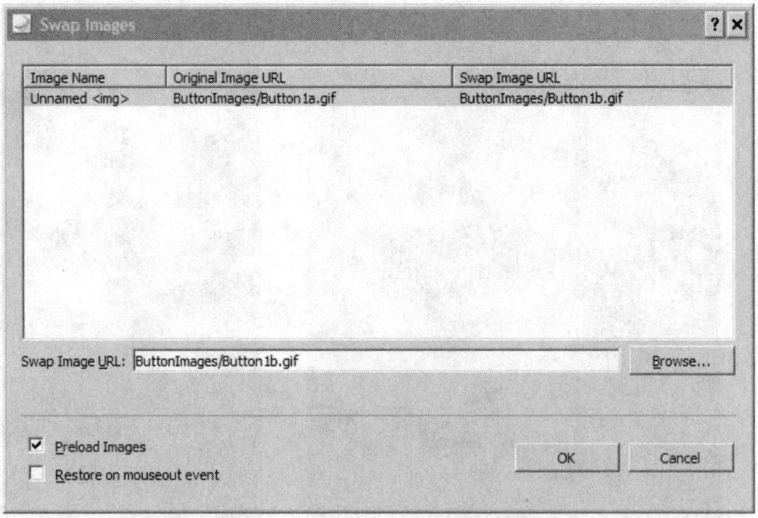

FIGURE 10-10 You can specify the images to swap with this dialog.

Summary

This chapter offers many many tools to make your web pages much more active. You can activate images, buttons, and other HTML items. You can add useful functionality by doing things such as validation checks.

In addition to the behaviors that are built into Expression Web 2, you can also download and use javascript code. In this way, the sky is the limit in what you can do.

11

Insert Media Elements

HOW TO...

- Understand Silverlight and create a web application
- Understand Flash
- Understand Windows Media
- Use podcasts

In Chapter 10 we talked about adding behaviors to HTML objects. These objects allow Expression Web 2 to allow web pages to be dynamic. And behind all of these behaviors is JavaScript—the language that can be added to HTML pages and interpreted by the browser.

JavaScript is a fantastic addition to static HTML. Instead of static pictures and text, users can experience a wide variety of rich interaction. But JavaScript can only go so far to create the kinds of dynamic and interactive pages that users of today expect. In this chapter we will talk about several new technologies including Silverlight, Flash, Microsoft Media, Java, and podcasts.

The technologies are all different and all meet different needs, and which you use depends entirely on your own needs. After going through each section, you will have a much better idea of when to apply each one.

Understand Silverlight

Silverlight is Microsoft's answer to Flash (which we will talk about later). It's a browser plug-in that displays rich content including animation, vector graphics, and audio-video playback. It was originally developed under the code name Windows Presentation Foundation/Everywhere. Most browsers support it since most browsers support plug-ins. There is an effort underway to support the Linux platform.

When we first learned about Silverlight, we wondered why anyone would want to compete with Flash since it is so firmly entrenched. We looked around and saw Silverlight being used on Microsoft's web sites but couldn't find it being used anywhere else. One of the authors was on a consulting assignment and when the question of whether to consider Silverlight was raised, the answer was that Silverlight was not worth the effort. He takes that back now. There are some good reasons to use Silverlight.

The authors of this book are competent C# programmers. However, Flash is difficult for them because they don't spend enough time creating Flash applications to be proficient. But Silverlight is different. That's because it can be created in Visual Studio, and coded in C#. So these skills can be leveraged to create Silverlight content without having to struggle to be good at Flash. Once you realize that you can create content as cool as our Flash friends with the skills that you already possess, you will see Silverlight in an entirely new light.

Use Silverlight Content

At this writing, Silverlight is up to version 2. When you build Silverlight content with Visual Studio, an XAP file is created. This file contains all of the files that Silverlight needs including the XAML file and the DLL files. The advantage of using XAP files is that all of the Silverlight application files are compressed and require less storage space and bandwidth. It's also very convenient to have everything collected into a single package.

In order to consume the XAP file, an object tag must be used in the HTML code. When you build your Silverlight content, a wrapper HTML file will be created. You can simply copy the object tag code and paste it into your HTML page. The following code is the object code that we copied from the HTML wrapper that Visual Studio created:

```
<object data="data:application/x-silverlight," type="application/x-
silverlight-2-b1" width="100%" height="100%">
<param name="source" value="HelloSilverlight.xap"/>
<param name="onerror" value="onSilverlightError" />
<param name="background" value="white" />

<a href="http://go.microsoft.com/fwlink/?LinkID=108182" style="text-
decoration: none;">
<img src="http://go.microsoft.com/fwlink/?LinkId=108181" alt="Get
Microsoft Silverlight" style="border-style: none"/></a>
</object>
```

In order to view the Silverlight content, just use a browser to open your HTML page. You will see this Silverlight application appear as shown in Figure 11-1. The further to the left of the content the mouse is, the darker the text. The further to the right of the content the mouse is, the lighter the text. For instance, if the mouse is at the extreme left of canvas, the text will be black. The XAP file and the project can be downloaded from http://rickleinecker.com/HTDE/Chapter11.aspx.

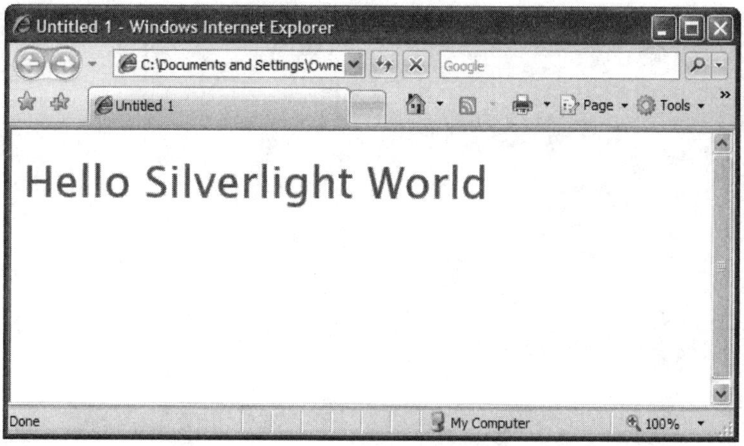

FIGURE 11-1 This Silverlight content responds to mouse movements.

There are also quite a few example files on McGraw-Hill Professional's web site at www.mhprofessional.com. The following files can be downloaded from this site:

- 1highway528.zip, Free sample flash script
- flashiness.zip, Free sample flash script
- HelloSilverlight.xap, Simple hello world Silverlight application
- HelloSilverlightPrj.zip, Simple hello world Silverlight project
- LearnSilverlightPrjCS.zip, Simple C# Silverlight project
- LearnSilverlightPrjVB.zip, Simple VB Silverlight project

There is an easier way to insert Silverlight content into your Expression Web 2 pages. From the Insert menu, select Media | Silverlight. A dialog box will appear, as shown in Figure 11-2, into which you must specify the folder where the Silverlight content resides. Once you do this, Expression takes care of all of the details for you. The object tag is inserted along with the correct values for the content.

Create Silverlight Content

We think the easiest way to create Silverlight content is with Visual Studio 2008. It allows you to leverage your knowledge of Visual Studio and C#. (You can also choose VB.NET with which to develop Silverlight content.) Visual Studio 2008 Express can be downloaded free from Microsoft at http://www.microsoft.com/express/download/. We are using the full version of Visual Studio 2008, but the results with the Express version should be the same. This section shows you how to get started creating Silverlight content with Visual Studio 2008.

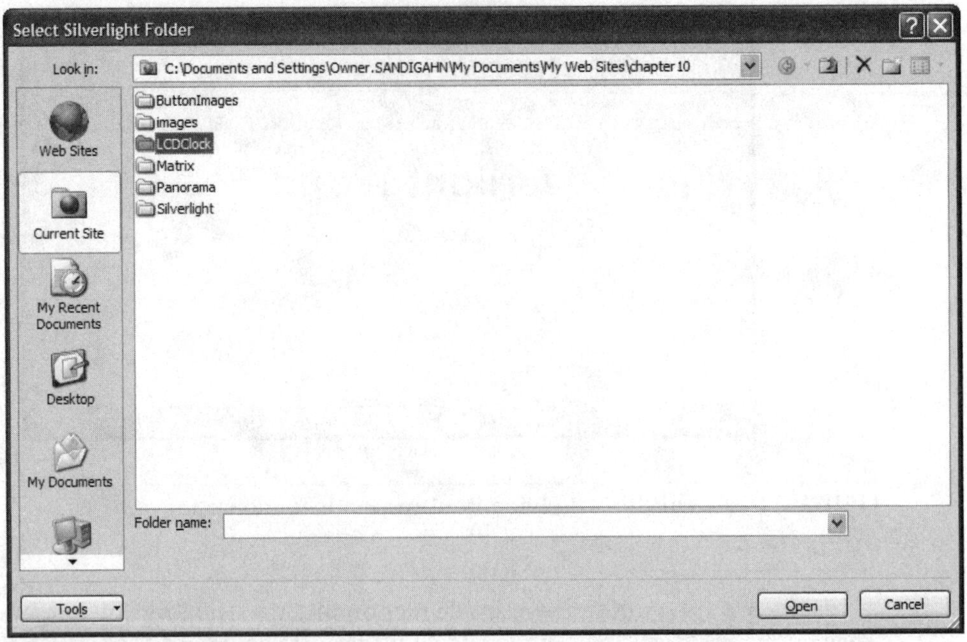

FIGURE 11-2 You must specify the folder that contains the content.

The steps to create a simple Silverlight web application are fairly straightforward:

1. Start Visual Studio 2008.
2. From the File menu, select New | Project.
3. Under the Visual C# language or the Visual Basic language, select Silverlight, as shown in Figure 11-3.
4. Give your application a name. For this example, we'll use LearnSilverlight.
5. When the dialog box appears as shown in Figure 11-4, select Generate an HTML Test Page to Host Silverlight within This Project. Visual Studio will create the Silverlight project.
6. Edit the XAML as follows:

```
<UserControl x:Class="LearnSilverlight.Page"
    xmlns="http://schemas.microsoft.com/client/2007"
    xmlns:x="http://schemas.microsoft.com/winfx/2006/xaml"
    Width="400" Height="200">
    <Grid x:Name="LayoutRoot" Background="White">
        <Button Width="80" Height="40"  Content="Do It"></Button>
        <TextBlock FontSize="25" Name="MyText"
           HorizontalAlignment="Center">No Button Press Yet</TextBlock>
    </Grid>
</UserControl>
```

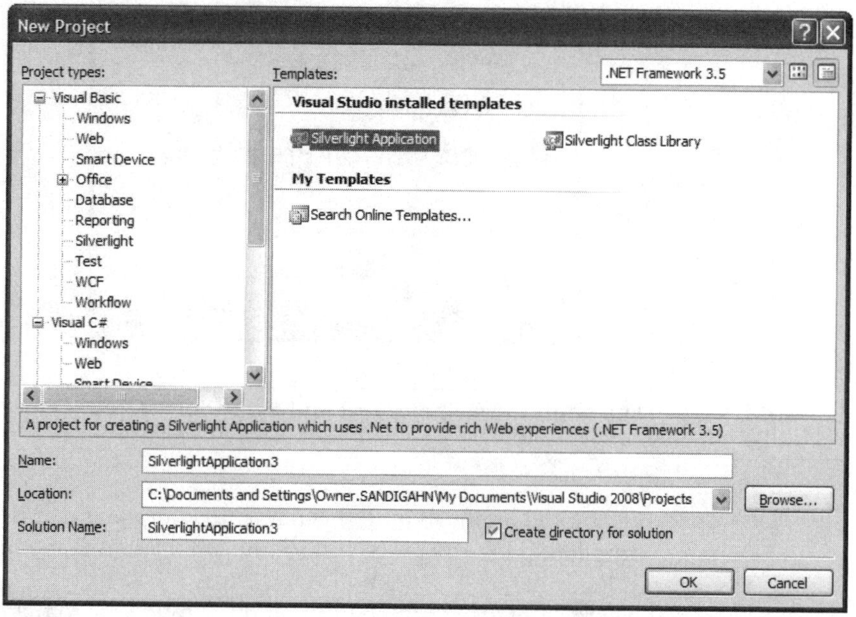

FIGURE 11-3 When you create a new project, choose a Silverlight application.

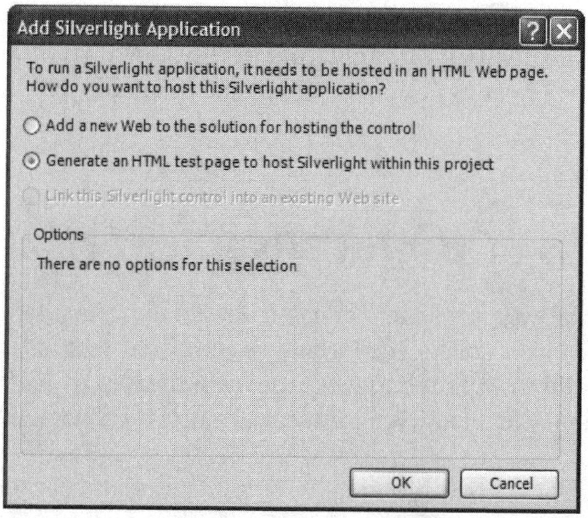

FIGURE 11-4 We will have the application hosted in an HTML page.

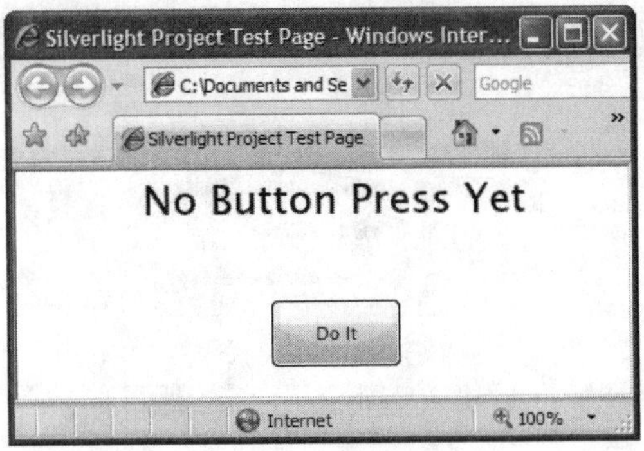

FIGURE 11-5 The application shows text and a button.

7. Compile and test the application to this point. To compile, press SHIFT-CTRL-B. Once it's compiled, press CTRL-F5 to run it. The application to this point will appear as in Figure 11-5.
8. Now we'll create an event for the button. Add the following to the button tag in the XAML.

```
Click="Button_Click"
```

The entire button tag is now:

```
<Button Click="Button_Click" Width="80" Height="40" Content="Do
It"></Button>
```

9. Open the code by right-clicking in the XAML window and selecting View Code. A CS or VB file will open and appear in an edit window.

How to... Find Lots of Useful Silverlight Applications

There is a great web site where you can download quite a few Silverlight applications. Many of them make source code available, too. That means you can learn from them and possibly modify them for your own use. The web site can be found at http://silverlight.net/community/communitygallery.aspx. It includes Silverlight applications for both versions 1 and 2.

There are also quite a few good Silverlight tutorials that you can find online. We recommend one by Scott Guthrie at http://weblogs.asp.net/scottgu/pages/silverlight-tutorial-part-1-creating-quot-hello-world-quot-with-silverlight-2-and-vs-2008.aspx.

The last recommendation we'll make is to get a book named *Microsoft Silverlight 2.0: A Beginner's Guide* by Shannon Horn (McGraw-Hill Professional, 2009). It will get you started in creating Silverlight applications.

10. Find the method named Button_Click and add the following code:
    In C#:

```
MyText.Text = "YES button press!!!";
```

    In VB:

```
MyText.Text = "YES button press!!!"
```

11. Compile and run the Silverlight application. When you press the button, the displayed text will change to "YES button press!!!"

Understand Flash

As with Silverlight, Flash requires a browser plug-in to host it. It's a technology that allows browsers to display rich content including animations, complex graphics, video, and much more. It's the most firmly entrenched of the rich technologies. Sites such as Disney.com are almost completely filled with Flash content, and even many sites that are predominantly HTML judiciously employ Flash.

One of the earliest uses for Flash was web site introduction pages, which appear before any other page in the web site. They display an animation sequence that gives the viewer a good idea of what the web site is about. These introductions are used to this day as a way to provide users with an overview to the experience that they will have on the web site. You could also say that it's a way to provide a free advertisement for the web site content.

Most Flash introduction content offers users a Skip option. This is almost always a small icon or short text indicating the option to skip the introduction.

You can view Flash intro content from the http://rickleinecker.com/HTDE/Chapter11.aspx page. Just click the word "Show" where you see the text "Show Flash Intro Page." You can also download the files necessary to use it in your own page by clicking the word "Download" where you see the text "Download the Flash content." You will need to have this content on your hard drive in order to work through the first exercise that follows.

Use Flash Content in Your Pages

In this section, we'll use Flash content in an HTML page. You can use any Flash content, but this set of instructions uses the Highway Animation Flash content that is available for download on the Chapter 11 page. Follow these steps to implement the Flash content:

1. Create a new HTML page named UseFlash.htm.
2. Add a title to the page such as "This Page Uses Flash Content."
3. From the Insert menu, select Media | Flash Movie.
4. Browse for and select Highway.swf, and a representation of the Highway.swf content will appear in the HTML page.

5. Right-click the Highway.swf content and select Flash SWF Properties.
6. Leave the Movie settings to their default values.
7. In the Size section, do the following:
   a. Deselect the Keep Aspect Ratio check box
   b. Set the Width to 800.
   c. Set the Height to 600.
8. Save the HTML page.
9. Open the Highway.txt file. It will appear as follows:

```
&varURL=          www.variableURL.com
&text1=your variable text 1 goes here
&text2=your variable text 2 goes here
&text3=your variable text 3 goes here
&url=http://www.wyomingwebdesign.com/index.html
```

10. Edit the Highway.txt file and save it. The edits that appear on the page are as follows:

```
&varURL=      http://rickleinecker.com/HTDE/Chapter11.aspx
&text1=         How to Do Everything with...
&text2=         Microsoft Expression Web 2
&text3=         by Donna Baker and Rick Leinecker
&url=http://rickleinecker.com/HTDE/Chapter11.aspx
```

11. Preview the page in Expression Web 2—it will appear as shown in Figure 11-6.

If you are interested in more Flash introduction scripts, we recommend you check out the web site at http://www.flashfair.com/. It has quite a few introduction scripts you can use free of charge, but there are also some premium introductions that you can purchase. If you do a web search on "Free Flash Intro," you'll get thousands of results. Many of these web sites give you material that you can use in your pages, and many of them give you ideas that you can use to create your own Flash introductions.

We recommend that you take some time now to download a Flash introduction and use it in a web page. This will give you good practice and reinforce what we just learned.

Use Flash Banners

In the early days of the Internet, many sites had those advertising banners at the top. At first they were all static images, but eventually many were animated. The animations during these early years were accomplished by using animated GIF images.

The days of animated GIF banners are all but dead. Today's animated banners are almost exclusively Flash. That's because Flash offers so many more possibilities for animation than the dated GIF animations. In this section we'll use some Flash banners in HTML pages. Follow these steps to experiment with Flash banners:

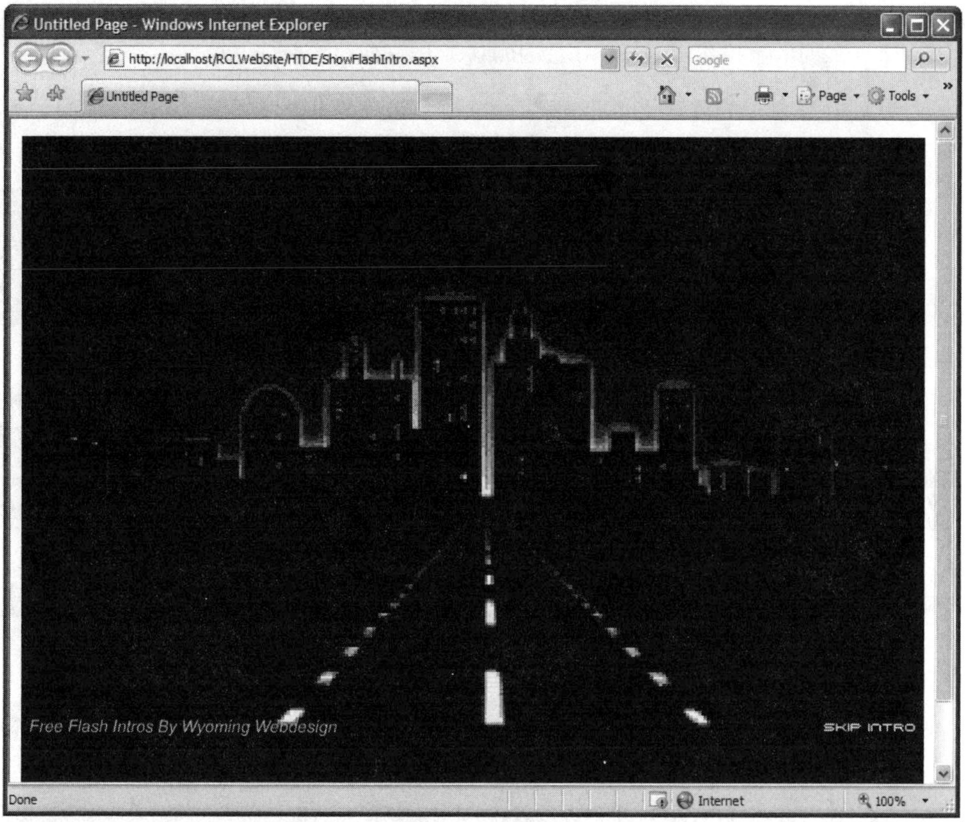

FIGURE 11-6 Your first Flash page will look like this.

1. Download and unzip the file from the Chapter 11 page. Click the word "Download" where it says "Download Flash Banner Content."
2. Create a page in Expression named UseFlashBanners.htm.
3. Add a title to the HTML page with text such as "Flash Banner Demo."
4. Insert the excuseme.swf and fsrays.swf Flash content.
5. Set the width to 728 for both banners.
6. Set the height to 120 for both banners.
7. Save the HTML page.
8. Preview the page as shown in Figure 11-7.

The second banner, fsrays.swf, loads in three JPG images. You can edit these images in order to give it a different look. From Expression, open fsraysimage.jpg. The image file will be opened for editing with Microsoft Paint. Using this program, you can edit the image and then save it. The newly edited image will then be displayed in the fsrays.swf Flash banner.

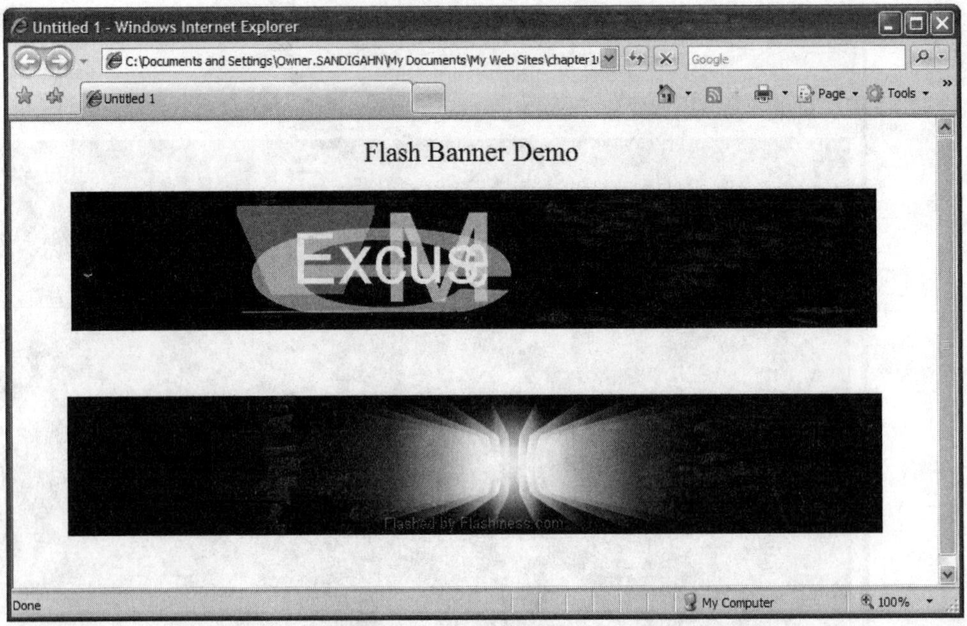

FIGURE 11-7 This page hosts two Flash banners.

Create Flash Content

You can try your hand at creating Flash content. The first thing you'll need is a Flash editing program. We suggest you download the trial version of Flash from http://www.adobe.com/downloads/. The program will be fully functional for 60 days and give you a good taste for creating Flash content.

The process we're going to work through right now assumes you've downloaded Flash and installed it. Follow these steps to create a simple animation script:

1. Run the Flash program.
2. Create a new Flash File (ActionScript 3.0).
3. Select the rectangle tool from the left toolbar.
4. Draw a rectangle in the Stage area as shown in Figure 11-8.
5. Select the Arrow tool from the left toolbar, and double-click the rectangle to select it.
6. From the Modify menu, select Convert to Symbol, name the symbol rect, and click OK.

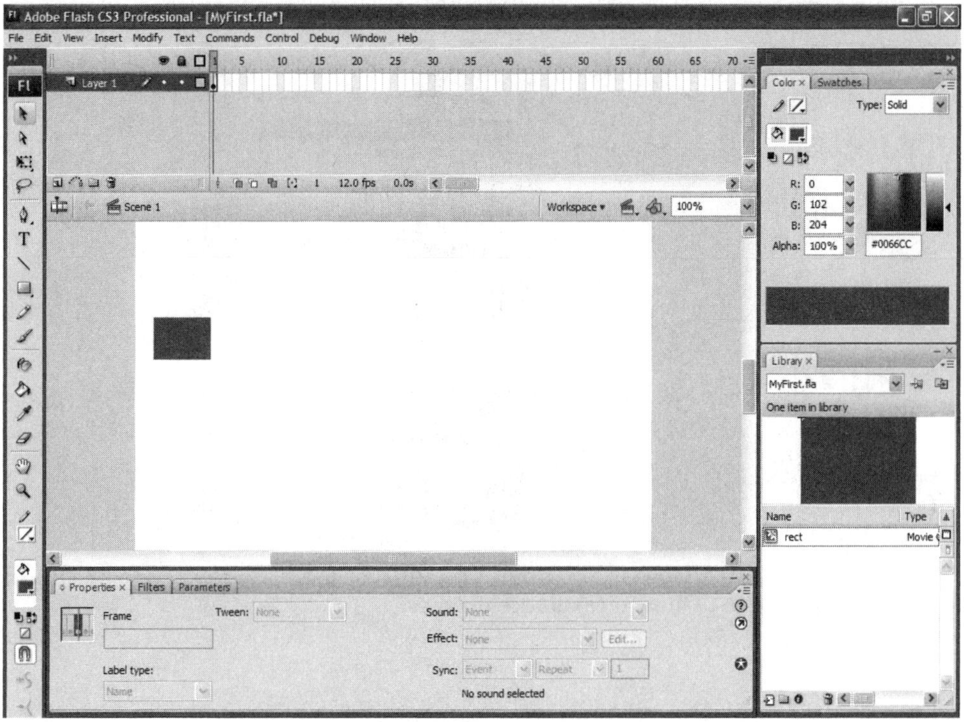

FIGURE 11-8 A rectangle has been placed into the Stage area.

7. In the timeline at the top of the Flash edit window, click the gray field below the number 10—this goes to frame 10 in the timeline.
8. Right-click the selected frame (under the number 10) and choose Insert Keyframe (see Figure 11-9).
9. Drag the rectangle in the Stage area to the right about three inches.
10. Click the timeline anywhere between frame 1 and frame 10.
11. Right-click and select Create Shape Tween.
12. From the Control menu, select Test Movie—the animation will display.
13. Close the Test Movie window.
14. Save the source code by selecting File | Save As and entering a filename such as MyFirst.FLA.
15. Save the SWF file by selecting File | Publish—the MyFirst.swf file is ready to use in your HTML page.

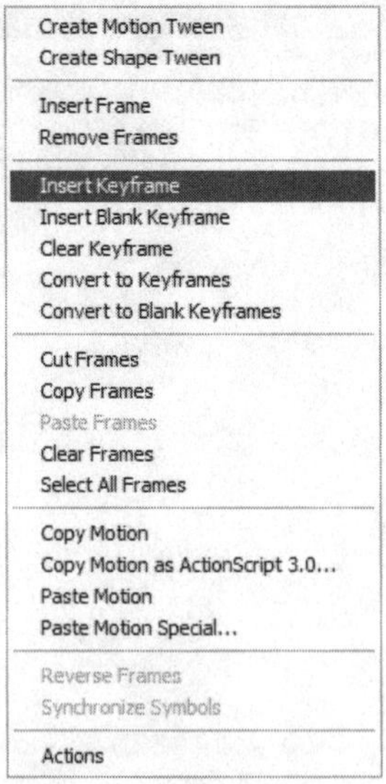

FIGURE 11-9 Choose Insert Keyframe.

Understand Microsoft Media

In this section you'll learn how to insert Windows Media files. The two file formats that are most common are WMA (Windows Media Audio) and WMV (Windows Media Video).

We'll start with an audio file. There's a sample audio file that you can download from the web site at http://rickleinecker.com/HTDE/Chapter11.aspx. The name of the audio file is WS_10043.WMA, and it is zipped on the server to reduce your download time. The next section assumes you have that file on your computer. Follow these steps to insert the Windows Media Audio file.

1. From the Insert menu, select Media | Windows Media Player.
2. Browse for and select the WS_10043.WMA file. The Windows Media Player object will appear in your web page.

Did You Know?

Some Versions of Firefox Need a Plug-in

Some versions of Firefox won't load Microsoft Media player files by default. If you are using Firefox and Windows Media files don't load and display, check the Firefox site for a Microsoft Media Player plug-in.

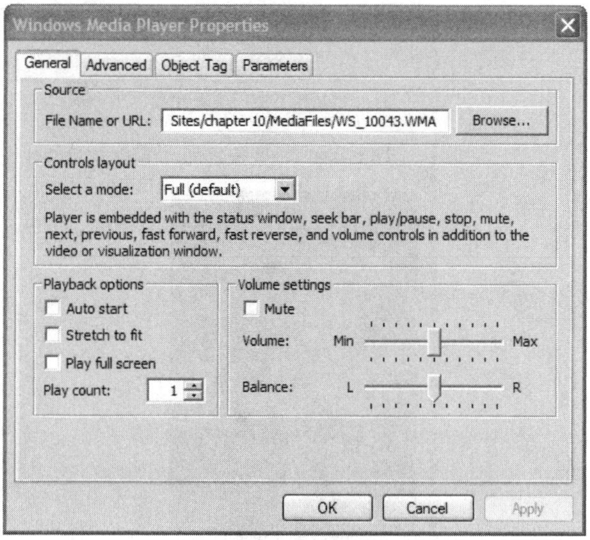

FIGURE 11-10 This dialog box allows you to set the Media Player properties.

3. Right-click and select ActiveX Control Properties. A dialog appears as shown in Figure 11-10.
4. Set the Media Player properties to your desired values. (We usually deselect the Auto Start check box.)
5. Save your page.
6. Preview the page. Windows Media Player will be available to play the audio file.

Now that we've used an audio file, we'll move on to a video file. It's just as easy as audio. There is a sample WMV file on the Chapter 11 page on the web site named Arrays.WMV. It's in a ZIP file on the server to reduce your download time. This section assumes that you've downloaded the file onto your local machine.

1. From the Insert menu, select Media | Windows Media Player.
2. Browse for and select the Arrays.WMV file.
3. The Windows Media Player object will appear in your web page.
4. Right-click and select ActiveX Control Properties. A dialog appears as shown in Figure 11-10.
5. Set the Media Player properties to your desired values. (We usually deselect the Auto Start check box.)
6. Save your page.
7. Preview the page. Windows Media Player will be available to play the video file as shown in Figure 11-11.

FIGURE 11-11 The video is played within Windows Media Player.

Use Podcasts

Podcasting is a technology that delivers audio content. While the audio content can be almost anything including music and speech, it is usually intended for instructional purposes and almost always consists of speech. The podcasting technology is divided into two parts: the digital audio files and the RSS (Really Simple Syndication) feeds.

Normally, the audio content and RSS feeds are stored on a web server and accessed over the Internet. All modern web browsers consume podcasts seamlessly—that is, they can play podcasts without any additional intervention by the user. There are many pieces of software that download, manage, and play podcasts. The most notable and most well-used software is iTunes, which is published by Apple and free. It can be downloaded from the Internet (http://www.apple.com/itunes/download/). Almost all MP3 devices now come with software that manages podcasts.

The audio files are almost always MP3 audio files. These are highly compressed files that take far less storage space and Internet bandwidth than uncompressed audio files. They undergo a two-step compression process. The first step is known as lossy compression. In effect, the lossy compression degrades the audio in order to eliminate a great deal of information in order to reduce the file size. (This is scientifically known as reducing the entropy of the information.) But the degradation of the audio data is done in such a way that the listener can't hear the degradation. A science known as psychoacoustics studies such phenomena and has pointed the way for the developers of the MP3 compression technology. The second phase of the compression process is known as lossless compression. The Huffman data compression algorithm is used to take the degraded audio content and make it much smaller.

The RSS feed is a relatively small text file that resides on the server. There is a process in which the client software subscribes to the RSS feed for any given group of podcasts. The podcast groups are an aggregation of like podcasts, which have been grouped by the creator of the podcasts. Once the subscription mechanism has been enabled, the client software periodically checks the server to see if any changes have been made to the podcast group. The RSS file stores its data in XML (Extensible Markup Language) format. The following is a sample RSS file taken from the RCC server.

A set of three podcasts are hosted in the Chapter 11 page. Here are the steps taken to create it:

1. Record all topics as audio files.
2. Convert them to MP3 files. (You can download a free tool from http://audacity.sourceforge.net/.)
3. Create links in the HTML page for each MP3 file.
4. Create the RSS feed file. (You can download a free RSS editor from http://www.download.com/RSS-Editor/3000-11745_4-10747276.html?tag=lst-2&cdlPid=10747275.)
5. Create a link to the RSS feed file.
6. Preview the Podcast links. Ours can be seen in Figure 11-12.

FIGURE 11-12 We posted some podcasts, including an RSS fee.

Summary

Media elements can give your web applications a way to provide rich content. This makes pages more expressive and conveys a lot of information. It's can also be very entertaining for viewers.

Given the content that's currently available, you'll have no shortage of media to use. You can also easily create your own media.

PART IV

Use Dynamic Pages and Publish Your Site

12

Collect and Validate Information with Forms

HOW TO...

- Understand the anatomy of a form
- Use form controls in Expression Web 2
- Insert fields into the form
- Style form elements with CSS
- Send form data to another page
- Save form results to a file or e-mail
- Validate form information
- Use required fields
- Compare fields
- Include regular expressions

There are lots of times when your web applications will need to ask the user for information. While there are different mechanisms to get information from users, it's almost always with a form that information is gathered. That's because forms offer different data types such as text fields and radio buttons, as well as a variety of ways to process the data. Expression Web 2 gives you the tools to easily validate form data.

This chapter will teach you about forms and how to use them in your web applications. We'll work through the basics, then we'll end with some advanced form validation techniques that can make your application much friendlier and efficient.

Understand the Anatomy of a Form

Forms are HTML objects; if you look at HTML code that has a form, it will start with a `<form>` tag and end with a `</form>` tag. Inside of a form are form fields, and they have their own tag pairs such as `<input></input>` and `<button></button>`.

Did You Know?

Form Information Is Delivered to the Server in the HTTP Header

When a form is submitted, the data that is contained in the fields is treated in a special way. It's extracted from the form fields in the page, consolidated, and then carried in the HTTP header. This is a very efficient method of transporting the submitted data to the server.

Form data is almost always sent to another page that processes the data. There are exceptions to this rule, but it is usually how they work. Most forms are sent to their receiving pages in response to a button in the form that is usually marked Submit. The browser actually packages the form data up and passes it to the next page in what's known as the HTTP header. This mechanism transfers the data behind the scenes.

HTML code within the form doesn't have to be a form tag, it can instead simply be some presentation HTML code that gives users instructions or decorates the form with pictures. There can be more than one form on a page. If there is, the form's name attribute will differentiate between the forms. For instance, you might have two forms as follows:

```
<form name="ContactInfoForm">
</form>
<form name="OrderInfoForm">
</form>
```

The data from only one form can be submitted to a destination page. If there are multiple forms on the page, only one form will be submitted. Only the data from the form in which the Submit button was clicked will be sent to the receiving page.

This may sound confusing, but it's very convenient. Let's say you have a page in which you offer lookups for domain names to the general public. Anyone can go to the page, type in a domain name, and find out who it is registered to. The domain name is entered into a form field, and a Submit button sends the data to a receiving page. But there might be additional advanced functionality that you only offer to subscribers. That means you also want to offer the opportunity to login, and this can be a second form. In this way, you can simplify things and have a single page that serves more than one function: logging in and searching for a domain name, in this example.

Use Form Controls

Adding forms to HTML documents is easy. Expression has a form control in the toolbox that you can place onto your HTML page while in Design mode. Follow these steps to add a form to an HTML page:

1. Create or open an HTML page.
2. Make sure that you are in Design mode, and make sure the Toolbox window is open (you can change its visibility from the Task Pane menu).

3. Open the Form Controls section.
4. Drag a form object onto the HTML page. The form is now ready to receive form controls.

Expression lets you set a number of options for forms. You can set all of these options in the HTML code, but the easiest way is to use Expression's dialogs. Start by right-clicking a form object, and then select Form Properties. A dialog box will appear as shown in Figure 12-1.

The top part of the dialog lets you determine where the form information goes. The options that are offered are destination files, e-mail, databases, and pages. While everyone's use of forms is different, most of the time a page is the destination for form data.

The bottom part of the dialog lets you name the form, and optionally name a target frame. It's fairly common to give forms names such as form1, form2, and form3. That's because most pages just have a single form or possibly a second form. The form name isn't usually necessary for programmers to differentiate between form objects and keep things organized in their minds. However, we recently started naming forms in a more descriptive way, with names such as ContactForm and OrderForm. Consider giving your forms descriptive names so that you and developers who come after you can easily identify the purpose of a form.

Use the Options Button

The Options button brings up a dialog as shown in Figure 12-2 that allows you to set three properties for your form: the action, the form method, and the form encoding type. We almost never alter these, but there are times when it is necessary, such as

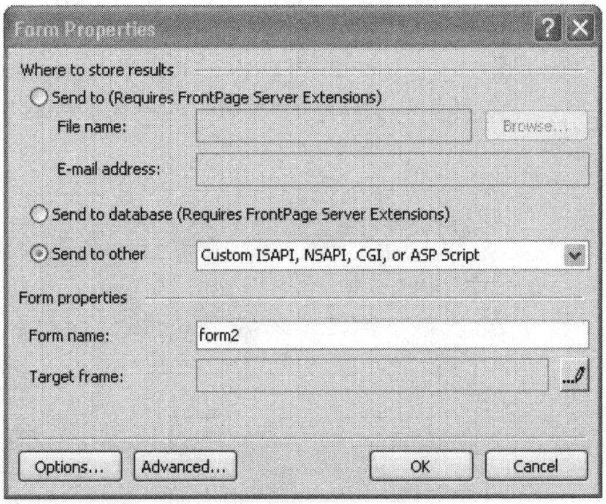

FIGURE 12-1 The Form Properties dialog box allows you to set form options without editing the HTML code.

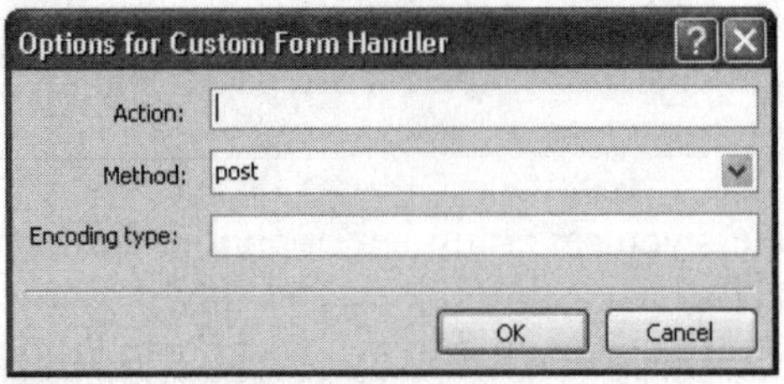

FIGURE 12-2 This dialog allows you to set some important form options.

when you need to retrieve (`get`) information from a database instead of filling out a form that would post information into a database.

- **Action** Specifies a JavaScript function that will fire in response to the form submission.
- **Method** Will be either `post` or `get`. You will use `post` in most cases, and consider `get` when the form is a pure query form.
- **Encoding type** Lets you determine the encoding type such as ASCII (encoding value ISO10646) or Unicode (encoding value UNICODE).

Use the Advanced Button

The Advanced button invokes a dialog, as shown in Figure 12-3, in which you can add and edit hidden fields. It might seem like a useless feature to add hidden fields to a form, but we have used them many times. Let's say that you have a number of forms in your web application. To simplify your development, many of the pages with forms go to the same recipient page that processes the data. This page then redirects to another page after the data has been processed. But the redirect page may be different and will probably depend on the page from which the form data originated. If there

FIGURE 12-3 You can easily add hidden fields to a form.

is a hidden field in the form data that contains the URL to which the browser should be redirected, then your job is easy. Just add hidden fields to the forms on each page with a form indicating where to redirect once the data has been processed.

The code for a simple form named ContactInfo that has a single hidden field looks like the following.

```
<form action="" method="post" name="ContactInfo">
   <input name="RedirectInfo" type="hidden" value="www.google.com" />
</form>
```

Insert Fields into the Form

A form itself won't do you much good. It needs controls in order to offer any usable functionality. Expression makes it easy to add form controls. Follow these steps to add form controls to a form:

1. Create or open an HTML page, and make sure you are in Design mode.
2. Make sure there is a form on the page, and add one if there is not.
3. Make sure the Toolbox window is open. (You can change its visibility from the Task Pane menu.)
4. Select the form control that you want to put into your form.
5. Draw the selected control onto the HTML form.

Now let's go through the process of creating a personal information form. Follow these steps:

1. Create an HTML page named PersonalInformation.htm.
2. Add a form and name it PersonalInformation.
3. Draw five input (text) fields onto the form.
4. Place text to the left of the added fields such as Name, Address, City, State, and Zip.
5. Add an Input (Submit) button to the bottom of the form.
6. Your form should appear as the one in Figure 12-4.

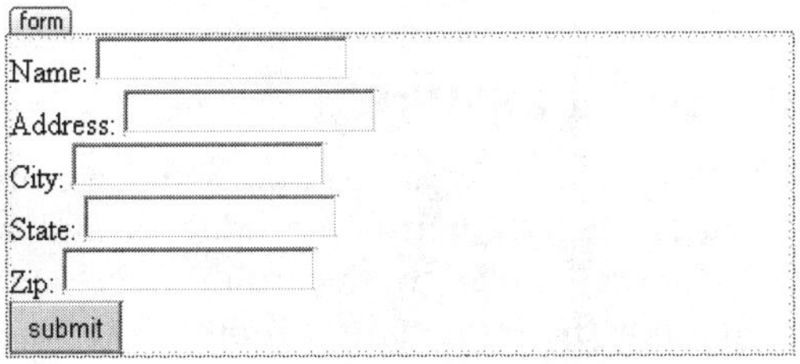

FIGURE 12-4 This form has five text input fields and a Submit button.

How to...

Align Form Items for a Better Appearance

You might have noticed from Figure 12-4 that the fields aren't lined up very attractively. In order to make them line up in a tidy way, you'll need a table inside of the form with six rows and two columns. The first five rows will contain the Name, Address, City, State, and Zip information. The sixth will have the Submit button but will have its colspan attribute set to 2. You can see a table inside of a form in Figure 12-5.

The code for this table within a form can be found on that page at http://rickleinecker.com/HTDE/Chapter12.aspx. When you use a table within a form, it is best to add the table first before adding any form controls.

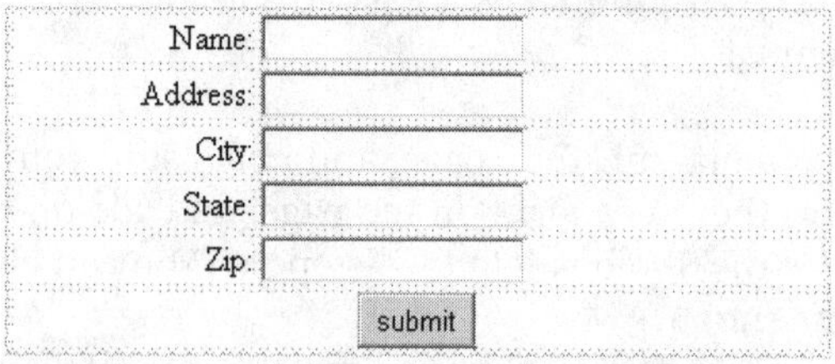

FIGURE 12-5 The table inside of this form lines everything up nicely.

Work with Different Form Types

There are 15 form controls that can be added to your forms. They offer users, among other things, the ability to type in text and numbers, select from a number of radio buttons, or choose from a list of options. In this section we'll go through them and talk about how to use them.

All form controls can and should have a name. As you use them, it's best if your form control names are descriptive of what the control does such as require an address, city, or state.

Use Input and Password Text

Form fields that allow users to type text are the most common. With these fields, users can enter information such as their name, address, and city. These fields are also used in e-commerce for items such as credit card numbers and billing information.

To get started, draw the form control Input (Text) onto your form. Right-click the control and select Form Field Properties. A dialog box will appear as shown in Figure 12-6.

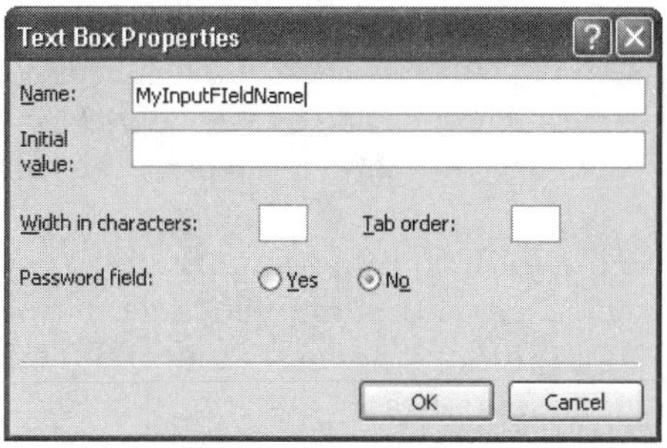

FIGURE 12-6 The Text Box Properties dialog allows you to specify attributes of an Input Text form control.

The Text Box Properties dialog allows you to set the name, initial value, width in characters, tab order, and whether it is a password field. Setting the initial value can be convenient if there is a default value that you would like to suggest. Or, you can set the width in characters so that the fields in your forms line up perfectly, including the right side of all fields. We don't usually set the tab order as the web browsers do a good job of this, but this option exists in case there is a compelling reason to explicitly set it. Setting it to a password field causes the typed-in characters to be masked and appear as bullet (•) characters or as asterisks (*) in Firefox.

When you use the form control Input (Password), you get a Text Box with the password radio button set to Yes.

Use the Submit, Reset, and Normal Buttons

Submit buttons are almost a requirement for forms since they are the main trigger for the submission of the form. To use a Submit button, select the form control Input (Submit) and drag it onto the form. Right-click the button and select Form Field Properties to invoke the Push Button Properties dialog box.

The fields that can be edited from the dialog are the Name (which is the HTML name and not what appears to the user), the Value/Label (which is the text that appears to the user), the Button Type (Normal, Submit, or Reset), and the Tab Order. We recommend naming the button something similar to the form name with a Sub or Submit appended. Note that HTML elements with identical names make it difficult for the browser to correctly act, so use unique names for all HTML elements. Setting the Value to something such as Submit, OK, or Save is usually a good choice. The button type will almost always be Submit, since after all this is a Submit button. We have never had occasion to set the tab order of a button, but the ability is there if you feel the need.

Note The tab order is important for people who do not like to use the mouse to move from field to field in a form before clicking the Submit button. If you do not insert tab order numbers, your user could possibly tab right over a field, depending on how the page is laid out. Well-thought-out tab order can help with accessibility issues.

When you use the form control Input (Button), you get a control identical to the Submit button, except that the button type is set to Normal. Similarly, when you use the form control Input (Reset), you get a control identical to the Submit button, except that the button type is set to Reset.

The Reset button clears out all the fields without submitting any information. Reset buttons are rarely ever used, although you will find these in every form.

Note There is an additional button control called the Advanced button. It is the same as the other three button types, except that you can explicitly set its width and height, whereas the width of the other three button types automatically adjusts to accommodate its text.

Allow File Selector Input

You can allow users to select files on the local machine. To do this, select the form control Input (File) and place it onto the form. When users click the button, they will have the opportunity to find a file on the local machine.

The only options you can set for this control are the Name, Width in Characters, and Tab Order options. Of these three, we set only the name in our HTML applications.

Insert Check Boxes, Radio Buttons, and Group Boxes

Check boxes allow users to give yes/no answers to certain things. For instance, a check box indicating that you want express shipping can be selected from an ordering form. Each check box is a yes/no decision that, unlike radio buttons, doesn't normally affect other HTML controls.

To use a check box, select the form control Input (Check box) and drag it onto the form. Right-click and select Form Field Properties. The Check Box Properties dialog appears. It allows you to name the control, specify its text (which appears as text to the user), decide whether the control is checked by default, and set the tab order.

Radio buttons give users a set of mutually exclusive choices—only one can be selected at a time. You might note that Expression uses radio buttons in the Push Button Properties dialog to let users select from Normal, Submit, and Reset.

Before using radio buttons, you might want to place a Group Box form control onto the form. This allows the user to see how radio buttons are grouped. To do this, select the form control Group Box and drag it onto the form. Right-click the group box and select Group Box Properties. The Group Box Properties dialog box will appear. This dialog allows you to set the Label (the text that appears to the user) and the alignment.

To use a radio button, select the form control Input (Radio) and drag it onto the form. Right-click and select Form Field Properties. The Option Button Properties dialog appears, which allows you to name the group to which the radio button belongs, give it a value (which does not appear to the user), decide whether the control is selected by default, and set the tab order.

Note It's important that at least one radio button in each group is selected. Decide which choice should be the default, and set its initial state to Selected.

Use a Text Area

Text areas allow users to type in, view, and edit more than one line of text. To use a text area, select the form control Text Area and drag it onto the form. Right-click the text area and select Form Field Properties. The Text Area Box Properties dialog will appear. This allows you to set the control's name, initial value, dimensions (in character width and height), and the tab order.

Use Images and Labels

We have never used the image and label form controls and find it much easier to use the normal HTML `<img>` and `<span>` tags to do the same thing. The HTML controls more flexible and easier to use and you don't have to memorize two different sets of image and label controls.

Style Form Elements with CSS

There are times when you will need to change the look of form controls in your HTML application. You might want to do this for the entire application, for several pages, or for a single page. We'll create a style sheet file with style information for form controls. We'll then use it in a sample page. Begin by creating an HTML page named ChangeFormStyles.html as follows:

1. Create a new HTML page named ChangeFormStyles.html.
2. Add a form control to the page.
3. Type **Your Name** and then add a form text box.
4. Add a Group Box with the label Sex.
5. In the Group Box add two radio buttons: Male and Female.
6. Below the Group Box type **Comments About Yourself** and then add a Text Area control.
7. Below the text area, add a Submit button.
8. Figure 12-7 shows the newly created page. (This page can be obtained from http://rickleinecker.com/HTDE/Chapter12.aspx.)

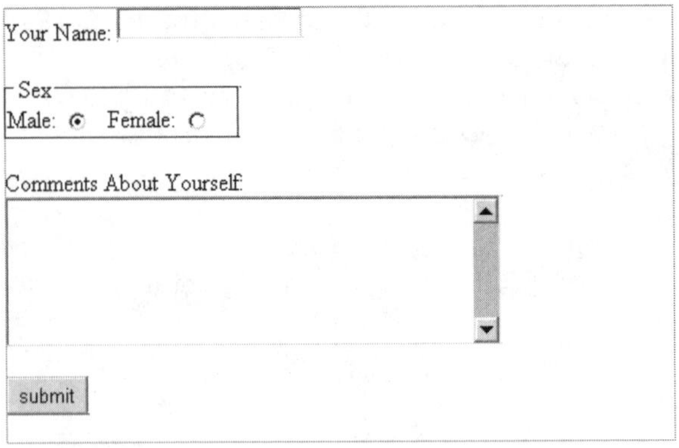

FIGURE 12-7 This new HTML page with a form will be used to learn how to change form styles.

Now you need a style sheet file. Follow these steps:

1. Make sure the Apply Styles task pane is opened.
2. Click New Style.
3. From the Define In drop-down, select New Style Sheet.
4. Select the Apply New Style to Document Selection check box.
5. Click OK.
6. You will be asked, "Do you want to attach the style sheet for the new style?" Answer yes, and Expression will add the link tag to your HTML page.
7. Save the new style sheet as FormStyles.css. You will note that this name has been updated in the link tag in your HTML page.
8. Edit the style sheet as follows.

```
.newStyle1
{
background-color:silver;
}
```

9. Save the CSS and HTML files.
10. Preview the page. You will see a silver background to the form.

You can also change the style of any element within the form. To change the background color of an input text field, create a class in the CSS file, edit its style information, and then add the class attribute to the input text field. Follow these steps:

1. Add this class to your CSS file.

```
.textinput
{
background-color:lime;
}
```

2. Add a class attribute to a text input field as follows:

```
Your Name: <input class="textinput" name="YourName" type="text" />
<br />
```

3. Save both files.
4. When you preview the HTML file the first input field's background color will be lime.

For more information about CSS and styles, refer back to Chapter 5.

Save Form Results

Forms aren't much good unless you can save the data somewhere, including sending it to another page for processing. In this section we'll talk about receiving form data from an ASPX page, saving form data to a file, and e-mailing form data to a recipient.

Send Form Data to a Page

Most often, forms submit their data to another page. The destination page processes the form data in any number of ways. For examples, you can set http://rickleinecker .com/HTDE/ShowFormData.aspx as your destination page and it will show you the form field names and their data.

The page is an ASPX page, and we will talk about how to write these in Chapter 14. The code snippet to display the form data can be seen on the http://rickleinecker.com/ HTDE/Chapter12.aspx page in case you want to use it.

To set a destination page, we'll use the form page that we created earlier in this chapter that asks for name, address, city, state, and zip. Follow these steps:

1. Right-click the form in the HTML page while in Design mode.
2. Select Form Properties. The Form Properties dialog appears.
3. In the Where to Store Results section, make sure that Send to Other is selected.
4. Click the Options button. The Options for Custom Form Handler dialog appears.
5. In the Action field, enter the destination URL as shown in Figure 12-8.

FIGURE 12-8 Set the destination URL in the Action field.

6. Click OK.
7. Save the page.
8. Preview the page.
9. Enter data in the form.
10. Click the Submit button and you can see the results as shown in Figure 12-9.

Send Form Data to a File

Sometimes it's more convenient to save form data to a file. This lets you collect the data and process it later. Follow these steps to save form data to a file:

1. Make sure that your web server has FrontPage extensions installed and running.
2. Verify that a folder named _private exists. If not, create it.
3. From Design mode, right-click the form.
4. Select Form Properties. The Form Properties dialog appears.
5. In the Where to Store Results section, select Send To (Requires FrontPage Extensions).
6. Enter a filename in the File Name field such as _private/MyInfo.txt. (Placing it in the _private directory prevents it from being viewable from a web browser.)
7. Click OK.
8. Save the page.
9. Preview the page.
10. Enter data in the form.
11. Click the Submit button. (If you don't have FrontPage Extensions available, you will get an error message.)

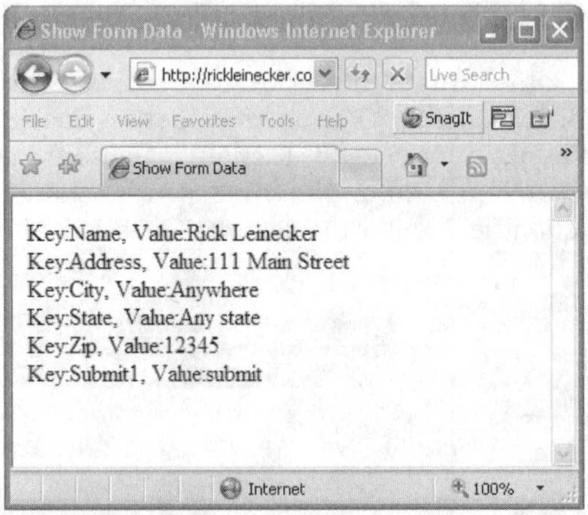

FIGURE 12-9 The form field names and data

Send Form Data to an E-mail Address

The process for sending form data to an e-mail address is almost identical to the process for sending form data to a file. The only difference is that instead of a filename, you will need a valid e-mail address in the E-mail Address field.

Validate Form Information

Unless you implement proactive measures, there is no guarantee that the information users submit in forms will be correct—you won't know if their name is correct, for example. However, you can know if their e-mail address is in the proper format or if two password fields match.

The trick is to know this before the form is submitted. Once it's submitted, then your code has the responsibility of checking the form data for correctness. If you catch the errors before the form is submitted and alert the user, then it is their responsibility to correct the errors. You are also saving server CPU time if the form data is validated before it gets to the server as the server won't have to perform checks on the data.

Check for Required Fields

The first thing your HTML form might need to do is check for fields that are required. Examples of this might be the e-mail address or user name. It's much easier and more robust if you check before the submit process happens. Your receiving code can be sure that the data is there, and this will save processing time on the server end.

Let's create a form similar to one we created earlier in this chapter that contains the fields Name, Address, City, State, and Zip. We'll require the Name field to have data by using a RequiredFieldValidator. Follow these steps to add this control to your form:

1. Create an ASPX page (the example is named UseForm.aspx).
2. Add five fields: Name, Address, City, State, and Zip.
3. Type the text such as Name, Address, and so on.
4. Add an ASP.NET TextBox object to the page and name it appropriately such as txtName, txtAddress, and so on.
5. Add an ASP.NET button to the bottom of the page and edit its text to say "Submit."
6. You can shorten the creation process by finding the basic ASP.NET code (without any validation controls) at http://rickleinecker.com/HTDE/Chapter12.aspx. This will save you from having to create the code yourself.
7. In the toolbox, open the ASP.NET controls.
8. Open the Validation Controls.

9. Drag a RequiredFieldValidator to the right of the Name field.
10. Right-click the newly added RequiredFieldValidator and select Properties.
11. Set the ErrorMessage property to "This is a required field."
12. In the ControlToValidate property, select txtName (or whatever you named your Name TextBox).
13. Save the page.
14. Preview the page.
15. Click the Submit button with nothing in the Name field and the message "This is a required field" appears.
16. Enter a name in the Name field.
17. Click the Submit button.
18. "Success!!!" appears below the button.

Compare Fields

Let's say that you have two fields that you need to compare. Maybe they need to be the same as with password fields, maybe you want them to be different. In any case, you can compare two fields to see if they are the same, different, greater than, less than, greater than or equal to, and less than or equal to. The following steps compare two fields, and notify the user if they are the same:

1. Open the page from the previous steps (the example is named UseForm.aspx).
2. Drag a CompareValidator control to the right of the Address field.
3. Right-click the CompareValidator and select properties.
4. Edit the ErrorMessage property to say "These are the same."
5. Edit the ControlToValidate property to txtAddress (or whatever you named your Address TextBox control).
6. Edit the ControlToCompare property to txtCity (or whatever you named your City TextBox control).
7. In the Operator property select NotEqual.
8. Save the page.
9. Preview the page.
10. If you still have the RequiredFieldValidator for the Name field, enter a name.
11. Now enter **Miami** in the Address and City fields.
12. Click the Submit button.
13. An error message appears saying "These are the same."
14. Now change the Address data to **111 Main Street**.
15. Click OK.
16. The error message disappears and the "Success!!!" message appears.

Use Regular Expressions

There are times when simple field comparisons aren't enough. Let's say you want to make sure that the format of an e-mail address or web address are correct. Or perhaps you want to make sure that the zip code is in the correct format. You can use the RegularExpressionValidator to check for the correct formatting in many common situations. And even if your situation falls outside of the common situations that arise, you can create your own regular expression to deal with your need. The following steps make sure that the zip code of our form is in the correct format:

1. Open the page from the previous steps (which I named UseForm.aspx).
2. Drag a RegularExpressionValidator to the right of the Zip field.
3. Right-click the RegularExpressionValidator and select Properties.
4. Edit the ErrorMessage property to say "Incorrect Zip Code Format."
5. Edit the ControlToValidate property to txtZip (or whatever you named your Zip Code TextBox control).
6. Click the ellipses (...) button at the right of the ValidateExpression property. The Regular Expression Editor dialog appears, as shown in Figure 12-10.
7. Select U.S. ZIP Code.
8. Click OK.
9. Save the page.
10. Preview the page.
11. Fill in other form data that is necessary (in case you still have the validators from the previous exercises).
12. In the Zip field, enter **1234**.
13. Click the Submit button.
14. An error message appears saying "Incorrect Zip Code Format."
15. Edit the Zip field to say **12345**.
16. Click the Submit button.
17. The error messages disappear and the "Success!!!" message appears.

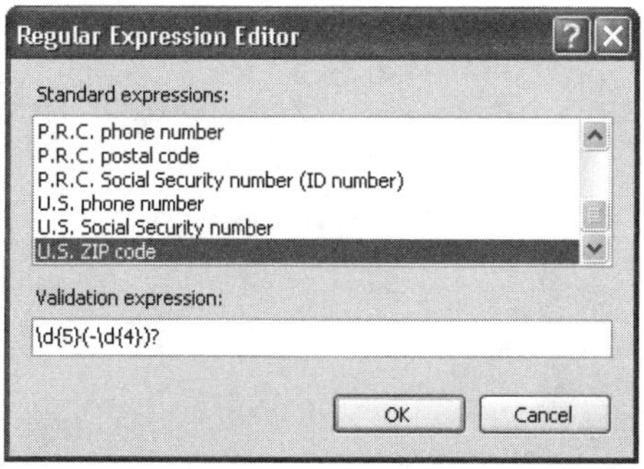

FIGURE 12-10 The Regular Expression Editor Dialog

Summary

Form field data validation is a great tool for creating web pages that work smoothly. It ensures that you get the data you want and have a smooth experience since it reduces the number of page redraws that can result from improper data. It also reduces the traffic to the server for pages with improper data. You should take advantage of this capability any time you can.

13

Build Dynamic Pages with PHP

HOW TO...

- Understand dynamic web pages
- Understand server requirements
- Add a PHP page
- Use PHP scripts

This chapter covers creating and editing PHP pages with Expression Web 2. We'll start with some background information about how PHP works and how to get it working on your server. We'll then give some simple examples to get you started. Finally, we'll add some more advanced scripts to give you great functionality.

Dynamically Create Web Pages

In Chapter 10 we talked about adding behaviors to HTML web pages. It's a way to create dynamic interaction on the client machine. Many times, adding similar behaviors is known as Dynamic HTML (DHTML).

But DHTML is a client-side behavior. In contrast to DHTML, technologies such as PHP, ASP.NET, and JSP create pages dynamically. It happens on the server, so this is a server-side process. Dynamically created HTML looks just like garden variety HTML when it arrives at the client machine. It is created by the server in real time based on data that's on the server. The data might be a PHP, ASPX, or JSP file. The code on the server might contain additional assets such as include files. The created HTML might also contain code that is retrieved from a data store. Dynamically created HTML is assembled on the server and sent to the client. In this way, it can respond to whatever situation is called for.

Let's say that I have a server with a database of all employees in the company. I decide to create an HTML page that offers the ability to search the database. It has various search criteria including name and department. When the user submits this page to the server, the server takes the search criteria, queries the database, and returns an HTML page with the appropriate data including a list of matching employees. This is a classic example of a dynamically created web page.

Now let's say that I maintain a web site that offers social networking content. Users can post any text, pictures, sounds, and other content. In order to make this possible, there's a database that can be queried to obtain everything that a given user has posted on their page. With this information, an HTML page can be assembled. It is formatted according to some rules on the server which might include XML and XSLT. Or it might just be formatted according to some CSS style sheets. But with the information obtained from the database, an HTML page is created and sent to the client machine. The client's browser receives the HTML and renders it—exactly the same as if it were originally a static HTML page.

Dynamically created web pages are an incredible tool for web developers. You can create weather web sites with the current weather. You can create web sites with the current phase of the moon. You can create web sites with biorhythms. You can do almost anything imaginable with dynamically created web pages. They are limited only by your creativity and imaging, the time you have to develop the application, and the resources needed to support the application. Figure 13-1 shows the basic process of dynamic page creation.

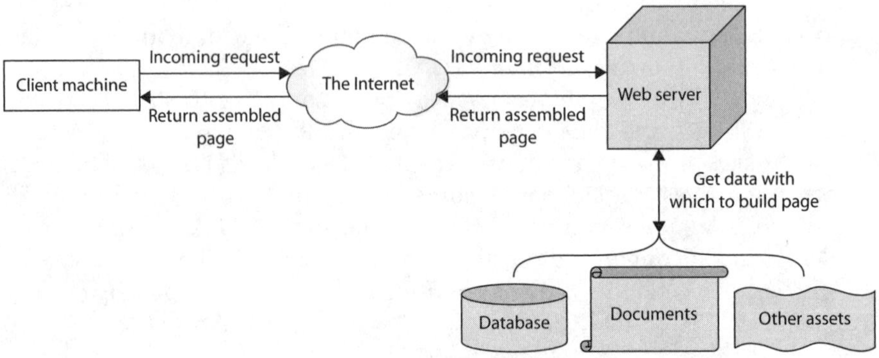

FIGURE 13-1 The basic dynamic page creation process

Understand PHP Server Requirements

At their core, web servers simply answer requests that come in from a TCP/IP connection that usually originates from an Internet connection. This involves analyzing the request to determine what document is being requested, loading the document from the hard drive, and sending the document to the client machine.

Web servers don't natively know how to create dynamic pages. A plug-in is necessary in order for the dynamic creation process. With the proper web server plug-in, web page requests for extensions belonging to that plug-in are managed by the plug-in.

Let's say for instance that the PHP web server plug-in is installed and a request for a file with a PHP extension is made to the web server. The web server recognizes the file extension as belonging to the PHP plug-in. Instead of loading the requested file from the hard drive and sending it to the requester, it passes the request off to the PHP plug-in. Once the PHP plug-in has processed the file and constructed the HTML code, it gives the data to the web server, which then sends it to the requester. A similar process is carried out for ASPX, JSP, CGI, and other dynamically created page types.

GoDaddy is one good choice for web site hosting. There are lots of others, including M&M and ASPSites. A web search will list thousands of others. GoDaddy has PHP installed on all of their servers whether Linux or Windows. To use PHP extensions, all you have to do is create a PHP page and upload it to the server.

Internet Information Server (IIS), the standard Windows web server, does not have PHP installed by default. In fact, Microsoft doesn't even ship PHP with IIS. In order to use PHP on your own Windows-based web server, you must install PHP. It is easy to do, and there is a web site with complete instructions and downloads.

How to... Get PHP for Your Local Computer

You must install PHP before you can develop PHP applications with Expression. To download PHP for Windows web servers, go to http://php.net/downloads.php.

For the complete web site with PHP information, go to http://php.net/. This site offers tutorials on PHP and lots of programming examples.

Add a PHP Page

In this section, we'll get started with PHP by creating a PHP page in Expression Web 2. The code for a PHP page is identical to the code for an HTML page, except that you can insert PHP code into the page. This PHP code performs the dynamic HTML content creation.

You will need to tell Expression where the PHP executable is. Before viewing PHP pages in Expression, make sure you install PHP. Then, you select Tools | Application Options. In the dialog box that appears, browse for and select the PHP executable, as shown in Figure 13-2.

You only need to tell Expression where the PHP executable is if you want to preview the page without actually uploading it to the server. The installation of PHP on your development machine is different than the installation of PHP on the server. Follow these steps to install PHP on your local machine:

1. When you develop pages in Expression that have PHP code, there must be a way for Expression to execute the PHP code. That's why the external PHP program must be installed. In addition, Expression needs to know where the PHP program is located so that it can properly execute it. Download the archive from php.net.
2. Extract the files.
3. Give Expression Web the path.
4. Rename the file named PHP.INI-recommended to PHP.INI.

Follow these steps to create your first PHP page.

1. Select File | New | PHP. A new page is created.
2. Go to Code view.

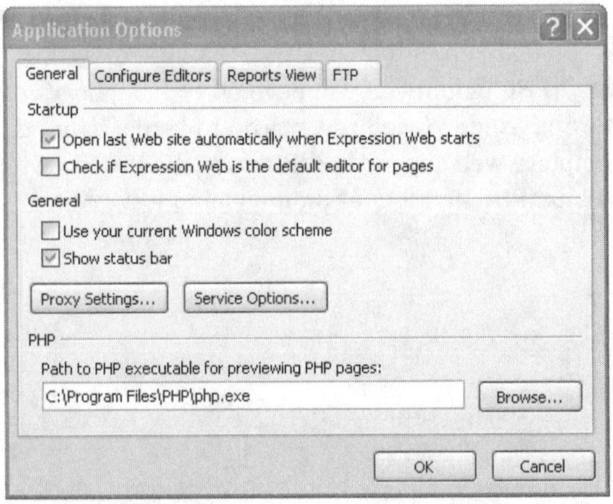

FIGURE 13-2 You must tell Expression where the PHP executable is located.

3. Inside the <body> tag, add <?php, indicating the start of PHP code, then insert ?>, indicating the end of PHP code. (This allows you to go in and out of PHP code as the need arises in the page.)
4. Between the start and end PHP indicators, add the code echo '<p>Hello PHP World!</p>'. Your page code should appear as follows:

```
<body>
<?php
echo '<p>Hello PHP World!</p>';
?>
</body>
```

5. Save the page.
6. Preview the page. (The first time that Expression previews a PHP page, it might ask to configure the PHP extensions. You should allow it to do the configuration.)
7. The text "Hello PHP World!" appears in the browser window.

There are quite a few PHP tutorials online that can help you learn the basics. You can also pick up a copy of *PHP 6: A Beginner's Guide* by Vikram Vaswani (McGraw-Hill, 2008).

You can start experimenting with the functions. Let's output the date and time. They both use the date function, each with different formatting strings. To output the date, use the following code:

```
echo date("m-d-Y");
```

To output the time, use the following code:

```
echo date("h:I A");
```

The code to output both the date and time is as follows:

```
<?php
echo date("m-d-Y");
echo "<br />";
echo date("h:i A");
echo "<br />";
?>
```

Did You Know?

Expression's IntelliSense Helps with PHP Syntax

Expression Web will give you a good bit of help via IntelliSense, which will list all of the available functions and variables. In order to invoke IntelliSense, the edit cursor must be within a PHP code block. Then, press CTRL-L to invoke the IntelliSense menu, as shown in Figure 13-3. Note also that if the cursor is in the middle of a quote or another PHP command, CTRL-L will just ding at you.

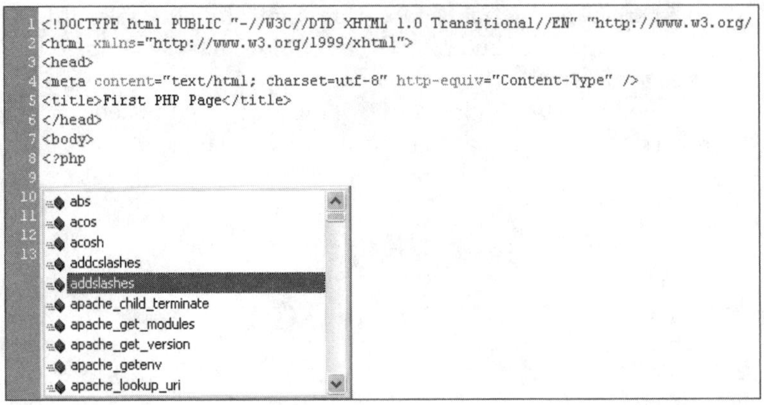

<!DOCTYPE html PUBLIC "-//W3C//DTD XHTML 1.0 Transitional//EN" "http://www.w3.org/
<html xmlns="http://www.w3.org/1999/xhtml">
<head>
<meta content="text/html; charset=utf-8" http-equiv="Content-Type" />
<title>First PHP Page</title>
</head>
<body>
<?php
abs
acos
acosh
addcslashes
addslashes
apache_child_terminate
apache_get_modules
apache_get_version
apache_getenv
apache_lookup_uri

FIGURE 13-3 IntelliSense shows you the available functions and variables.

You could also combine the date and time in the same function call:

```
echo date("m-d-Y h:I A");
```

An excellent reference for PHP date and time formatting can be found at http://www.w3schools.com/PHP/func_date_date.asp.

Create Useful PHP Pages

In this section we'll take a few more steps toward PHP mastery. The first thing we'll do is show some information that the server makes available to PHP applications. Next, we'll use a page with a form to perform some calculations.

Use PHP Server Variables

When you write PHP applications, there is a lot of information available in server variables. For instance, you can easily get the browser type, the current date, and the IP address. All of the server variable information that's available won't be useful to every application, but you can pick and choose what you use.

In order to show the current server date, you add the following code to your page:

```
echo $_SERVER['HTTP_USER_AGENT'];
```

The echo command sends whatever follows to the display. The $_SERVER represents the collection of server variables. The 'HTTP_USER_AGENT' string identifies the server variable that you are referencing.

There are quite a few server variables that you can use; Table 13-1 lists them.

TABLE 13-1 Server Variables That You Can Use from PHP

Variable Name	Description
'PHP_SELF'	The filename of the currently executing script, relative to the document root.
'GATEWAY_INTERFACE'	Which revision of the CGI specification the server is using; for example, 'CGI/1.1'.
'SERVER_ADDR'	The IP address of the server under which the current script is executing.
'SERVER_NAME'	The name of the server host under which the current script is executing. If the script is running on a virtual host, this will be the value defined for that virtual host.
'SERVER_SOFTWARE'	The server identification string given in the headers when responding to requests.
'SERVER_PROTOCOL'	The name and revision of the information protocol via which the page was requested; for example, 'HTTP/1.0';.
'REQUEST_METHOD'	Which request method was used to access the page; for example, 'GET', 'HEAD', 'POST', 'PUT'.
'REQUEST_TIME'	The timestamp of the start of the request. Available since PHP 5.1.0.
'QUERY_STRING'	The query string, if any, via which the page was accessed.
'DOCUMENT_ROOT'	The document root directory under which the current script is executing, as defined in the server's configuration file.
'HTTP_ACCEPT'	The contents of the Accept: header from the current request, if there is one.
'HTTP_ACCEPT_CHARSET'	The contents of the Accept-Charset: header from the current request, if there is one; for example, 'iso-8859-1,*,utf-8'.
'HTTP_ACCEPT_ENCODING'	The contents of the Accept-Encoding: header from the current request, if there is one; for example, 'gzip'.
'HTTP_ACCEPT_LANGUAGE'	The contents of the Accept-Language: header from the current request, if there is one; for example, 'en'.
'HTTP_CONNECTION'	The contents of the Connection: header from the current request, if there is one; for example, 'Keep-Alive'.
'HTTP_HOST'	The contents of the Host: header from the current request, if there is one.
'HTTP_REFERER'	The address of the page (if any) which referred the user agent to the current page. This is set by the user agent. Not all user agents will set this, and some provide the ability to modify HTTP_REFERER as a feature. In short, it cannot really be trusted.

TABLE 13-1 Server Variables That You Can Use from PHP *(Continued)*

Variable Name	Description
'HTTP_USER_AGENT'	The contents of the User-Agent: header from the current request, if there is one. This is a string denoting the user agent that is accessing the page. A typical example is Mozilla/4.5 [en] (X11; U; Linux 2.2.9 i586). Among other things, you can use this value with get_browser() to tailor your page's output to the capabilities of the user agent.
'HTTPS'	Set to a nonempty value if the script was queried through the HTTPS protocol. Note that when using ISAPI with IIS, the value will be off if the request was not made through the HTTPS protocol.
'REMOTE_ADDR'	The IP address from which the user is viewing the current page.
'REMOTE_HOST'	The host name from which the user is viewing the current page. The reverse DNS lookup is based off the REMOTE_ADDR of the user.
'REMOTE_PORT'	The port being used on the user's machine to communicate with the web server.
'SCRIPT_FILENAME'	The absolute path name of the currently executing script.
'SERVER_ADMIN'	The value given to the SERVER_ADMIN (for Apache) directive in the web server configuration file. If the script is running on a virtual host, this will be the value defined for that virtual host.
'SERVER_PORT'	The port on the server machine being used by the web server for communication. For default setups, this will be '80'; using SSL, for instance, will change this to whatever your defined secure HTTP port is.
'SERVER_SIGNATURE'	The string containing the server version and virtual host name that are added to server-generated pages, if enabled.
'PATH_TRANSLATED'	The filesystem- (not document root–) based path to the current script, after the server has done any virtual-to-real mapping.
'SCRIPT_NAME'	Contains the current script's path. This is useful for pages that need to point to themselves. The __FILE__ constant contains the full path and filename of the current (that is, included) file.
'REQUEST_URI'	The URI that was given in order to access this page; for instance, '/index.html'.
'PHP_AUTH_DIGEST'	When running under Apache as a module doing Digest HTTP authentication, this variable is set to the 'Authorization' header sent by the client (which you should then use to make the appropriate validation).
'PHP_AUTH_USER'	When running under Apache or IIS (ISAPI on PHP 5) as a module doing HTTP authentication, this variable is set to the user name provided by the user.

TABLE 13-1 Server Variables That You Can Use from PHP *(Continued)*

Variable Name	Description
'PHP_AUTH_PW'	When running under Apache or IIS (ISAPI on PHP 5) as a module doing HTTP authentication, this variable is set to the password provided by the user.
'AUTH_TYPE'	When running under Apache as a module doing HTTP authentication, this variable is set to the authentication type.

You can now create a page that displays a lot of valuable information. You can see several server variables at http://rickleinecker.com/HTDE/Chapter13.aspx. (This page hosts a PHP document within an IFrame.)

Use a Form from PHP

In order to use forms in PHP, you'll need to create normal forms. (For more information about forms, see Chapter 12.) The page where the form resides doesn't have to be a PHP page—it can be HTML or ASPX or any other valid document type that supports forms. For this section, though, we're going to have a PHP file as the destination for the form. Let's take a quick look at a simple form.

```
<form action="DestDoc.php" method="post">
<input type="text" name="firstfield" /><br />
<input type="text" name="secondfield" /><br />
<input type="submit" value="Submit" />
</form>
```

When this form is submitted to the receiving PHP document, you can easily access each form field with $_POST['fieldname']. So, for the simple form we just showed, the destination document will display the form contents as follows:

```
<?php
echo $_POST['firstfield']
echo $_POST['secondfield']
?>
```

If you have fields that contain numbers, you can cast the field as the numeric type that it is. The following multiplies two numbers first as integers, then as doubles (floating point numbers).

```
<?php
echo (int)$_POST['firstfield']*(int)$_POST['secondfield']
echo (double)$_POST['firstfield']*(double)$_POST['secondfield']
?>
```

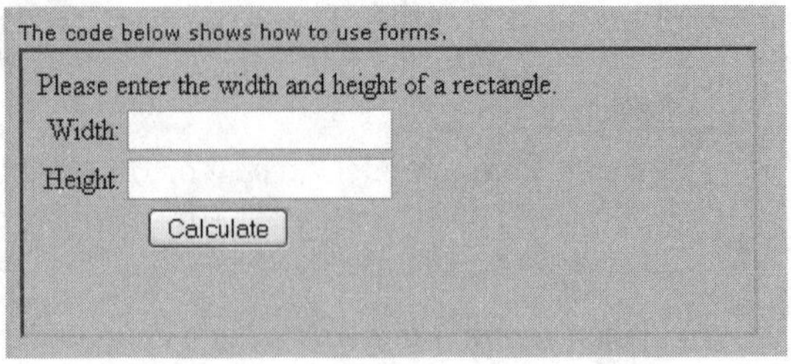

FIGURE 13-4 This application takes the width and height of a rectangle.

We created a pair of PHP documents. One contains a form and accepts the width and height of a rectangle, and the second is the destination for the form data, which calculates the area and perimeter of the rectangle. The application can be seen in Figure 13-4.

The application and the source for both of these files are at http://rickleinecker.com/HTDE/Chapter13.aspx.

Use PHP Scripts

There are a lot of PHP scripts already written to do many of the things you need to do; you can search the Internet for free PHP scripts and find thousands. In this section, we'll use full PHP applications and also incorporate small scripts.

Use Full PHP Applications

There are quite a few fully developed applications that you can download and use. One of the best repositories can be found at http://webscripts.softpedia.com/. In this section, we'll walk you through the process of downloading and using the GBook script, a nice guest book application written in PHP. Follow these steps:

1. Create a directory in your web application named GB.
2. Navigate to http://webscripts.softpedia.com/script/GuestBooks/GBook-42.html.
3. Click the Download link.
4. Click the Download From: Homepage link.
5. Now click the Download link again.
6. A new screen appears explaining their policies, and the download begins in about 10 seconds. When it's finished, unzip the files to your GB directory.
7. Open the settings.php file.
8. Edit anything in the file that you want, including the domain of your web site.
9. Make a link to the GBook.php file inside of the GB directory.

10. Save and preview your web application.
11. Link to the guest book application by clicking on the link you added.

The guest book application is very easy to set up and use; you should be able to set it up in less than five minutes, including uploading it to your server. You can see an example running inside of the page at http://rickleinecker.com/HTDE/Chapter13.aspx. The application can be seen in Figure 13-5.

Use Small PHP Scripts

Many times, you need something simple for your web site. In these cases, there are lots of small PHP scripts you can use without having to deal with an entire PHP application. The one we'll use for this example displays the weather for any U.S. Zip code. Follow these steps:

1. Create a directory in your web application named Weather.
2. Navigate to http://webscripts.softpedia.com/script/Miscellaneous/US-Weather-45974.html.
3. Click the Download link.
4. Click the Download From: Homepage link. The download will begin.
5. Extract the files to your Weather directory.
6. Add a link to your web application that opens Weather/index.html.

FIGURE 13-5 This guest book application is easy to use and has many good features.

7. When you click the link to the weather script, it will give you the chance to enter a Zip code.
8. Click the Check the Weather button and the current weather will be displayed.
9. Place the weather application in the following IFrame in order to keep the weather within one of your pages:

```
<iframe width="400" height="150" src="weather/index.html"></iframe>
```

Take Advantage of Expression's Built-in PHP Support

Expression has some built-in support for PHP pages so you don't have to know that much about PHP to use it. If you are editing an PHP document, try selecting PHP under the Insert menu. You'll find a submenu with several choices, including Form Variables, URL Variables, and If/Else. Feel free to experiment with this Expression Web feature. However, we find it much easier just to type in the PHP code.

Summary

PHP is another tool in your arsenal. It dynamically creates HTML code that's sent to the client machine. In this way, each user can have a customized experience. And there are many PHP examples that you can take advantage of to give your web site some great functionality.

14

Work with ASP.NET

HOW TO...

- Understand the ASP.NET architecture
- Understand ASP.NET master pages
- Understand controls and events
- Talk to a database
- Make pages responsive with AJAX

This chapter will teach you how to create ASP.NET web pages. They are different from static HTML pages in that the server creates the HTML on-the-fly based on the ASP.NET code that is stored on the server. For a complete explanation about dynamic pages, read the section in Chapter 13 entitled "Dynamically Create Web Pages."

Underneath ASP.NET is the .NET Framework. There are several versions in use as of this writing including 1.0, 1.1, 2.0, 3.0, and 3.5, and to create ASP.NET pages, you'll need to have one of the latest .NET platforms installed. The examples in this chapter use .NET version 3.5 since it is the latest and greatest. Upgrading your code to later versions is practically automatic and should not pose any problems. However, if you want, you can use .NET 2.0 to assure that everyone can take advantage of your code.

At the heart of .NET is the Common Language Runtime (CLR). This is the bedrock that contains all of the functionality that makes it easy to program. Before the CLR, many tasks required a high degree of skill and lots of code. Now, the plumbing is taken care of, and many things that were formerly extremely difficult can now be done with a few lines of code—you can spend more time programming business logic instead of worrying about how to perform something such as interprocess communication.

Besides the wide array of foundation code that the CLR offers, it makes it easy to use any .NET language you choose without any penalty. It used to be that Visual Basic was easy to use but performed poorly and that Visual C++ performed well but took much more time to use. Now you can use any .NET language, whether it's Visual

Basic .NET, C#, or J#, and get the same results. You can also write different pieces of an application in one language and other pieces in another language. The CLR offers true language agnosticism.

ASP.NET Architecture

ASP.NET is a technology that is built on the .NET runtime. Everything that the .NET Framework has to offer can be used within an ASP.NET page. This means that ASP.NET pages can be written in any .NET language including VB.NET and C#, and you can take advantage of the richness of the CLR base classes.

Internet Information Server (IIS) is normally used to manage ASP.NET pages, but other simplified web servers can be used, too. Let's say you have a server with IIS that is acting as a web server for your web sites. Here is the simplified process that IIS uses to manage the pages:

1. A user makes a request for a web page by typing it in the browser address bar or clicking a hyperlink.
2. The browser resolves the DNS address of the web page that is to be requested to an IP address. For instance, rickleinecker.com resolves to 208.109.181.49.
3. The browser sends the page request to the server at the IP address. The request is an HTTP header that includes (among other things) the document that is being requested.
4. The web server loads the requested page from the hard drive. (This is not technically correct since most web servers cache pages for improved performance, but this is theoretically how it works.)
5. If the page is a simple HTML page, it is sent to the client machine making the request.

Did You Know?

Postbacks Happen When a Page Calls Itself in Response to User Interaction

There is one more important ASP.NET concept that's important to understand, and that's the notion of a PostBack. Many ASP.NET controls can be used to perform tasks such as calculations or data alteration on other controls in the page. In many cases, this is done by making a request for the same page to the web server. But you wouldn't want the web server to simply send you a fresh copy of the same page: you want it to reflect any changes that the users intend to make. IIS and ASP.NET have a page request mechanism that handles this, where IIS knows that the request should not be answered with a fresh copy of the web page and should instead reflect any appropriate changes. This is called a PostBack. We'll talk more about PostBacks later in the chapter.

6. If the page is an ASP.NET page, a number of steps are performed in order to dynamically generate the HTML that will be sent to the client machine. This includes rendering any ASP.NET controls with the proper attributes such as color and text size. For many controls, this includes populating them with data from a database.
7. When the client machine gets the HTML data, it renders it within the browser window.
8. There is almost always a need to request additional elements such as images to fully render the web page in the browser window.

Note Expression Web 2 has its own built-in server that it uses to manage the ASP.NET pages in a way similar to the way IIS manages them.

Get Started with ASP.NET Pages

Let's get started now and create an ASP.NET page. First, create a new ASP.NET page. From Expression's File menu, select New | ASPX. When the page is created, it will be blank. You might want to save it with a file name that you can refer back to, such as UseASPNET.aspx. (Note that ASP.NET pages have an .aspx extension.)

If you go to the Code view in the editor window, you'll see code similar to the HTML code you've seen up until this point. However, there are two things that are very different, which ASP.NET needs to function properly. The first is the page directive that specifies the language. By default the language is C#, but this can be changed by simply entering a different language. For example, to use the Visual Basic .NET language, just change "C#" to "VB". The following two examples are page directives for the C# and Visual Basic .NET languages:

C# Language:

```
<%@ Page Language="C#" %>
```

Visual Basic .NET Language:

```
<%@ Page Language="VB" %>
```

Find the Expression Toolbox window. Drill down into the section entitled ASP.NET Controls, as shown in Figure 14-1. You'll see the following categories:

- Standard
- Data
- Validation
- Navigation
- Login
- WebParts
- AJAX

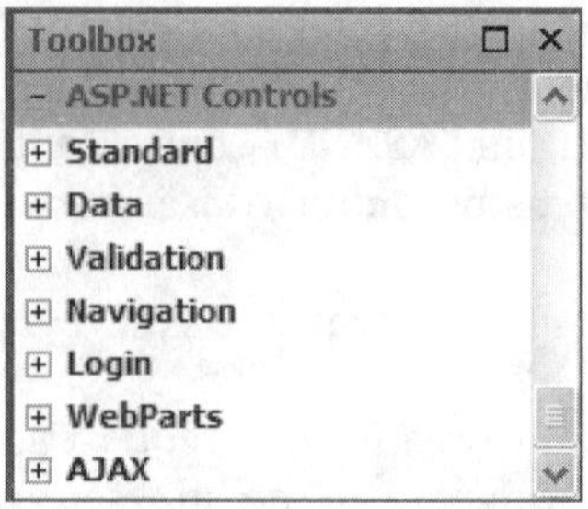

FIGURE 14-1 The ASP.NET controls can be found in the Toolbox.

We'll spend most of our time with the Standard controls. Drill down into the Standard controls. Make sure that the editor is in Design mode. Drag a label control onto your web page. You will see a Tag Properties window that contains the properties for the newly added label. Set the Text property to "Hello ASP.NET World". Set the Forecolor property to another color such as Fuchsia. When you save and then preview the page, you'll see the label control rendered in the HTML.

If you look closer and open the editor's code window, the label is represented with code that isn't standard HTML, as follows:

```
<asp:Label id="Label1" runat="server" ForeColor="Fuchsia"
   Text="Hello ASP.NET World"></asp:Label>
```

But when you preview the page, the label control has been transformed to normal HTML code, as follows:

```
<span id="Label1" style="color:Fuchsia;">Hello ASP.NET World</span>
```

Seeing the ASP.NET label code replaced by the standard HTML code illustrates what ASP.NET web servers do: they take the ASP.NET server control code and transform it into the appropriate HTML code.

Of course, the code you've seen so far isn't too exciting. You could have easily done it with some simple HTML text. The next step is to show you how to write code that modifies the label control. The code we're going to write is totally different than the HTML or ASP.NET control code. It's language code that doesn't get rendered but performs manipulation and calculation on your behalf.

Note Special markings are used to indicate where language code starts and ends. The characters `<%` indicate the start of code, and the characters `%>` indicate the end of code.

Here's an example of adding code to an ASPX page. If you add the following code right above the body tag in the file we're currently working on, it will change the way the page renders:

```
<%
    Label1.Text = "Hi mom!";
%>
```

Instead of seeing "Hello ASP.NET World", you will now see "Hi mom!" That's because the language code executes and changes the label's text to something different than what's in its Text property. We can do something more useful, though, and tell the user if it is morning or afternoon, as follows:

```
<%
    if( DateTime.Now.Hour < 12 )
    {
        Label1.Text = "It is morning.";
    }
    else
    {
        Label1.Text = "It is afternoon.";
    }
%>
```

Add a Button and a Button Event

Now we'll add a button to the page, create an event, and put some code into the event handler method on the same page we've been using. First, remove the code before the body tag. The next steps show how to add a button and an event handler for the button, and then how to put code into the button's event handler that changes the label text.

1. With the editor in Design mode, add an ASP.NET button below the label.
2. Edit the button Text property to say "Do It".
3. Change the editor to Code view.
4. Position the cursor to the right of the text asp:Button and to the right of the blank space.
5. Press the SPACEBAR, and IntelliSense appears.
6. Find the OnClick event, as shown in Figure 14-2.
7. Add the code OnClick = "Button1_Click". The entire tag should appear as follows:

```
<asp:Button OnClick="Button1_Click" id="Button1" runat="server"
Text="Do It" />
```

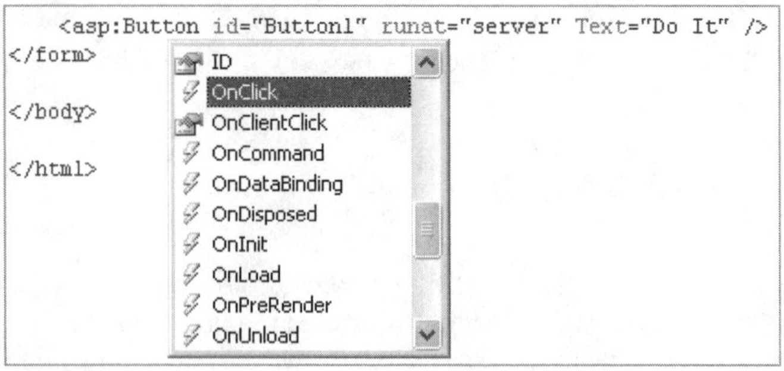

FIGURE 14-2 The OnClick event will appear within IntelliSense.

8. Add code for the button click event handler somewhere between the <head> and </head> tags, as follows:

```
<script type="text/c#" runat="server">
protected void Button1_Click(object sender, EventArgs e)
{
   Label1.Text = "You clicked me!";
}
</script>
```

9. Save the page, and preview it. When you click the button, the label text changes to "You clicked me!".

If you followed the instructions, you have an ASP.NET web page that responds to a button event. Let's take a closer look at it, as this will give you a better understanding of the ASP.NET architecture, especially the PostBack notion.

When you first preview the page, it is converted to HTML that all browsers can display. This is done by the development web server that's built into Expression. It scans the ASPX file for all ASP.NET controls, directives, and code. The directives instruct the conversion process in the details such as the .NET language to user. The controls are converted to their HTML counterparts based on how their properties have been set, and the code executes when necessary.

When the button is clicked, it generates a PostBack to the server. Essentially, it requests that same exact page, but tells the server what event is being responded to and what data is in the page controls. The server executes code based on the event that triggered the PostBack. The server then sends the altered HTML data back to the client. The following process describes what happens in this example.

1. The initial request for UseASPNET.aspx is made to the server.
2. The server scans the page for directives and finds that the C# language is used.
3. All controls are converted to HTML equivalences.

4. Any code execution that is required is performed.
5. When the user clicks the button, a PostBack request is sent to the server: the server is told the state of all controls, user-editable data fields, and that the PostBack is due to a button event.
6. The server performs the code for the Button1_Click event.
7. The updated HTML code is sent to the client.

Perform Calculations on User Data

In this section, we'll work through an example that performs calculations after the button is pressed. The user enters a width and height into textbox controls, and then a label is populated with the area and perimeter calculations.

To start, create an ASP.NET page named CalcAreaPerimeter.aspx. Add a title, a textbox for the width, a textbox for the height, a label for the calculation results, and a button. You can download the page and see this example working at the http://rickleinecker.com/HTDE/Chapter14.aspx page. You can see the web application working in Figure 14-3. You can also find the example files from McGraw-Hill Professional's web site at www.mhprofessional.com in a file named CalcAreaPerimeterPage.zip.

You will notice that the text "Width:" and "Height:" are not ASP.NET controls but simple HTML text. This is the best choice for anything that is static and unchanging because the web server doesn't have to do any transformation for straight HTML code, only for ASP.NET controls. Straight HTML data will save the web server some CPU time.

It's a good idea to name the ASP.NET controls with descriptive, meaningful names. By default, the ASP.NET controls get names (IDs). However, if your page gets long,

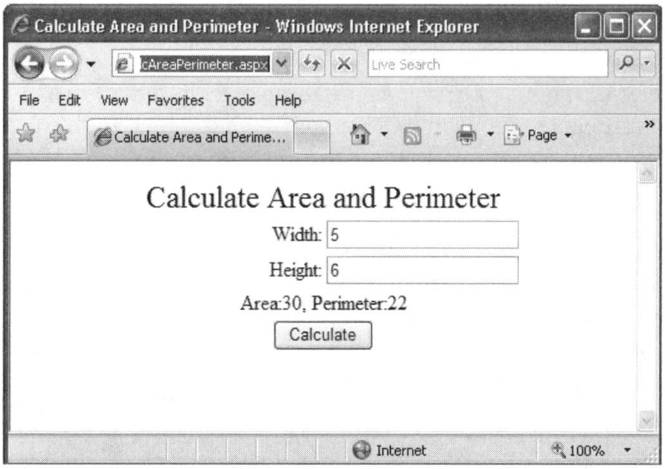

FIGURE 14-3 This page demonstrates using ASP.NET controls and an event.

you'll have a hard time remembering the difference between Label1 and Label3, and textBox1 and textBox17. You can also precede the control names with something that indicates what it is. For instance, we named the width textbox txtWidth. The txt preceding modifier lets everyone know that it's a textbox.

We created an event handler for the button, and the method is named btnCalculate_Click. The ASP.NET button control has the attribute OnClick="btnCalculate_Click" so that the button fires off the correct code when it's clicked.

If you look at the HTML source from within your browser, you will see how ASP.NET carries out some of its magic through a hidden field named __VIEWSTATE. This field is where all information that's used for PostBacks is kept. The following is the hidden information that the CalcAreaPerimeter.aspx page creates after calculations:

```
<input type="hidden" name="__VIEWSTATE" id="__VIEWSTATE" value="/wEPDwULLT
ExNzE0NTIxNTUPZBYCAgQPZBYCAgUPDxYCHgRUZXh0BRVBcmVhOjU2LCBQZXJpbWV0ZXI6MzBk
ZGQ8Br3tanjfygjVpBl6Eho16jQM5A==" />
```

Use Master Pages

In the old days of development, developers used server-side includes and user controls to create a page template feel for their web sites. Using the ASP.NET master page feature, you no longer have to copy and paste repetitive code into your web pages to create a template effect.

Although you could create page templates in early versions of ASP.NET, you needed some coding expertise. Now, Expression Web has support for master pages. The master page looks and feels like any web page, with two major differences:

- Master pages aren't called from the browser.
- The ContentPlaceHolder control on the master page is replaced with content from a content page.

Think of the master page as the template for your web site. Any content that you want repeated on each of your web sites is added to this page. For example, add the header and footer and any navigation element to your master page. After you associate your content pages with your master page, those elements appear on all your content pages.

Let's walk through an example of creating a web site based on a master page. You can download the entire web site project from the Chapter 14 page on http://rickleinecker.com/HTDE/Chapter14.aspx. You can also find the example files from McGraw-Hill Professional's web site at www.mhprofessional.com in a file named LiteraryGeniusPrj.zip.

1. Start by creating a new web site named LiteraryGenius.
2. Create a master page as shown in Figure 14-4 and save it as site.master.

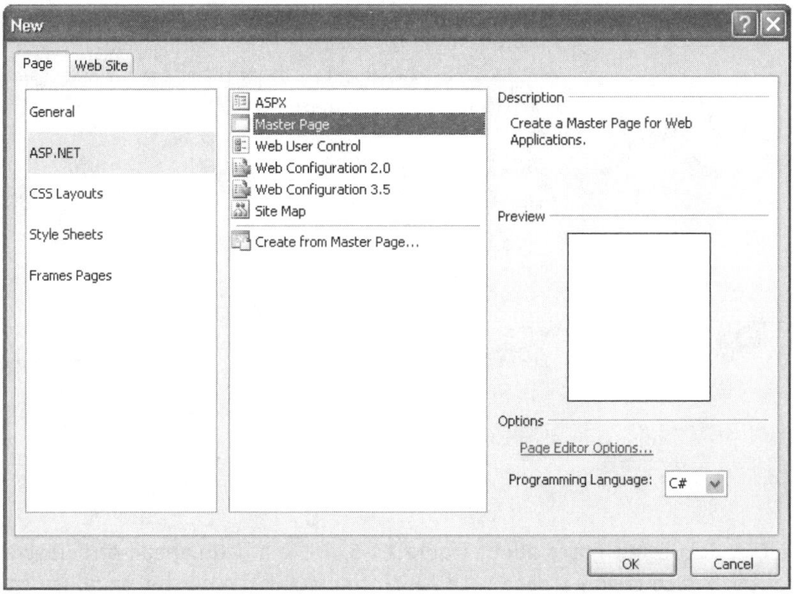

FIGURE 14-4 You must add a master page for this example.

Use the style sheet named stylesheet.css with the following line within the <head></head> tags:

```
<link rel="stylesheet" type="text/css" href="stylesheet.css" />
```

3. Add some code so we can see the general layout of the page. The following code was the result after adding the basics to the site.master page. (You can download this exact code from the Chapter 14 page under the heading "site.master page with the basic code".) Your page will resemble Figure 14-5.

```
<%@ Master Language="C#" %>
<!DOCTYPE html PUBLIC "-//W3C//DTD XHTML 1.0 Transitional//EN"
"http://www.w3.org/TR/xhtml1/DTD/xhtml1-transitional.dtd">
<html xmlns="http://www.w3.org/1999/xhtml">
<head runat="server">
    <title>Literary Genius</title>
    <link rel="stylesheet" type="text/css" href="stylesheet.css" />
</head>
<body>
    <div id="wrapper">
        <form id="Form1" runat="server">
              <div id="header">
                  <span class="title">Literary Genius</span>
                  <span class="breadcrumb">Todo: Breadcrumb will go here...</span>
```

```
            </div>
            <div id="content">
              <asp:ContentPlaceHolder ID="MainContent" runat="server">
              </asp:ContentPlaceHolder>
            </div>
          <div id="navigation">
              Todo: Menu will go here...
          </div>
      </form>
    </div>
    <div id="footer">
      <a href="http://rickleinecker.com/HTDE">How To Do Everything With Expression
Web 2</a>
    </div>
</body>
</html>
```

Note Just a few notes about Figure 14-5. We're a little ahead of ourselves because we had to create a page with which to display the master page. We'll talk about that shortly. Also, there is no content, so the figure is slightly edited to reflect this.

4. Now we will add the pages, starting with the main page, which we'll name Default.aspx. Select File | New | Page to open the dialog box shown in Figure 14-6.

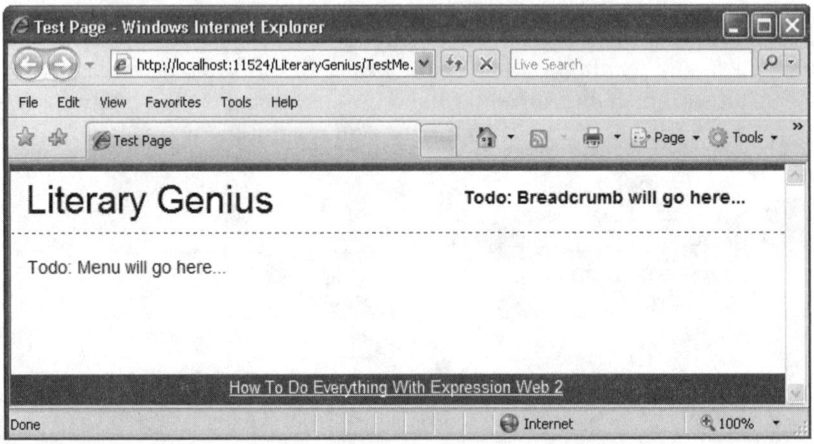

FIGURE 14-5 This master page has just the basics.

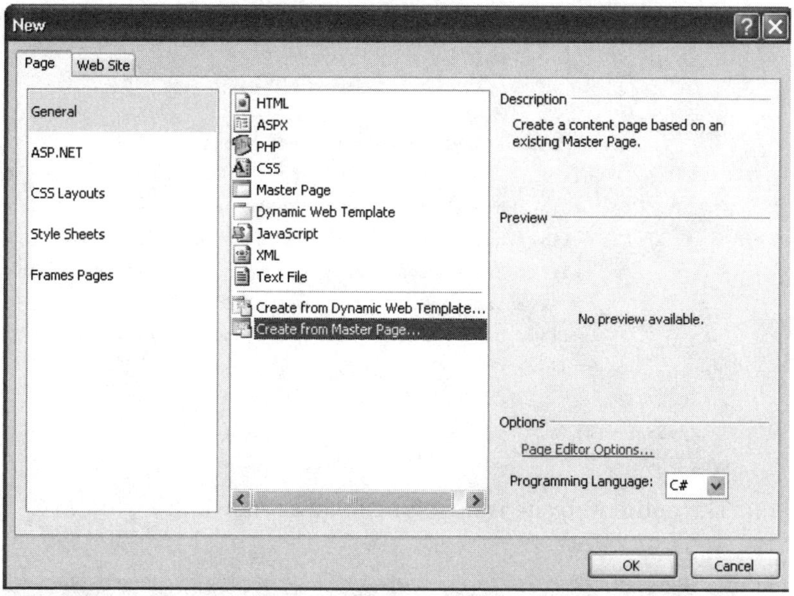

FIGURE 14-6 This dialog will appear, allowing you to create each page from the master page.

5. Make sure you're set for an ASPX page by selecting ASPX rather than the other choices.
6. You will now be prompted to select a master page: yours should be site.master.
7. Save the new file as Default.aspx.
8. In the editor's Design view, you will see the MainContent control. Select Create Custom Content.
9. Put your content into the control that is labeled MainContent.
10. Add the remainder of the pages. For this example, the files are Dickinson1.aspx, Dickinson2.aspx, Dickinson3.aspx, Dickinson4.aspx, Frost1.aspx, Frost2.aspx, Frost3.aspx, and Frost4.aspx.
11. Add content to each page as you did with Default.aspx.
12. The next thing we must do is create the navigation with the following code:

```
<div id="navigation">
  <ul>
    <li><a href="default.aspx">Home</a></li>
      <li>
        <span class="style1">Emily Dickinson</span>
          <ul>
            <li><a href='Dickinson1.aspx'>The is Another Sky</a></li>
            <li><a href='Dickinson2.aspx'>I'm Nobody! Who Are You?</a></li>
            <li><a href='Dickinson3.aspx'>Because I Could Not Stop For
                - Death</a></li>
```

```
            <li><a href='Dickinson4.aspx'>Nobody Knows This Little Rose</a></li>
           </ul>
         </li>
        <li>
          <span class="style1">Robert Frost</span>
            <ul>
              <li><a href='Frost1.aspx'>The Road Not Taken</a></li>
              <li><a href='Frost2.aspx'>Nothing Gold Can Stay</a></li>
              <li><a href='Frost3.aspx'>Stopping By Woods on a Snowy
                 Evening</a></li>
              <li><a href='Frost4.aspx'>Fire and Ice</a></li>
            </ul>
       </li>
    </ul>
</div>
```

13. The entire web site is now functional as shown in Figure 14-7.

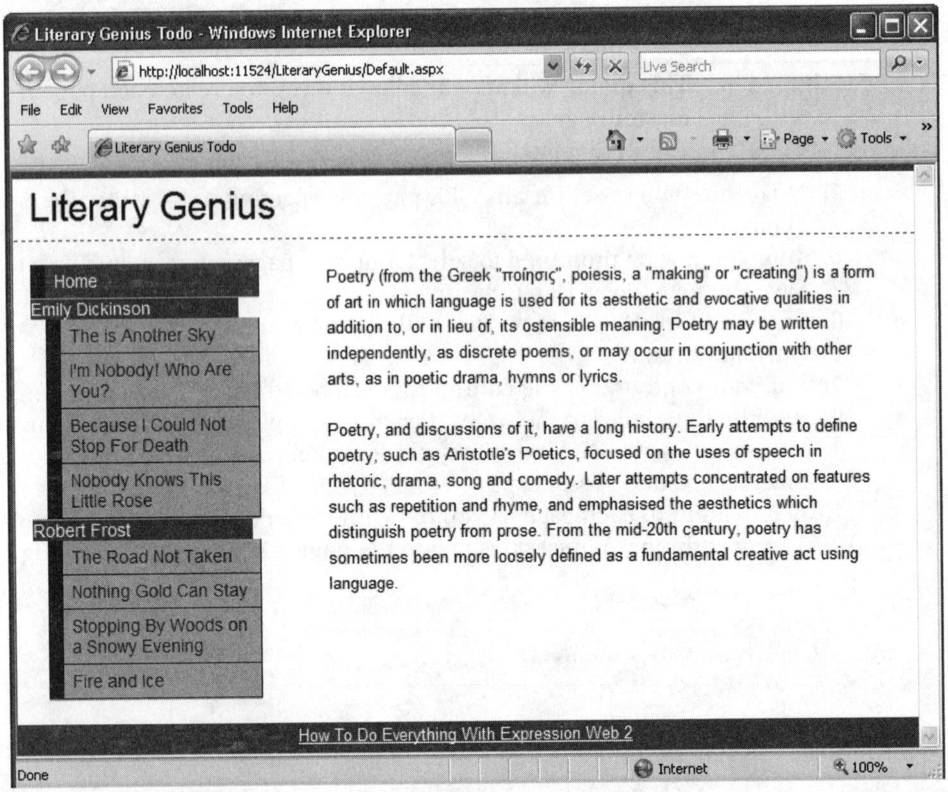

FIGURE 14-7 The entire web site is now functional.

Access Data from ASP.NET Pages

Most web sites access data in one way or another. ASP.NET makes it extremely easy to access data stores, and Expression Web fully supports the ASP.NET data access functionality. This section shows how to display data on a web page. It uses a sample access database, but connecting with SQL Server is just as easy if you need to do that.

We'll walk through the simplest possible database access to get warmed up. After the first example, we'll add some more complexities and demonstrate more of the power of ASP.NET.

Display the Contents of an Access Database

There is a sample database with the file name of FPNWIND.MDB that comes with Access that we'll use for all of the examples in this chapter. You can download it from the Chapter 14 page on the web site. The following steps walk you through the process of displaying contents of an Access database. You can also find the database on McGraw-Hill Professional's web site at www.mhprofessional.com in a file named FPNWIND.zip.

1. Create a new .aspx page named ShowSampleData.aspx.
2. Make sure that the FPNWIND.MDB file is in the web site's directory. (This isn't absolutely necessary, but it will keep things consistent for this walkthrough.)
3. In the Toolbox, open the ASP.NET Controls section and then open the Data section.
4. Add some title text to the page such as, "This page displays data from a sample database".
5. Drag an AccessDataSource control onto your page. It may warn you that you don't have visual editing for this control turned on. Select Yes to turn it on if this is the case.
6. Select the ASP.NET check box nonvisual controls from the Visual Aids selection under the View menu.
7. You will see a small box with the " > " symbol at the upper right corner of the control, as shown in Figure 14-8. Clicking this will display your configuration choices.
8. Select Configure Data Source. A dialog box opens as shown in Figure 14-9.

FIGURE 14-8 There is a small box that allows you to configure the control.

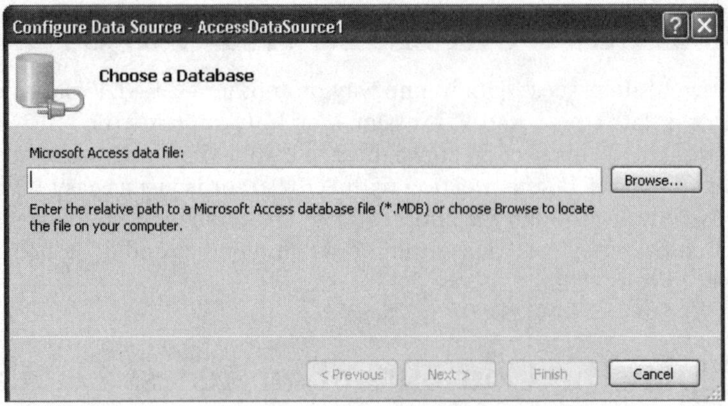

FIGURE 14-9 A dialog box appears that allows you to configure the data source.

9. Browse for the FPNWIND.MDB file and click the Next button.
10. In the next dialog box, select the Specify Columns from a Table or View radio button, leave Categories selected in the Name drop-down box, select the check box next to the asterisk (*) character, then click the Next button, as shown in Figure 14-10.

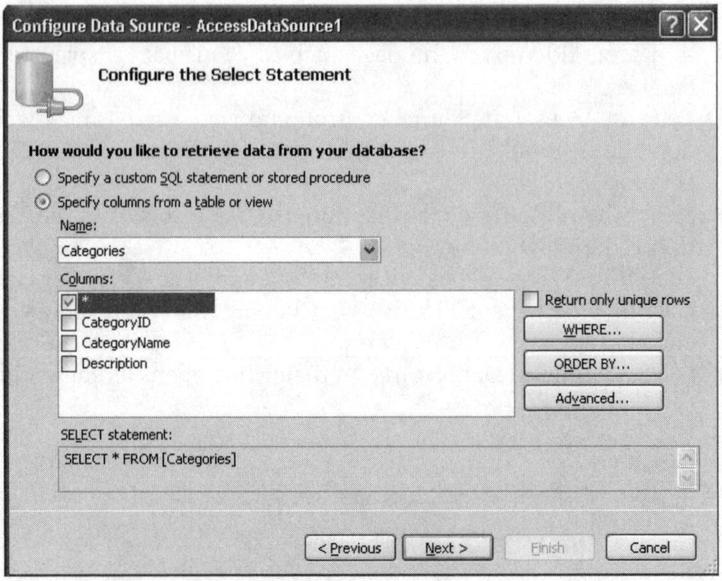

FIGURE 14-10 This is how the configuration should be for this example.

11. In the Test Query dialog box, click the Finish button. You will see the AccessDataSource control appear in the page.
12. In the AccessDataSource control's properties, set the ID to FNDWindDataSource.
13. Draw an ASP.NET DataList control onto the page right below the AccessDataSource object.
14. From the Choose Data Source drop-down, select FNDWindDataSource.
15. Save and preview the page. It will appear as shown in Figure 14-11.

Get More Control with the ListView Control

In this section we'll go further by using the ListView control, which allows you much more control. We'll do some formatting, too. Follow these steps to use the ListView control:

1. Create a new ASPX page named MoreDataDisplay.aspx.
2. Make sure that the FPNWIND.MDB file is in the web site's directory.
3. In the Toolbox, open the ASP.NET Controls section and then open the Data section.

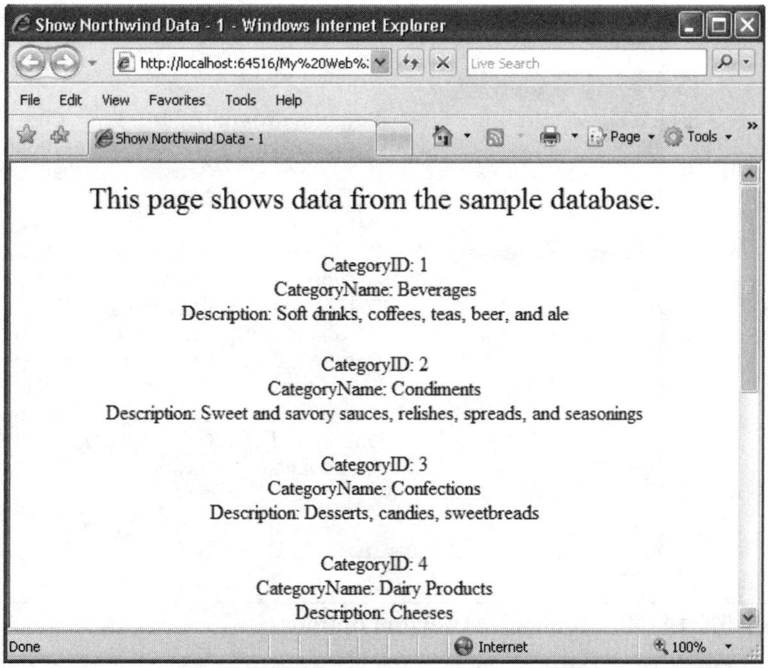

FIGURE 14-11 This example displays the contents of the Category table.

4. Add some title text to the page such as "More Data Display".
5. Drag an AccessDataSource control onto your page. It may warn you that you don't have visual editing for this control turned on. Select Yes to turn it on if this is the case.
6. Select Configure Data Source.
7. Browse for the FPNWIND.MDB file and click the Next button.
8. In the next dialog box, select the Specify Columns from a Table or View radio button, leave Customers selected in the Name drop-down box, select the check box next to Company Name, Address, City, Region, Postal Code. Click the Next button.
9. In the Test Query dialog box, click the Finish button. You will see the AccessDataSource control appear in the page.
10. In the AccessDataSource control's properties, set the ID to CustomerData.
11. Add a DataList control right below the AccessDataSource control.
12. In the Choose Data Source drop-down select CustomerData.
13. Select Configure ListView.
14. In the dialog, select Colorful, as shown in Figure 14-12, and click OK.
15. Save and preview the page. It will appear in your browser as in Figure 14-13.

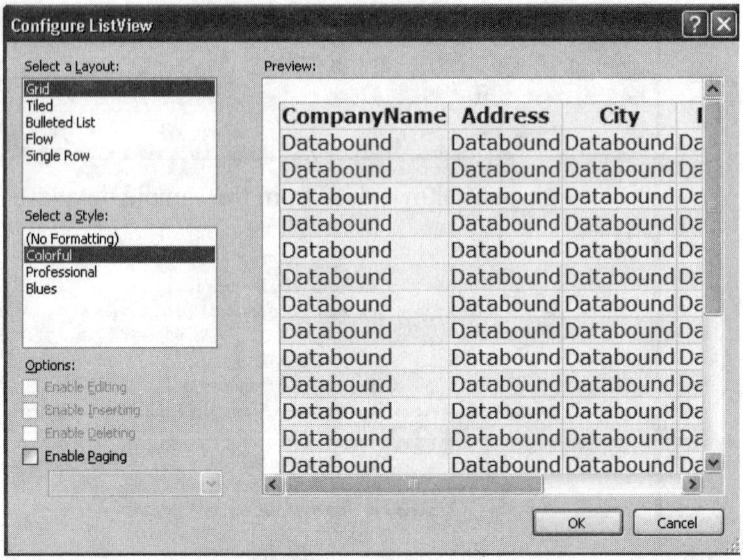

FIGURE 14-12 You can set several options.

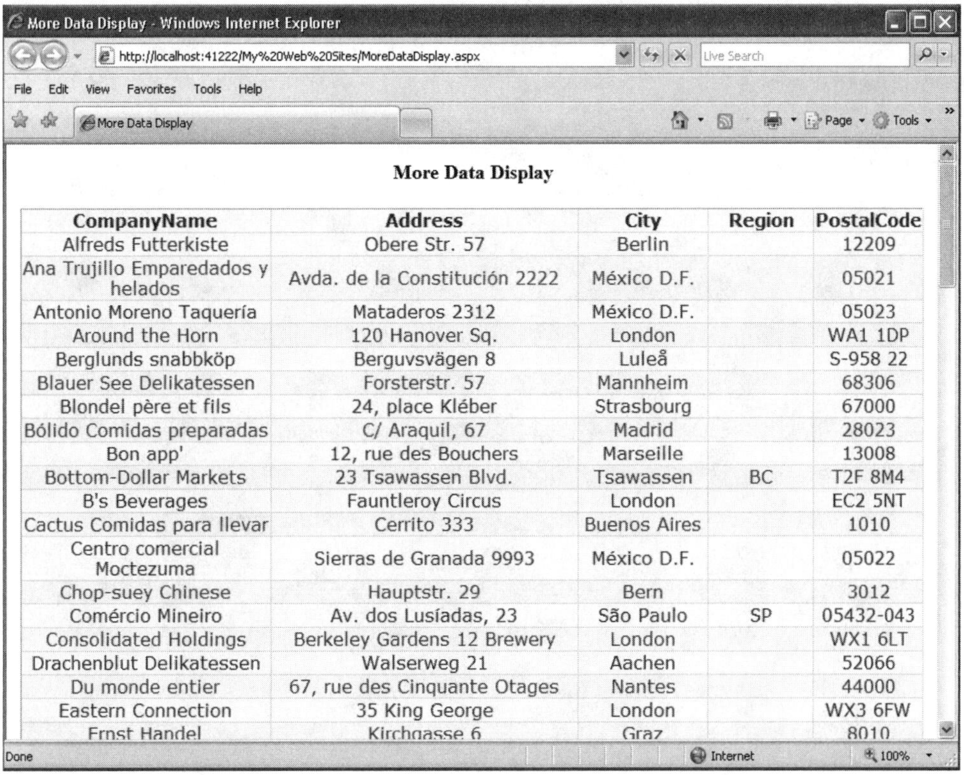

More Data Display

CompanyName	Address	City	Region	PostalCode
Alfreds Futterkiste	Obere Str. 57	Berlin		12209
Ana Trujillo Emparedados y helados	Avda. de la Constitución 2222	México D.F.		05021
Antonio Moreno Taquería	Mataderos 2312	México D.F.		05023
Around the Horn	120 Hanover Sq.	London		WA1 1DP
Berglunds snabbköp	Berguvsvägen 8	Luleå		S-958 22
Blauer See Delikatessen	Forsterstr. 57	Mannheim		68306
Blondel père et fils	24, place Kléber	Strasbourg		67000
Bólido Comidas preparadas	C/ Araquil, 67	Madrid		28023
Bon app'	12, rue des Bouchers	Marseille		13008
Bottom-Dollar Markets	23 Tsawassen Blvd.	Tsawassen	BC	T2F 8M4
B's Beverages	Fauntleroy Circus	London		EC2 5NT
Cactus Comidas para llevar	Cerrito 333	Buenos Aires		1010
Centro comercial Moctezuma	Sierras de Granada 9993	México D.F.		05022
Chop-suey Chinese	Hauptstr. 29	Bern		3012
Comércio Mineiro	Av. dos Lusíadas, 23	São Paulo	SP	05432-043
Consolidated Holdings	Berkeley Gardens 12 Brewery	London		WX1 6LT
Drachenblut Delikatessen	Walserweg 21	Aachen		52066
Du monde entier	67, rue des Cinquante Otages	Nantes		44000
Eastern Connection	35 King George	London		WX3 6FW
Ernst Handel	Kirchgasse 6	Graz		8010

FIGURE 14-13 The data is displayed within a table.

Summary

ASP.NET is one of the most powerful tools for creating dynamic and interactive web sites. Expression Web 2.0 provides an easy interface to the ASP.NET controls, so it's a snap to use them. Once you get started using ASP.NET controls, you'll never stop.

15

Make Your Site Available to Everyone

HOW TO...

- Understand the importance of accessibility
- Design pages and sites for accessibility
- Use the Accessibility Checker
- Produce accessibility reports for reference

In this chapter, we'll talk about accessibility. The term has come to mean a lot of things to a lot of people, but here, we'll understand it to mean that as many people as possible have access to something. And for the purposes of this book, that "something" refers to web sites.

Don't confuse accessibility with usability. Usability refers to the extent to which something can be used by specified users to achieve specified goals with effectiveness, efficiency, and satisfaction in a specified context of use. If a web site is really slick and smooth and easy to use, we say its usability is high. If almost every person can use it (whether smoothly or not), then we say its accessibility is high.

When web sites are correctly designed, developed, and edited, all users can have equal access to information and functionality. For example, when a site is coded with semantically meaningful HTML, with textual equivalents provided for images and with links named meaningfully, this helps blind users using text-to-speech software. When text and images are large, it is easier for users with poor sight to read and understand the content.

Understand the Importance of Accessibility

Creating highly accessible web sites is important for a few compelling reasons. Out of respect to visually impaired visitors, we all want to make information available to everyone, despite difficulties they may experience. Economics is another reason, as enabling more people to view and enjoy your web site provides a larger base for e-commerce. There are legal reasons for accessibility too: you must adhere to a number of accessibility laws if you are developing government web sites.

An Accessibility Scenario

You work for ACME Widgets, Incorporated. Imagine your marketing department is charged with increasing sales by 10 percent. They can do this with a big effort and lots of resources. It may take months or even years, but a 10 percent growth would please many CEOs.

Now imagine you're the chief web developer for ACME. You get a letter from a potential customer who explains that she has poor vision. She says that when she increases the text size in her browser, everything on the web site runs together. You realize that this customer will probably not become a customer because the web site is so hard to read.

You walk down to the mailroom and ask if they've ever gotten similar letters. The clerk tells you that they receive dozens of similar letters each week but discard them since there is no company policy for what to do with such letters. This gets you to thinking hard.

You go back to your team and discuss ways to adjust the web site presentation so that users who increase the text size can easily read it. In two weeks the job is done. Alerting the mailroom to monitor the incoming letters that are similar to the one you got, they tell you at the end of the month that they haven't gotten any. In a staff meeting, marketing is ready to launch the new advertising campaign to get sales up by 10 percent. The company accountant tells everyone that sales are up by 4 percent already. You realize that your efforts to attract the customers who couldn't successfully read ACME's web site have provided a quick boost in sales.

You consult with a web accessibility expert and get a prioritized list of suggestions for the web site. Your web development team implements them, and within three months of your first accessibility efforts, company sales are up 15 percent: 10 percent of that is probably due to your efforts, and 5 percent is probably due to marketing's efforts. Of course, they get the credit, but you get the warm fuzzy feeling inside that you did the right thing.

Legal Issues

Let's say that you are the web developer for a governmental agency. You will absolutely need to adhere to accessibility guidelines. If you don't, there is a possibility that you will be notified of infractions. If you don't fix them within a short period of time, you will be subject to fines. It's better to get it right from the beginning. If accessibility issues come to light and you're in the middle of a large project, you might not have the time to deal with them. That means either you will have to pay someone to fix the problems, or incur the fines.

Did You Know?

Entire Businesses Are Built on Identifying Accessibility Infractions

Here's the scary part of designing nonaccessible web pages for governmental agencies. There are companies that are in business to find noncompliant governmental web sites. Once they find them, they report them and offer to fix them. If the original developer can fix it, they do. But in most cases, the original web developer is scheduled for the next six months and has no hope of finding time to fix the problems. The company who finds and identifies the problem gets paid for the fixes, and you will either have to pay for it or risk losing future web development business with that governmental agency.

We strongly recommend that all of your web sites, whether governmental, e-commerce, or just informational, are accessible. It pays to do it right and costs to do it wrong.

Note You can find the legal guidelines at www.access-board.gov. They are maintained by a US government agency know as the United States Access Board. The specific pages for web accessibility can be found at the following two links: http://www.access-board.gov/telecomm/index.htm and http://www.access-board.gov/508.htm.

Design Pages and Sites for Accessibility

In this section we'll talk about the four principles and the twelve guidelines you need to keep in mind when you design and develop your web sites in order to keep them accessible. We took the guidelines from www.access-board.gov and will summarize them here for you with our own insights. They are pretty much bureaucracy-speak in their native form.

Accessibility Principles

At the very top of the list are four principles that provide the foundation for web accessibility: perceivable, operable, understandable, and robust. We'll talk about those in this section. Under the principles are guidelines. The 12 guidelines provide the basic goals that authors should work toward in order to make content more accessible to users with different disabilities. These guidelines are not testable but provide the framework and overall objectives to help authors understand the success criteria and better implement the techniques. These guidelines are sometimes referred to as Web Content Accessibility Guidelines (WCAG).

Principle 1: Perceivable

This principle implies that all user interface components are perceivable to users.

The first guideline requires that you provide text alternatives for any nontext elements. For instance, images should all have Alt Text so that screen readers and other software can communicate their value to users.

The second guideline requires that you provide alternatives for time-based media. These are mostly audio and video files. The alternatives that are most commonly provided are text equivalences for the content.

The third guideline requires that content which is more complex can also be presented in a simpler way without losing any of the content. There are many ways to do this, including tabbed content and tooltips that appear.

The fourth guideline is to make the colors distinguishable. The hardest thing for anyone to read is dark text on a black background: even someone with 20/20 vision can find that difficult, so imagine how someone with visual challenges would fare. Make sure that your colors contrast well enough so that text is easy to read.

Principle 2: Operable

This principle implies that all user interface components are operable and easy to use.

The first guideline requires that all functionality is available from a keyboard. Fortunately, most browsers support keyboard shortcuts for moving from field to field and for selecting a button or link. But anything the browser doesn't make accessible is your responsibility. Many developers tend to use the keyboard shortcuts most of the time anyway, as they are easier for us than the mouse.

The second guideline is that users must have enough time to read and use the content. Make sure, if there is anything time-based such as a sound or a video, that users can replay, pause, or stop it. If you redirect from a page for any reason after a set period of time, make sure that users can read what is on the page before you continue. The JavaScript timers that were found in the example which changed font colors over time in Chapter 10 must be used carefully, as they can cause you to violate this guideline.

The third guideline is that your content can't cause seizures. This may sound like a strange thing, but repeated flashing on the screen can in some cases cause seizures. The recommendation is to limit flashing content to three flashes only.

The fourth guideline requires that navigation be clearly available and understandable. For example, web pages should have titles that relate to their purpose and the fields in the HTML page should follow a well-thought-out focus sequence. In addition, there should be multiple navigation paths to pages, links should clearly make their purpose clear, and there should be section headings that group navigational items.

Principle 3: Understandable

This principle states that all information and the operation of the user interface must be understandable.

The first guideline requires the text content to be readable and understandable. That is, the page language should be clear, there should be a way for users to identify and understand unusual words, and abbreviations should be clear or a way to look them up should be provided. It's advised that the reading level required should be at the lower secondary education level.

The second guideline states that pages should be predictable. This mostly has to do with the consistency of the web site. Navigation and user interface should be consistent, and the look and feel of the web site should be consistent.

The third guideline is that the web site should help users avoid and correct mistakes. When an input field is in the incorrect format, you should alert users to this. (For more about form field validation, see Chapter 12.) Suggestions should be provided when an error has been detected. Help should be provided whenever possible.

Principle 4: Robust

This principle states that the content must be robust enough that it can be interpreted reliably by a wide variety of user agents, including assistive technologies.

The first and only guideline requires that the user interface components be clearly identified in the HTML code. This includes a combination of Name and ID attributes. Duplicate attributes for each HTML tag must be avoided.

Note Several of these principles/guidelines are illustrated at http://rickleinecker.com/HTDE/Chapter15.aspx.

Use the Accessibility Checker

Fortunately, Expression Web 2 comes with an Accessibility Checker. It will take a look at your web site and identify any issues that it finds.

To find the Accessibility Checker, select Accessibility from the Task Panes menu. The Accessibility Checker will appear as in Figure 15-1.

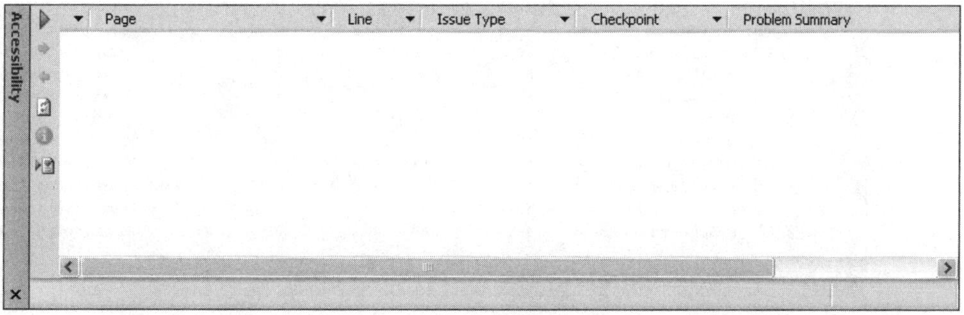

FIGURE 15-1 The Accessibility Checker window opens after you select Accessibility from the Task Panes menu.

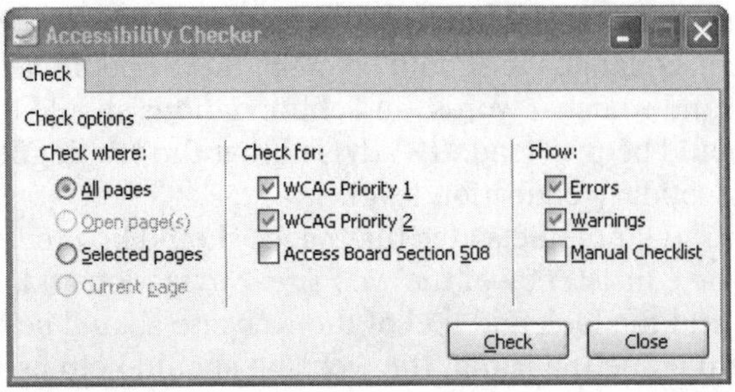

FIGURE 15-2 You will have the chance to select your options before the Accessibility Checker gets started.

When you click the green arrow that gets the Accessibility Checker started, a dialog will appear in which you can select the appropriate options as shown in Figure 15-2. The principles and guidelines that were presented earlier in the chapter are from the WCAG Priority 2 standard. We suggest you check this check box, along with the WCAG Priority 1 check box for additional checks.

It's also a good idea to show both errors and warnings as warnings can easily become errors after edits, and you should be aware of them.

Let's try an experiment. Create a blank web page. Enter the text **This is a test**. Now run the Accessibility Checker for the current page. You should get no errors or warnings.

Now make the text background color yellow and the text foreground color the same yellow. When you re-run the Accessibility Checker, it will give you a warning. That's because it realizes that the text is unreadable since its foreground and background colors are the same.

Figure 15-3 shows the Accessibility Checker after it is done. For each error or warning, it shows you the page, the line that's being referred to, the issue type (warning or error), a link to the WCAG guideline that covers the issue, and a summary.

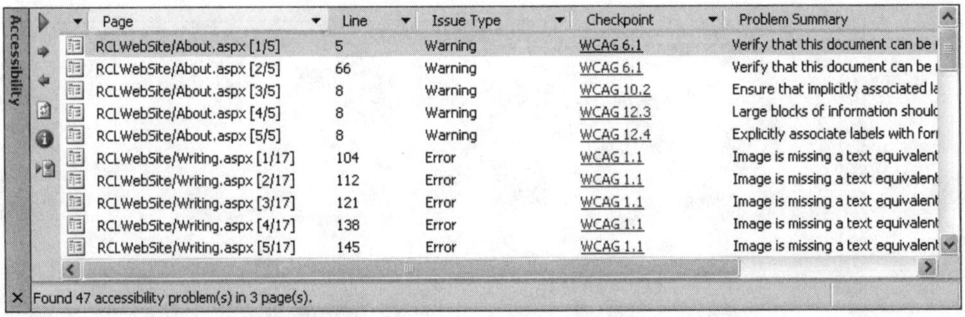

Accessibility
Page
Line
Issue Type
Checkpoint
Problem Summary
RCLWebSite/About.aspx [1/5] 5 Warning WCAG 6.1
RCLWebSite/About.aspx [2/5] 66 Warning WCAG 6.1
RCLWebSite/About.aspx [3/5] 8 Warning WCAG 10.2
RCLWebSite/About.aspx [4/5] 8 Warning WCAG 12.3
RCLWebSite/About.aspx [5/5] 8 Warning WCAG 12.4
RCLWebSite/Writing.aspx [1/17] 104 Error WCAG 1.1 Image is missing a text equivalent
RCLWebSite/Writing.aspx [2/17] 112 Error WCAG 1.1 Image is missing a text equivalent
RCLWebSite/Writing.aspx [3/17] 121 Error WCAG 1.1 Image is missing a text equivalent
RCLWebSite/Writing.aspx [4/17] 138 Error WCAG 1.1 Image is missing a text equivalent
RCLWebSite/Writing.aspx [5/17] 145 Error WCAG 1.1 Image is missing a text equivalent
Found 47 accessibility problem(s) in 3 page(s).

FIGURE 15-3 The Accessibility Checker gives you very complete information.

How to... Produce Accessibility Reports for Reference

Having the Accessibility Checker show you all of the problems it found in a task pane is nice, but you might need more. Suppose, for instance, you need to print the issues out to bring to a meeting. Or you might need a mechanism with which you can track the issues and the progress toward fixing them.

Expression can create an HTML report based on the Accessibility Checker's findings, as shown in Figure 15-4. You can print this report for your records or for distribution, save it and use it to track your progress, e-mail it, or save it on your company's intranet. Some even have check boxes that you can use to keep track of the items that have been addressed.

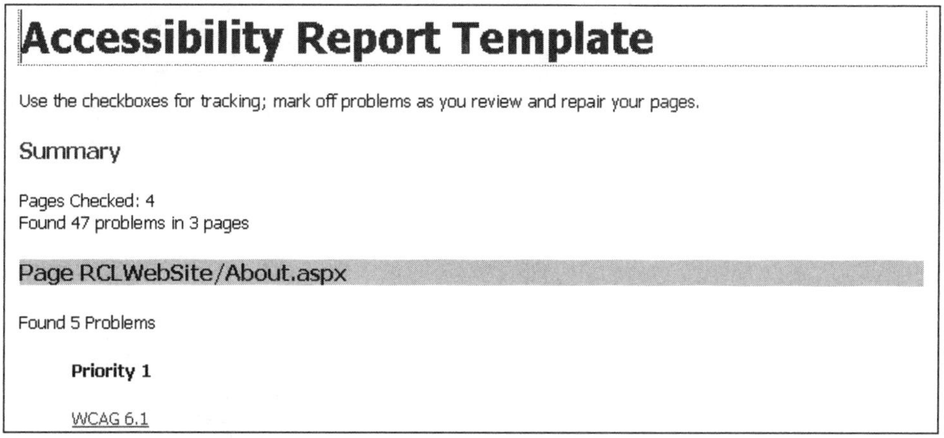

Accessibility Report Template
Use the checkboxes for tracking; mark off problems as you review and repair your pages.
Summary
Pages Checked: 4
Found 47 problems in 3 pages
Page RCLWebSite/About.aspx
Found 5 Problems
Priority 1
WCAG 6.1

FIGURE 15-4 Expression creates a very useful HTML report.

Summary

Accessibility is very important for web sites. Expression Web 2 makes it easy to check pages for adherence to the WCAG guidelines. This will help your web applications' commercial viability, and will make sure that governmental web sites are in compliance.

16

Test and Publish the Site

HOW TO...

- Optimize files for efficiency
- Validate XHTML
- Set up the remote site
- Define pages for publishing
- Upload pages to the Web

Several years ago, one of the authors, Rick, was trying to get one of the local hospitals to let him create and maintain their web site. A visit was scheduled with their chief operating officer and the network administrator. They said that they were satisfied with their web site, and that the network administrator was doing all of the content creation and maintenance.

Pulling up the web site was a slow process. The main page, which was almost entirely composed of a single image, came up slowly. Looking at the HTML and retrieving the image, it was revealed that it was a 5MB GIF image. The sheer size of the image bogged down the loading of the main page. How many of their dial-up visitors waited? In addition, using a GIF image for a picture is a big mistake since they only support 256 simultaneous colors.

After his experience at the hospital, he realized that anyone can put up a web site, but if they don't understand some optimization principles, the experience provided to users might be poor. This chapter talks about optimizing web sites for optimal performance and balancing performance with practical reality. We'll provide you with some good advice that isn't obvious when you develop and deploy web sites.

We'll also talk about the mechanisms for setting up and uploading to a Web. This one hurdle has prevented countless would-be web developers from creating an Internet presence.

Optimize Files for Efficiency

In this section, we'll go over some good strategies for optimizing the performance of your web site files. This ranges from which image file formats to choose to how to streamline HTML.

Choose the Best Image File Format

Over the years we have been absolutely amazed at the number of technically competent people who knew nothing about the differences in image file formats. Knowing which format to choose for a given situation can make all the difference in whether your web site has the appearance you want and whether it performs at its best. We'll set some guidelines in this section so that you can make wise choices.

There are several types of image files that web browsers will load. Many browsers may have plug-ins that load additional image types, but we'll limit this section to the major four: BMP, GIF, JPG, and PNG images. BMP images are native to the Windows operating system; GIF stands for Graphics Interchange Format; JPG (sometimes JPEG) stands for Joint Photographic Experts Group; and PNG stands for Portable Network Graphics. All of these image file formats offer different advantages and disadvantages. What we'll do right now is describe the image file formats and discuss the advantages and disadvantages of each. Deciding which image to use in which setting will be important.

BMP Image Files

BMP image files are native to the Windows operating system. While the file format did not originate on the Windows platform, it gained its greatest acceptance and use there.

BMP files are uncompressed bitmaps that represent any type of graphics. They faithfully reproduce photographic images as well as crisp line art. There is no image degradation when BMP files are saved to and reloaded from disk.

Unfortunately, BMP files are uncompressed. There is a compression mechanism that exists in the file format specification, but it is rarely implemented in software. For this reason, BMP images are very large. Their large size makes them very impractical for web sites since the transfer time is large and makes web pages load slowly.

Note While BMP files are supported on all Windows platforms, not all browsers support them. Internet Explorer is pretty consistent, but earlier versions of Firefox and other browsers may not load BMP files.

GIF Image Files

The GIF format is a creation of CompuServe and is used to store multiple bitmap images in a single file for exchange between platforms and systems. GIF is a widely used format for storing multibit graphics and image data. Even a quick peek into the graphics file section of most Internet servers seems to prove this true. Many of these are high-quality images of people, landscapes, and cars. The vast majority of GIF files contain 16- or 256-color quality images. Grayscale images such as those produced by scanners are also commonly stored using GIF, although monochromatic graphics such as clip art and document images rarely are.

Although the bulk of GIF files are found in the Intel-based MS-DOS environment, GIF is not associated with any particular software application. GIF is not created for any particular software application need, either, although most software applications that read and write graphical image data such as paint programs, scanner and video software, and most image files display and conversion programs usually support GIF.

GIF uses a lossless compression method called LZW, which stands for Lempel, Ziv, and Welch, the three men who invented it. (More correctly, Lempel and Ziv created the early version and Welch made modifications later on; but we digress.) The compression method that GIF uses does not degrade the picture quality at all. Every time you save and load the same GIF image, it is recreated with 100 percent integrity. For this reason, if you have an image that must be crisp and clear and reproduced with the absolute highest quality, GIF should be your choice.

One limitation of GIF in certain circumstances is that it is limited to 256 simultaneous colors. Although the 256 colors are selected from a palette of millions of colors, GIF files can only use 256 of those colors at a time. For most web applications, there's a commonly accepted palette known as the browser-safe palette that many GIF images now use. If you use this browser-safe palette, your GIF images are almost guaranteed to have the best reproduction on systems all over the world. However, if you use some custom palette that is not easy to match on all systems, your image may not look the same and may suffer when it is displayed on another system. One big advantage of GIF files is that one GIF file can store multiple images, and the multiple images can be displayed in sequential order within a browser. These are called animated GIFs, and are very popular on the Web.

JPG Images

JPG refers to a standards organization (Joint Photographic Experts Group), a method of file compression, and also a file format. The JPG file interchange format is designed to allow files containing JPG and coded data streams to be exchanged between otherwise incompatible systems and applications. For instance, a Macintosh and an IBM compatible computer can share the same file. JPG files, unlike GIF files, use a compression method that degrades the image at least somewhat. This is called lossy compression: that is, there is a certain amount of loss every time the file is saved. For this reason, if you need an exact replication of the original image, JPG is not necessarily the choice you need to make.

One advantage of JPG, however, is that even with the image degradation you get, for photographic images, you really can't tell much of a difference. It does a great job in images of near photographic quality as opposed to those with crisp, sharp edges.

JPG images are also composed of 24-bit colors. Each pixel in a JPG image can be one of a different color selected from a palette of millions. This is far better than the limitation of 256 colors in a GIF palette. In this case, a JPG image can consist of millions and millions of simultaneous colors.

Did You Know?

JPG Files Have an Adjustable Level of Compression

JPG images can be compressed in a variable way. More compression gives greater image degradation; less compression gives greater image integrity. Consider this tradeoff when you decide where on the continuum that your image needs to be.

PNG Image Files

The PNG file format was designed to overcome the limitations of the GIF file format, the most important being the restriction of 256 simultaneous colors. PNG can support millions of colors similar to JPG. (There are also some other limitations that PNG overcame, such as legal issues and additional transparency modes.)

PNG files use lossless compression and will sometimes compress even better than an exact image saved in the GIF file format. The one thing that PNG images are missing is the ability to have multiple images and support animation.

Image File Format Comparisons

Let's compare image file formats, starting with BMP files. Although they work for web pages, we highly recommend against using them under any circumstances because of their large size. We have used them in the past only when under duress and without access to graphics software that could be converted to an image, and needed to get something posted on a web site immediately.

We use GIF images often. We almost always select a GIF image for a small icon that must be saved with no image degradation as well as for any drawings with lines, rectangles, or other shapes that must remain crisp. Usually, images with shape drawings don't have many colors, and the 256 color limitation doesn't factor in.

We use JPG images any time we need to display a photographic image, including portraits, landscapes, and scans of art. Many of the games that are written use JPG images for backgrounds and landscapes. For these types of images, the glossy compression (and the resulting data degradation) aren't perceivable. JPG compresses images to a fairly small size, so the load time for your web pages will be quick.

PNG is a fairly new addition to the developers' arsenal. We tend to use the PNG file format for images that must remain crisp, yet need more than 256 colors. Many report images now use sophisticated shading techniques that require many colors. If you reduce these images to GIF (with 256 colors), they lose much of their attractiveness.

General Web Page Optimization Tips

In this section we'll talk about tips that will help keep your web pages running smoothly. These tips range from reduced HTML payloads to optimized delivery.

Combine External Files

There are many times when you will use external files in your web pages. Combining them doesn't necessarily reduce the amount of data that comes in, but it reduces the number of HTTP requests that the browser makes. Each HTTP request carries overhead that you should avoid whenever possible.

Many times, multiple style sheets can be combined into a single style sheet. Using one style sheet instead of three reduces the number of HTTP requests by two.

External JavaScript files can often be combined. Here again, the fewer the external files, the faster the web page loads.

Another less obvious technique is using image maps that combine the functionality of several images. If, for instance, you have four images that all function as clickable links, you can create one large image and use an image map.

Move All Style Sheets to the Top of the HTML Code

You are allowed to load style sheets just about anywhere within your HTML code. However, if you put the style sheet reference within the `<HEAD>` tag, it will appear to load faster because it allows the document to render progressively.

Move All Scripts to the Bottom of the HTML Code

Moving all your scripts to the bottom of the HTML code probably seems like a strange suggestion. However, when the browser loads script, all parallel downloads are blocked. Parallel downloads allow simultaneous downloading of multiple components, and therefore speed up the content delivery.

Reduce Unnecessary Characters in JavaScript and CSS

It is easy to add extra characters to JavaScript and CSS. We do it often so that content is more readable, and therefore more maintainable, to us. While that sounds nice, it also means that there are lots of extra formatting characters. We often indent and add blank lines to our JavaScript functions, but the browser doesn't need this, and it just adds to the downloadable payload. Rick wrote a program that strips unnecessary characters from my code so that you can keep the well-formatted code for editing. We haven't found a similar utility, and it is now posted to the rickleinecker.com/HTDE/Chapter16.aspx page.

Avoid Scaling Images in HTML

You can easily add width and height attributes to `<IMG>` tags. These attributes allow you to scale a large image down to a smaller image (and the reverse). However, the entire image still needs to be downloaded. A better alternative when you want to display a smaller image than the original is to scale it with a graphics program such as Gimp, Paint Shop Pro, or Adobe Photoshop. The downloaded image will be much smaller and the overall payload will be reduced.

How to... Get a Free Paint Program

Gimp is a paint program that is completely free. It does most everything that you will need to do such as create, load, and save images, edit images, perform some image processing, and manipulate bitmaps. To find this program, go to http://www.gimp.org/ and follow the links to download the program.

Validate XHTML

We've been talking about HTML throughout the entire book, but what is XHTML? It's an update to HTML that solves a number of problems that HTML hasn't been able to shake.

Has your web browser ever stopped to complain about errors in HTML code that it encounters on a page? We know you often get JavaScript errors, but that is a totally different animal. Web browsers have been expected to render HTML code, regardless of how poorly formed it is. Even with tons of errors, your browser renders a page to the best of its ability. The HTML parser must be lenient when it comes to dealing with HTML code. Now, imagine how much unnecessary demand this places on the browser as it performs handsprings to make things work.

Even if the HTML code is perfect, though, there are some issues that make it more difficult to use. Many tags, most notable `<BR>` and `<IMG>` tags don't have closing tags. Idiosyncrasies such as this make it harder to parse. XHTML is a way to fix the idiosyncrasies and to enforce better HTML code.

The first thing you might have noticed after creating an HTML page with Expression Web and looking at the code is a Document Type Declaration (DTD), sometimes referred to as a doctype, at the top of the code. It might looking something like this:

```
<!DOCTYPE html PUBLIC "-//W3C//DTD XHTML 1.0 Transitional//EN"
    "http://www.w3.org/TR/xhtml1/DTD/xhtml1-transitional.dtd">
```

A doctype declares to the browser which DTD the document conforms to. A DTD should be placed before the root element.

Expression Web will alert you to XHTML errors by making the background of a noncompliant tag yellow. For instance, if you add a <BR> tag to the code, its background will become yellow. If you change it to the newer, XHTML compliant version of <BR />, its background will return to normal. The following common HTML errors will cause Expression Web to flag you.

- Not closing empty elements (elements without closing tags in HTML 4):
  - Incorrect:
  - Correct:

  Note that any of these are acceptable in XHTML:
</br>, <br/> and <br />. Older HTML-only browsers interpreting it as HTML will generally accept <br> and <br />.

- Not closing nonempty elements:
  - Incorrect: <p>This is a paragraph.<p>This is another paragraph.
  - Correct: <p>This is a paragraph.</p><p>This is another paragraph.</p>
- Improperly nesting elements (this would also be invalid in HTML):
  - Incorrect: <em><strong>This is some text.</em></strong>
  - Correct: <em><strong>This is some text.</strong></em>
- Not putting quotation marks around attribute values:
  - Incorrect: `<td rowspan=3>`
  - Correct: `<td rowspan="3">`
  - Correct: `<td rowspan='3'>`
- Using the ampersand character outside of entities:
  - Incorrect: <title>Cars & Trucks</title>
  - Correct: <title>Cars & Trucks</title>
- Using the ampersand outside of entities in URLs (this would also be invalid in HTML):
  - Incorrect: <a href="index.php?page=news&style=5">News</a>
  - Correct: <a href="index.php?page=news&style=5">News</a>
- Failing to recognize that XHTML elements and attributes are case sensitive:
  - Incorrect: <BODY><P ID="ONE">The Best Page Ever</P></BODY>
  - Correct: <body><p id="ONE">The Best Page Ever</p></body>
- Using attribute minimization:
  - Incorrect: <textarea readonly>READ-ONLY</textarea>
  - Correct: <textarea readonly="readonly">READ-ONLY</textarea>
- Misusing CDATA, script-comments, and xml-comments when embedding scripts and style sheets. This problem can be avoided altogether by putting all script and style sheet information into separate files and referring to them in the XHTML head element.

Expression can easily check the compatibility of your web pages. Go to the Tools menu and select Compatibility Checker. A dialog will appear as shown in Figure 16-1 which gives you the choices that are available.

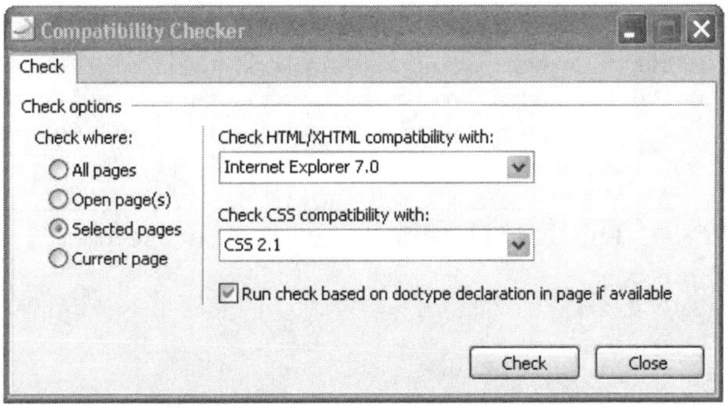

FIGURE 16-1 You have a number of choices when checking the compatibility.

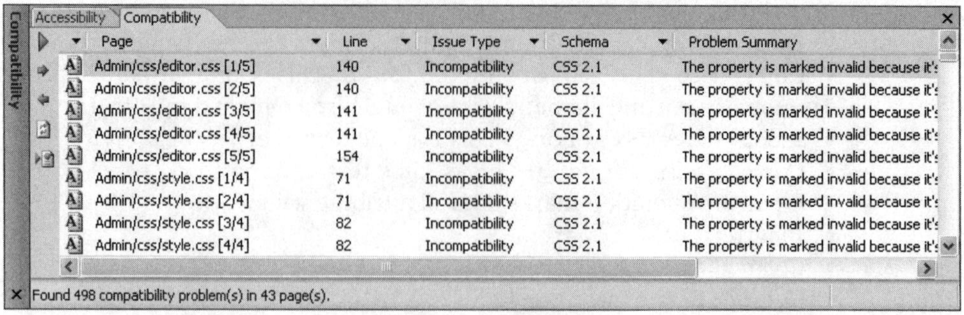

Accessibility
Compatibility
Page
Line
Issue Type
Schema
Problem Summary
Admin/css/editor.css [1/5] 140 Incompatibility CSS 2.1 The property is marked invalid because it's
Admin/css/editor.css [2/5] 140 Incompatibility CSS 2.1 The property is marked invalid because it's
Admin/css/editor.css [3/5] 141 Incompatibility CSS 2.1 The property is marked invalid because it's
Admin/css/editor.css [4/5] 141 Incompatibility CSS 2.1 The property is marked invalid because it's
Admin/css/editor.css [5/5] 154 Incompatibility CSS 2.1 The property is marked invalid because it's
Admin/css/style.css [1/4] 71 Incompatibility CSS 2.1 The property is marked invalid because it's
Admin/css/style.css [2/4] 71 Incompatibility CSS 2.1 The property is marked invalid because it's
Admin/css/style.css [3/4] 82 Incompatibility CSS 2.1 The property is marked invalid because it's
Admin/css/style.css [4/4] 82 Incompatibility CSS 2.1 The property is marked invalid because it's
Found 498 compatibility problem(s) in 43 page(s).

FIGURE 16-2 The Compatibility Checker shows you the results in a task pane.

The Compatibility task pane will appear and list the issues that were found. You'll see the document, the issue summary, and other information, as shown in Figure 16-2.

You can create an HTML report from the Compatibility Checker as shown in Figure 16-3. This is a big help when you need to distribute the results in a meeting or to the development staff.

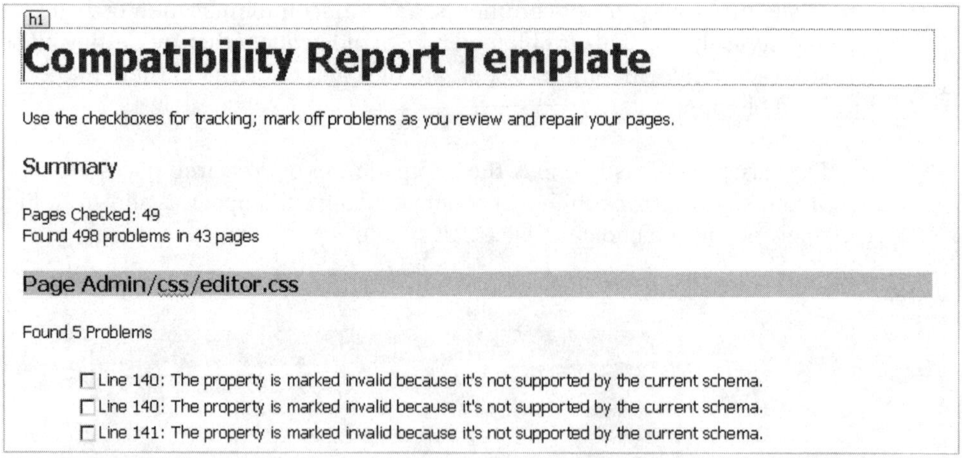

h1
Compatibility Report Template
Use the checkboxes for tracking; mark off problems as you review and repair your pages.
Summary
Pages Checked: 49
Found 498 problems in 43 pages
Page Admin/css/editor.css
Found 5 Problems
Line 140: The property is marked invalid because it's not supported by the current schema.
Line 140: The property is marked invalid because it's not supported by the current schema.
Line 141: The property is marked invalid because it's not supported by the current schema.

FIGURE 16-3 This HTML report is extremely useful.

Set Up the Remote Site

This section will guide you through setup of your web site and deployment of the content. Two approaches are discussed: setting up a web site on a machine with Internet Information Server, and using a third-party hosting service. There are many more options, but these are the two most common and, arguably, the two most practical.

For both approaches, you will need to register a domain name. There are many available, and the authors have used quite a few different services over the years. We prefer GoDaddy for its relatively low price and its easy-to-use interface.

We'll use the fictitious domain name of HTDEExpressionWeb2.com. Go to your selected domain name provider and find a domain name that is not already in use. Register the domain name and pay the fees. Now enter the IP address of the server that will host the web site. If you don't know the IP address when you register, you can specify it later. Your domain name provider will implement a parking page until you point the domain entry to your IP address.

Set Up a Web Site on Internet Information Server

This section covers Internet Information Server (IIS) versions 6 and 7. Version 6 comes with Windows XP (a limited version) and Windows 2003 Server. IIS 7 comes with Vista and Windows 2008 Server.

To start with, make sure IIS is installed. By default for Windows XP and Vista it is not installed. You will have to go to the Control Panel, select the Install Software icon, and add a Windows Component. Windows 2003 Server usually has it installed, but by default (for security reasons) it is not running. IIS must be installed and running before you can set up a web site.

IIS 6

To use IIS 6, start by creating a folder on the hard drive in which the web site content will be placed. It is usually within the c:\inetpub\wwwroot folder, but that isn't a requirement. For our fictitious domain we'll create HTDEExpressionWeb2.

Copy all web content into the newly created folder. (The destination path for this example is now c:\inetpub\wwwroot\ HTDEExpressionWeb2.) To set up IIS, follow these steps:

1. Open the Control Panel.
2. Open Administrative Tools.
3. Click the Internet Information Services icon. The IIS management window appears.
4. Drill down until you find the Default Web Site as shown in Figure 16-4.

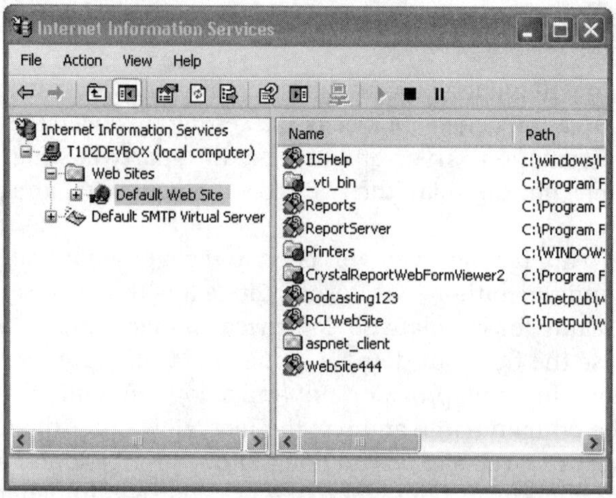

FIGURE 16-4 Drill down to the Default Web Site.

5. Right-click Default Web Site and select Properties. The Default Web Site Properties dialog box appears as shown in Figure 16-5.
6. Click the Home Directory tab, and put your content directory in the Local Path field as shown in Figure 16-6.

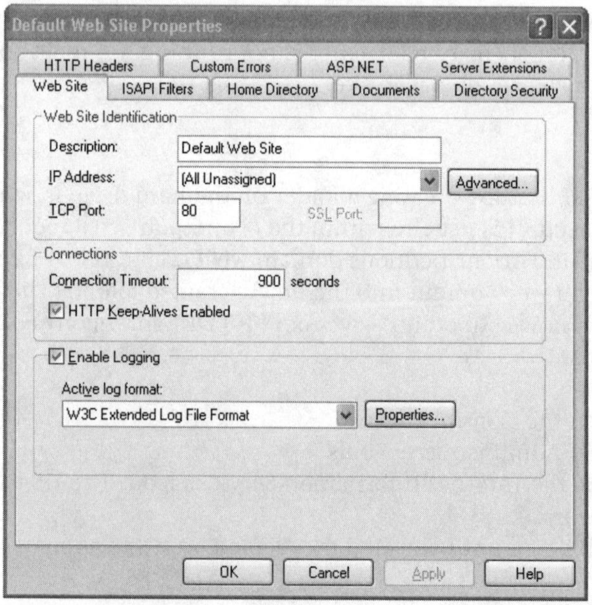

FIGURE 16-5 Open the Default Web Site Properties dialog box.

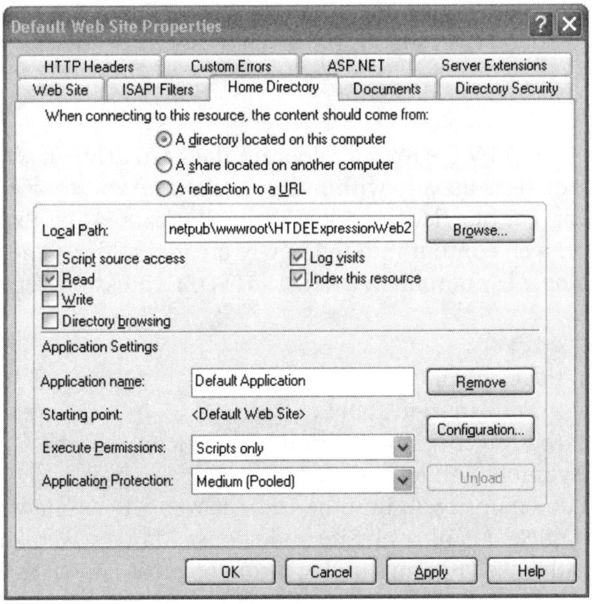

FIGURE 16-6 Put your local content directory here.

7. Go back to the Web Site tab and click the Advanced button.
8. Now click the Add button and do the following:
   - In the IP Address selector, leave it All Unassigned.
   - In the TCP Port text box enter 80.
   - In the Host Header Name text box enter your domain name as HTDEExpressionWeb2.com.
   - The dialog box will appear similarly to the one shown in Figure 16-7. Click OK.
9. Now repeat step 8 for the www version of your domain. In other words, add another host header for www.HTDEExpressionWeb2.com.

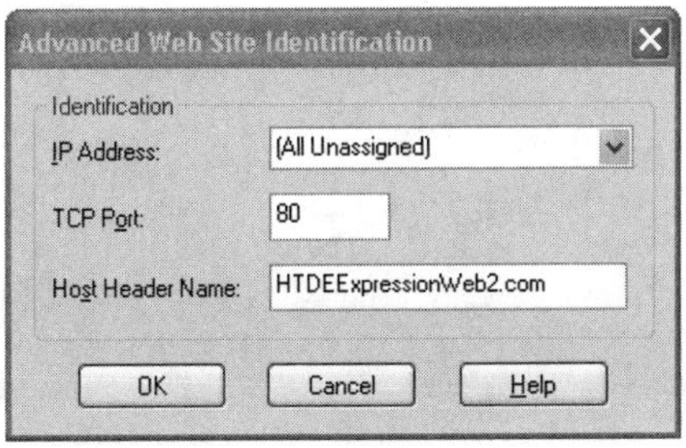

FIGURE 16-7 Enter the host header for your domain.

With your domain name correctly registered and the correct IP address in your domain provider's DNS server, IIS will now serve as a web server for your content.

IIS 7

To use IIS 7, start by creating a folder on the hard drive in which the web site content will be placed. It is usually within the c:\inetpub\wwwroot folder, but that isn't a requirement. For our fictitious domain we'll create HTDEExpressionWeb2.

Copy all web content into the newly created folder. (The destination path for this example is now c:\inetpub\wwwroot\ HTDEExpressionWeb2.) To set up IIS, follow these steps:

1. Open the Control Panel.
2. Open Administrative Tools.
3. Open the Internet Information Service icon (not the 6.0 Manager). The IIS management window appears.
4. Drill down until you find the Default Web Site as shown in Figure 16-8.
5. Right-click Default Web Site and choose Manage Web Site | Advanced Settings. The Advanced Settings dialog box appears as shown in Figure 16-9.

FIGURE 16-8 Drill down to the Default Web Site.

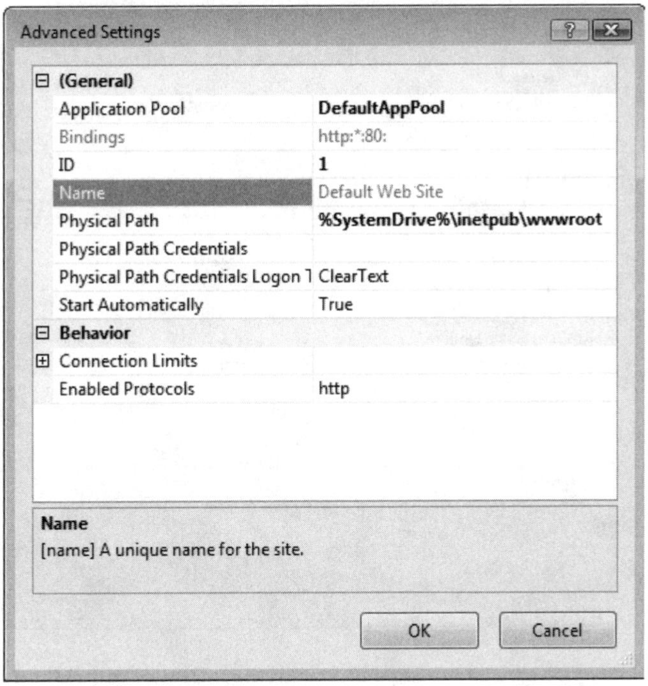

FIGURE 16-9 Open the Advanced Settings dialog box.

6. Edit the Physical Path field and put your content directory in it by typing it in or browsing to it as shown in Figure 16-10.
7. Click OK.
8. Right-click Default Web Site and select Edit Bindings. The Site Bindings dialog box will appear.
9. Click the Add button and do the following:
   - In the IP Address selector, leave it All Unassigned.
   - In the TCP Port text box, the value should be 80.
   - In the Type selector, the value should be http.
   - In the Host Name text box enter your domain name as HTDEExpressionWeb2.com.
   - The dialog box will appear similar to the one shown in Figure 16-11. Click OK.
10. Now repeat step for the www version of your domain. In other words, add another host header for www.HTDEExpressionWeb2.com.

With your domain name correctly registered, and the correct IP Address in your domain provider's DNS server, IIS will now serve as a web server for your content.

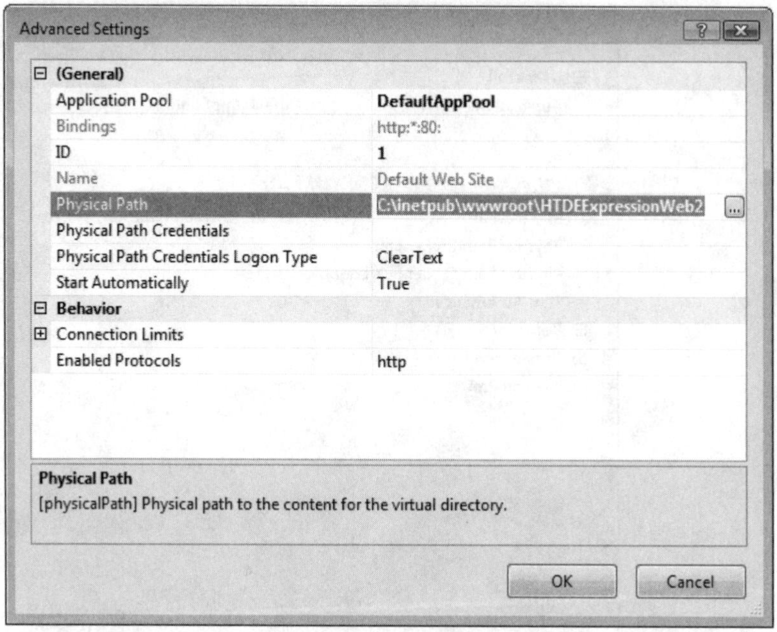

FIGURE 16-10 Enter your local content directory here.

Set Up a Web Site on a Third-Party Hosting Service

We've already talked about setting up our own web server by installing and configuring IIS. This section talks about using a third-party hosting service.

At one time, Rick wouldn't have considered using a hosting service. Why not? Because he has his own servers and can easily host them. It gave him bragging rights

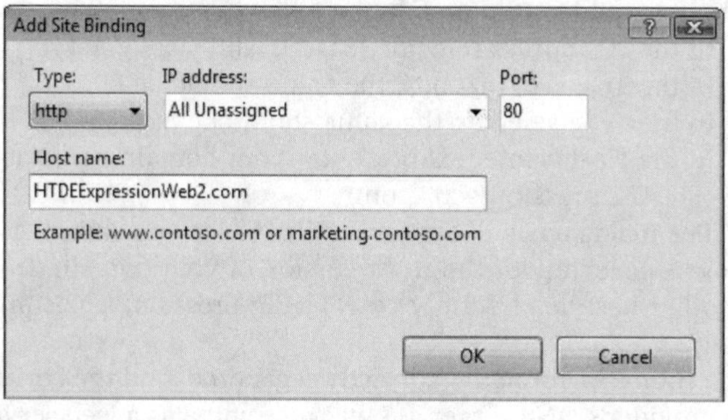

FIGURE 16-11 Enter the host header for your domain.

when everyone asked who hosted his web sites and he replied that he hosted them on his own space. But his desire to do his own hosting has eroded to the point that he has only some simple and fairly insignificant web sites hosted on his own servers.

You may be wondering what eroded Rick's desire to host. Every power outage was like the Chinese water torture. The first hundred drops don't hurt, but eventually every drop is painful. That's the way power outages are, they get more painful. Yes, you can buy a larger UPS (uninterruptible power supply), but there's a point where even that doesn't help. There are also the hackers who use zero day attacks to compromise your server. Then there are the constant operating system upgrades. We could go on for quite awhile, but suffice it to say that we probably won't host any more new web sites. We have been through quite a few third-party hosting services. Many of them are good and provide their service at a reasonable price, but more than half of the hosting services we've tried turned out to be bad experiences. As we've already mentioned, we have settled in with GoDaddy. We are able to do everything we need to do for 99 percent of our web site applications. We've never experienced downtime for any of our web sites. Their management tools are easy to use, their prices are very reasonable, and, since we believe that GoDaddy is a good choice for most hosting needs, we'll talk about using GoDaddy for hosting in this section.

Create a GoDaddy Account

To begin the process, log on to GoDaddy.com and create a new account.

Get a Domain Name

Next, you'll need to find and register a domain name. From the main GoDaddy page, enter a domain that you would like to use in the Start Your Domain Search Here! text box. If the domain has not been taken, you'll see the message "MyDomain.com is available!" There will be quite a few additional choices that GoDaddy suggests (nothing like suggestive sales), but we never buy these and only buy the domain name that we've already chosen.

If the domain you want has already been taken, you'll see the message "MyDomain.com is already taken." Other related domain names will be suggested. In some cases, you will found a suitable domain name among the suggested alternatives. You can also click the Use a Domain Buy Agent to Get This Name link, but there are no guarantees that an agent can get the domain that you want, and even if the current owner is willing to sell, the price might be very high.

Select a Hosting Plan

From the GoDaddy main page, select Hosting & Servers | Web Site Hosting. You can evaluate your choices and get the type of hosting you need. For many simple web sites, the economy plan works well. Just make sure that you select a Windows operating system instead of the default Linux choice. You will need a Windows operating system in order to take advantage of many of Expression's Microsoft-centric features such as the ASPX pages.

Managing Content

There are two ways to put content onto your GoDaddy web site. One is by using the Microsoft FrontPage Extensions. This allows Expression Web (as well as many other programs) to edit files that are on the server just as if they are local files. The other method is by simply send files via FTP to the server.

You must turn FrontPage Extensions on since GoDaddy's default is to have them off. Navigate to the Manage Account link for your web site and click it—the Hosting Control Center will open up. Click the Settings tab and then the FrontPage Extensions icon; the FrontPage Extensions configuration section will open up. Click the check box and turn the FrontPage Extensions on. When they are turned on, the FrontPage Extensions configuration section will appear similarly to what you see in Figure 16-12.

Now you will need to connect to the web site from Expression Web 2. Select File | Open Site. In the Site Name text box, enter your domain name preceded by **http://**, such as **http://rickleinecker.com**. Expression will go to the server and attempt to open the web site. Unless you've already opened this site and selected to store the password, you will have to provide login credentials. The user name can be seen from the Hosting Control Center section of GoDaddy, and the password can be managed from the Account Login icon under the Settings tab.

Once you've opened the site with the FrontPage Extensions, you can edit files just as if they were on your hard drive.

Expression has File Transfer Protocol (FTP) built in. This allows you to easily send files from your hard drive to the web site. The difference between this and using the FrontPage Extensions is: If you use FTP, you create and edit the web site on your computer, and then send files to the server. With FrontPage Extensions, you work from the server.

FrontPage Extensions Google Webmaster Tools

FrontPage Extensions

Current Install Status Installed

Select Installation Option ☐ Reinstall FrontPage Extensions
 ☐ Uninstall FrontPage Extensions

FrontPage Email Address

Enter FrontPage Email rick@jsventures.com
Address

 Continue Cancel

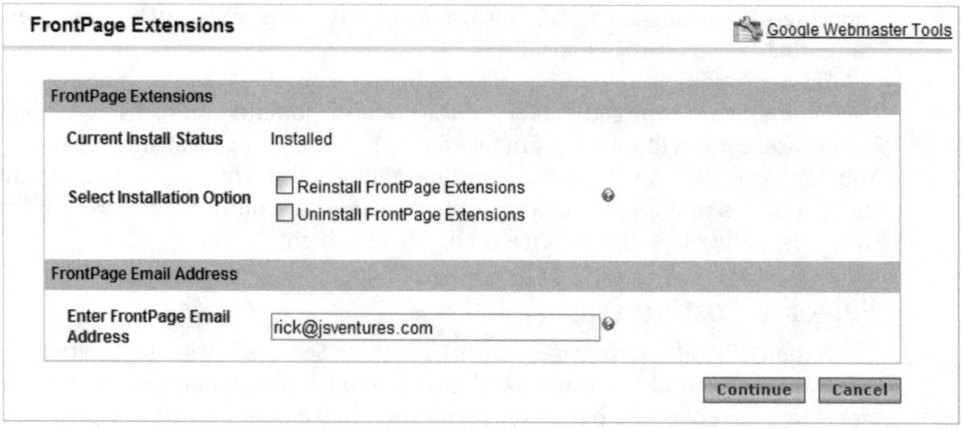

FIGURE 16-12 This shows that the FrontPage Extensions are turned on.

We suggest FrontPage Extensions for simple web sites and FTP for web sites that need to be tested before they go live on the server.

Summary

Creating a great web application is the first part of the equation. The second part is the web application's hosting. It's not that difficult, but you need to know how to upload and maintain files on a server.

There are lots of hosting options. Find one that is cost effective, easy to use, and reliable. These comprise the main criteria for selecting a hosting service.

PART V

Appendixes

A

XHTML Tag Attributes

HOW TO...

- Identify and define XHTML tags
- Name colors

One of the basic building blocks of the Web is XHTML. In this appendix, you can view XHTML tags categorized by functional area. You can also review the list of color tags that validate by name.

XHTML Tags

In this section, you'll read about different categories of tags. *Deprecated* tags—those considered outdated and replaced by newer constructs—are not included in the tables. At the current time, browsers support deprecated elements for backward compatibility, but this should be avoided.

Meta Information

A range of information is included within the nondisplayed content found in the <head> tag of a web page.

Tag	Definition
<base>	A base URL for all the links in a page, part of the <head> element
<head>	Contains the nondisplayed meta-information in a document
<html>	The root element of each XHTML document; doesn't include *X*
<meta>	Lists generic meta information; part of the <head> element

Tag	Definition
<address>	An address element used to provide contact information for the document author
<title>	Defines the document title, part of the <head> element

Basic Tags

Format much or all of the content on the average web page using basic tags. Read about using basic tags in Chapter 2.

Tag	Definition
<body>	Contains the document's displayed content
<h1> to <h6>	Heading levels 1 through 6
<p>	A block element displaying one paragraph
 	Empty element, forces a line break
<hr />	Empty element, displays a horizontal rule
<!-- ... -->	A comment hidden within the XHTML on the page; the enclosed text (symbolized by the ellipses) isn't displayed on the page

Blocks

This category includes a variety of items that represent text used for specific purposes, such as quotations and cites.

Tag	Definition
<acronym>	Identifies an acronym
<abbr>	Identifies an abbreviation
<blockquote>	Displays a long quotation; generally more than one line
<q>	Defines a short quotation used in line
<cite>	Indicates a citation or reference to other work
<ins>	Identifies content inserted on a page in order to update the document
<del>	Identifies content deleted from a page in order to update the document

Character Format

Use tags to identify specific characters, such as subscripts or superscripts, or to point out words or phrases using bold or italic text.

Tag	Definition	Tag	Definition
<b>	Bold text	<strong>	Strong text
<i>	Italic text	<small>	Small text
<em>	Emphasized text	<sup>	Superscripted text
<big>	Big text	<sub>	Subscripted text
		<bdo>	The direction of text display

Images

Use images to illustrate or present information on a web page visually. Discrete areas, defined on an image called an image map, contain hyperlinks. Read about using images in Chapter 3.

Tag	Definition
<img>	An image included in a web page
<map>	A client-side image map
<area>	A defined area inside an image map

Links

Links are the basis for web functionality and interactivity. Read about linking in Chapter 4.

Tag	Definition
<a>	Anchors one document or location to another, such as a hypertext link
<link>	A media-independent resource reference, part of the <head> tag

Lists

Web pages, like other written publications, commonly present information in list form. Use unordered lists to present a series of items in any order; use ordered lists to provide a sequence of items in a specified order.

Tag	Definition
<ul>	Defines an unordered (bulleted) list
<ol>	Defines an ordered (numbered) list
<li>	An item in a defined list, either <ol> or <ul>
<dl>	A definition list
<dt>	A definition term used within <dl>
<dd>	A definition description used within <dl>

Styles

Use style tags to define the presence of styles in a web page. Define arbitrary block and inline structures to receive style rules.

Tag	Definition
<style>	A style definition, part of the <head> element
<div>	A block level language/style container in a document
<span>	An inline language/style container in a document

Tables

The XHTML tags for tables describe and identify the individual unit or compound structure in a table.

Tag	Definition
<table>	A table
<caption>	A table caption
<th>	A table header
<tr>	A table row
<td>	A table cell
<thead>	A table header

<tbody>	A table body
<tfoot>	A table footer
<col>	Attributes for table columns
<colgroup>	Groups of table columns

Frames

Frames identify subwindows in a page referencing other pages. Frames use specific dimensions and arrangements. None of the tags are valid in XHTML 1.0 Strict.

Tag	Definition
<frame>	A subwindow (a frame)[a]
<frameset>	A set of frames[a]
<noframes>	A noframe section[b]
<iframe>	An inline subwindow (frame)[b]

[a]XHTML Frameset only

[b]XHTML Transitional and Frameset

Input

Input tags on a form that provide for user interaction and transference of data or information.

Tag	Definition
<form>	A form
<input>	An input field
<textarea>	A text area
<button>	A push button
<select>	A selectable list
<optgroup>	An option group
<option>	An item in a list box
<label>	A label for a form control
<fieldset>	A fieldset
<legend>	A title in a fieldset

Output

Use tags to define a variety of types of output ranging from code to variables.

Tag	Definition
<pre>	Preformatted text
<code>	Computer code text
<tt>	Teletype text
<kbd>	Keyboard text
<var>	A variable
<dfn>	A definition term
<samp>	Sample computer code

Programming

Several tags identify programming language inserted into a web page.

Tag	Definition
<script>	A script
<noscript>	A noscript section
<object>	An embedded object
<param>	A parameter for an object

HTML Colors

You can define a color to use for any part of your web page using RGB or hex values. The following table lists the 16 color names that validate for XHTML and CSS using a text name rather than their corresponding hex values.

Color Name	Hex Value
Aqua	#00FFFF
Black	#000000
Blue	#0000FF
Fuchsia	#FF00FF

Gray	#808080
Green	#008000
Lime	#00FF00
Maroon	#800000
Navy	#000080
Olive	#808000
Purple	#800080
Red	#FF0000
Silver	#C0C0C0
Teal	#008080
White	#FFFFFF
Yellow	#FFFF00

B

Style Properties and Values

HOW TO...

- Read style properties
- Understand style property definitions

Cascading Style Sheets format the visual appearance of elements on a web page. CSS offers timesaving features and provides a consistent appearance to a site's pages. Access a style object from the document or apply it directly to an element.

The tables in this appendix list a range of style properties; applicable values vary according to the property.

Text Properties

Since communication online is predominantly text based, there are many styles for configuring and customizing the appearance of text on a page. Some styles are designed to write a shorthand style for items such as for text or an object's borders.

Property	Description
`color`	Sets text color
`font`	Sets all font properties in one
`fontFamily`	Sets a text element's font name
`fontStyle`	Sets an element's font-style, such as `italic` or `oblique`
`fontVariant`	Displays text using a small-caps font
`fontWeight`	Sets the level of text boldness
`fontSize`	Sets the font size of a text element
`fontSizeAdjust`	Sets or adjusts text size

Property	Description
fontStretch	Specifies an amount to condense or stretch a font laterally
lineHeight	Sets distance between lines of text
letterSpacing	Sets character spacing
textAlign	Aligns a block of text
textIndent	Indents the first line of a text block
textTransform	Sets capitalization effects
textDecoration	Sets text decoration options, such as blink or overline
textShadow	Sets shadow effects
quotes	Sets the type of quotation marks to use
whiteSpace	Specifies how line breaks and white space display in a block of text
wordSpacing	Sets spacing between words in a block of text

Background Properties

Backgrounds are used for many page elements, ranging from headings and images to form fields and tables. Styles provide for precise positioning of backgrounds as well as general image or color properties.

Property	Description
background	Sets all background properties in one statement
backgroundColor	Sets an element's background color
backgroundImage	Sets an element's background image
backgroundRepeat	Defines if or how to repeat a background image
backgroundAttachment	Specifies whether a background image scrolls with the page or is fixed at a single location
backgroundPosition	Defines the placement coordinates for a background image
backgroundPositionX	Specifies the X-axis coordinates for the background's position
backgroundPositionY	Specifies the Y-axis coordinates for the background's position

Border and Margin Properties

Borders are a convenient means to draw attention to particular messages or items on a page. There are many styles available for setting border, margin, outline, and padding appearances. CSS allows several shorthand properties to define multiple properties in one statement, including specifying different values for different sides of an element.

Property	Description
border	Sets all properties of all four borders
borderColor	Sets the color of all four borders
borderStyle	Sets the style of all four borders
borderWidth	Sets the width of all four borders
borderTop	Sets all properties for the top border
borderTopColor	Sets the top border's color
borderTopStyle	Sets the top border's style
borderTopWidth	Sets the top border's width
borderBottom	Sets all properties for the bottom border
borderBottomColor	Sets the bottom border's color
borderBottomStyle	Sets the bottom border's style
borderBottomWidth	Sets the bottom border's width
borderLeft	Sets all properties for the left border
borderLeftColor	Sets the left border's color
borderLeftStyle	Sets the left border's style
borderLeftWidth	Sets the left border's width
borderRight	Sets all properties for the right border
borderRightColor	Sets the right border's color
borderRightStyle	Sets the right border's style
borderRightWidth	Sets the right border's width
margin	Sets all the margins of an element
marginTop	Sets an element's top margin
marginBottom	Sets an element's bottom margin
marginLeft	Sets an element's left margin
marginRight	Sets an element's right margin

Property	Description
outline	Sets all outline properties in one
outlineColor	Sets an element's outline color
outlineStyle	Sets an element's outline style
outlineWidth	Sets an element's outline width
padding	Sets all the padding of an element
paddingBottom	Sets an element's bottom padding
paddingLeft	Sets an element's left padding
paddingRight	Sets an element's right padding
paddingTop	Sets an element's top padding

List Properties

Bullets don't have to look like round dots aligned at the left of list items. Use styles to specify the type of marker, or an image to use instead of a text marker.

Property	Description
listStyle	Sets multiple properties for a list
listStyleImage	Sets an image for the list-item marker
listStylePosition	Sets the position for the list-item marker
listStyleType	Sets the type of list-item marker

Table Properties

In addition to visual characteristics common to any element, such as borders and margins (listed in the earlier section, "Border and Margin Properties"), tables have a few specific styles.

Property	Description
borderCollapse	Sets whether the table borders are collapsed into a single border
borderSpacing	Sets the distance separating cell borders
captionSide	Specifies the location of the table's caption
emptyCells	Sets whether or not to show empty cells in a table
tableLayout	Sets the method used to display table cells, rows, and columns

Positioning Properties

Use positioning properties to define the location of objects on a page in relation to other objects. Specify objects in 2D or 3D axes.

Property	Description
top	Sets how far the top edge of an element is above/below the top edge of the parent element
bottom	Sets how far the bottom edge of an element is above/below the bottom edge of the parent element
left	Sets how far the left edge of an element is to the right/left of the left edge of the parent element
right	Sets how far the right edge of an element is to the left/right of the right edge of the parent element
position	Places an element in a static, relative, absolute, or fixed position
zIndex	Sets the stack order of an element

Layout Properties

Styles are used to define criteria for display and layout of elements on a page. Styles range from height and width variations to whether the content is visible to how element content is managed under different conditions, such as floats and overflows.

Property	Description
content	Specifies metadata information
visibility	Defines whether an element is visible or not
height	Defines an element's height
minHeight	Defines an element's minimum height
maxHeight	Defines an element's maximum height
width	Defines an element's width
minWidth	Defines an element's minimum width
maxWidth	Defines an element's maximum width
cursor	Defines the type of cursor to display
direction	Defines text direction of an element
display	Defines how an element displays

Property	Description
clear	Defines an element's sides where other floating elements are disallowed
cssFloat	Defines where an image or a text appears, or floats, in another element
clip	Defines an element's shape
overflow	Specifies how content that doesn't fit in an element box is treated
verticalAlign	Defines vertical alignment of an element's contents
markerOffset	Defines the distance between the nearest border edges of a marker box and its principal box
marks	Defines whether to render cross marks or crop marks outside a page box's edge
counterIncrement	Defines a list of counter names, followed by an integer indicating how much the counter is incremented for each occurrence of an element. The default is 1.
counterReset	Defines a list of counter names, followed by an integer indicating how much the counter is set to for each occurrence of an element. The default is 0.

Printing Properties

Use styles to define printing properties. As in defining print criteria for other documents, use styles to define page breaks, page sizes, and widow/orphan controls.

Property	Description
page	Sets a page type to use for display
size	Defines page size and orientation
pageBreakBefore	Sets how a page breaks before a specified element
pageBreakAfter	Sets how a page breaks after a specified element
pageBreakInside	Sets how a page breaks within a specified element
widows	Specifies a minimum number of paragraph lines allowed at the top of a page
orphans	Specifies a minimum number of paragraph lines allowed at the bottom of a page

Scrollbar Properties

Internet Explorer allows for scrollbar styling. Similar to the scrollbars seen on a program interface, styled scrollbars include 3D and shadow properties.

Property	Description
`scrollbar3dLightColor`	Sets the color for left and top sides of arrows and scroll boxes
`scrollbarArrowColor`	Sets the color for the scrollbar arrow
`scrollbarBaseColor`	Sets the scrollbar base color
`scrollbarDarkShadowColor`	Sets the color for right and bottom sides of arrows and scroll boxes
`scrollbarFaceColor`	Sets the color for the front of the scrollbar
`scrollbarHighlightColor`	Sets the color for the left and top sides of arrows and scroll boxes, and scrollbar background color
`scrollbarShadowColor`	Sets the color for the right and bottom sides of arrows and scroll boxes
`scrollbarTrackColor`	Sets the scrollbar background color

Index

Note: Page numbers referencing figures are italicized and followed by an "*f*." Page numbers referencing tables are italicized and followed by a "*t*."

D

Q

R

S

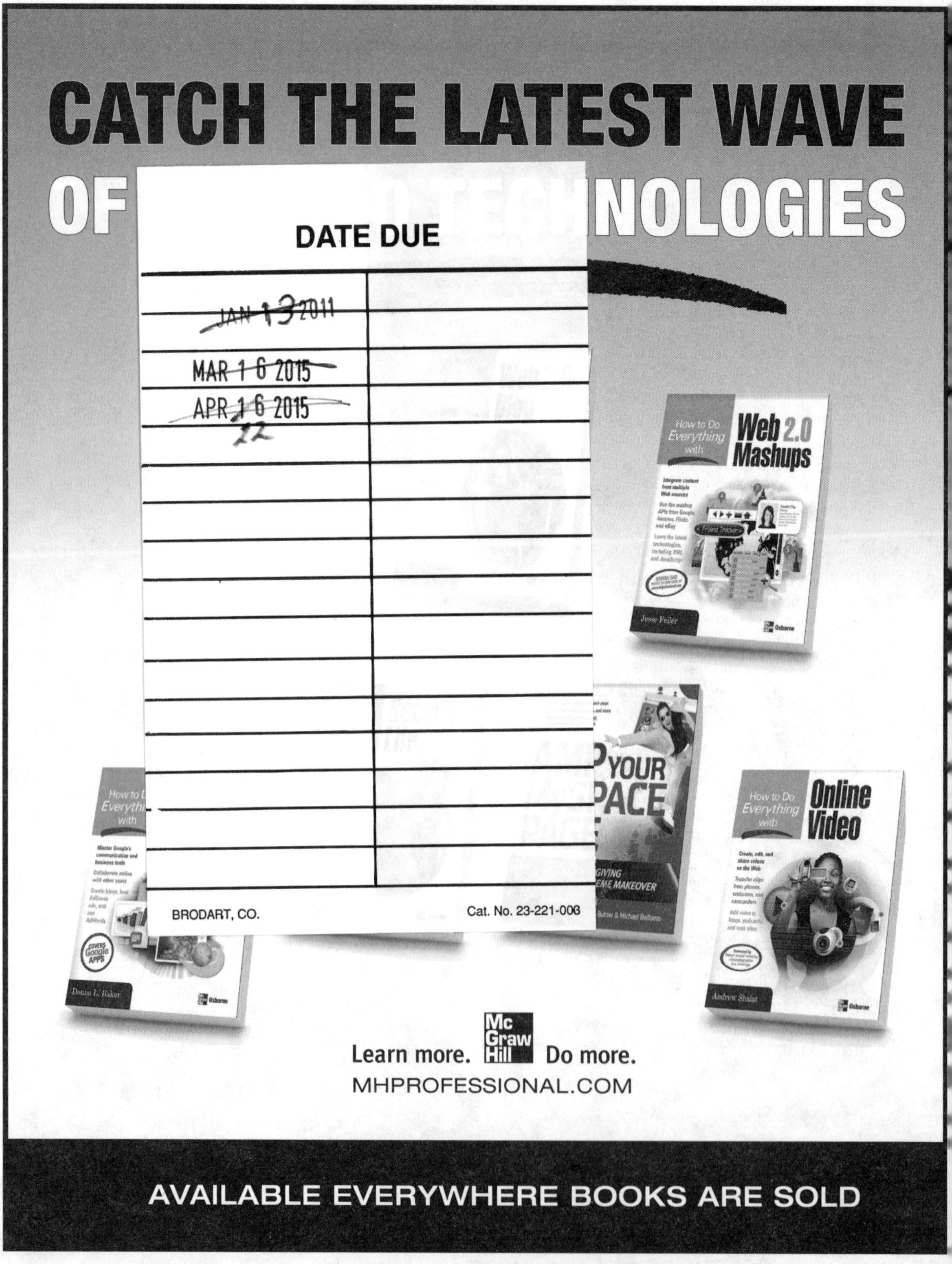
CATCH THE LATEST WAVE
OF
NOLOGIES
How to Do Everything with
Web 2.0 Mashups
Jesse Feiler
YOUR
PACE
How to Do Everything with
Online Video
Andrew Shalat
Donna L. Baker
Learn more. Do more.
MHPROFESSIONAL.COM
AVAILABLE EVERYWHERE BOOKS ARE SOLD